Direct Licensing and the Music Industry

Ivan L. Pitt

Direct Licensing and the Music Industry

How Technology, Innovation and Competition Reshaped Copyright Licensing

Springer

Ivan L. Pitt
Former Senior Economist
American Society of Composers,
Authors and Publishers
New York, NY, USA

ISBN 978-3-319-17652-9 ISBN 978-3-319-17653-6 (eBook)
DOI 10.1007/978-3-319-17653-6

Library of Congress Control Number: 2015940119

Springer Cham Heidelberg New York Dordrecht London

Printed on acid-free paper

Springer International Publishing AG Switzerland is part of Springer Science+Business Media (www.springer.com)

Preface

Technological change, legislation and consumer preferences have created new challenges and business models in the music industry because music consumers are moving from one new trend to the next. The ability of digital technology to reduce the transaction costs of music copyright licensing has destroyed the old-media business models of incumbent Performing Rights Organizations (PROs), music publishers, record labels, radio and television stations. In economic literature, much of the analysis has focused on the traditional blanket form of music content licensing because digital streaming of music and the use of smart phones for music were not major issues until recently.

This book was written to explain the "big picture" and the brand new competitive landscape in music licensing with an emphasis on songwriters and composers. It was necessary because there are so many astonishingly fast changes that are sweeping the music industry, including consumers who prefer a music access/subscription model to an ownership model; the consolidation of the major music publishers (even as smart phones, streaming, cloud services, iTunes, and YouTube have changed the way that music is consumed and distributed and new artists are discovered); new business models (direct licensing and the aggregation of performance, mechanical and synchronization licenses); the proliferation of music streaming services (Pandora, Spotify, and Beats Music); and the rise of independent music labels such as Kobalt (without the legacy baggage of the old music publisher). Furthermore, music piracy, that was emotionally out of proportion with economic reality when it came to these forces that are reshaping the music industry, is now receding.

New marketing innovators such as Apple's iTunes, Pandora, and Netflix have all aggregated licensed music and video content—something that the incumbents could not easily replicate—and provided the legal means for consumers to download content. In addition, Apple's iTunes disaggregated music content by decoupling singles from albums. Consumers no longer needed to purchase an entire CD to get the one or two songs that they desired for their libraries. Social media—such as Facebook and YouTube—created mass-appeal while lowering the transactions costs associated with distributing music, and in the process changed the conventional role played by radio and television. Traditional broadcast TV is now struggling to reinvent itself because Netflix created a viable on-demand video streaming service that transformed the way that consumers watch television and movies (on smart phones and iPads) and the distribution window in which films are released. Like music streaming services, Netflix global growth has been stymied by its inability to secure licensing rights to content from some copyright holders.

For some of the music licensing agencies that have been around for a century change would not come easy in the digital era. The incumbent PROs are now considered sunset licensing operations who are struggling to justify their existence in a digital world that exposed their inefficiencies, internal bureaucracy problems and unaccountability in royalty payments. Competitors, without the legacy costs, are now out-maneuvering the PROs and increasingly their survival is in doubt. Aggressive and pioneering new firms—such as TuneCore and Kobalt—have developed creative and original licensing models from the ground up. The PROs digital strategies could be the difference between becoming a third-party licensing agency for small publishers who cannot negotiate their own licensing deals and permanent extinction. There is also a widening gap between PROs and songwriters in the true value that these agencies provide.

The Internet age brought a similar upheaval in the music industry that the introduction of terrestrial radio caused in circa 1920. Radio was then described by others as "a powerful and interactive piece of technology." With the introduction of radio and telephone networks, the first "mass" market with national marketing and distribution was being developed in which an entire continent could be served. Radio was also seen as one of the "cash cows" in the nascent music licensing industry in the decades before the development of television and the Internet. The cash cow mentality would persist decades later when practically every conceivable business enterprise that played music was preyed upon for licensing fees. Terrestrial radio remains one of the largest sources of licensing revenue for some PROs. Internet radio is now the latest powerful, interactive, and *global* technology that caters to practically every mood, taste, and genre.

In 1923, and barely 9 years old, ASCAP would file one of its early infringement lawsuits against a retail store and a radio station. There were two major boycotts that occurred in the music industry in the 1940s and each boycott had significant long-term consequences for songwriters and composers. In both boycotts, the issue was the distribution of royalty payments, an issue that would persist to today. In the first boycott in 1941, ASCAP led an unpopular boycott of radio in which stations could not perform any of the one million musical compositions that ASCAP controlled in its repertory. The boycott was perceived as an alleged extortion racket by a monopolist PRO to extract higher radio licensing fees because ASCAP was dominated by the major Tin Pan Alley songwriters and music publishers whose works couldn't be licensed elsewhere. The ASCAP boycott proved to be a "disastrous failure" and was undermined by BMI—that was set up in 1939 by radio executives who were members of the National Association of Broadcasters (NAB)—to weaken the monopoly powers of ASCAP. BMI increased its market exposure by providing radio stations with alternative musical compositions from its own distinct repertory.

In the second boycott in 1942, a strike by the musicians' union meant that no new sound recordings could be made. After the musician's strike was settled, vocalists would eclipse the big-band musicians, and eventually DJs playing records on the radio would force the demise of live big-band music on the radio. The demise of big-band music on the radio would also affect Broadway shows, and the Tin Pan Alley songwriters whose works when featured on radio broadcasts served as publicity for Broadway shows. DMX and music publishers (some of whom are members of the PRO's board of directors) would later undermine both ASCAP and BMI with their direct licensing business models as music streaming became popular.

The sinking of the Titanic and The Great War (now referred to as World War I) led to the increased consumer demand for news and information because Americans had relatives on the fateful voyage and others had relatives who served overseas in the war. As the adoption of radio exploded, the market for phonograph records declined because consumers switched to listening to music in a new way using the latest affordable technology. A distinct pattern to the life cycle of music products in which consumers replaced older technology with newer ones will repeat itself over and over again. The real estate bubble, international debt crisis, bank failures, corporate bankruptcies, stock market crash and the Great Depression throughout the 1920s and 1930s would have an enormous economic (deflationary) impact across the United States, including the sale of recorded music and radios. The same has been observed in 2008, in which the so-called Great Recession replaced The Great Depression. In both eras, the vast expansion of debt left lending institutions with impaired loans that could not be repaid and insolvent borrowers when the crash occurred. As a result, every form of consumption, including the sale of recorded music, music players, and concert tickets began to decline.

In both eras, older executives were out of touch with the music preferences, tastes, demands, values and cultural shift of a younger generation of music fans fascinated with the radio, Internet, or smart phones. This meant that some of the status quo business models were unprofitable. Entirely new services, products, payment systems, processes, and networks in the music industry had to be built or redesigned. In every case, technology, innovation, and competition caused the permanent weakening of the incumbent monopolists in a complex market that was constantly evolving. In some cases, court action—following lengthy litigation—was required to settle patents, infringement, and royalty disputes before the benefits of competition became widespread in the industry. Clairvoyant and forward-thinking executives were able to anticipate the changes and adapt accordingly.

In addition, there are pending revisions in copyright law led by the Copyright Office and the consent decrees led by the Department of Justice that are expected to simplify the accounting treatment for copyright administration, by (perhaps) including a *maximum statutory fixed-rate* and other terms for musical performances on terrestrial radio and television that are *similar in scope*, but not exactly the same, to the rate structure or price discovery mechanism for mechanical licensing. Similar in scope because there is a statutory prohibition on using sound recording rates in determining a rate for a license for the public performance of a musical work. This could become one of guiding principles to make sure that there is a quick, accurate, and *direct distribution* of royalty payments to songwriters, composers, and other copyright holders.

A maximum statutory fixed-rate formula for musical performances as a price discovery mechanism—as opposed to just a fixed or penny rate—is just one of the many solutions on fixing the copyright problem and would ensure that songwriters and composers are *directly* paid the maximum (whether fixed per song or per-minute of playing time) for any future increases in the statutory rate. There is always a time dimension when people listen to music, even with the electronic delivery of digital compositions. It would make it easier to amend future copyright changes that are the result of technological changes or mergers because the "price of a musical performance" or price discovery mechanism would be known and it would be hard to manipulate the price.

ASCAP and BMI may charge the same percentage of revenue for the cost of obtaining a blanket license under their consent decrees, their convoluted royalty payments formulas are different. As a result, there is a variation in royalty distribution payments to copyright holders, and this can affect the income of songwriters and composers. There is no consistent and equitable standard in the valuation of a musical performance and this is another area that future changes to copyright laws should fix. A standard that should be able to accommodate future technological changes, innovations, mergers, new business models and changing consumer preferences without an adverse impact on songwriters and composers. (Congress is also debating a *public performance right for sound recordings* bill that we discuss briefly in the context of Clear Channel's direct licensing deals in Sect. 8.6 on page 235.)

Although there are no legal mandates for PROs to produce and publish licensing fees (revenue) and royalty payment (income) deflators, there is a need for such data on a regular basis that could be republished in *Statistical Abstract of the United States*. Furthermore, with all of the traditional and non-traditional (online advertising) changes in advertising-industry dynamics caused by digital devices, social networks, demographics, and the demands of advertisers, there were hardly any white papers or peer-reviewed statistical analysis published by US PRO chief economists on the impact on songwriters' income.

Songwriters—tend to focus on the artistic rather than on the commercial exploitation of music and cannot ignore how these two endeavors complement each other—have had to adapt to new terms and conditions such as fixed fees or percentage-based royalties in contract negotiations as technology changed the music industry. It is often the case that songwriters and composers may go unpaid because there are no industry-wide, certified accounting and auditing requirements provided by law that royalty payments should be made public to ensure that PROs, record labels, and music publishers are all acting in good faith. The ease in which music can now be digitally distributed means that the process for obtaining copyright clearances should be automatic, transparent, and simplified to minimize protracted licensing negotiations between parties that are often shrouded in confidentiality agreements in which the financial terms and conditions are not disclosed to songwriters, composers, and other parties.

All of these rapid changes and the disruption caused by new technology are going to have an impact on the royalty income stream and on the livelihood of songwriters and composers. There are lessons to be learned from the telecommunications industry in which technology, deregulation, and competition reshaped that industry. After more than a 100 years in business, AT&T—the former monopoly—no longer exists in its original form after its consent decree was abolished. Eventually, a new equilibrium was established that brought with it new leadership, competitors, business models, customer segments, and revenue streams. Similar changes can be expected in the music industry.

A musician can create the most wonderful, imaginative, creative, and artistic songs with all of his/her heart and soul, but unless the songs can generate revenue from paid downloads; ringtones; interactive streaming; merchandising; concert tours; and performance, mechanical and synchronization licensing very few publishers would be interested in adding them to their catalogs. The naive might believe that music is all about "art" and not about the money, but it is always about the money and who gets to control and allocate the spoils of copyrighted music. We have seen that although technology has changed music distribution and licensing, it has not changed the creative art of producing great songs in which the copyrights can be exploited. However, technology has created a lot of tension between songwriters/composers and music distributors as the dominance of the latter has been receding for years.

Due to the adversarial relationships among songwriters, PROs, record labels, and music publishers, there is no unified solution on how to solve many of the problems in the music industry. It is important that the focus of new copyright laws or revisions to consent decrees should be on increasing the bargaining leverage of *individual* songwriters and composers, the actual content creators in music, who should have a greater share of revenue when their copyrighted songs are exploited by PROs, record labels, music publishers, and music users. PRO collective bargaining on behalf of songwriters, composers, and music publishers may not be the only viable licensing model in the future as songwriters regain control of their copyrights. Increasingly, the collectivity function of PROs is being questioned by their own members as to who exactly is benefiting as discussed in the Bruce Springsteen case study below.

Performance royalty income is important to songwriters and composers because it is the only source of income that is almost never recoupable, and it may be the only means of financial stability after their copyrighted music is no longer sold in stores. The major music licensing agencies such as PROs, record labels, and music publishers are looking to protect the status quo, their perks, and revenue streams, and it seems as though the songwriter or composer is just an afterthought. The harsh reality in the music industry is that the executives used to the old marketing, old technology, old distribution, and old licensing methods are now facing difficult choices when it comes to their livelihood because they are losing control to technology, innovation, and competition. Their failures to adapt to the changing technological environment meant that entrepreneurs with more youthful instincts were going to replace them.

For example, the Harry Fox Agency (HFA) is now slowly sinking into irrelevance because mechanical licensing revenue has dried up due to the decline in the reproduction and sale of physical records such as CDs, and from RightsFlow, a new online competitor. The days of the PROs are also numbered due to direct licensing, and new entrants such as TuneCore and Music Reports Inc. (MRI). The music business is not on its deathbed, if you believe some of the rhetoric. The music industry is simply changing due to innovation and technology, just like it did with the introduction of the player piano, radio, juke boxes, television, and the Internet.

The Structure of the Book

This monograph is in two parts. In Part I, we examine the economic aspects of direct licensing as an alternative to the traditional blanket license for copyrighted musical compositions. Direct licensing is a serious threat to the survival of the incumbent and protected monopoly PROs because music publishers are increasingly (partially) withdrawing digital rights from the PROs and negotiating direct licensing agreements with music users, eliminating the intermediate layer of PROs in the process. The partial withdrawal of digital rights is designed to increase the royalty rates for music publishers over licensing fees that are restricted by rate courts under consent decrees imposed on PROs. Two recent court cases in which DMX, a background/foreground music user, prevailed over both ASCAP and BMI in a direct licensing lawsuit revealed the economic and anti-competitive barriers to entry put in place by the PROs to prevent the development of innovative services in the music industry. Direct licensing has further economic implications for future business models in the music industry that we discuss in the Part II.

In Part II of this book, we examine a selection of the new publishing business models in the music industry and the role of direct licensing in creating a competitive market for copyright administration. These new models demonstrate that the old music industry business model in which intermediaries, such as record labels, kept a disproportionate share of songwriters' gross revenue may be a practice of the past. Songwriters may sell fewer units under some of these new licensing models, but they get to keep a larger percentage of revenue that is not shared with intermediaries. These new models encompass greater price transparency, on-time royalty payments and a shift to where intermediaries serve the interests of the recording artist and not the other way around. In addition, we speculate on the role a merger among several companies could play in bringing new competition to the music industry. This hypothetical merger reinforces the intent of the ASCAP and BMI consent decrees of maintaining reasonable licensing fees, fostering competition, and reining in the inherent pricing and market power of the two leading incumbent PROs. In addition, such a merger could intensify innovation and competition in the music industry.

It is thinking ahead to a possible future consolidation in the music industry in which consent decrees may be abolished, and copyright laws are revised to make sure that songwriters and composers are not adversely affected when the old and new laws are compared. This book adds to the growing literature on the economic effects of directly licensing music in the industry, particularly as the competitive Internet landscape is moving in the direction of handheld mobile devices and applications. The reader of this monograph will notice the recurring themes of: predatory behavior; self-destruction; preserving the status quo; active resistance to industry reform; cartels; inefficiencies; secrecy; scarcity; out-of-date business models; a lack of transparency; barriers to entry; control of information and price discovery mechanism are presented and discussed in a very pragmatic way. It was not possible to cover every topic in detail, but there are several excellent books and articles that are cited throughout the text that should be helpful. In the course of writing this monograph, other important works may have been overlooked and for that the author offers his apologies.

Intended Audience

This monograph is intended to be used by economists, music executives, musicians, songwriters, composers, law experts, business consultants, and students who are interested in understanding how technology, innovation, and competition have reshaped the music industry. This book was also written to be readable by the layperson and with enough detail that researchers in copyright law, business, and economics should find it helpful.

New York, NY, USA Ivan L. Pitt

Important Disclaimer

The information, data, and tables presented here do not contain or convey legal or accounting advice and should not be used or relied on with regard to any particular facts, circumstances, or situations. Laws, processes, strategic plans, business models, consumer demand, copyright owners, URLs, and market share can rapidly change, and some of the source material discussed here could be out of date by the time the monograph has been published. Given this time lag, the reader is advised to consult with legal counsel for expert advice and interpretation of US Copyright Laws and conduct their own research for the most current data on any subject matter presented here. Furthermore, the opinions and generalizations developed here over the course of decades and expressed here are solely those of the author and should not be construed to represent any particular organization or person.

Acknowledgments

The monograph builds on decades of work experience, and throughout those years, I have had the great pleasure of working with many people whose ideas are still empowering so many decades later. It is almost impossible to thank all these people who helped me to refine the ideas presented in this monograph. On most occasions, it was just the art of listening and asking questions that generated new ideas. First and foremost, I would like to thank the readers for purchasing either the hardback or a digital version of this monograph. Without you and your purchasing choices, this monograph would not have been possible. I would particularly like to thank Bryon Morgan for his comments on an earlier draft of the manuscript. I would like to thank Lorraine Klimowich, the economics editor at Springer, for all her help in getting the monograph approved for final publication. I would also like to thank Silembarasan Panneerselvam and Anthony Charles. Springer for their help in the final production of the monograph.

Contents

List of Figures

List of Tables

Part I
How Direct Licensing Increased Competition

Chapter 1
Introduction

In recent years, technology, innovation, competition, corporate policies, and government regulation have caused dramatic changes in the music industry. These changes have resulted in new global music business models. In particular, digital technology reshaped the way music is created, licensed, distributed, sold, and consumed. Music consumption is the many ways that people "experience" music by listening, watching, streaming, and downloading of musical compositions. Digital technologies have made the worldwide distribution of music, books, film, newspapers, and magazines much easier and cheaper, while significantly lowering the operating costs in those industries. The music industry has been the fastest to adopt and monetize digital formats. As Table 1.1 shows, close to 60 % of recorded music revenue—when revenue from some performing rights organizations, touring and merchandising are excluded—is now derived from digitally distributed formats—such as downloads, streaming and ringtones—while it is less than 25 % in films, books, newspapers, and magazines, but growing year over year. The music industry is now adjusting to these changes in digital technology by focusing on maximizing copyright revenue from existing music content (music publisher catalogs) and future content creation using a more efficient distribution system or supply chain.[1]

As the digital distribution of musical compositions transformed the music industry, the infrastructure of large distributors of physical records—such as manufacturing plants, warehouses, sales and promotion personnel, distribution networks, inventory control systems, and supply chains—was no longer needed. For example, most of the stand-alone, brick-and-mortar record retailers (like Tower and Virgin Records with a massive inventory) are now defunct, except for a few dwindling

[1]The term "distribution" as used in this monograph can have three different meanings depending on the context. First, a distribution can mean the quarterly royalty payments made by PROs to songwriters, composers, and music publishers. A second use can be a statistical distribution. Finally, the use of term can mean the physical or digital delivery of a product or service over a network.

I.L. Pitt, *Direct Licensing and the Music Industry*,
DOI 10.1007/978-3-319-17653-6_1

Table 1.1 Year over year change (%) in digital distribution revenue

Industry	2011	2012	Change
Recorded music	51 %	59 %	8
Films	18	21	3
Books	12	16	4
Newspapers	10	11	1
Magazines	7	11	4

Sources: News and Notes on 2013 RIAA Music Industry Shipment and Revenue Statistics: http://www.riaa.com/media/2463566A-FF96-E0CA-2766-72779A364D01.pdf.
Music Industry Continues To Lead the Way in Digital Adoption, With A Bit of Vinyl On The Side, June 14, 2013, https://www.riaa.com/search.php.

specialty physical record retailers. As the sale of music on CDs continues to plummet (along with the record labels' operating costs), it is big-box retailers such as Walmart and Target who are now handling most of these music sales.[2]

Practically overnight, A&R (artists and repertoire) people, marketing (product management, pricing, sales, distribution networks, and promotion), production, manufacturing, financing, and legal issues concerning both domestic and international copyright licensing clearances had changed. The old music business model of exploiting the momentum from hit singles to sell millions of albums using radio airplay became increasingly difficult. It became a struggle for some start-up music publishers to sustain themselves without a substantial catalog of master recordings and performance royalty income during the music industry's digital transitional phase.

Surprisingly, it is Apple's iTunes music distribution model that has now become the biggest online retailer of digital music in the United States because consumers are no longer interested in owning a physical copy of a song on a CD; consumers saw no value in purchasing an entire CD with just one or two good songs; or consumers wanted access to their music on "cloud-based storage" platforms for easier mobility. In essence, Apple's iTunes became one of the first legal alternatives to music piracy even though there was strong resistance from record labels and music publishers who had failed to capitalize on the trends in music downloading and streaming.[3] It is surprising in the sense that it took innovators from outside the music industry to

[2]Some of these defunct record retailers have a small online operation. It was not just the digital shift that destroyed stand-alone record retailers, but also stiff price competition among big-box chains like Walmart, Target, and Best Buy that sold goods other than music that could subsidize the music discounts. The same can be said about PROs with infrastructure (and the associated sunk costs) in multiple states where doing more of what was once considered efficient makes little sense in the new digital environment.

[3]Google Play, eMusic, and Amazon MP3 are some of the other digital retailers of music.

create the new music distribution model because the incumbent music publishers or record labels were unable to develop a viable business for online sales. The new online-distribution model threatened the outdated business models and leverage (bargaining power) in contracts that so many media executives had built their careers on.[4] In some cases, the early digital strategy to control markets, technology and preserve the (unsustainable) status quo appeared to have been to file copyright infringement lawsuits; offer lucrative financial incentives to existing music suppliers or other vested interests upon contract renewals/supplemental licensing agreements or including punitive measures in licensing agreements for music users in order to prevent emerging businesses, new business models and innovations from reaching consumers.[5]

As Patry (2011, p. 46) observes on the creative and financial development of new technologies in the music industry, "[n]ot a single penny was contributed by the music industry to the creation, manufacture or marketing of iTunes, the iPod, or the iPad. Not a single penny was contributed by the copyright industries to the development of the Internet or to any search engine even though the copyright industries could not exist without either." The monopolist-as-gatekeeper mindset among PRO executives made it difficult—if not impossible—for new entrants in the PRO industry and they adapted anti-competitive measures to discourage competition and limit economic growth.[6] However, as the digital revolution transformed the music industry, it became apparent that the survival of legacy PROs—the gatekeepers of performance rights licensing and their outdated business models keeping them afloat—were in doubt because digital technologies reinvented the way music was composed, presented, managed, distributed, stored, streamed, and licensed.[7]

PROs were left in dire need of fresh executive talent and struggled to adapt to all of the new and evolving business models in the music industry as the tsunami of competition, innovation, and digital technology began to emerge. You would be hard pressed to find a PRO with warehouse and distribution networks, inventories, stores, patents or major fixed assets, and yet they still exist as monopolies with tough barriers to entry. PROs do not share ownership of the copyrights of musical

[4]See Verrier (2014) and Ulin (2014). It is not just music that is digitally distributed, but movies as well. Paramount Pictures became the first major Hollywood movie studios to distribute movies entirely in a digital format—without the use of 35 mm film or film reels on which the industry depended on for over a century.

[5]See these important early court cases on peer-to-peer file sharing in: Langenderfer and Cook (2001). See also Ulin (2014, pp. 76–90) for his analysis of the seminal Grokster case and the novel copyright issues that were raised, just as Apple's economic model was beginning to dominate the music industry. *MGM vs. Grokster*, US Court of Appeals for the Ninth Circuit, Case No. 04-480, argued March 29, 2005 and decided June 27, 2005.

[6]It is often the case of semantics when PROs are described. Academics view the PROs as monopolists—with the usual textbook examples—while the public tends to view the incumbent PROs as a *cartel*—with a sinister implication—whose intent is to restrict competition, raise prices, and erect regulatory barriers.

[7]See DiLorenzo (1996).

compositions in their repertories that have been registered by songwriters, composers, or music publishers. There was nothing absolutely unique about the PROs' status quo business models that could not be easily and cheaply replicated with a central registry of copyrighted song data and digital processing technologies. PROs "intangible assets" were mainly in making direct royalty payments to songwriters, composers, and music publishers, placing the (songwriters' and composers') royalty payments beyond the reach of (record labels' and music publishers') recoupable agreements. In a competitive environment, the double-digit margins that these PROs skim off the top of licensing fees should have started to erode with the introduction of digital technologies that replaced the manual processing of song-title registration and performance data.

Self-delusional executives were demoralized and unprepared for the faster adoption rates of new technologies, new ways in which music, books, and videos were now consumed, the alternative access methods to content, and the convergence on multi-media platforms such as smart phones and tablet computing devices. This was going to play a major role in the lack of foresight in developing business models in the digital era that were a consequence of their role as gatekeepers to maintain the status quo. In addition, the mobility features of smart phones and tablets were replacing the older practice of watching scheduled television programming at home and disrupted the old mass-market advertising model. Consumer were looking for lower monthly bills, flexibility, à la carte access to video content and were no longer willing to pay for a bundled full subscription to cable networks, all of which affected the business models in the media industry. Flexibility meant that consumers did not care whether they were accessing content on a computer, tablet, television set or some other device, Table 1.2 shows the worsening economic situation for licensing agencies dependent on their outdated status quo business models and the new media consumption patterns as terrestrial radio and television continued their steep decline in users, ratings and revenue. Traditional television viewership dropped nearly 4 %, while radio listening declined by 3 % last quarter. The growth in content distribution using digital platforms is growing dramatically with a 60 % increase in online video streaming, due in part to subscription-based video-on-demand services such as Netflix and consumers dropping their pay-television subscriptions.

Table 1.2 Composite monthly time spent by medium (minutes): quarterly Y/Y change 2013–2014

Medium	Q3 '13	Q3 '14	Change	Change (%)
Watching video on the internet	401	642	241	60.10
Using App/web on a smart phone	2,144	2,855	711	33.16
Watching video on a smart phone	85	106	21	24.71
Traditional TV	8,821	8,479	−342	−3.88
Radio AM/FM	3,642	3,533	−109	−2.99

Source: Based on data from: *The Total Audience Report: December 2014*. The Nielsen Company, p. 12.

The table also shows how much smart phones have penetrated the market for content distribution, retail and entertainment and they are giving consumers control over where, what, and when they watch television. With a few exceptions, when compared to television, laptops and tablet media devices, smart phones have become the largest single-screen medium around the world in terms of the minutes of daily screen use because they are miniature Internet-connected computers for people on the go.[8]

In some cases, the incumbents' determination to control the new music industry did not result in practical, consumer-friendly policies, or very good leadership. Given the apocalyptic rhetoric that suited their own self-serving and vested interests that was floating around the industry, it appeared as though the music industry was afflicted with a new, deadly and cyclical crisis and in its last throes (again!) following the introduction of digital technologies that were driving structural changes in music creation, production, sales, distribution, and licensing.

1.1 How to Divide the Spoils of Music

The economics of streaming in the music industry is now focused on the way in which streaming is cannibalizing download music sales. It is a familiar life cycle and consumption pattern in which consumers switching to a new medium or digital platform cause sales and revenue to decline in the older medium. Download music sales are now declining due to streaming services such as Spotify, just iTunes was a major factor in the decline of CD sales and CD sales were a major factor in the decline of vinyl records. The economic reasoning used by consumers in their decision-making process is also the same; why pay $10 to download a single album on iTunes when a monthly subscription to a streaming service cost the same for unlimited streams of cloud-based music libraries, curated playlists or customized music based on taste, lifestyle, mood swings or day of the week. The big question for copyright holders—who earned their income from recording sales associated with physical media (such as CDs), mechanical royalties and downloads—was how they were going to be compensated when consumers switched to online streaming and music subscription services? Streaming revenue is lower than the revenue generated by digital downloads or performance royalties. Furthermore, streaming once favored the major labels and their mainstream recording artists whose popularity enabled them to generate substantial royalties from a large audience when their musical compositions were publicly performed or distributed on streaming services such as iTunes, Pandora, and Spotify.

In the early days, it was often the case that the increase in revenue from the sale of digital music did not offset the decline in revenue, and the lost and cannibalized

[8]See *AdReaction: Marketing in a Multiscreen World* by the consulting firm Millward Brown and available here: http://www.millwardbrown.com/AdReaction/2014.

Table 1.3 Selected music industry revenue by segment: 2012–2013 in ($Millions)

Segment	2012	2013	Change	Change (%)	Segment share (%)
Synchronization					
Synchronization[a]	$191	$190	−1	−0.47	1.36
Digital subscription and streaming					
Paid subscription	$400	$628	228	57.06	
On-demand streaming (ad-supported)	171	220	49	28.73	
Subtotal	571	848	277	48.58	6.06
Physical recordings					
CD	$2,486	$2,124	−362	−14.57	
CD single	3	2	−1	−25.00	
Other	283	319	36	12.53	
Subtotal	2,772	2,445	−327	−11.81	17.48
Performing rights					
ASCAP[b]	$942	$945	4	0.39	
BMI[c]	899	944	45	5.03	
SoundExchange	462	590	128	27.71	
SESAC	NA	NA	NA	NA	
Subtotal	2,302	2,479	177	7.68	17.73

Digital permanent downloads					
Single	$1,624	$1,569	−55	−3.36	
Album	1,205	1,234	29	2.38	
Ringtones and ringbacks	167	98	−69	−41.52	
Other	25	23	−2	−6.53	
Subtotal	3,020	2,923	25	0.81	20.90
Touring					
Live concerts (North America only)	$4,300	$5,100	800	18.60	36.47
Merchandising					
Live concerts	NA	NA	NA	NA	
Amazon	NA	NA	NA	NA	
Fan club					
Membership dues	NA	NA	NA	NA	
Grand total	$13,156	$13,985	$829	6.30	100

Sources: *News and Notes on 2013 RIAA Music Industry Shipment and Revenue Statistics*: http://www.riaa.com/media/2463566A-FF96-E0CA-2766-72779A364D01.pdf.

[a]RIAA recorded music data only. Synchronization worldwide revenue was estimated to be around $2.5 billion in 2011.

[b]Fiscal Year ending in December 31: http://www.ascap.com/about/annualreport.aspx.

[c]Fiscal Year ending June 30: http://www.bmi.com/press/entry/563077.

Pollstar: http://www.pollstar.com/news_article.aspx?ID=808976

http://www.pollstar.com/news_article.aspx?ID=803803.

sales from physical records. However, revenues from synchronization licensing to television, video, and movie production companies were growing rapidly. In addition, synchronization licensing to social media services like Facebook and Twitter was increasing as they added video advertising with background music to their sites.[9] It is in the total value (price and quantity) of music streaming that the economic rivalry among record labels and recording artists; music publishers and songwriters; and PROs developed.[10] This economic conflict focused on who collected and distributed the billions in royalty revenue from streaming music services. In the competitive scramble to collect streaming royalty income—due in part to no one wanting to relinquish control—each group believed that their share of the royalty income pie would decrease if the other groups were paid more.[11]

Table 1.3 shows the revenue from various segments in the music industry—an industry that is controlled by a few gatekeepers in every segment—and this is essentially where the battles are being fought on how to distribute the spoils of copyrighted music.[12] The music industry revenue pie is shrinking in certain segments, while growing in others. It is an enormous amount of revenue and there is no apparent transparency in the process on *how* some of the revenue is distributed to songwriters, composers, and artists, judging from artists' complaints that they are not receiving their fair share of revenue. This has caused songwriters, composers, and performers to become skeptical about the economics of music licensing and in this environment some artists have begun to remove their catalogs from streaming services. They are arguing for a greater share of licensing revenue because they are the content creators or the performers who brought the music to life. The table shows the overall revenue picture in the music industry in which we can clearly see the year over year decline in revenue for both physical CDs and digital downloads, while growth is occurring in digital subscriptions and streaming. Live concerts are by far the greatest generator of revenue in the music industry and that is depicted in Fig. 1.1.

For example, in 2013, music streaming services that competed with terrestrial radio stations generated \$1.4 billion in revenue that consisted of \$628 million (43.67 %) from subscription services; \$220 million (15.3 %) in advertising from on-demand streaming; and \$590 million (41.03 %) in licensing fees paid to SoundExchange. Digital paid subscription and streaming revenue grew 48.58 % from the year 2012—offsetting some of the revenue from the rapid decline in CD sales and downloads—and it shows how fast streaming is being monetized because advertisers are interested in the demographic that spends a disproportionate share of their leisure time online and interacting with friends on social media. In addition, the table shows the \$1.89 billion that ASCAP and BMI collected in licensing fees in

[9] See Wixen (2014, p. 107).

[10] See Copyright Royalty Board (2012).

[11] See Christman et al. (2013), *BMI vs. Pandora Media Inc.* (2013), and *US vs. ASCAP & In re Petition of Pandora Media* (2014).

[12] See DiCola (2013) for his survey results on musician's self-reported income.

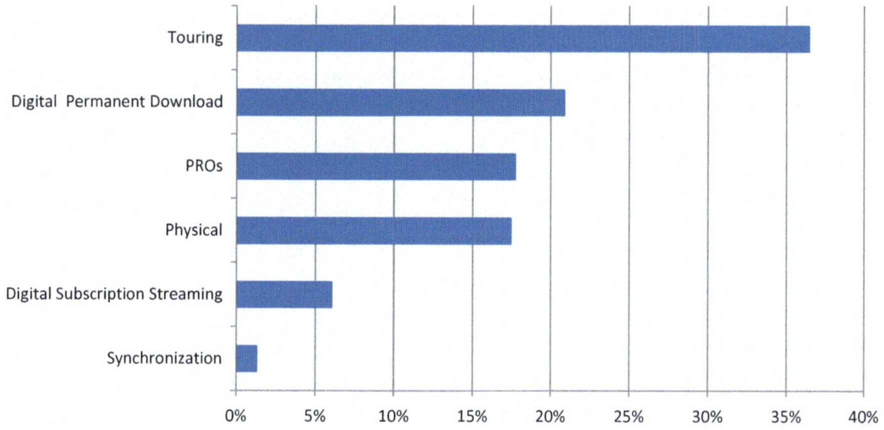

Fig. 1.1 Revenue share by industry segment 2013

2013 for distribution to songwriters, composers, and music publishers. Overall, the US market is estimated to be around $14 billion in revenue from various sources—with a significant amount from royalty fees that is distributed by the PROs—and this figure excluded revenue from merchandising and other segments. SESAC does not disclose financial data and revenue numbers are not reported. Moody's Investors Service estimated that SESAC's revenue had grown to $182 million in 2014 from $167 million in 2013.[13]

1.2 Who Is Really Getting Paid?

There is an industry perception that the sound recording royalty payment (record labels) process is inequitable to the performance royalty payment (music publishers) process, and vice versa, depending who is collecting and distributing royalty payments. This is a direct reflection of the outdated *Copyright Act* that has not kept up with all the digital changes that have occurred. Quite often, the record label is a subsidiary of the major music publisher and so it depends on how the royalty pie is sliced up and distributed. There have been countless amendments to the *Copyright Act* and various consent decrees over the years (and most have been well-intentioned), yet songwriters and composers—the actual content creators—have been complaining that the changes never seem to improve their incomes or leverage. Billions in revenue are generated each year and it appears as though musicians not getting a fair and equitable share of revenue that is generated from

[13]See *SESAC Buys the Harry Fox Agency*, Billboard Magazine, July 7, 2015, https://www.billboard.com/articles/news/6620210/sesac-buys-the-harry-fox-agency.

their song creations. One reason for the inequitable distribution of royalties is that the pricing mechanism—price discovery—for determining the value of a musical performance across all terrestrial and digital music platforms is not transparent and fixing it will require a complete overhaul of the *Copyright Act* and consent decrees.

Currently, some recording artists have been voicing concerns about how they are being compensated by streaming services, a process in which *direct* payments to songwriters, composers, and artists are not an industry standard. However, the same concerns about the amount of control and leverage that songwriters have in the copyright exploitation of their music can be made about the other music revenue segments that are collecting and distributing royalties. Some artists may focus more on their creative credibility and not enough on their business acumen. The gatekeepers are handsomely rewarded—even though digital technologies have made many of the functions of PROs, music publishers, and record labels redundant—but songwriters, composers, and artists are left to fend for themselves. For example, ASCAP and BMI split performance royalties 50/50 with songwriters and music publishers, even though song plugging by music publishers has been practically extinct since the demise of Tin Pan Alley. Songwriters have taken on more of the functions of music publishers by first being discovered on YouTube and creating their own fan-base, yet the 50/50 share still persists. It is possible that the entire music licensing bureaucracy that is over 100 years old needs to be rebuilt from the ground up with an emphasis on the songwriter, composer, and artist.

On Forbes Magazine annual listing of the top earning musicians in 2014, shown in Table 1.4, the top earner that year was Dr. Dre with $620 million—whose income was mostly related to the one-off sale of Beats Music to Apple and is reported to have given him the biggest single-year payday of any musician in history. Bruce Springsteen was ranked in the top 5 with earnings of $81 million. Taylor Swift was ranked number 11 with approximately $64 million in earnings from touring and album sales. The table also reveals that most of the top earners' (highly-skewed) income came from live performances, touring and other ventures and the top 5 musicians raked in more than 50 % of the $1.9 billion in earnings in the selection shown.[14]

[14]One of the major threats to live touring appears to be the practice of vocal performers miming or lip-syncing—the use of pre-recorded vocals in a live concert without the knowledge of the audience. It has been claimed that unlike previous generations of "real" singers who mastered the art of singing, today's generation often relies on Auto-Tune and other digital voice-enhancing technologies that are capable of transforming mediocre singers into perfectly in-tune vocalists in the studio, and increasingly the technology is now being shifted from the studio to live concerts. It has been reported that the standard of perfection created by the widespread use of Auto-Tune software in a recording studio is almost impossible to hit in reality, even for some artists with great vocals. See *Miming Will Be The Death of Live Music Performance*, The Telegraph, January 23, 2013, http://www.telegraph.co.uk/culture/music/rockandpopmusic/9821284/Miming-will-be-the-death-of-live-music-performance.html and *Britney Spears is a pop queen. And pop queens don't need to sing*, Vox, July 11, 2014, http://www.vox.com/2014/7/11/5888535/britney-spears-without-autotune-horrible.

Table 1.4 Top 20 of the world's highest paid musicians in 2014

Rank	Musician	Amount ($M)	Share (%)	Cum. share (%)	Source of income
1	Dr. Dre	$620	32.63 %	32.63 %	Sale of Beats Music to Apple and producer
2	Beyoncé	115	6.05	38.68	Touring, album sales and endorsements
3	The Eagles	100	5.26	43.95	Mostly touring
4	Bon Jovi	82	4.32	48.26	Mostly touring
5	Bruce Springsteen	81	4.26	52.53	Mostly touring
6	Justin Bieber	80	4.21	56.74	Mostly touring
7	One Direction	75	3.95	60.68	Touring and endorsements
8	Paul McCartney	71	3.74	64.42	Mostly touring
9	Calvin Harris	66	3.47	67.89	Albums, DJ and producer
10	Toby Keith	65	3.42	71.32	Own record label, beverages and restaurants
11	Taylor Swift	64	3.37	74.68	Album sales and touring
12	Jay Z	60	3.16	77.84	Stadium co-bills and financial ventures
13	Diddy	60	3.16	81.00	Mostly endorsements
14	Bruno Mars	60	3.16	84.16	Mostly touring
15	Justin Timberlake	57	3.00	87.16	Touring, acting, restaurant and clothing
16	Pink	52	2.74	89.89	Touring
17	Michael Bublé	51	2.68	92.58	Live performances
18	Rihanna	48	2.53	95.11	Album sales and touring
19	Rolling Stones	47	2.47	97.58	Mostly touring
20	Roger Waters	46	2.42	100.00	Mostly touring
	Total	$1,900			

Sources: Based on data from: Forbes Magazine, December 29, 2014 and accessed online: http://www.forbes.com/pictures/eeel45fdddi/the-worlds-30-highest-paid-musicians-of-2014/.

The revenue disbursement process—how artists are paid and the billions in revenue distributed—is opaque, and the payments to songwriters, composers, and artists are often commingled with record labels and music publishers. Digitalization with its massive amount of readily available music performance and financial data exposed the problems associated with the music licensing process. With a few exceptions such as in some performance royalty payments, the current convention in music licensing is that royalties are first paid to record labels and music publishers, who then pass a share of royalties on to songwriters, composers, and artists. It is in this intermediary pass-through and commingling royalty payment system to record labels and music publishers—often subject to recoupment—in which the payments to songwriters, composers, and artists are not readily transparent; there is no proper public accounting on a timely basis; licensing fees, rates and terms are hidden in confidentially agreements; and this is the source for the bitter controversy over royalty payments. This is one of the areas in which there needs to be more forward-thinking and changes to the current conventional licensing process (such as doing away with the commingling of royalties) to the *Copyright Act*, consent decrees and licensing agreements are needed to ensure that songwriters and composers who may lack the leverage in contract negotiations can receive their fair share of licensing revenue. In some cases, streaming services negotiate licensing deals with record labels and it is the label's responsibility to distribute royalties to their artists based on statutory requirements, signed agreements, and recoupment practices. There are also intermediary collecting societies (ASCAP, BMI, SESAC and SoundExchange) that are collecting royalties for later distribution to artists, often months after a public performance of their music.

Table 1.5 shows the estimated revenue and market share data for the major streaming services and this represents about 6 % of music industry revenue. Pandora, is the largest Internet radio service and the majority of royalty payments to SoundExchange comes from Pandora. Pandora, Spotify, Vevo, and YouTube control about 65 % of the market for streaming services.[15] There are complaints about the streaming services' business models—a combination of listening to music for free but with advertising messages and paid subscriptions without advertising—on how to turn listeners into paid subscribers. The incremental revenues from streaming services have not been able to offset the cannibalization of CD sales, but they appear to offset some of the decline in digital sales, even though there is growth in the overall consumption of music.

1.2.1 Streaming Services Controversy

Recent press reports revealed that Taylor Swift, a singer who writes most of her music and has a crossover appeal in both country and pop music, believes that

[15] See Pham (2014) and Lyons (2014).

Table 1.5 Estimated streaming music market 2013

Digital service	Est. royalty revenue ($)[a]	Share (%)[b]	Cum. share (%)
Pandora	$431,400,000	30.00 %	30.00 %
Spotify	251,650,000	17.50	47.50
Vevo	143,800,000	10.00	57.50
YouTube	107,850,000	7.50	65.00
Rhapsody	100,660,000	7.00	72.00
Cricket/Muve	81,966,000	5.70	77.70
Microsoft	67,586,000	4.70	82.40
iTunes radio/match	53,206,000	3.70 %	86.10 %
Google Access	28,760,000	2.00	88.10
eMusic	28,760,000	2.00	90.10
Slacker	21,570,000	1.50	91.60
Radio	14,380,000	1.00	92.60
TouchTunes	10,066,000	0.70	93.30
Apple's Beats Music	5,752,000	0.40	93.70
Others	90,594,000	6.30	100.00
Streaming total	$1,438,000,000		

Sources:
[a]Based on SoundExchange, paid subscription, and on-demand streaming (ad-supported) revenue data from Table 1.3.
[b]Estimated market share data from Lyons (2014).

her fans should be purchasing (at Target, perhaps) or consuming entire albums (as opposed to single downloads to create their own libraries of songs) because the value of *her* music and art can only be appreciated in an album format. Purchasing her music is to be considered an *investment*, and it is not clear if the ROI is monetary or just listening pleasure.[16] This thinking represents the old CD model in which fans were forced to purchase CDs with one or two good songs until Apple's iTunes disaggregated the songs on an album to sell singles (while aggregating the repertories of the record labels). Ms. Swift withdrew her entire catalog from Spotify—with around 50 million users worldwide in which 25 % are paid subscribers—in September 2014 to protest royalty compensation rates from music subscription services that often pay less than downloads and physical CDs and to boost album and download sales (initial impulse buys) of her newly released album entitled (*1989*) on other digital platforms and physical outlets by restricting her music on Spotify's paid tier, which the streaming service refused to do. Ms. Swift's action could be described as "windowing" in which she attempted to maximize payouts from the release of her album by providing exclusive access to selected distributors while restricting her music on other platforms.

[16]See *Artists weigh in on music streaming services*: https://news.yahoo.com/artists-weigh-music-streaming-services-174801043.html that appeared November 24, 2014.

Spotify was in a difficult financial and competitive position of running a business that was subjected to the whims and fancies of copyright holders who in some cases can overestimate the value of their works. This created a *churn* situation where a substantial music catalog with the most popular music could disappear overnight from its streaming service. Paid subscribers would abandon the service and flock to competitors for their music consumption, creating a financial drain in the process and lower revenue that resulted in even lower compensation for recording artists.[17] The music service would then have to devote more financial resources to acquire new customers to make up for the losses or to retain existing customers in a loyalty program.

Ms. Swift's back catalog was available on other streaming services such as YouTube (where it is still free); Beats Music and Rhapsody in which consumers pay for premium access to albums; and Rdio whose free version is based on custom radio stations that do not allow full on-demand listening. Her new album, *1989*, was said to be the fastest-selling in 12 years with nearly 1.3 million sales in the first week and 3.66 million total in 2014 due to the clever use of social media marketing on Tumblr, Twitter, and Instagram. About one-third of the first-week album sales were reported to have occurred at Target retail stores that had an exclusive physical-album sales deal that included bonus tracks and deluxe versions, despite the fact that streaming services help to boost music sales by consumers who prefer to stream entire albums or just purchase one or two hits from a new album, extending consumption into ownership. Indeed, skeptics would ask whether the true aim to restrict music access on Spotify was to enhance album and merchandise sales by increasing consumer traffic at Target outlets.[18]

Royalty compensation, sustainable business models, windowing and competition were important issues on the monetization of streaming services that were raised by the Swift/Spotify and the Pandora/music publishers/PRO controversies, and these issues had both sort-term and long-term financial consequences in the music industry. The first issue raised is that of the current streaming royalty compensation system for recording artists, songwriters, composers, record labels, and music publishers. This may be, in part, due to the lack of transparency in royalty compensation across all music segments; streaming payments may never reach the right copyright holders; there is no direct or up-front payments to songwriters and composers; or a song may have multiple songwriters that share in royalty compensation. When compared to streaming services, there is the perception among artists that they may be better compensated from other music formats such as downloads and album sales on iTunes, and from performance royalties collected and distributed by ASCAP and BMI. In other words, royalties paid by streaming services may be comparatively too low, just pennies for millions of streams. However, Pandora, the radio streaming service, has been suing ASCAP and BMI seeking lower performance royalties rates

[17]The compensation for the company executives would be an entirely different matter and can probably be found in SEC quarterly filings for public companies.

[18]See *Taylor Strikes a Chord*, Time Magazine, November 24, 2014, pp. 42–48.

because they believe that performance royalty rates charged by the PROs are too high. The disparity between sound recording and performance royalties payments by licensing agencies has been at the heart of the digital withdrawal movement among music publishers who believe they can directly negotiate higher licensing fees for the both the sound recording and performance rights, bypassing the PROs in the licensing process. Digital withdrawals may be the final nail in the coffin for incumbent PROs who are struggling to remain relevant. The stumbling block in music publishers directly licensing music has been the consent decrees that may prohibit the publishers from refusing to grant licenses over fee disputes and require that fee disputes to be settled by a rate court.

The second issue is the business models used in streaming services and the expectations of younger consumers. YouTube is one of the biggest sources of music consumption and until recently it was available for free without a paid tier. It is often difficult to get some younger consumers to pay for music subscription services when they have grown up with Internet, and the expectation that music should be free and made available across a wide variety of platforms, including smart phones and tablets. Music was always free to listen to on advertising-supported radio networks. Differentiating between the "free versus paid access" models used by various streaming services—and how should music content be made available to consumers when streaming services offer both free on-demand and premium tiers—is often financially difficult because there are more free users than paid subscribers. The paid-tiered customers are often subsidizing some of the free on-demand users, even though free on-demand may be ad-supported. It is not only the "free versus paid access" models that are problematic, but differentiating between streaming music services themselves in a market that is over-saturated with everyone essentially having the same access to acquired content from the three major music publishers and independent labels. Other music service business models, like Muve Music, focus less on direct subscription models, but more on bundles involving pre-paid mobile subscriptions (that include voice, text, and Internet access) along with the convenience of unlimited music downloads.

The third issue is windowing—the model often used in movie distribution in which movies first appear in theaters, then on-demand, and later on broadcast television and cable networks—that is, what is the time frame (immediately upon album release or at a later date) when albums should be made available to free streaming services? Artists and labels are seeking to maximize royalty payments on new releases by making content exclusive, like Ms. Swift's latest album, to distributors by requiring additional payments or other terms.[19] Finally, there is the long-term issue of the survival of streaming services, given the current level of competition and growing losses in music streaming. The financial model in place today appears to focus on the short-term upside growth in customer acquisition (funded by Wall Street speculators) rather than long-term profitability,

[19]See *Why Streaming (Done Right) Will Save the Music Business*, Billboard Magazine, November 29, 2014, p. 15.

in a similar model that is used by Amazon. Subscription-only or paid-only models, like Rhapsody, are struggling to generate sustaining or significant profits in order to acquire or convert all those free users in a rapidly changing competitive market. It is not entirely clear when most of these streaming services will be become profitable, given rising content acquisition costs, and stiff competition from some new entrants with deep pockets to sustain loses. A fair number of marginal streaming services are now defunct, due in part to the high cost music content acquisition that could not be offset by revenue.[20]

Google has launched a new paid music services called—YouTube Music Key—to complement its free service and to compete directly with Spotify and Apple's Beats Music. Music Key will start with a built-in base of more than one billion monthly viewers, the largest group of people who listen to music and watch videos on the Internet. In order for Spotify, Rhapsody, and other streaming services to compete effectively, they would have to spend marketing dollars to acquire such customers. "[T]he wide availability of free music on YouTube was a big part of the reason why CDs sales—and more recently downloads too—have been falling. Though such worries are widespread in the music industry, that has not stopped Merlin [a licensing agency that represents independent record labels] and the three big record labels—Universal, Sony and Warner—from agreeing to let YouTube make significant enhancements to its free tier in conjunction with the launch of the paid one... YouTube's enhanced free service was likely to attract people who pay for downloads, and in doing so it would cannibalize the most lucrative part of the music industry."[21] The net effect is that the new competition is likely to erode even further the price that consumers are willing to pay for music—which is practically very little—creating further financial problems for music services and the perceived value of music subscription services.

Table 1.6 shows the estimated revenue, based on a low of \$0.006 and a high of \$0.0084 per stream, for the top ranked streams on Spotify for the period January through October 2014. For the 3,029 billion streams, it was estimated that Spotify paid about \$25.54 million in royalties on the high end of the range, essentially pennies for millions of plays.[22] However, not all of that money went to the artists listed in the table; most likely, the royalty payments were made to the record labels who share the copyright ownership of the sound recordings or to SoundExchange who is collecting digital royalties. It is after this royalty pass-through payment

[20]See the section, *Web Music's Bleak History* for a list of defunct music services that included Napster (bought by Rhapsody) and Sony Connect in the following article: *Eclipsed by Rivals, Rhapsody Reduces Staff and Ousts Key Managers*, The Verge, September 16, 2013 that is available here: http://www.theverge.com/2013/9/16/4735512/eclipsed-by-rivals-rhapsody-reduces-staff-and-ousts-key-managers.

[21]See *YouTube Launches Music Subscription Service*, Financial Times, November 12, 2014, http://www.ft.com/cms/s/0/4c26b2d0-6a78-11e4-bfb4-00144feabdc0.html#axzz3L836mpOE.

[22]See Johnson (2014) and Copyright Royalty Board (2012).

Table 1.6 Spotify's top ranked streams January–October 2014: and estimated royalty payments

Rank	Song	Artist	Streams (millions)	Share (%)	Cum. share (%)	Payout ($000)
1	*Summer*	Calvin Harris	203	6.70 %	6.70 %	$1.700
2	*Dark Horse*	Katy Perry	196	6.47	13.17	1.600
3	*All of Me*	John Legend	194	6.40	19.58	1.600
4	*Waves*	Mr. Probz	178	5.88	25.45	1.500
5	*Counting Stars*	OneRepublic	166	5.48	30.93	1.400
6	*Problem*	Ariana Grande	165	5.45	36.38	1.400
7	*Timber*	Pitbull	160	5.28	41.66	1.300
8	*Rude*	MAGIC!	155	5.12	46.78	1.300
9	*Fancy*	Iggy Azalea	153	5.05	51.83	1.300
10	*Am I Wrong*	Nico and Vinz	152	5.02	56.85	1.300
11	*Rather Be*	Jess Glynne	151	4.99	61.84	1.300
12	*Chandelier*	Sia	139	4.59	66.42	1.200
13	*Stay With Me*	Sam Smith	138	4.56	70.98	1.200
14	*Demons*	Imagine Dragons	135	4.46	75.44	1.100
15	*A Sky Full Of Stars*	Coldplay	135	4.46	79.89	1.100
16	*Bad*	Vassy	134	4.42	84.32	1.100
17	*Pompeii*	Bastille	125	4.13	88.45	1.100
18	*Wiggle*	Snoop Dogg	119	3.93	92.37	1.100
19	*Riptide*	Vance Joy	116	3.83	96.20	0.970
20	*Radioactive*	Imagine Dragons	115	3.80	100.00	0.970
Total			3,029			$25.540

Source: Based on data from: http://time.com/3590670/spotify.

Table 1.7 Digital downloads vs. streaming 2014 (billions)

	2013	2014	Change	Change (%)
Digital songs	1.26	1.1	−0.16	−12.70
Streamed songs	106	164	58	54.72

Source: Wall Street Journal, January 2, 2015, p. B2.

system that the artists are paid after recoupment by the record labels and copyright administration fees by SoundExchange are deducted.

Whether artists will be hurt or helped by withdrawing their music from streaming services—given that streaming services represent changing media and post album-launch music consumption habits—will probably be determined by a decision that Billboard Magazine has made in modifying its traditional chart ranking methodology into a multi-metric consumption model that will include digital and streaming data. The change was necessary due to the growth in streaming services that benefited Spotify, and the continued decline in digital album and download sales that affected iTunes as is highlighted in Table 1.7. Digital songs declined by 12.70 % to 1.1 billion in 2014, from a high of 1.26 billion in 2013, while digital album sales is said to have decreased by 9 % in the same period. Streaming grew sharply from 106 billion in 2013 to 164 billion songs in 2014, a 54 % increase for the period and benefited music streaming services such as Spotify.

Billboard's 200 albums chart is highly regarded as one of the most important barometers of album sales in the music industry. Billboard will add a new chart that measures not only an album's popularity in sales, but music consumption activity by media platform as well. The chart will cover digital sales and on-demand streaming to more accurately reflect how people listen to and purchase music, and in the process extend the life cycle of albums in their ranking system as consumers enjoy them through their favorite streaming services. For example, under Billboard's chart ranking formula—1,500 song streams from services like Spotify, Beats Music, Rdio, Rhapsody, and Google Play will now be the equivalent to a single album sale, and ten downloads of individual tracks will equal one album. Billboard's new ranking system is expected to benefit artists whose streaming and digital song sales have been outperforming their album sales, and hurt older artists whose music is not streamed or sales occur through other channels.[23]

[23]See also Christman (2014), Blacc (2014), and Sisario (2014a,b).
Billboard 200 Makeover: Album Chart to Incorporate Streams & Track Sales: http://www.billboard.com/articles/columns/chart-beat/6320099/billboard-200-makeover-streams-digital-tracks, November 19, 2014.

1.3 SoundCloud's Business Model

Independent artists—who faced a much tougher challenge when it came to earning royalty income from streaming because they lacked a larger fan base and their music may not have been appealing to a mainstream audience—are now turning to new services such as SoundCloud. SoundCloud is a social *sound* platform where independent musicians or anyone can create, upload, and share audio content privately with friends or publicly to blogs and social networks such as Twitter, Tumblr, Facebook, and Foursquare in a system that is similar to that of YouTube. The SoundCloud platform is accessible from anywhere with the use of smart phone apps. It was reported that in a market saturated with mainstream competitors such as iTunes, Spotify, and Pandora, SoundCloud has managed to become the world's largest audio streaming service that reaches a huge global audience of about 350 million listeners a month with a catalog of unusual and exclusive audio-musical content. SoundCloud's demographic is highly skewed towards younger listeners under the age of 25 and about 69 % of listeners are said to be male, a young-and-male demographic profile that is appealing to advertisers.

SoundCloud's business model consists of allowing users to upload content—at a rate of about 12 h of sound every minute—for *promotional purposes* only and as a result the company is not yet required to pay royalties, but that is expected to change. SoundCloud has avoided paying royalties because until recently they didn't sell advertising.[24] SoundCloud's financial picture looks like some of the other streaming services, that is, there is insufficient revenue to cover all of their overhead, debt service, taxes, or operating costs as shown in Table 1.8—where the currency is denominated in euros. However, unlike Spotify and Pandora, SoundCloud's losses are occurring even before they have started to make royalty payments and it is not entirely clear if they will ever become profitable in the long run, like so many of the other streaming services. For now, most of these streaming services are focused on subscriber growth and less on profitability. SoundCloud's losses were more than twice its revenue in 2013 and before the implementation of an advertising business model and licensing deals with the major music publishers. SoundCloud's historical financial data paint a similar picture of widening losses between 2010 and 2013 and questions about their viability as a going concern. For example, "SoundCloud's revenues were €1.37m in 2010, €4.32m in 2011, €8.04m in 2012 and €11.28m in 2013. However, its net losses grew from €1.55m in 2010 to €3.74m in 2011, €12.43m in 2012 and €23.11m in 2013. Or, to put that another way, SoundCloud's losses were 113 % of its revenues in 2010, 87 % in 2011, 155 % in 2012 and 205 % in 2013."[25] What all of this means is that the music streaming financial landscape (negative cash flow) for SoundCloud is likely to worsen when royalty costs are added to their business model that may not be totally offset by advertising or subscription revenue.

---

[24]See Peoples (2014).

[25]See Dredge (2014).

Table 1.8 SoundCloud's consolidated profit and loss YE 2012–2013

	2012 €(000)	2013 €(000)	Change	Change (%)
Revenue	8,040	11,277	3,237	40.26
Cost of sales	3,950	5,908	1,958	49.57
Admin. expenses	16,489	28,461	11,972	72.61
Sub-total expenses	20,439	34,369	13,930	68.15
Operating profit (loss) before taxes, interest and other	(12,399)	(23,092)	(10,693)	86.24

Source: Based on data from: Dredge (2014).

Given the size of SoundCloud's audience, SoundCloud is reported to be negotiating licensing agreements and equity stakes with the major publishers and independent labels instead of litigating over past copyright infringement issues.[26] SoundCloud is expected to start paying royalties once advertising and subscription revenue are added to their business model and licensing deals are completed with all of the major record labels. Warner Music Group became one of the first music publishers sign to a licensing deal with SoundCloud in November 2014 and will begin to pay royalties for the first time.[27] Could the equity stakes signal that it may not be worth the legal costs to fight this overlooked force in digital music distribution among independent artists because they cannot win and its better for music publishers and record labels to join forces with services such as SoundCloud?

1.4 Digital Privacy

There may be a serious tradeoff between what consumers believe is a free service—social networks, search engines and apps—and the private data that is collected from advertising—supported sites on the Internet or with the use of smart phones. Consumers may be paying a high price for "free" services in terms of the loss of individual privacy and the lack of control over the private information that is collected and shared with third parties. Internet sites and smart phone companies are collecting vast amounts of what is called users' experience data—that is, their personal browsing, location and demographical data—every time that a PC, smart phone or tablet is turned on or personal information (including photographs) is uploaded to social networking sites. The users' experience data, in most cases, is an important differentiator when there is no perceivable difference among the various features offered by smart phone manufacturers or even the music content available at music streaming services. The private information that is collected—which in

[26]See Sisario (2014c).

[27]See Sisario (2014b).

itself may be more valuable than the ads themselves—is then sold to third parties to be used for tracking and targeted advertising without the permission of users, a practice that some consumers may find objectionable. Unwittingly, consumers may be agreeing to the collection of personal browsing habits on the Internet when they sign up for free or even paid online services and accept their opaque privacy policies. Although the free information from websites may be valuable to consumers, many object to the private data collection practice in which little information is disclosed on what is collected and consumers given a transparent choice on whether to opt in or out. Internet users may not have control over the way in which third parties (such as employers, law enforcement agencies, ex-spouses, stalkers, ad servers, hackers, data brokers, trackers, and marketers) may access or use the information gathered and stored by websites. There is a huge disparity among privacy policies associated with an online advertising business model on the Internet, and it is very similar to the criticisms of the *Copyright Act* in which regulatory efforts have not kept up with the use of emerging technologies. The loss of privacy and the lack of control over personal browsing data are made even worse by the cloud-based storage of such data. There is a huge concern that cloud-stored data does not have the same Fourth Amendment legal protections that it would have if it were stored in a desk drawer, desktop computer or other local storage device. There are now legislative efforts underway to address many of the inadequacies of he outdated *Electronic Communications Privacy Act of 1986* (ECPA) to further protect the online privacy of consumers.[28]

1.5 New Industry Structure

It is curious in retrospect to see how their own myopic assumptions, decisions, and natural reaction—caused by insecurity, inertia, suspicion, impatience, fear, greed, anxiety or ambition—led music executives and their subordinates to see only looming threats rather than greater opportunities and new jobs that were being created by digital technologies. In the digital age, executives saw new technology as a threat, while entrepreneurs saw it as an opportunity for a much better future. This antipathy—probably dating back to the first introduction of player pianos and later radios—would always remain to divide consumers and prevent the rapid introduction of new technology in the television and Internet eras. As the transition to a new structure in the music industry was occurring, the interminable battle plans—with its built-in bias towards litigation and its high costs of enforcing copyrights as a deterrent—were soon drawn up and old economic rivalries were forgotten in order for "defenseless" conglomerates to fight the new enemies that they all had in common: music thieves or "pirates," technology and entrepreneurs.

---

[28]See *The 5 Biggest Online Privacy Threats of 2013*, PC World, April 8, 2013, http://www.pcworld.com/article/2031908/the-5-biggest-online-privacy-threats-of-2013.html.

All of this has been somewhat peculiar (if not for the later and inevitable consequences) because they had no control over the rapid adoption rates of smart phone technology as the dominant single-screen in usage for consumers who were no longer tied to the home or car; collapsing sales of physical media such as CDs at retail outlets; or convincing radio stations to perform the dormant works of long-forgotten recording artists that were locked away in the libraries of music publishers. As it turned out in some court cases, outside counsel and expert witnesses collected huge fees for work that was of dubious value in protecting the status quo. Purportedly, under the guise of providing objective legal and economic advice, these experts were really covers for an internal lack of brainpower and a convenient scapegoat to be blamed for losing lawsuits. The relationship between the PROs and these experts became one that can only be described as epiphenomenal, that is, the secondary relationship was short-lived and risky. Old business models—that were once revenue drivers, in place for decades and now difficult to replicate—were now exhausting themselves. Litigation could not stop the internal hemorrhaging as consumers embraced the ubiquitous spread of digital technology around the world.

As in the past whenever a change in equilibrium caused by new technology occurred in the industry and threatened vested interests, the old battle plan with a few minor tactical adjustments and a change in alliances would be dusted off and reused: Pressure and mobilize Congress to enact new legislation to deter rampant music theft, prevent the collapse of the status quo, and hinder the pace of badly needed *consumer-driven* reforms in copyright laws. It was the predictable spectacle of would-be reformer, lobby and special interest groups manipulating public opinion using public relations techniques and funded by the PROs, music publishers, record labels, media companies, and others. In the endless public debates that followed between the *cause de cèlébres* and tech-savvy *social gadflies* participants—who already controlled access to print, Internet and broadcast media—promoting their own agendas and tailor-made for Congress, a complex and controversial issue was often reduced to a sound-bite description "piracy" in the media.[29] These divisions reinforced the negative and widespread perception that consumers held of record labels, PROs, and music publishers. Piracy, an overly simplistic mantra, became the obvious suspect for all the self-serving excuses and self-serving behavior in the music industry, even though the statistics and empirical evidence (illegal downloads versus legal buys) on the scale and dynamics of music theft was often lacking, unreliable or inconclusive.[30]

It was assumed that by solving the "piracy" problem, every imaginable business issue or economic problem in the music industry would vanish. Of course, even with this myopic way of thinking, the predatory practices and the self-destructive nature of these agencies hardly led to improved economic performance, lower debt levels, fewer layoffs, or better decision making in the industry. Most consumers

---

[29]The millions in annual lobbying expenditures spent by media companies can be found here: https://www.opensecrets.org.

[30]See Patry (2011, p. 51) and Ulin (2014, p. 366).

were left bewildered by all the confusing and unreliable news stories that were circulated because the only "pirates" that they came into contact with were probably the decorated pirate cakes at their children's birthday parties. The sharp decline in revenue from CD sales did have a negative impact. In some cases, the losses were spread out among the low-level people in marketing, sales, production, manufacturing, and other business services who lost their jobs, and on recording artists who no longer received royalty income from record sales. However, the losses were hardly conspicuous among the few highly overpaid executives who were immune from the crisis and still received their huge annual bonuses, perks, and retirement benefits.

The music industry is now past the first (disruptive) phase of the digitization of music in which consumers switched from vinyl records to CDs and then on to digital downloads. In the next digital phase, some consumers have decided they may no longer wish to own music, but to access music across a wide variety of platforms using cloud services and their smart phones. All these transformations from technological innovations have resulted in new business models, new consumer behaviors, the changed perception in the value of music, conflicts over the distribution of royalties to content creators and a new industry structure.

1.6 The Demise of a Monopoly: Growth Versus Value

The final collapse of AT&T was a long process that was driven by both internal and external dynamics. AT&T was heavily invested in the sunk costs and processes associated with the proprietary Public Switched Telephone Network (PSTN), and lacked the essential digital processes and flatter organizational structure needed to compete with various new entrants in the changing telecommunications landscape. AT&T's Long Distance executives were deluded into thinking—by Madison Avenue advertising executives, public relation hacks, Wall Street speculators, and probably every known consultancy—that even though the company and its various subsidiaries were in business for over a century with a prestigious brand name, consumers would be willing to pay a "premium" for its legendary attention to Bell Labs quality. The AT&T brand name still resonates today and that is, perhaps, why on purchasing the "old" AT&T's assets following its demise, SBC Communications (SBC) renamed itself, AT&T.[31] Quite shockingly after their rather dubious and expensive consulting advice, customers willingly switched to MCI for cheaper telephony service that they perceived as a better value. The tradeoff or sacrifice—even if the service was relatively inferior with annoyances such as electrical interference or noise on the line during a connection and poor customer service—was worth the lower price. As AT&T found out when MCI unleashed its innovative "friends and family" marketing program—a loyalty program in which customers

[31]Most the author's comments concern the old AT&T Consumer Services unless stated otherwise.

and friends received discounts if both callers were MCI customers—the advertising resources that AT&T had spent to build its brand-switching costs or loyalty—the things that made consumers "sticky" or reluctant to leave to try a new brand—could not overcome cheaper price discounts offered by MCI and other carriers. The benefits of AT&T's brand loyalty, if it ever existed for the majority of customers, quickly evaporated.

Today, it appears completely absurd, but in the parlance of Wall Street myopia, AT&T following deregulation was seen as a "growth" company—a company in the growth phase of one of its product's lifecycle—with the expectation that it met unrealistic double-digit growth in revenue, profitability, and stock price appreciation in a market, regardless of economic conditions. The US market for dial-tone service was mature and close to 95 % or more fully penetrated in most areas. Growth and value stocks are measured by price-to-earnings ratios (the price of a stock divided by the current year's earnings per share) or by a price-to-book ratios (share price divided by book value per share) relative to other firms in the industry. Growth stocks tend to have high price-to-earnings and price-to-book ratios, while value stocks do not. With a growth stock, the investment strategy is to buy low with the expectations that the stock will continue to rise and it can be sold for a profit at a short-term date. A value stock, on the other hand, is stock of a company in which business fundamentals, such as new technology, new competitors, economic conditions, business cycles, new markets, new customers, product lifecycle or other condition, may have altered its growth trajectory and a higher value may emerge at anytime, if ever. Amazon, the online retailer, may be a mysterious exception to these rules. Amazon's stock has risen despite its lackluster earnings performance. In general, growth and value stocks tend to move in opposite directions and are used by investors to diversify their risk portfolios.

The vast majority of US households already had a landline and the last loop or direct connection to a customer's premise was actually controlled by Local Exchange Carriers (LECs) who provided local (INTRA–LATA) service that did not include long distance (INTER–LATA) service. Various regulatory requirements—such as the federal Universal Service Fund (USF)—ensured that phone service rates were reasonable for those living in rural and high-cost areas, income-eligible consumers, rural health care facilities, and schools and libraries. Combinations of several LECs were called Regional Bell Operating Companies (RBOCs). Before the days of the widespread use of cell phones in which LATA designators are mostly irrelevant, phone service areas were broken up into Local Access Transport Areas (LATA) based on the geographical distance from the home by some telephone companies. LATAs may still be in use for the remaining customers who have retained a landline, but are using a cell phone for other calls. The geographical regions were sometimes referred to as the LEC areas. Local Exchange Carriers were responsible for originating and terminating long distance calls within their LATAs. Long distance carriers were charged originating and terminating access fees by LECs. Access charges were a significant input cost for long distance carriers and eroded their already thin margins on every long distance call so much so that strategies were being developed to bypass the LECs and these charges altogether.

It is one of the reasons why AT&T rushed in to purchase TCI, a cable Multiple System Operator (MSO), without a timely and proper engineering due diligence. AT&T discovered that TCI's headends needed a massive capital infusion on top of the hefty purchase price to provide voice, video, and data.

For Competitive Local Exchange Carriers (CLECs) that sprung up after the passage of the *Telecom Act* to compete with incumbent LECS in local markets, FCC and Public Service Commissions mandated rules and fees—such as access charges, subscriber line charges, and End User Common Line Charges (EUCL), along with hefty markups on payphone and directory assistance calls—were often their only major sources of revenue because few were able to grab enough market share from the incumbent LECs to succeed. CLECs without a switching infrastructure or their own 5ESS switches relied instead on "wholesaling," that is, reselling LEC services that were discounted under a different name, a marginal business at best. INTRA–LATA calls or "local toll" or "local long distance" were calls that originated and terminated in the same LATA or geographical area and did not involve a long distance carrier. INTER–LATA calls were calls that originated within one LATA and terminated in a different LATA, and were carried by a long distance company. All international calls were classified as INTER–LATA and completed by a long distance carrier. Today, all of the major stand-alone long distance carriers (AT&T, MCI and Sprint) have vanished or incorporated as other entities, and the RBOCs (following consolidations and mergers in the industry) provide long distance as part of a bundle of services that now include video. Most direct connections to homes in densely populated urban areas may be fiber optics, but in some rural areas the copper-pair still exists. In addition, a second connection into the home may be owned and controlled by cable and satellite operators.

AT&T was nothing more than a so-called "value" company that was in the decline phase of its product life cycle that made pennies from millions of customers placing phone calls on a daily basis, paid a reliable dividend for decades and in the process of being liquidated. However, it was managed as though it was a growth company and egged on by Wall Street speculators. Due to inertia, millions of customers remained with AT&T following deregulation—particularly elderly homeowners and others who remained on a basic plan without price discounts—and were not exploiting the system to take advantage of "winback" checks to switch long distance carriers as price competition dramatically increased. Winback was the insane and unprofitable marketing practice in which customers were paid to switch from one long distance carrier to the next and the amount of the check often exceeded the value of the calls placed by some of these customers. For example, a customer may be enticed to switch with a check for $200 dollars, but may only make $100 in long distance calls in a given time period. The same manner in which value companies were managed—as growth companies—would be used for CLECs as well that served mostly rural areas without the population density that would support private investment in fiber optic technology.

1.6.1 McKinsey and Company

McDonald (2013) placed the blame for AT&T's metaphorical death at the hands of the McKinsey consultancy for its faulty research. It is only a partially accurate account—although McKinsey did inflict critical wounds in which the company could not fully recover—and a cautionary tale of what can go wrong when companies outsource their strategic thinking to fresh MBAs just out of business school with very little knowledge of a business enterprise.[32] Most of today's digital technologies that involve sending electrical signals across a network at one point or another had its early start at AT&T's famous research laboratory called Bell Labs. There were considerable *cultural*, internal AT&T barriers that had to be overcome before new products could be successfully launched and those products had to match AT&T's vision, a luxury that would be considered quaint today. AT&T telephone products were meant to last decades or more with incremental and predictable breakthroughs that would not be considered game-changing technology. Rotary-dial phones that were first introduced circa 1904 weren't replaced with push-button keypad dialing technology until the 1960s. It is unlike today in which smart phones and computers can become not necessarily obsolete but dated after a year or so. Bell Labs scientists worked on projects that may never have become commercially viable, but there was academic prestige from doing so. Research and Development (R&D) has since been shifted to the so-called Silicon Valley in which venture capitalists determine which products are funded, products that are not immediately and commercially viable are quickly extinguished. However, there is still a fair amount of taxpayer-financed scientific research that is conducted by all of the major universities and funded by agencies such as the National Science Foundation (NSF).

Among the cultural, internal barriers that had to be overcome were such things as: (a) product development that may take years, if not decades; (b) protecting AT&T's corporate image and Bell Labs quality and reliability; (c) products that had to leverage the existing copper-wire infrastructure without undertaking a costly alternative (such as fiber optic cables to the home, wireless towers, or microwave stations); (d) services had to compliment markets that the incumbent wanted to enter or were already in; and (e) inventors had to deal with a large and often bureaucratic organization that shunned risk takers with new ideas that could cause disruption. These internal barriers were some of the reasons why even though the technologies were often invented at Bell Labs, AT&T was never able to capitalize on the inventions and lagged behind other companies. There was a certain amount of internal inertia, complacency, and inefficiency that came from a large and incumbent monopoly in which technological innovations were pursued only if it protected a status-quo business model that once made a lot of money. Some employees were always skeptical about deploying new technologies even with bandwidth limitations. They were never sure that markets existed for their products

[32] See also Alchian and Demsetz (1996), Cairncross (1997).

and services beyond voice and as most monopolists could not envision how new competitors were likely going to disrupt their business until it actually occurred. Internal economic barriers to entry—such as economies of scale and scope; financial resources; entrenched management; vertical integration; R&D labs; a large base of both residential and business customers; a highly educated workforce; brand name recognition; a large sales force for commercial customers; and dozens of call centers—were thought to be formidable obstacles for any new competitor to easily replicate. It was always an entrepreneur who exploited the inventions developed at Bell Labs, created new choices for consumers fed up with the existing product or service, lead the change, and later reaped the rewards.

In AT&T's monopoly era, the company did not have to sell or market telephony services because if consumers wanted telephone service they had no choice but to choose AT&T. As a result, the company had little or no expertise in acquisition–retention–loyalty marketing that is common today. The data for such marketing analysis were there, but the internal computer systems were not necessarily designed to easily capture and analyze such data. AT&T's mass advertising was done more or less to soften the image of a high-priced monopolist, something that MCI would later exploit with its own memorable and successful advertising of consumers in tears from seeing their telephone bills while reaching out to touch their relatives. As the competitive landscape shifted dramatically, AT&T began an internal transformation, heavily influenced by outside consultants, Wall Street shenanigans, and marketing experts. The ill-fated acquisition of NCR, a manufacturer of point-of-sale terminals, cash registers and computers—just as prices that had anything to do with electronic computing were falling due to worldwide competition, but the power of the machines was growing exponentially—was supposed to find some sort of synergy with telephone services. IBM had to eventually abandon the personal computers market due to the fact that proprietary parts and the PCs themselves became obsolete quickly; stiff price rivals meant "IBM clones" flooded the market; and portable computers (laptops) eventually outsold desktops for both home and business use.[33] The open architecture design of personal computers—in which technical specifications were made public instead of being proprietary—meant that it was easy to modify, add, upgrade, swap, and repair components with parts purchased at RadioShack. Open architecture meant that personal computers could be easily reversed-engineered and recreated—particularly by third-party hardware and software developers—to produce functional copies without costly infringement lawsuits, a change that was to produce the widespread innovations that we see today. Wall Street investment bankers and attorneys benefited in two ways from investment fees in such deals that married old-world companies with new-era companies. Fees were paid for advising on the merger or acquisition itself to the investment part of the bank, while the commercial side of the bank in some cases was busy floating

[33]IBM was another company that faced a lengthly 13-year long antitrust lawsuit for their practice of bundling software and services with hardware. The lawsuit was eventually dropped in 1982. Microsoft faced a similar lawsuit for bundling their Internet browser with their operating system.

equity or bond schemes to pay for the acquisition. Later on when the synergies did not materialize as envisioned, fees were again paid for dissolving the union.

During this transformation, an organization that was heavily influenced by its own engineers, subject-matter experts, and Members of the Technical Staff (MTS) and their depth-and-breath experience in technical areas, particularly for process analysis, gave way to newly hired managers from the financial, public relations, and food packaging industries. It was not unusual for financial consultants to become senior managers only after a brief consulting stint with the company, and in the process, they occupied a coveted position that an insider had long aspired to attain. Marketing long distance services, a commodity that was hard to differentiate—because you couldn't touch, feel, or taste the service—was now going to be similar to the way ketchup was packaged, distributed, and sold, including retail store outlets in which AT&T had no experience.[34] Unlike ketchup in which customers made purchasing decisions based on quality factors such as whether the product contained refined sugar or high fructose corn syrup and fresh tomatoes versus tomato paste, the quality and technology in long distance relied on the LECs providing the so-called last mile connection or dial tone in order to originate and terminate long distance calls. Marketing was made consistent across the organization and everything about a product or service was documented in a LBGUPS (pronounced ELBEE–GUPS) marketing plan. LBGUPS were the various descriptive sections—Learn, Buy, Get, Use, Pay, Service—in the marketing plan on how customers were going to learn about a service and the fulfillment process involved, common sense repackaged in a single document that could be easily shared in a Powerpoint presentation. LBGUPS was another innovation by an outside consulting group to match the famous system at Proctor and Gamble.

This is where a major conflict (GRPs versus revenue) occurred within AT&T and is related to its enormous advertising budget that was probably wasted in most instances to get customers to "Learn" about its consumer services. The return on investment and response rates from direct mail campaigns was dubious as the costs often exceeded revenue. The results almost never really matched the "gains charts" that were produced by the direct mail agencies prior to a campaign. The sponsoring of a prestigious golf tournament was most likely done so that star-struck executives could hob-nob with golf professionals in the clubhouse. The outside advertising agencies were more concerned about their performance measure or metric, Gross Rating Points (GRPs). GRPs measured reach and frequency during an advertising campaign by specific medium or schedule and often expressed as a percentage. GRPs were greeted with a healthy dose of skepticism because it was never made clear how GRPs contributed on a quarterly basis to generating revenue, the metric most important to sustaining AT&T. Millions of customers could have repeatedly seen an ad on television or on outdoor billboards and received a direct

[34] AT&T's advertising campaigns in the 1980s did feature a "reach out and touch someone" tag-line though it was meant for customers do so by calling the person.

mail promotion—which to an advertising agency is all that mattered—but it hardly translated into new customers signing up for long distance service.

In fact, in the days when calls were rated and per-minute charges applied, the telephone industry had more in common with the airline industry, another highly regulated industry that was eventually deregulated. Both industries had an elaborate short and long haul network system that catered to business and leisure customers with peak and off-peak-time-sensitive commitments, and required a sophisticated billing system to do so. Capital equipment (airplanes and network switches) may have taken a decade or more to amortize and required expensive maintenance to remain reliable. For example, phone calls were more like airline seats, in that they were considered perishable. A call not made today or an empty airline seat on takeoff meant lost revenue. Airlines, like phone companies, had to balance peak and off-peak traffic across a network—including domestic and international—in which the weather, natural disasters, and holidays were seasonal factors. There is a lot of travel around the Thanksgiving holiday and call volumes spiked on Mother's Day. Price-insensitive business travelers booked expensive seats at the last minute and did not care about the cost of long distance calls because they were billed to their expense accounts. Price-sensitive leisure travelers traveled at off-peak times on discounted tickets, while cost-sensitive phone customers placed their calls during off-peak hours when the rates were lower.

The turf battles over his or her "directorate" was an amusing tale in organizational dysfunction as the self-promoting flunkies who had flourished under the monopoly system could not understand the demands of a new competitive industry in which customers were not interested in paying a premium just for a brand name in telephony services. With the rents (revenue) that came from monopoly pricing, it was always easy to paper over inefficiencies, greed, and incompetence. Ideas that flowed from the bottom rungs were only welcomed if it propelled an ambitious director to the next level. Everyone ran around with Powerpoint "decks" all labeled "AT&T Proprietary" with precise instructions on page size, fonts, and headings, a McKinsey innovation. It was a serious matter if a document did not have a proprietary marking in which there were various levels. It became a guessing game as to which proprietary level should be placed on documents, typically the ones marked "Proprietary Restricted" might contain something useful but became outdated as long distance prices dropped dramatically and new competitors entered into the industry on a daily basis. Most of it was inane nonsense with a "key takeaway" and some bulleted items from even low-level managers with too much time on their hands and not enough critical thinking skills. Most of the prized decks came from outside consultants. Everyone was always curious to get a copy because it was assumed that the report—particularly if it was annotated with an executive's handwriting to some underling—was reviewed by the senior executives, and therefore everyone had a faint idea as to what they were thinking, what had to be immediately implemented or more likely what the consultants were peddling to a captive audience in the CEO suite in a state of panic. None of the tactical and strategic planning consultants had envisioned a world in which a digital platform such as the smart phone was going to become the driving force for growth in later years. Most of the consultants peddled material that was learned from AT&T's experts and process leaders and regurgitated to executives who did not have the quantitative intelligence to ask for the data or analysis in a format that was easy to comprehend. It was an error in poor management to require only a high-level overview of anything when competing rivals in the industry shortened the response time to product marketing.

AT&T was an early pioneer and an excellent training ground in what later became known as "big data" or data science from handling billions of calls each month, rating those calls based on time of day and complicated tariffs, billing millions of customers, and collecting payments. A young economist on joining the company could immediately call on the scientists at Bell Labs for their expertise in a wide variety of areas, a major benefit at the time. The problem was that the data were dense; data comprehension was difficult; the computer systems were complicated to use and required a technical computer programming and statistical background to retrieve the data; mainframe time and storage were expensive; and the tools in place were limited to effectively and efficiently communicate and present critical information with clarity, something that the consultants accomplished with their visual design skills. Indeed, the consultants help in the creation of things like dashboards and scorecards for rapidly monitoring the sub-processes in providing telephony service and providing immediate critical feedback vastly improved the intuitive thinking and communication skills of all managers, regardless of cognitive or scientific reasoning abilities. Developing a process map or a visual flow chart, essentially drawing a picture of a complicated process in both parallel and sequential stages—something that computer programmers already knew—was the best advice that the consultants imparted on other AT&T employees. The consultants cut through layers of management, competing agendas, turf wars and simplified the data for easier consumption. Of course, the consultancies that worked for AT&T's, worked for competitors as well and so their information ("competitive analogs") might contain some fleeting insight into a rival's strategy gleaned from their work. Generally, the information was presented in a bubble-graph format with details omitted so that, perhaps, the same presentation could be sold to other clients.[35] Presumably, it also worked in reverse in which AT&T's data were shared as well in that small incestuous world of consulting. Security checks were conducted at night to make sure no documents with proprietary markings were left out for prying eyes to read. Office doors, desks, and file cabinets had to be locked, fearing that either an employee or the cleaning staff might be corporate spies. The obsession with proprietary levels and secrecy was more than marking documents for whatever reason. It was more of a mindset or an unsustainable business model of proprietary products and services used by monopolies to restrict and control markets, and it becomes more apparent in the Internet era that ushered in the wider adoption of open-source software and the ability of companies to grow rapidly and profitably.

[35]The word "analog" was probably chosen to reinforce AT&T's mindset of an analog world of technology.

Fortress AT&T was in a battle to the death with MCI, Sprint, and hundreds of resellers who were decimating the long distance market, and any loose lips could easily sink that Titanic.

1.6.2 Valuation Metrics

In the early 1990s, metrics—Total Quality Management (TQM), Activity Based Costing (ABC), Economic Value Added (EVA), and Six Sigma—became all the rage that the consultants were peddling to clients—particularly for a former monopolist that was regulated on a "rate of return" basis in which a rate of return was added to artificially inflated input costs without adjusting for productivity and needed to align declining revenue with the new industry cost structure. A brazen upstart called MCI (initially treated with disdain) was a major cause of concern. The above-mentioned metrics were all the (deceptive) ways that consultants allegedly used to turn a lumbering conglomerate like GE into a nimble Wall Street darling with Strategic Business Units (SBUs) that were supposed to encourage innovation. AT&T had to try some of the metrics and the SBU concept, if only because the financial press were idolizing GE and IBM, and touting the benefits. MCI did not have the legacy costs of an incumbent so naturally their operating costs were much lower. The aim was to match MCI's cost structure and naturally, AT&T had a good idea on network, equipment, and capital costs from their own operations, the one remaining variable input was labor related and this was baffling to AT&T who could not understand how MCI functioned without a massive head count. To provide AT&T with a competitive edge, it has been alleged that consultants were sent out to count the actual number of cars in a MCI parking lot to estimate head count. As competition took hold, there was a renewed short-term focus on meeting Wall Street's unrealistic quarterly churn estimates of the number of customers gained versus the number that left, an important metric in the long distance price wars. In this frenzied atmosphere, it was any wonder that any long-range planning was done when every other week there was a new organizational structure.

In a free market with price discovery and without central bank manipulation and debt expansion, unreliable telecom operators would never have received funding and dubious mergers might not have occurred. The Federal Reserve monetary and liquidity policies (lowering of interest rates) provided the relatively cheap financing that made the bubbles, speculative distortions and mal-investment in telephone equipment, dotcom stocks and housing possible. Financial deregulation with the repeal of the *Glass-Steagall Act* that separated commercial and investment banking enabled the banking system to become even more risky with banks being able to leverage their balance sheets by getting into stock trading and hedge fund activities. Following the bailout of Long Term Capital Management (LTCM), risky banks had nothing to fear because the Fed allegedly came to their rescue through its various debt monetization schemes in which losses were socialized, that is, covered by taxpayers, while profits were privatized. With the removal of the so-called "Chinese

Wall" that separated investment and commercial banking, while the investment side of the house was busy artificially inflating "new economy" Internet stocks with obscene valuations, the commercial side was busy loading up the companies with debt through bond offerings. The money raised during an Initial Public Offering (IPO) almost immediately had to go toward debt servicing. McKinsey and other consultants also had a major role by laying the ground work for "financialization" with the aggressive introduction of shareholder value management by convincing CEOs that "value-based planning," "economic value added" (EVA), or "shareholder value metrics" would reverse their company's economic decline. EVA theory and concepts were neatly laid out in a text entitled *Valuation: Measuring and Managing the Value of Companies* that was written by McKinsey consultants. The book was a repackaging of well-known discounted cash flow (DCF) analysis—which had previously been used to help companies with buy or build decisions for capital investment—with the aim of creating value that was mostly limited to double-digit returns on dividends, stock price appreciation, and ROI for shareholders that Wall Street speculators endorsed. There was added pressure on executives and employees to maximize shareholder value, that is, to meet or exceed aggressive and unrealistic earnings estimates by a wide margin, and quite often financial and accounting fraud was used to achieve such expectations.

Executives relied on Wall Street analysts from investment banks and their stock ratings for guidance on how to run a company (into the ground) based on "top-line and bottom-line" growth. Every company wanted to be rated as a growth stock because growth stocks had a higher valuation than value stocks that languished, the stock could be used as currency for acquisitions and supposedly the market value of a company was reflected in the stock price. Higher stock valuations meant that it could be used as collateral for external bond or equity funding. Just the mere announcement of a layoff sent stock prices up, presumably on the assumption that resources that were not spent on wages and salaries could be used for other functions such as paying down debt or increasing dividends. Missing Wall Street's cooked-up earnings estimates sent stock prices plummeting. Routine layoffs, restructuring, and the off shoring of living-wage jobs raised corporate profits and, thereby, the incomes of shareholders and executives. Financial fraud centered on artificially inflating the bottom like revenue and earnings per share (EPS) for Wall Street's quarterly presentations that at the same time was boosting the executives' stock-based compensation.

CEOs loved the EVA concept because it produced a perverse performance-based compensation plan in which they derived the most benefits; their compensation (including income and bonus) was based on stock grants and stock price appreciation that they could cash out at timely intervals with or without insider knowledge of a company's health. Furthermore, with a stock-based compensation plan, income could now be taxed at the much lower capital gains tax rate. For all other employees, they were encouraged to load up their 401K plans with the company stock for the long run—in a buy and hold strategy—and when the stock eventually became worthless, their retirement savings vanished. Every employee had to take a course on EVA to make sure that they knew all of the "drivers" of shareholder value and the concepts were institutionalized. Old-line industrial companies (General Electric (GE) and General Motors (GM)) in which growth was stalled and/or slowing due to market saturation or maturity were using financial engineering through their financial subsidiaries to mask their industrial decline while the CEOs were becoming fabulously wealthy. Unlocking shareholder value meant that the wealth of certain short-term institutional investors and executives at certain times increased dramatically, while at the same time it reduced the aggregate wealth of individual shareholders due to the increased number of shares outstanding that were issued to acquire companies.[36]

AT&T's entry into revolving financial services consisted of the *AT&T Universal Card*, a *credit card* (not to be confused with a calling card) that came without an annual fee, an innovation at the time. Both industrial GE and GM required government bailouts during the 2008 financial crisis for the losses associated with GE Capital and GMAC, a GM subsidiary that financed car loans and mortgage business. The Universal Card was sold off to Citibank and that bank needed to be bailed out as well. GE and GM were more or less banks or hedge funds (without the regulatory and capital constraints of banks) that were masquerading as industrial companies and finance was used to mask their industrial decline.

In later years, the EVA concept evolved into company share buyback programs that were funded mostly by debt rather retained earnings and euphemistically referred to as returning capital to investors. Capital that could have been spent on building new manufacturing facilities, new equipment, or increasing stagnant wages. Share buybacks were another form of financial engineering in which inflated stocks (as a currency) were no longer used to fund dubious acquisitions. Share buybacks—using cheap debt made possible by unnaturally low Fed rates—was just another ploy to artificially boost earnings in certain cases by shrinking the number of shares outstanding or the denominator in an EPS calculation—when some companies were experiencing poor financial performance. Unnaturally low interest rates distorted the price discovery mechanism in financial markets by inflating the price of bonds, stocks, and housing. Even profitable companies with enough retained earnings to fund share buybacks and were in no danger of being rapidly liquidated were using debt to do so. Executives—whose compensation was stock-based—and shareholders benefited from the program because share buybacks did not have the dilutive effects of issuing shares to fund acquisitions, and it temporarily boosted the stock price and incomes of shareholders.[37]

---

[36]See Stout (2012) for her critique of shareholder value.

[37]Share buybacks is discussed here because it was once suggested by an outside counsel to a PRO that one of the new business models for PROs could include a share flotation program to the public. Whether songwriters and composers would be wiling to place their royalties at risk in a stock market and Wall Street speculators is an entirely different matter.
See *ZIRP and QE: Central Bankers' Narcotics of Choice*, http://www.economonitor.com/blog/2012/11/zirp-and-qe-central-bankers-narcotics-of-choice.
Apple Expands Capital Return Program to $200 Billion, https://www.apple.com/pr/library/2015/

1.6.3 Early Internet Service

In the early days of the Internet, consumers accessed the Internet using dial-up modems from their homes and this dramatically increased the demand for second phone lines that mostly benefited the RBOCs. Long distance carriers with no local connections to homes—in order to offer nationwide dial-up Internet service with local access numbers so that customers avoided long distance phone charges—had to purchase local access phone lines from the RBOCs, a strategy that was not only costly, inefficient, and probably unprofitable, but a sure sign of AT&T's pending liquidation. It was too painful to watch as silly marketing plans included combing long distance service, a calling card, a credit card, a loyalty rewards card, Internet service, and whatever else into a ridiculous bundle—without local, video or cellular service—that baffled customers. The so-called "AT&T Bundle" could not save that lumbering dinosaur with no agility on its deathbed. Customers were looking for a bundle that included voice, video, and data from a single entity and on the same bill, something that laggard AT&T could not deliver in time.

For AT&T, their "innovation" at the time was to recombine long distance and local charges on a single bill—something that customers received before deregulation—and was a costly process that wasn't worth the time and effort required to synchronize with RBOC billing systems. Customers could now be charged a fee for the privilege of a single combined bill of services. The slow speeds and the limitations of dial-up modems were followed by digital subscriber lines (DSL) which was yet another attempt to extend the life of the hundred-year old copper infrastructure—a phone line that transmitted voice as an analog signal on a pair of copper wires. DSL was a short-term alternative to the expensive and delayed capital investment in fiber optic technology to the home, something that cable operators were already doing. As the demand for interactive services, e-commerce, video-on-demand, data-rich images, music, and video increased, it became clear that the cable operators were way ahead of the incumbent phone companies that lagged behind by decades in providing affordable high-speed broadband service—including voice, video, and data—to the home using fiber optics.

The rise of the open Internet—the network infrastructure that supported numerous and faster online services (email, file transfers, high-definition video, games, telephony, remote data centers, and electronic commerce)—and the web—which provided a common user interface—accelerated the shift from away the proprietary Public Switched Telephone Network (PSTN) to a public Internet, a generational tectonic shift that even McKinsey could not have predicted. There were significant regulatory changes and technological advances in new hardware, software, and support services that transformed entire industries, including the music industry. The disruptive impact of the Internet was felt in several ways. First, AT&T was

04/27Apple-Expands-Capital-Return-Program-to-200-Billion.html.
About 70 % of the $200 billion was allocated for share buy backs and the rest for dividends.

deregulated—it was no longer a public utility with strict government oversight—and its economic outlook deteriorated with every passing year. AT&T Long Distance without a local network infrastructure and who relied on the LECs for a direct connection to a customer's premise was doomed. It was this lack of a local infrastructure to originate and terminal calls and the fact that distance no longer mattered that spelled the end for AT&T. In retrospect, had AT&T been broken up into the original seven RBOC regions, but with each RBOC allowed to complete both local and long distance calls, and the telephone equipment arm turned into an independent entity, the competitive landscape would have been vastly different than it is today.

Second, the Internet—a wider commercial and open source application that enabled Internet companies such as iTunes, eBay, Google, Amazon, Pandora, and Netflix—replaced the proprietary PSTN. The PSTN was designed for two-way analog voice communication between two copper-wire endpoints, and the costs varied with the location of each endpoint and the distance between the two endpoints. The Internet—with a higher bandwidth capacity—was designed for a wider variety of uses, and included a transit network that moves data and a network of computers, which allow anyone to access, retrieve, process, and store all manner of information in a digital format (e.g., voice, video, documents, and images). The biggest difference is that broadband is now defined as the ability to transmit data at speeds greater than 25 megabit per second (Mbps), fast enough for streaming today's ultra high-definition video to smart devices. The greater need for higher and higher bandwidth capacity is driven, in part, by all of the unforeseen and new streaming services and cloud-based applications.[38]

Third, the Internet undermined the business models of practically every so-called brick-and-mortar business, particularly businesses whose products could be digitalized and distributed over the Internet. Independent record stores that catered to mostly music customers, such as Tower Records, met their untimely demise. Music publishers and record labels had to develop digital strategies. New business models included income from digital advertising, licensing fees, and subscription revenue. New metrics such as "page hits" and the number of downloads were to become commonplace.

Finally, the Internet created the process where hardware, software, and support services were *unbundled* and each component could be sold separately. Domestic customer support services could now be outsourced to international call centers where labor rates were lower. Unbundling may have eliminated higher prices, proprietary dependencies, and inflexibility associated with a single vendor that integrated hardware, software, and support services. Before AT&T was deregulated, local and long distance service, and network and handset equipment were all bundled. IBM and Microsoft had at one point in time bundled hardware, software,

---

[38]See *The Internet and the PSTN: Disparities, Differences, and Distinctions*, Internet Society, http://www.internetsociety.org/sites/default/files/The%20Internet%20and%20the%20Public%20Switched%20Telephone%20Network.pdf.

or support service into a single package. The Internet created new competition and entire new businesses started providing networking equipment and servers; software and services; web publishing; search engines; portals; and social networks.

MCI would again beat AT&T and other ISPs to the punch with another innovation that undermined their business models. In 1994, MCI launched its "InternetMCI" service in which they provided 20 h of monthly Internet access for $19.95, a service that was less expensive than the per-minute charges of AOL and Prodigy. AT&T would play catch-up years later with its own Worldnet product, too little too late. Eventually, the industry standard became $19.95 for *unlimited* access and consumers could browse, shop or download music to their heart's content. "Subversive teenagers" no longer needed to use college and university computers to create Internet apps; they could now do so from the comforts of their homes. Shawn Fanning was only 18 years old when he developed Napster in 1998, one of the first popular and widespread peer-to-peer file sharing platforms. As bandwidth increased dramatically with the transformational shift from dial-up and DSL copper telephone wires to fiber optic cable, entrepreneurs created the new, faster, and unforeseen online services.

AT&T's cost-cutting measures of eliminating layers of management were often portrayed as an attempt to become more nimble and better prepared to meet the digital onslaught as fiber optic technology replaced the hundred-year old copper wire infrastructure that turned a once high-priced service into a commodity. With increasing competition in the long distance market, the company focused on sustaining revenue by: (a) acquiring new customers (the very same ones that had left for cheaper service elsewhere a month or so prior and were being paid to switch carriers); (b) getting existing customers to pay more (by exploiting the regulated tariff system in which customers not on a basic rate plan paid more and essentially subsidized those on a discounted pricing plan); (c) to raise prices (which was almost impossible, except for customers on a basic rate tariff); or (d) by offering new products and services (credit card, loyalty rewards, and Internet service). It would take years for the old AT&T to become "nimble" (which it never did) until its eventual demise.

1.6.4 The Birth of Cellular

As McDonald (2013, pp. 178–179) recounts, AT&T had invented an earlier version of wireless technology and in 1980 was interested in marketing the technology. However, the company was worried about capital investment costs in erecting radio towers, the double-digit return on investment (that included the prime rate, equity market risk and company bond rating) to meet or exceed Wall Street's expectations, bandwidth costs, profitability, and a clunky and expensive handset that appealed to the very wealthy and corporate executives. The McKinsey consultancy was called in to help executives develop a feasibility study for AT&T's entry into the wireless market, an undefined market that was probably limited to luxury cars and those who could afford it (like the executives who wanted to talk to each other in their limousines to and from their weekday golf games). A crude form of cellular service was already in commercial use by long-haul truckers and local police patrol cars using Citizens Band (CB) airwaves, a technology that has been replaced with smart phones and tablets in some cases. "McKinsey, as always, carefully studied the issue and came up with an estimate that was, to say the least, laughably off the mark: In the year 2000, McKinsey deduced, the total market would be less than one million subscribers… However, this was clearly a blunder, and a very costly one. AT&T dropped the project, dooming the company to playing catch-up in wireless and necessitating its eventual sale to SBC Communications in 2005. That is the consultant's equivalent of a malpractice case, in which the patient dies an awful, avoidable death."

In 1973, a small upstart and equipment manufacturer named Motorola had already tested a rudimentary device that weighed 2.5 pounds, had a battery life of a few minutes, cost close to $4,000, and intended as a voice-only application, but AT&T, still a monopolist that controlled telephony equipment as well as service, probably thought that its clout would have been a significant barrier to entry for any new competitor, big or small.[39] The thinking was no company could possibly compete with the resources of an AT&T pre-and-post deregulation, and even if they did, at some point the upstart would have to connect to some part of the Bell System network that AT&T still owned and controlled or faced a patent infringement lawsuit. AT&T's cellular efforts were aimed mostly at the narrow car phone market. With a pay phone installed on every street corner in America, why would consumers want to walk around with a clunky device anyway, besides they already had a phone in the home and the handset was Bell Labs certified for quality and reliability. Landlines in the United States still functioned even in the case of an electricity blackout because Bell System engineers had built in a backup and un-interruptible power supply into the system that was independent from other utilities. This is not true today with cordless or wireless phones that require electricity for charging. On the other hand, Motorola envisioned a more *portable* device that could be placed in the hands of consumers with the device becoming lighter, talk-time increasing and affordable, the forerunner to today's smart phone that is really a computer with high-end components. Motorola would prove that cellular service did not need the resources of a monopolist to succeed and the cell phone market could be competitive, further paving the way for the development of e-commerce in which information was free, ubiquitous, and easily shared.

To AT&T's executives an unproven technology like cellular that was not certified 100% reliable and efficient by Bell Labs standards; a huge capital investment project that would require a double-digit ROI to meet Wall Street expectations of a "growth" company; a potential market of a mere one million cellular customers; a possible new network infrastructure that had to be created; a service that they could not

---

[39]See *The Verge Interview: Marty Cooper, father of the cellphone*,https://www.theverge.com/2012/2/20/2811861/marty-cooper-interview.

tightly control; and a risky job that could entail failure and eliminate some from becoming CEO were all unfathomable. One million cellular customers would have appeared as a mere blip to AT&T that controlled a majority of the 100 million or so long distance customers at the time. Prior to the break-up circa 1982, AT&T was considered a place of lifetime employment and everyone memorized their service date, that is, the day in which they started at the company and every anniversary was duly noted. There were steady pay raises, a slow climb up the corporate ladder and at retirement, you collected a gold pen or some other trinket and a pension. It is also likely that McKinsey was not really hired to help AT&T executives create the market for cellular service, but rather to confirm their narrow, status quo thinking that cellular service was never really going to take off beyond the luxury car market. It is possible that McKinsey may have limited its selectivity in data gathering and simply regurgitated what they heard in the CEO suite, and later found some study to confirm their pre-ordained conclusions. Long distance was always supposed to be the most lucrative segment—particularly the international long distance segment—because executives built their careers on climbing the Bell System corporate ladder and had invested all of their time and energy in a switched-based analog network. The McKinsey study could then be used as a deceptive form of independent thinking by outsiders adding something "fresh" to a debate in order to form an internal consensus, and later, if necessary, become the scapegoat for poor executive decision-making in which they could not be held accountable when it became apparent that no contingency plans were in place. McKinsey's goal was always to expand and deepen their engagements with clients, and they were hardly going to include any radical thinking or vulnerable information that was going to upset the status quo and their future billings. In the days before IPO, stock options and get-rich quick madness that followed Internet stocks, very few of AT&T executives were going to jeopardize their posh life in Basking Ridge to oversee a risky cellular project that may or may not work. A young engineer wanting to take a risk and experiment with a cellular network trial would not get past the AT&T cloudy "vision thing" and the elaborate business case process that required layers and layers of approval, becoming frustrated at the lack of interest by his superiors, and eventually forced to leave to form a start-up company in California, which is what most risk-takers did.

According to reports, in 1981 Craig McCaw came across an AT&T document about the future of cellular telephony that included McKinsey's prediction that by the start of the twenty-first century there would be close to a million cellular subscribers in the United States. For someone like McCaw in the mushrooming cable business, a million subscribers would have been an enormous potential and dynamite that made AT&T vulnerable, if only McKinsey had included the cable industry in their study. The new cable industry was essentially replicating the telephony infrastructure in which a headend (similar to a central office switch) was going to all serve customers in the same geographical area, and instead of voice traffic, it was video traffic over coaxial cable wiring. MCI was also in the process of using microwave technology to challenge AT&T's dominance in the telephone industry. A critical assessment of the nascent cable industry—particularity the delivery of a satellite feed to a headend—and MCI's new competitive strategy would have been illuminating for AT&T executives. Intrigued by the possibilities, McCaw began by acquiring the licenses for cellular spectrum that were being sold at $4.50 per "pop," that could be used to build a base for future subscribers for very low cost and quickly capture a foothold in the emerging market. By 1983, McCaw Communications had purchased licenses in six of the 30 largest US markets. McCaw then succeeded in using the licenses, collateral and AT&T's market projections to buy billions of dollars of spectrum. In 1992, as AT&T was now desperate to enter the new wireless market, they agreed to purchase one-third of McCaw Cellular for $3.8 billion (it was now cheaper to buy rather than build), which at the time was generating $1.75 billion in annual revenue, and had two million Cellular One subscribers—far more customers than AT&T's earlier projections for all cellular use in the US. In 1994, AT&T purchased the rest of McCaw Cellular for $11.5 billion—at that time the second largest merger in US history—creating AT&T Wireless Group, which was at that time the largest cellular carrier in the US.[40]

Interestingly enough, some of the senior executives responsible for the debacle—mal-investment, bloated corporate structure, a failure to conduct the proper due diligence on certain acquisitions, bureaucratic in-fighting, and a reliance on outside consultants for strategic thinking and their flavor-of-the-month ideas—were never really held accountable for their own mistakes or the residual effects such as mass layoffs. The transformational and tectonic shift from analog to digital technologies—and with it the rapid increase in speed and capacity and lowered costs for information processing—destroyed the old market structure. In hindsight, had AT&T not been deregulated, the benefits from the smart phone that we see today would not have occurred because the monopolist would have wanted to extend the life of its existing infrastructure and slowed the pace of innovation.

1.6.5 The Convergence of Telecommunications, Technology, and Media

By 2000, AT&T Long Distance was in its sunset days in corporate America after more than a century in business because (a) the Bell System was totally demolished; (b) the prestige of the Bell System logo meant nothing except to nostalgia buffs; (c) distance no longer mattered in telephony; (d) its prospects as a stand-alone entity with no local access capabilities and a dated analog switch-based network infrastructure that required maintenance were diminishing on a daily basis; (e) its business model was obsolete; (f) consumers preferred voice, video, and data from a single entity that cable operators provided; (g) *packet-switched networks* in which data are moved in separate, small blocks or packets based on the destination address in each packet and reassembled in the proper sequence once it reached its destination replaced *circuit-switched networks* that require dedicated point-to-point connections

[40]See http://en.wikipedia.org/wiki/AT%26T_Wireless_Services.

during calls and were in existence for over a hundred years; (h) open Internet-based systems replaced proprietary equipment; (i) data traffic surpassed voice traffic; (j) its expensive cable acquisitions failed to deliver broadband service as promised; (k) its debt load had skyrocketed and its triple A rating was being downgraded; and (l) tens of thousands of loyal employees would lose their jobs. Cellular companies were more interested in selling "data packages" with voice thrown in for free. Rivals—such as cable MSOs and the rapidly consolidating RBOCs in both the deregulated telephone equipment and services segments—were gaining market share, and eventually AT&T's equipment arm was spun off as the new Lucent so that the remaining enterprise could focus on its "core competencies," another flavor-of-the-month idea peddled by consultants and a prelude to massive layoffs.

As the liquidation of AT&T was gaining momentum, it was not just the organization that had to figure out its core competencies, but managers had to know theirs as well. It was all part of the mirage that human resource management could turn around a company that was collapsing at its hollowed-out core in an industry that was shrinking.

In the early days of terrestrial cable, MSOs were monopolists within their particular regions and very few MSOs served overlapping areas. With the exception of RCN whose attempts were negligible, the so-called over-builders that were supposed to compete with terrestrial cable never materialized. This meant that very little competition occurred in the cable industry to drive down expensive monthly subscription fees and rental equipment until satellite and phone companies and streaming services like Netflix began competing. In the event that an acquisition caused two MSOs to become competitors in an area, cable swaps occurred to make an area contiguous for only one operator. Cable operators were notorious for their poor service quality and skyrocketing prices and it is still true today. The early bundling of voice (phone service), video (cable television), and data (Internet) was an innovation in itself because (a) customers received a discount for purchasing these multiple services from a single provider instead of individual services from multiple providers; and (b) it sometimes made it harder for new entrants who could not offer all three services to acquire customers because bundling increased loyalty and retention for the incumbents and prevented switching. In later years, bundling of these services produced "sticker-shock" as the rate of price increases in subscription fees began to surpass the rate of inflation. Consumers began abandoning the cable operators in the so-called cord-cutting fashion for streaming services such as Netflix to lower their monthly bills. Table 1.9 shows AT&T's ill-fated cable buying binge between 1998 and 1999 in its attempt to build a nationwide broadband network for information, data and video entertainment. The rapid pace of the acquisitions left many wondering if a proper engineering due diligence was conducted in a timely manner because some cable operators were further along their broadband capital improvements than others at the time. The acquisitions occurred just as the dotcom/telecom equipment bubbles were nearing their peak and every stock that could be tied to the so-called new economy was overly or artificially inflated. In 1998, AT&T rushed in to purchase TCI, a cable MSO and soon discovered that some of TCI's decrepit headends that were cobbled together needed a massive capital

Table 1.9 AT&T cable acquisitions

Year	Buyer	Company bought	Amount ($B)	Subscribers (000)
1998	AT&T	TCI	$54	11,000
1999	AT&T	MediaOne	$45	5,000
1999	AT&T	Lenfest	$2	1,500
2001	Comcast	AT&T broadband	$45	8,000[a]

Source: Selected financial data from New York Times, May 27, 2015, p. B6
Debt may not be included in the amounts shown
Subscriber data is estimated and may vary due to swaps and other agreements
[a]Comcast subscribers

infusion on top of the hefty purchase price to provide voice, video, and data. In quick succession in 1999, AT&T then purchased MediaOne and Lenfest in order to rapidly offer broadband service and overcome some of the technical problems with integrating its purchase of TCI.

AT&T cable acquisitions were then folded into a new subsidiary called AT&T Broadband that combined other consumer units and a clash of corporate cultures soon ensued that made integrating the cable acquisitions difficult. The cable industry was more accustomed to a decentralized form of organization with considerable autonomy given to managers in local areas, while AT&T's corporate structure was more formal and centralized. Decentralization occurred in the cable industry out of necessity because cable systems were often not contiguous within or across multiple states and subjected to various state and local regulations. There were exceptions to this rule as in the case of Cablevision, Adelphia, and others that were controlled by a family. One cable executive "commuted" from the West Coast on a weekly basis using a corporate jet and it was apparent that a commitment to make AT&T a stronger national cable player was not going to be made. The only interest was the massive bonus payments that came from the acquisitions and the shock that came later as stock prices collapsed and various asset bubbles deflated. Denver at the time was the heart of the cable industry and Basking Ridge, New Jersey in close proximity New York City's financial district could hardly suffice. A director level position at AT&T came with a plush office, a chief of staff position needed to manager the director's daily calendar, division managers, district managers, staff managers, staff supervisors, and other support staff, while the same position from an MSO could have been a cubicle with no support staff. By 2001, the stock market was in its self-correcting mode and all the bubble stocks imploded. The value of AT&T's acquisitions had to be written down to reflect the new reality. Comcast put AT&T out of its misery by purchasing AT&T's heavily discounted cable assets after AT&T's unsuccessful attempt at providing broadband service ended up increasing its debt load by as much as $65 billion and its debt was being downgraded by the ratings agencies. After more than one-hundred years in providing many telephony innovations, AT&T's role in delivering the fat pipes that was driving entertainment and information in the digital age had drawn to a close. It was the end of the line for Ma Bell!

The Lucent spin-off occurred just as the end of the old telecom equipment lifecycle in which analog was replaced with digital, copper-wire with fiber, landlines were replaced with wireless, and circuit switches were replaced with packet switching. Staffed with some of the hold-over executives from AT&T, Lucent's demise came rapidly, a mere four years after the spin-off, and did not survive the *Telecom Reform Act of 1996* and the dotcom boom-and-bust bubble implosion that followed in which marketing gimmicks (accumulating and monetizing eyeballs) or financial engineering (vendor financing and asset sales) were the new norms.[41] Lucent's growth in its initial stages came from providing network equipment *and* vendor financing to new CLECs who could not afford the equipment; were not profitable and were not going to be profitable in the near future; and were never going to become significant competitors to the incumbent LECs. Some of the CLECs remained viable only until the proceeds that were raised from their recent IPO—the process in which a privately-held company becomes a public company that sells stock or equity to the public on one of the financial exchanges—and funds from their debt offerings that immediately followed their IPOs ran out by which time Wall Street speculators and insiders had cashed out in the familiar "pump and dump" valuations from that era. Some of these CLECs engaged in accounting fraud called "swapping" of equipment or parts of an over-built fiber optic network that were "lit," that is, it had the capacity to carry traffic but had no customers and was not generating revenue while interest costs mounted. The swaps resulted in a so-called net zero balance between the two companies involved, but they "booked" these swaps as revenue to artificially inflate their quarterly income statements to fool Wall Street speculators into thinking that they were meeting revenue targets, while most were in the stages of financial collapse. Lucent already had a viable business providing network equipment, maintenance and upgrades to the incumbent LECs—the value companies that paid a reliable dividend—but it was a mature business without double-digit growth that was marginally profitable.[42]

In 2010, CenturyTel, one of the struggling rural CLECs, eventually acquired Qwest (the former US West) and one of the last remaining RBOCs in a market dominated by the new AT&T (SBC) and Verizon, and their bundle of voice, video, and data services. The Wall Street Journal described the merger as a gamble caused by a desire to fight off the relentless decline in the local-phone business by getting bigger. The two companies were still in the business of measuring progress by the declining growth in the once-reliable landline business instead of wireless. In rural or sparsely populated outlying areas—some areas that may be still without direct-dial technology—offering telephone services with a traditional switched-based system would have been economically challenging connecting just a few residential customers to a central office. Business customers who were willing to

---

[41]See Cassidy (2002).

[42]See Doug Pitt's article, *What Really Happened to Lucent Technologies?*, http://usphoenix.net/science,%20technology/what_reallyhappened_to_lucent_t.htm (no relation to the author) and *Lessons from the Lucent Debacle Think Twice About What You Promise Wall Street. And Don't Send a Lumbering Old Company to do a Startup's Job*, http://archive.fortune.com/magazines/fortune/fortune_archive/2001/02/05/296152/index.htm.

pay for expensive T-1 service would have the necessary bandwidth. Qwest's territory consisted of mostly Western areas of the United States that were more or less sparsely populated and its major population density was in areas such as Denver and Seattle. It is the one of the reasons why it was the last remaining RBOC to be acquired. CenturyTel was started in the backwoods of Monroe, Louisiana and it is said to be the birthplace of Delta Airlines. Delta Air provided limited air service there to maintain its lineage and if you missed the one or two scheduled flights, you were stuck in purgatory. At the time of the announcement, neither company had a significant wireless business, had largely missed out on the cellular boom, and was forced to rely on profits from slower growing or declining businesses. Consolidation was not likely to significantly boost the growth prospects of the combined entity, and this was more or less a farce to delay the inevitable liquidation following the accumulation of massive debt, another sad occurrence of a value company run as though it was a growth company.[43]

1.6.6 Free Calls

Cisco Systems would later emerge as one of the dominant networking equipment manufacturers in the digital era providing the digital information switches for the new telecommunications infrastructure that now included broadband, cellular, and WiFi networks. The combination of broadband and wireless technology meant that thousands of seemingly unrelated objects—such as home security and utilities, cars, and appliances—could be collectively monitored from a distance. AT&T was able to retain some of their landline customers when they began offering wireless service, but in a market that was highly competitive and included competition from cable operators and Internet-based communication companies offering WiFi and VoIP (voice over Internet protocol). VoIP meant that electronic communications, including voice, were now bypassing the PSTN—that had kept AT&T and LECs in business for more than a century—for the public Internet network and available on smart phones and computers. Telephone calls, particularly expensive international calls, were now free with an Internet subscription even though the quality may not have matched the older analog network.

1.6.7 Free Music

In the music industry, the same analog versus digital phenomenon took place with every advance in digital music such as CDs, MP3, iPods, and downloads in

[43]See *CenturyTel Gambles on Qwest Merger*, Wall Street Journal, April 23, 2010 and accessed online: http://www.wsj.com/articles/SB10001424052748703876404575200042559183812.

Table 1.10 Major broadband acquisition deals 2014–2015

Year	Company bought	Buyer	Amount ($B)
2014	DirecTV	AT&T (SBC)	$49
2015	Time Warner Cable & Bright House Networks	Charter communications	$67
2015	Dish Network[a]	T-Mobile	NA

DirecTV and Dish Network are cable satellite operators
[a]Preliminary merger stage and the deal amount was not available at the time of writing

which there was a debate whether the latest music format degraded the (analog) sound quality of recorded music when compared to vinyl in exchange for lower prices, convenience, and ease of production and distribution. Early CDs were made from vinyl masters that contributed to the poor quality on the medium and it is unlike today in which original sound recordings have been remastered, vastly improving the sound quality. The perceived sound quality in music hardly mattered to teenagers because they did not have to purchase expensive turntables, and an entire album collection of music was now stored on a hard drive or portable device, although without the fancy cover art that accompanied vinyl records. With the sale of vinyl records increasing—and may include a free digital download of the album as well—vinyl records and digital music are happily coexisting for some audiophiles; they can listen to vinyl records while at home for its sound quality and when on the road they have the convenience of their digital libraries. Prior to the creation of iTunes and paid downloads, file sharing services such as Napster allowed digital music to be easily downloaded which in most cases was free for users with an Internet connection. Interestingly enough, digital technologies would increase the consumption of music regardless of the tradeoff between vinyl and digital.

Now that the fat pipes for delivering broadband are in place, there is a convergence of television, broadband, and wireless as shown in Table 1.10. Pending regulatory approval of the mergers and acquisitions, the video entertainment sectors are consolidating into a few major wireless carriers and a few cable operators. Broadband is said to be one of the principal components of these deals because traditional video subscription has been declining due to the proliferation of new (and cheaper) streaming services in which only a broadband or wireless connection is needed. Video content is said to be "king" because smart phones have dramatically changed the way in which consumers watch and pay for entertainment.[44]

[44]See *Dish Network in Merger Talks With T-Mobile*. Wall Street Journal, June 4, 2015, http://www.wsj.com/articles/dish-network-in-merger-talks-with-t-mobile-us-1433383285.

1.7 How Innovation, Competition, and Technology Changed Music Licensing

Two major technological breakthroughs that occurred in the computer industry were the miniaturization of computing hardware systems, or platforms and the commoditization of computer hardware over time, as shown in Table 1.11. Both breakthroughs eroded economic barriers to entry in the computer industry in which competition increased dramatically, prices fell, and entire new consumers services were created.[45] Miniaturization is the process that transformed computers from a device that once needed hundreds of square feet of space to a device that fits in the palm of your hand. One of the important benefits of miniaturization is portability; it is now easier to do most of the things of a personal computer on a tablet or smart phone. More importantly, the smart phone is all-important content consuming device, that is, consumers can have instantaneous access to their music, reading or video entertainment wherever they want.

Commoditization is the process in which a market or segment for a proprietary, premium, or branded product is transformed into a market based on undifferentiated price competition. In computers, it was the processing power of computers (microprocessors, increased memory, and a large hard drive) and mobility (laptops, tablets, and smart phones) that were once differentiators. Lower prices and mobile wireless capabilities increased the sales of laptops and smart phones as the desktop market matured. Some firms in the PC industry were negatively impacted from the shift to commoditization as price competition eroded operating margins and profits.

Table 1.11 Miniaturization and commoditization of Computer Systems

Period	Hardware	Brands	Proprietary Standard	Differentiation[a]	Audience
1950s/1960s	Mainframes	Univac, ENIAC & IBM-600	Closed	High	Scientific, businesses & government
1970s/1980s	Minicomputers	IBM-360, DEC & Wang	Closed	High	Small businesses
1980s	PCs	IBM-PC & Clones	Open	Low	Home/Office Users
1980s/1990s	PDA & cell-phones	Palm Pilot	Open	Low	Consumers
1990s/2000s	Smart phones & tablets	Apple, Android, & Amazon	Open[b]	Low	Consumers
2015	Mobile Apps	Twitter	Open	Low	Consumers

[a]Prices and specifications

[b]Apple's smart phone technology is proprietary, but Google's Android is open source

[45]See Campbell-Kelly and Garcia-Swartz (1997), Yost (2005).

Companies that were not able to reinvent themselves as this important shift—in which lower prices were the differentiator—occurred went out of business.

As these important shifts took place over the last 60 years or so, computer hardware became much smaller, but extremely powerful and the price of a computer fell dramatically and that paved the way for today's smart phone. In early 1950s and 1960s, mainframe computers were limited to large educational, manufacturing, and government enterprises that could afford the steep monthly fees. Following developments in transistor technology, the minicomputer was introduced in the 1970s, and the target markets were small to medium size businesses that could not afford the costs of a mainframe. In the 1980s, there was another major leap in technology in which the personal computer (PC) was introduced that targeted both home and business use. In the late 1980s and early 1990s a personal handheld and mobile PC called a Personal Digital Assistant (PDA) was introduced, along with the widespread mass marketing of cell phones. By the late 1990s, the functions of a PDA and a cell phone were turned into a smart phone.

Along the way, proprietary bundles of hardware, support services, and software—in which a company owned, controlled, and profited from key components of a technology—gave way to open standards and unbundled components that rapidly increased the widespread adoption of computers; fueled the collaboration of software projects from thousands of miles away and increased the competition for apps. As computer hardware became a commodity, the core of the computer industry shifted from hardware to apps and changed the perception of a computer. Brand loyalty was unimportant and lasted until the next yearly or bi-yearly product cycle in which the latest gadget was announced. Phones, like other commodities, were now bought, used, and discarded as soon as they outlived their usefulness. In the process new markets, products, services, and businesses were created. Apps—exclusive to a particular smart phone operating system—would soon become an important product differentiator for smart phone manufacturers as prices fell. For cellular carriers, relatively expensive data plans became an important source of revenue because they could charge more for different levels of intensive music and video data usage, while unlimited voice and text messaging services were offered for a flat fee. Savvy smart phone users are now looking to lower or eliminate their monthly data costs—bypassing their conventional cellular carriers—by using Wi-Fi-enabled phones, laptops, tablets, and other devices in most areas in which data charges do not apply.[46]

Miniaturization and commoditization were soon embodied in a smart phone developed by Apple that eroded the sale of PCs as the dominant computing device for many users. Apple's iPhone solved a major problem at the time and that was consumers were walking around with too many gadgets such as a cell phone, a PDA, a digital camera, a music player, and a GPS device. All of these gadgets were soon integrated into a single universal computer—a bundle that

[46]*See Can you ditch your smart phone data plan for Wi-Fi?*, http://www.cnet.com/news/can-you-ditch-your-smartphone-data-plan-for-wi-fi/.

Table 1.12 Mobile apps market dominance in 2013

	Google	Apple	Microsoft	Total
Store	Google Play	iTunes app	Windows Store	
Platform	Android	iOS	Windows	
All devices sold[a] by platform (%)	65	13	22	
Apps Revenue[b] ($ billions)	$10	$14	Na	
Number of users (in millions)	900	600	12	1,512
Number of apps (in thousands)	800	1,250	160	2,210
Number of developers (in thousands)	150	235	45	430
Number of downloads (in billions)	48	50	0.65	98.65

[a]Estimated based on one billion Android devices sold in 2014
[b]Estimated 2014

many consumers preferred—with a friendly touch-screen interface that was also an Internet communicator and entertainment device. The iPhone revolutionized the way to wirelessly download music from the iTunes store or the Internet.

With the widespread proliferation of smart phones, the competition has now shifted from hardware to software or apps developers in which their third-party applications are developed after the phones have been manufactured and now the driving force for the growth of smart phones. As shown in Table 1.12, apps are now product differentiators for the sale of smart phones by various competitors. Android devices have outsold both Apple and Microsoft product in 2014, but Apple has a bigger share of apps revenue. Apple is estimated to have approximately 235,000 developers who have built 1,250,000 apps that have been download 50 billion times and used by 600 million customers. Apple may be the leader in terms of the numbers of apps and developers, but Google has more users. Google provides its Android operating system free of charge to a wide variety of phone manufacturers and that has led to a surge of new entrants making less expensive smart phones (that often compete with Google's own products). Apple's operating system is exclusive to its own devices.[47]

1.7.1 Transformation of the Music Industry

The music industry was one of the first sectors in the entertainment business to confront the technological shift to digital products and services and the adverse effects of what was called "piracy," the unauthorized online sharing of copyrighted

[47]Selected data from *How Much Do Average Apps Make?*, http://www.forbes.com/sites/tristanlouis/2013/08/10/how-much-do-average-apps-make;
Planet Android's Shaky Orbit, New York Times, May 28, 2015, p. B1; and
Tech Giants Make Move in Mobile Payments, New York Times, May 28, 2015, p. B1.

music. Electronic music was easy to produce and distribute, and Napster—one of the early file sharing services that allowed users to exchange MP3 files—demonstrated how the digital transition was going to occur, although in the absence of a digital, legal framework for copyrighted music that had not kept pace with technology. It was the end of another product lifecycle in music and the beginning of a new one. The online sharing of music threatened the survival of record labels, music publishers, music licensing agencies, and record stores and revealed their incredibly slow response to the digital transition in order to maintain the status quo. It was similar to the way the incumbent and laggard phone companies had hoped to extend the useful life of copper wire systems as fiber optic technology was introduced. As cell phones became widely available, customers abandoned their landlines and few were ever going to own such equipment again. The phone companies had to deal with plummeting sales of landline services.

The online piracy issue camouflaged several industry problems. The industry's first response to Napster was to file copyright infringement lawsuits seeking outlandish damages in order to eliminate the service rather than focus on a legal digital download service that combined the music repertories of all the records labels and music publishers. As bandwidth capacity increased that enabled the faster downloading of large files, the movies and video entertainment and book publishing sectors faced the same infringement issues as the music sector, but they had the lead time to learn from the mistakes of the music industry. Copyright infringement lawsuits paralyzed the music industry for years and delayed the rapid introduction of digital technologies in order to protect the obsolete status quo business models. The industry's court victories were often described as pyrrhic and only a short-term solution. Napster was eventually shut down, but it was too little to late because Napster would become the inspiration for e-books, iTunes, Spotify, Pandora, YouTube, and other decentralized peer-to-peer file sharing services. Peer-to-peer file sharing services, such as BitTorrent, were hard to ban because it was worldwide and there was no central server that could be shut down to solve the problem. Shutting down all file sharing services would have meant shutting down the entire Internet.

Just like IBM was forced to unbundle hardware, software, and support services, AT&T had to unbundle local and long distance services; Microsoft unbundled its operating system from its browser; and Craigslist unbundled classified advertising from newspapers and made the service free for users—the music industry was also confronted with an unbundling issue as well. Digital music meant that consumers no longer had to purchase entire album or CD of songs created by music distributors—which can be considered a bundle of songs—in order to get one or two good songs that they liked. Purchasing digital singles to create their own albums meant album sales were going to plummet and new digital downloads and streaming business models were now needed. Apple's iTunes would later create the market for the legal downloading of music that combined the repertories of all the major music publishers. The business model for digital singles centered around $0.99 a song with the record labels earning about a 70 % margin on each song for a product that was essentially a commodity. Consumers were no longer going to pay $19.95 for a prepackaged music CD, when a digital album that they can create themselves would cost less and hundreds of CDs of their favorite music could easily fit on an iPod for easy portability. There is now another digital transition in music that is occurring as digital downloads (owning) may be near the end of its product lifecycle and it is to be replaced with streaming (subscription). With the rise of Netflix, the movie and video entertainment sectors—in learning from the mistakes of the music sector—have been comparatively quicker in developing the licensing and sales business models for the ways in which Americans watched and paid for digital programming.

Digital technology has been a double-edged sword in the industry in which digital music can be distributed around the world in lightening speed with little to no marginal cost, while the PROs, record labels, and music publishers have been rendered practically redundant by the same technology that has lowered the labor-intensive costs of music production, distribution, and licensing. The rapid adoption rates of new technologies like smart phones and its functionality have outpaced the business models of many sectors in the music industry. The *Innovator's Dilemma* facing the music licensing industry—due to the emergence of new technology and new entrants—is similar to watching the helplessness and despair of a slow-motion collapse of the celebrated 100-year-old established order being swept away, even as a new and direct one took its place. Technology and innovation are slowly eliminating the intermediate role of licensing agencies and most may not even be around in their original form in the next decade. The incumbent licensing agencies like ASCAP, BMI, SESAC, and Harry Fox Agency (HFA) are no longer the exclusive agencies for music licensing because copyright holders began bundling performance, mechanical and synchronization licenses, and negotiating their own licensing agreements, further weakening these organizations.[48]

1.7.2 The Demise of the Harry Fox Agency and Its Failure to Survive the Digital Transition

The HFA, a mechanical licensing agency, has been struggling to reinvent itself and remain relevant after the downloading of music and streaming services eliminated a source of income and the need for mechanical licensing required for the manufacturing, reproduction and distribution of copyrighted sound recordings on physical media such as vinyl, cassette tapes and CDs. Harry Fox has been facing declining revenue from mechanical licensing for years, and its recent estimated annual revenue on average was said to be in the $150 million range, half of what it

[48]See Christensen (1997) and Lepore (2014). The Innovator's Dilemma occurs when new (disruptive) technologies displace the incumbent competitors in an industry. In an ironic twist to history, BMI was formed in 1939 by radio executives to weaken ASCAP's stranglehold on performance royalty licensing by providing radio stations with non-ASCAP songs. Now both agencies have erected barriers to prevent new entrants from entering the music licensing business.

was in prior years. The HFA as a stand-alone mechanical licensing agency came to an abrupt end on July 7, 2015, when it was announced that SESAC had agreed to purchase the agency for the reported sum of $20 million. SESAC's strategy behind the deal is to bundle mechanical and performance licensing in a single agency—something the other two incumbent PROs have been clamoring to do in revisions to their consent decrees. Bundling performance and mechanical licensing make it much easier, simpler, and efficient for streaming music services on digital platforms when both licenses are applicable in an industry where licensing rights were fragmented until now.[49]

The demise of the Harry Fox Agency couldn't be stopped, even if the statutory fixed-rate pricing for a mechanical license was abolished and the underlying causes for its demise were overlooked. HFA could not escape the uncertainty, sunk infrastructure expenses, and economic consequences that the digital era unleashed; the better, faster, simpler, cheaper, efficient, and easier methods for processing mechanical licenses.[50] Before being acquired by SESAC in 2015, HFA had become a third-party licensing administrator—for mostly small music publishers and others who had not negotiated direct monetization (revenue sharing) deals with YouTube—after being forced to adapt to the speed of technological change brought on by *exogenous* factors. However, revenue from HFA's role as a third-party licensing administrator failed to reverse its economic decline and its financial struggles ended with the sale to SESAC.[51]

Direct licensing, open-source software (OSS), and cloud-based services are having the same detrimental effects on PROs that streaming services did to HFA, even though the actual demand for digital musical compositions on various media platforms (smart phones, Internet, iPods and iPads, satellite radio, etc.) has skyrocketed. New entrants were able to replicate almost all of the essential functions of a PRO, including their competitive advantage, specialized knowledge and technical expertise of music licensing, music rights administration, performance

[49]See Wixen (2014, p. 51); *SESAC Buys the Harry Fox Agency*, Billboard Magazine, July 7, 2015, https://www.billboard.com/articles/news/6620210/sesac-buys-the-harry-fox-agency.

[50]See Schumpeter (1939). This happens all the time in American business and it is also often described as Schumpeter's *Creative Destruction*. In other words, old business models, structures, companies, processes, markets, and jobs are destroyed as new ones are created with the introduction of new technologies.

[51]See http://www.youtubelicenseoffer.com for additional details. As this manuscript went to press, it was reported that SESAC had agreed to purchase Harry Fox for an estimated price of slightly more than $20 million in a deal that has to be ratified by the members of the National Music Publishers' Association (NMPA), a trade group that has long owned HFA. See *SESAC Buys the Harry Fox Agency*, Billboard Magazine, July 7, 2015, https://www.billboard.com/articles/news/6620210/sesac-buys-the-harry-fox-agency; *Music Rights Group Is Buying Harry Fox Agency*, New York Times, July 7, 2015, http://www.nytimes.com/2015/07/08/business/media/music-rights-group-is-buying-harry-fox-agency.html?_r=0.

data collection, and royalty accounting.[52] In the process, the new entrants were able to change the structure of the music licensing industry by taking market share from the incumbent PROs.

In the first part of this monograph, we review and discuss the economic implications of two important rate court rulings on direct licensing that were significant because they re-defined copyright music licensing as administered by the two leading incumbent performance rights agencies in the US. In upending the PRO status quo, *US vs. ASCAP & In Re Capstar (DMX)* (2010) and *BMI vs. DMX* (2010) revealed the often-secretive economic demands and barriers to entry put in place, not just by PROs, but by record labels as well, that made profitability difficult for some music users in the industry. In addition, the court rulings revealed the diminishing returns from a "litigation as a business model" as these organizations sought to sustain themselves. As adverse rulings in the rate court cases increased, operating costs skyrocketed as well, and litigation expenses became a financial drain on the various organizations that further reduced royalty income for songwriters and composers. These two court cases and others discussed in the text exposed some of the opaque, anti-competitive, hypocritical, corrupt, inefficient, and unaccountability practices in PROs that have long been suspected but not widely documented, and explain *why* there are real concerns about openness and full transparency in the administration of copyright licensing.

Patry (2011, p. 236) suggests, when copyright holders [in this case the large multinational music publishers and record labels, and to a large extent PROs who do not own the copyrights that they license] are frightened by new technologies that they cannot control, they often seek new laws to protect them from a new world that destroys long-established business models. The rate court judges' decisions added (pricing) transparency, direct auditing, and further flexibility in adapting the traditional blanket licensing process to meet a changing competitive market place driven by modern technology. However, there is still the need for more reforms in the industry.

References

Blacc, A. (2014). 'Streaming Services Need to Pay Songwriters Fairly'. *Wired.* November 14, accessed online: http://www.wired.com/2014/11/aloe-blacc-pay-songwriters.

BMI vs. DMX (2010). No: 08 Civ. 216 (LLS), S.D.N.Y. July 26, accessed online: http://www.leagle.com/decision/In%20FDCO%2020100727985.xml/BROADCAST%20MUSIC,%20INC.%20v.%20DMX,%20INC , pp. 1–33.

BMI vs. Pandora Media Inc. (2013). No: 13-cv-04037 (LLS), S.D.N.Y. December, accessed online: http://docs.justia.com/cases/federal/district-courts/new-york/nysdce/1:1964cv03787/58544/61/0.pdf?1387564284, pp. 1–14.

Cairncross, F. (1997). *The Death of Distance.* Harvard Business School Press.

[52] See Wixen (2014, p. 60).

Campbell-Kelly, M. and Garcia-Swartz, D. (2015). *From Mainframes to Smart phones: A History of the International Computer Industry*. Harvard University Press.
Cassidy, J. (2002). Dot.Con: The Greatest Story Ever Sold. Harper.
Christensen, C. (1997). *The Innovators Dilemma: When New Technologies Cause Great Firms to Fail*. Harvard Business School Press.
Christman, E. (2014). 'The Digital Decline: What's Behind the First Downturn of the iTunes Era? And Can Streaming Save the Day?'. *Billboard Magazine*. January 18 issue, pp. 34–36.
Christman, E., Pham, A., and Peoples, G. (2013). 'Special Report: The Pandora Wars'. *Billboard Magazine*. August 10 issue. pp. 20–25.
Copyright Royalty Board (2012). *Adjustment or Determination of Compulsory License Rates for Making and Distributing Phonorecords: Motion to Adopt Settlement, Docket No. 2011-3 CRB Phonorecords II*. April, accessed online: http://www.loc.gov/crb/motions/parties_motion_adopt_settlement_041112.pdf, pp. 1–33.
DiCola, P. (2013). Money from music: Survey evidence on musicians' revenue and lessons about copyright incentives. *Arizona Law Review, forthcoming*. Accessed online: http://papers.ssrn.com/sol3/papers.cfm?abstract_id=2199058.
DiLorenzo, T. (1996). The myth of natural monopoly. *Review of Austrian Economics*, 9(2):43–58.
Dredge, S. (2014). 'SoundCloud Financials Reveal Widening Losses'. *MusicAlly.com*. October 13, accessed online: http://musically.com/2014/10/13/soundcloud-financials-widening-losses.
Johnson, D. (2014). 'See How Much Every Top Artist Makes on Spotify'. *Time.com*. November 18, accessed online: http://time.com/3590670/spotify-calculator.
Langenderfer, J. and Cook, D. L. (2001). Copyright Polices and Issues Raised by A&M Records vs. Napster: "The Shot Heard 'Round the World" or "Not with a Bang but a Whimper?". *Journal of Public Policy and Marketing*, 20(2):280–288.
Lepore, J. (2014). 'The Disruption Machine: What the Gospel of Innovation Gets Wrong'. *New Yorker Magazine*. June 23 issue, accessed online: http://www.newyorker.com/magazine/2014/06/23/the-disruption-machine.
Lyons, D. (2014). 'The Real Reason Apple Needs Beats: It May Not Be the Headphones or the Streaming'. *Billboard Magazine*, pages 6–7.
McDonald, D. (2013). *The Firm: The Story of McKinsey and its Secret Influence on American Business*. Simon & Schuster.
Micklethwait, J. and Wooldridge, A. (1996). *The Witch Doctors: Making Sense of the Management Gurus*. Random House.
Patry, W. (2011). *How To Fix Copyright*. Oxford University Press, New York.
Peoples, G. (2014). 'Pumping Profits Into SoundCloud's Bottom Line'. *Billboard Magazine*. November 1 issue, p. 14.
Pham, A. (2014). 'Streaming Made Up One-Fifth of U.S. Recorded Music Revenue in 2013'. *Billboard Magazine*. March 18, accessed online: http://www.billboard.com/biz/articles/news/digital-and-mobile/5937634/streaming-made-up-one-fifth-of-us-recorded-music.
Schumpeter, J. (1939). *Business Cycles: A Theoretical, Historical and Statistical Analysis of the Capitalist Process*. McGraw Hill, New York.
Sisario, B. (2014a). 'Chief Defends Spotify After Snub by Pop Star'. *New York Times*. November 12, p. B1.
Sisario, B. (2014b). 'Paying to Press Play: Premium Service for Music Coming From YouTube'. *New York Times*. November 13, p. B1.
Sisario, B. (2014c). 'Popular and Free, SoundCloud Is Now Ready For Ads'. *New York Times*. August 21, p. B3.
Stout, L. (2012). *The Shareholder Value Myth: How Putting Shareholders First Harms Investors, Corporations, and the Public*. Berrett-Koehler.
Ulin, J. (2014). *The Business of Media Distribution: Monetizing Film, TV, and Video Content in an Online World*. Focal Press, second edition.
US vs. ASCAP & In Re Capstar (DMX) (2010). No: 09 Civ. 7069 (DLC), S.D.N.Y. December 1, accessed online: http://www.leagle.com/decision/In%20FDCO%2020101209735 , pp. 1–87.

US vs. ASCAP & In re Petition of Pandora Media (2014). Nos: 12 Civ. 8035 (DLC), 41 Civ. 1395 (DLC), S.D.N.Y. March 14, accessed online: http://www.business.cch.com/ipld/PandoraUSASCAP031414.pdf, pp. 1–136.

Verrier, R. (2014). 'End of film: Paramount first studio to stop distributing film prints'. *Los Angeles Times*. January 17, accessed online: http://www.latimes.com/entertainment/envelope/cotown/la-et-ct-paramount-digital-20140117,0,5245137.story#ixzz2qnhjeuov.

Wixen, R. (2014). *The Plain & Simple Guide to Music Publishing*. Hal Leonard, third edition.

Yost, J. (2005). *The Computer Industry (Emerging Industries in the United States)*. Greenwood Press.

Chapter 2
Music Licensing Process

Digital technologies have irrevocably altered the entire music process from song creation to royalty distribution, and the result has been total chaos in the music industry. New laws, including digital rights, new processes and new business models are rapidly changing in an effort to return the music process to an equilibrium level. The licensing of music content is fundamentally complicated because it is not a simple input and output process that is easy to illustrate. Unlike other processes in which once a product or service is created and sold in a store, the process more or less ends there with the consumer consuming the product or service. After music is sold or downloaded, an entirely new sub-process begins in royalty collection and compensation to the copyright owners, particularly when the song is performed on television, radio, or the Internet. As long as that song is being performed—which requires a license and is an overly complicated process in itself—the copyright owners are being paid performance royalties even if the song is no longer sold or downloaded. Quite often, performance royalties are the only source of income for songwriters and composers.

This sub-process in royalty collection and distribution is complicated by several input factors: the creativity of songwriters and composers (the actual content creators); the outdated Copyright Act and consent decrees; new digital rights, the exploitation of music by record labels and music publishers; new competitors; the collection of royalties by PROs; the business plans; and content acquisition costs of music users and the distribution of music content on various media platforms based on consumer preferences. (A comprehensive analysis of the PRO sub-process is discussed in Pitt (2010) and in the Appendix section, there is a flow chart of a PRO sub-process.) A simplified process of music licensing is shown in Fig. 2.1 with an emphasis on content creation. Figure 2.1 shows a process that is a cycle of several inputs that are related to content creation, however, it fails to show how a single piece of intellectual property, a copyrighted song, must be divided up among

I.L. Pitt, *Direct Licensing and the Music Industry*,
DOI 10.1007/978-3-319-17653-6_2

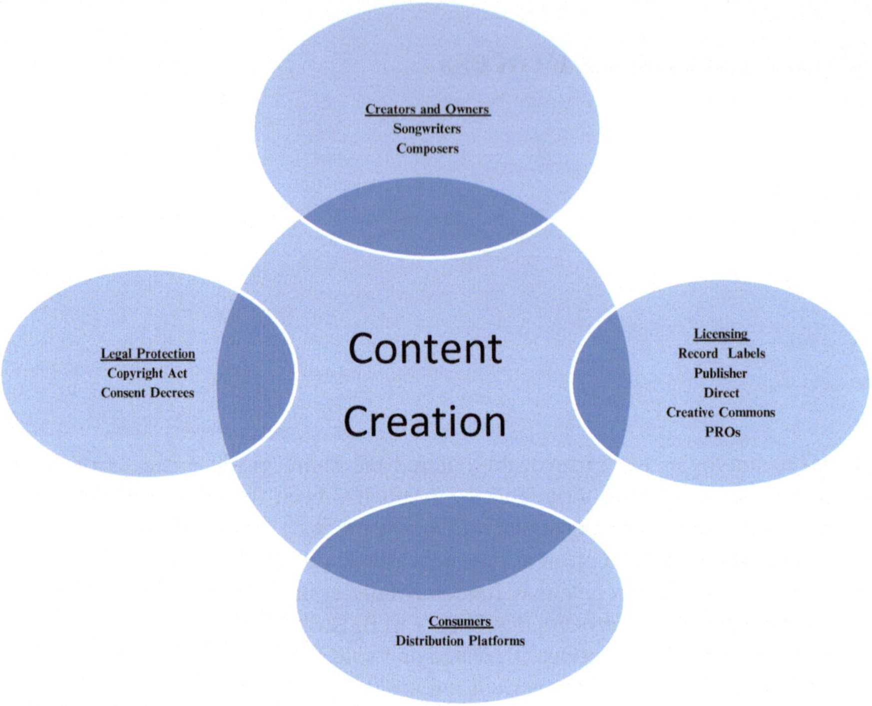

Fig. 2.1 Simplified music licensing process

the many owners and licensing agencies, often leaving song creators without a hit with very little royalty income. In Chap. 3, we will discuss the more complicated licensing process from a copyright law perspective. (See Fig. 3.1 on page 117.)

With the decline in CD sales, performing artists are now turning to touring and merchandising to increase their incomes.

2.1 Songs

Songs, once created and committed to a tangible form (the melody, lyrics, and the sound recording) begin the licensing and exploitation process by third-parties, or by music creators themselves on YouTube. To illustrate the complexity of music licensing and the economic underpinnings of the industry, we will use an actual example that is shown in Table 2.1. The table shows the top ranked songs and their corresponding units sales at year-end 2013 that teenagers and others were downloading and purchasing; songs that are not marching band, Broadway standards or big-band era music, nor are they nostalgic acts that make money from

Table 2.1 Top digital songs, songwriters and sales year-end 2013

Rank	Song	Songwriters/Composers	PRO	Record labels & publishers[a]	Performers/Artists	Sales in units
1	*Blurred lines*	Clifford Harris (T.I.) Robin Thicke	ASCAP ASCAP	Star Trak, IGA, Interscope, Deyjah'S Daddy Muzik, EMI April Music Inc, I Like 'Em Thicke Music, More Water From Nazareth	Robin Thicke T.I. Pharrell	6, 498, 000
2	*Thrift shop*	Ben Haggerty Ryan Lewis	BMI BMI	Macklemore, ADA, Ryan Lewis, Warner Bros	Macklemore Ryan Lewis Manz	6, 148, 000
3	*Radioactive*	Alexander Grant Benjamin A. Mckee Joshua F. Mosser Daniel C. Reynolds Daniel W. Sermon	BMI BMI BMI BMI BMI	Kidinakorner, IGA, Interscope, Universal, Imagine Dragons, Jmosser Music, Universal	Imagine Dragons	5, 496, 000
4	*Cruise*	Tyler R. Hubbard Brian Kelley Joey Moi Chase Rice Jesse K. Rice	BMI BMI SOCAN BMI BMI	Republic , BMLG, Sony/ATV, Big Loud Mountain, Big Red Toe Music, Dack Janiels Publishing, Deep Fried Dreams	Florida Georgia Line	4, 691, 000
5	*Royals*	Joel Little Ella Yelich-O'Connor	APRA APRA	Lava, Republic	Lorde	4, 415, 000
6		Lukasz Gottwald Martin Max Bonnie L. Mc Kee Katy Perry Henry Russell	ASCAP STIM BMI ASCAP ASCAP	Capitol, Bonnie Mckee Music, Songs of Pulse Recording, Where Da Kasz At	Katy Perry	4, 410, 000

(continued)

Table 2.1 (continued)

Rank	Song	Songwriters/Composers	PRO	Record labels & publishers[a]	Performers/Artists	Sales in units
7	*Just give me a reason*	Jeffrey Bhasker	BMI	RCA, Sony/ATV,	Pink	4, 310, 000
		Alecia Moore	BMI	EMI Blackwood,	Nate Ruess	
		Nathaniel Ruess	ASCAP	Pink Inside		
8	*Can't hold us*	Ben Haggerty	BMI	Macklemore,	Macklemore	4, 260, 000
		Ryan Lewis	BMI	Ryan Lewis Publ.	Ryan Lewis	
					Ray Dalton	
9	*When I was your man*	Peter Hernandez	ASCAP	Atlantic AG,	Bruno Mars	3, 928, 000
		Philip Lawrence	ASCAP	BMG Gold Songs,		
		Ari Levine	ASCAP	Mars Force Music,		
		Andrew Wyatt	BMI	Northside Ind.,		
				Roc Nation Music,		
				Toy Plane Music,		
				Universal,		
				WB Music Corp		
10	*Stay*	Mikky Ekko	BMI	SRP, Def Jam,	Rihanna	3, 854, 000
		Justin Parker	BMI	IDJMG		

Sources: Based on data from Christman (2014c).
http://repertoire.bmi.com, http://www.ascap.com/Home/ace-title-search and http://www.songfacts.com.
[a]Additional publishers may apply and some publishers listed may be licensing administrators, who perform the role of a publisher for a fee instead of copyright ownership.

mostly touring, long after consumers stopped purchasing their sound recordings. These are the songs that consumers are demanding, and not, necessarily, the songs that record labels are able to push on to consumers.

2.1.1 Songwriters and Composers

The songwriters, composers, and lyricists—the actual creators of music content—shown in the table are, generally, unknown to the general public, except if the songwriter is also a performer, a singer/songwriter. For example, Clifford Harris—known by his stage name as T.I.—is not only a songwriter, but also a performer who is well-known. Ryan Lewis is not only a songwriter, but a performer as well as the owner of his own music publishing firm. He is a self-publisher in which some of the administrative functions involved may be performed by a traditional publisher for a commission instead of a share in copyright ownership. More importantly, the table shows the influential and younger generation of songwriters and composers, the actual content creators, and their respective PRO affiliation—who are now well-positioned to revitalize PRO boards. Most of these younger songwriters seem to have a stronger affinity for BMI, and none of SESAC's songwriters made the list.

2.1.2 Performers, Artists, and Vocalists

Performers, such as Rihanna, who are not credited songwriters—at the least in the table presented here, but she may be on other songs—are hired as vocalists to bring the music of a songwriter and composer to life. Some songwriters may not be accomplished singers and may not like to perform in public. For example, if the song, *Stay*, is performed on terrestrial radio and television, the songwriters Mikky Ekko and Justin Parker, and the credited music publisher(s) are the ones paid performance royalties by BMI, while Rihanna, the vocalist, will *not* have a share in the performance royalty distribution. However, Rihanna, as the featured recording vocalist, along with the record labels and background musicians, will receive digital performance royalties from SoundExchange under a different provision of the *Copyright Act* for digital performances on certain digital platforms. Music publishers will *not* share in this type of digital performance royalties. To complicate matters even worse, the record label is often a subsidiary of the major music publisher and often a source of tension because of the difference in the royalty fees set by different governing bodies. (See Table 8.1 on page 224 and Table 8.7 on page 227.)

Table 2.2 Growth of the royalty network 2000–2014

	2000	2014	Change (%)	Services
Clients & songwriters	100	600	83	Copyright administrator,
Song catalog	5,000	65,000	92	Co-publisher and
Commission fee		10–15 %		Synchronization licensing

Sources: Based on data from www.roynet.com and Billboard Magazine, November 1, 2014, p. 75.

2.1.3 PROs, Record Labels, and Music Publishers

The Traditional third-party licensing agents are the PROs (ASCAP, BMI, SESAC, and SoundExchange, including foreign agencies such as SOCAN, APRA, and STIM), record labels (Interscope), and music publishers (Sony, Universal, and Warner). Record labels (sound recording) and music publishers (performance) share in the copyright ownership of a song, the PROs do not and their only role is that of a royalty collection agency acting on behalf of the copyright owners. Copyright ownership, protection against infringement, and rights are provided by provisions in the Copyright Act. Record labels and music publishers play (almost different roles) in the music exploitation process that we will discuss in Chap. 7. There are also independent publishers and copyright administrators such as Kobalt and The Royalty Network whose business models are different from the traditional music publisher and their costs and budgets are a fraction of the legacy publishers and PROs. Table 2.2 shows the growth of The Royalty Network, a copyright administrator, that is one of the new competitive options for self-publishing songwriters who may have outsourced their publishing and other income streams generation to a copyright administrator for a commission, instead of the standard 50 % cut and copyright ownership.[1]

2.1.4 Sales in Digital and Physical Units

Consumers play a big role in determining how a song may be exploited by deciding the price propensity at which they may be willing to purchase a song and the media platform that is more convenient for them. The year-to-date sales figures shown in

[1]The Royalty Network is able to compete with other licensing agencies with the help of specialty music software companies such as Counterpoint Systems.
According to their website, Counterpoint provides specialist rights and royalty management software for the music, entertainment, and brand licensing industries that helps their customers to track rights relating to their intellectual property, such as feature films, television programs and formats, songs, sound recordings, games, characters and entertainment or corporate brands.
They also help customers calculate participations and royalties associated with the content they are exploiting, and managing all the financial aspects of their rights and royalties business.
See http://www.counterp.com/aboutus.

the table include both digital and physical units and it shows just how many people and agencies are sharing in the licensing revenue and exploitation of a single song. In addition, personal managers, business managers, attorneys, agents, and various members of a performer's entourage are also paid. Ancillary revenue is also earned from fan-club membership fee, touring and merchandising.

2.1.5 Demand for Music and New Revenue Streams

On-demand streaming and cloud services for music and video content are now ubiquitous and convenient and this is the area in which an explosive growth in various media sectors is occurring. Music is exploding all over the Internet, but there is a greater demand for the newer songwriters and their musical compositions shown in the table, and not the Tin Pan Alley writers' music (used as background, underscores or theme songs), something that the status quo PROs failed to grasp. In addition, many in the music industry believed in the *Long Tail* theory that was popularized by Chris Anderson. In Anderson's theory, there is a market for any digital information file—including digital music–and no matter how obscure. This led many music executives to believe that the dormant or niche works in their catalogs could be easily monetized and there was a huge opportunity for incremental revenue. Anderson's theory has mostly been abandoned in the music industry because empirical research has shown that millions of songs available for purchase have never found a buyer, and the record labels are still focused on producing hits more than ever before.[2]

2.2 Competition

The Royalty Network, TuneCore, CD Baby and others would soon develop alternative business models that sold music; and tracked, collected, and distributed royalties on a fee-based system for independent musicians who were not affiliated with a record label or music publisher. Furthermore, as YouTube, smart phone apps, and streaming services became more popular for musical performances and were monetized, these competitors devised programs to collect a share of licensing fees or ad revenues directly from the platforms, bypassing the royalty collection agencies in the process.

CD Baby's catalog of three million tracks, 300,000 artists and 850 unique music genres would rival those of the incumbent PROs. These new competitors would

[2]See Anderson (2008); Page and Garland (2009).

differentiate themselves from the incumbents by offering independent musicians several income-revenue streams, weekly royalty payments, and instant access to sales and performance data, giving musicians control over their music.

2.3 Copyright Act

Table 2.1 also illustrates why the monetization of music has been made difficult in the music licensing process because the entire process is fragmented and burdensome for music users—caused in part by the outdated *Copyright Act*—and even though the exact same songs and songwriters are involved, the media platforms may be different and the royalty payment structure is also different. This fragmentation leads to digital royalty (statutory) rates set by the *Copyright Royalty Board*, a group of three judges appointed by the Library of Congress—SoundExchange, the digital performance rights organization, is collecting digital royalties—while the licensing fees for terrestrial radio and television broadcasts are set by a rate court judge under consent decree regulations—ASCAP, BMI, and SESAC are the PROs.[3]

2.3.1 *Royalty Income Streams*

Table 2.3 shows an example of the various sources of royalty income for a hit song based on the number of plays that was compiled by Kobalt, one of the fastest growing and influential music publishers. The name of the hit song that reached

Table 2.3 Sources of royalty income for a 2013 hit song worldwide

Medium	Number of plays	Share (%)
Streams	780,000	86.67
Radio	55,250	6.14
Broadcast TV	40,000	4.44
Downloads	15,000	1.67
Other	6,750	0.75
Physical albums	3,000	0.33
Total plays	900,000	
Royalty amount collected	$4,760,000	
Average per play	$5.29	

Source: Based on data from New York Times, June 8, 2015, pp. B1–B4

[3]See Bacharach (2014); Blacc (2014) in which these songwriters call for changes in the outdated licensing process in separate editorials.
SESAC is a for-profit organization and is not legally bound by a consent decree.

No. 1 was not revealed in order to protect the privacy and financial data of the songwriters. In typical fashion of following the dollars, the songwriters earned most of their royalty income from streaming services such as YouTube, Spotify, Pandora, iTunes, Google Play, and Amazon. Radio and broadcast plays—the largest revenue generators for PROs—were a distant second and third, respectively, and both have surpassed paid downloads. Kobalt's accounting revealed that for the 900,000 recorded plays, a total of $4.76 million in royalty payments were collected for an average of $5.29 per play. However, there is a vast difference in the amounts collected by the licensing agencies and the amounts distributed to songwriters and composers. When royalty payments are passed from one PRO to another around the world, each takes a cut in the form of taxes and fees for copyright administration. These taxes and fees can vary from 50 % to a whopping 75 % of the original royalty amounts collected and they can drastically reduce the final amount paid to songwriters and composers for their copyrighted music. Recordings artists may blame music services for the tiny amounts that they receive in royalty income, but it is also the current PRO payment process that is rife with inefficiencies, delays, and hidden costs. There are now calls for a new structure to handle a faster and more transparent process in the digital world. For example, YouTube and Spotify could link their music performance or plays data to a single and centralized database of copyright ownership information, eliminating dozens of royalty collecting intermediaries, so that songwriters and composers can be paid greater amounts and in much quicker time frame.[4]

2.4 The Problems with Music Licensing Agencies

Aggressive and costly litigation—including advocacy—designed as an incentive to force copyright compliance—in which some copyright holders (songwriters and composers) have been ill served—is not the only criticism of the anachronistic licensing agencies.[5] Critics allege that some of these licensing agencies are often opaque organizations lacking in public accountability, effectiveness, purpose, responsibility, and they may not reflect the way current markets and technologies work. The delayed development of innovations and competition in the music industry were often caused by incumbents seeking to protect the status quo—even as their strategic advantages were no longer sustainable—using a long

[4]See *Kobalt Goes to the Ends of the Earth to Get the Biggest Returns on Music*, New York Times, June 8, 2015, p. B1.
The article reveals that there is rising skepticism and resistance to the current music licensing process and the solid reasons why regulatory reforms are needed.

[5]Ill served because the lawsuits represented a significant amount of financial resources that could have been better used to pay royalty income to struggling songwriters. While the PROs had limited control over increasing revenue, they had total control over how much money was spent on litigation and advocacy expenses. See the extensive citation list on the problems and potential of collective licensing in the notes section of Patry (2011, pp. 302–304).

and costly litigation strategy that turned into an economic drain on corporate resources, and invariably the *individual* songwriter and consumers were the ones harmed. Critics have questioned whether such a litigation strategy was the worth the opportunity cost, given other choices and alternatives that might have been available. "Like all monopolists, they will use every last resource to lobby to maintain their monopolistic privileges, but the potential gains to consumers of free markets are too great to justify them."[6] We take a selective look below at some of the other widespread allegations of inefficiencies, corruption, incompetence, and inept leadership often cited as examples of the abusive, monopolistic, and predatory practices that the collective licensing agencies used in administering copyright licensing.[7]

2.5 Self-Preservation and the Status Quo

The collective licensing agencies often behave in a self-preservation or status quo manner when new technologies are introduced in the industry and they often lose sight of their original purpose of serving songwriters and composers. The collecting agencies are often resistant to industry innovation when such innovations threaten existing business models; the financial interests, salaries and pension benefits of the agencies' upper management, other vested interests, or the royalty income of a few influential and already successful songwriters and composers.[8]

Generically speaking, when these organizations become self-serving (often a gradual process over time), a few vested interests seek to maximize their own personal share of financial resources. It marks the beginning of internal rot and the vitality of the organization erodes from within even as new technology unleashes its pervasive and disruptive forces.[9]

The old, modest, long-established practices and manageable way of life in which organizational change occurred slowly is suddenly called into question and replaced with a rapid, unsettling, and complex set of diverse economic challenges that the executives are incapable of controlling or adapting to the speed of change. This leads to a general internal-resistance-to-change mentality or a new-guard (the new hires and independent thinkers with a broad range of managerial and industry experience) versus old-guard mentality (the ones who spent decades doing a single mundane task that is easy to automate and never worked in a competitive or publicly traded firm).

The problems and tensions inherent between the two groups become increasingly polarizing in an organization. Out of a combination of bureaucratic inertia and

[6]See DiLorenzo (1996).

[7]See Patry (2011, pp. 177–188) and Cardi (2007) among others.

[8]See Patry (2011, pp. 177–188) and Cardi (2007).

[9]See Christensen (1997) for analysis of his theory on how disruptive competitors may emerge and Lepore (2014) for her critique of disruption theory.

an insidious fear that their status and hold on power are undermined due to technological advances and challenges from new competitors, the old-guard locks away all the institutional memory and knowledge of the organization in their heads for their own security and control, when clearly the old methods and processes are failing. The old-guard is terrified that their knowledge and expertise would soon evaporate—in an open-source-technology world where secrecy no longer guarantees control of any process—if they delegated authority and that led to, accountability, new ideas, attitudes, and a different way of doing business.

As the old-guard becomes isolated, their ineffective decision-making becomes apparent to everyone in the organization. They behave in a constant state of panic with frequent (and often mindless) organizational restructuring because they are incapable of adapting to new markets and technologies. Within the organization, competent managers are pushed aside as a threat to the erratic, incoherent, and self-serving leadership and replaced with sycophants and their mastery of bureaucratic politics. It is often the case that managerial resources are squandered on the futile effort of preserving the existing status quo because of the risky nature of innovations and other changes that threaten those seeking to line their pockets. In essence, innovative ideas are often buried or shelved, and those people within (the 95 % doing the real work) or outside the organization with new processes, technical expertise, and business models are ignored, tossed out, or punished.

Clinging to the self-serving status quo leadership can also be considered a form of corruption in itself because of the harmful repercussions that may follow when it comes to implementing new technologies, new ideas, new innovations, or complex and multi-year capital projects such as computer system upgrades that may involve the specific contributions of individual team members to ensure that a project is successful. There is often no cross-fertilization of skills when projects depend on the creativity of employees. This can lead to risk-avoidance and morale problems among talented people with new ideas or innovations who might be reluctant to share them within their organization for fear of being marginalized, purged, demoted, passed over, or fired. It can be demoralizing to employees when they observe that no one among the inept leadership team is held accountable for past managerial and accounting mistakes, weak internal controls, litigation blunders, poor judgment, incoherent decision-making, and a lack of imagination and creativity. Consequently, the prestige of the organization (whether fairly or unfairly) is damaged by these grievances and internal divisions because conformity to the status quo was being rewarded and talent purged from the organization.

2.5.1 Natural Monopoly as a Barrier to Entry

The collecting agencies are alleged to be "natural monopolies," because *in the past* they were considered the most efficient method of administering the blanket license for some copyrighted works. These monopolies are able to use their inherent market power to protect their status quo (and often outdated) business models and prevent potential competitors from entering the industry. Due to the lack of competition and the concentration of ownership and licensing in a few hands, collecting societies can exercise a disproportionate amount of leverage against smaller music users, who may not have an alternative in obtaining music licensing clearances.[10] However, as digitization has taken hold, the enormous gains in productivity, efficiency, and other lower costs have eroded many of the natural monopoly advantages of PROs and left them saddled with the high overhead costs of maintaining a multi-state infrastructure (including international offices) that may not be needed in the digital era.

Each PRO controls a distinct music catalog in which the performance rights cannot be licensed elsewhere or they must be obtained in separate licensing agreements that entail separate administration fees for music users. The fragmentary approach to music licensing in which multiple licenses must be obtained from multiple agencies is often cited as a source of confusion, administrative inefficiency, increased costs, and a weakness in copyright law because there is no simple or streamlined method to obtaining performance, mechanical and synchronization rights to a song from a single agency in the United States.[11]

Performance licensing fees are set by a rate court, typically as a percentage of advertising revenue or a flat rate in some years. In the past, the benchmark rate for an ASCAP blanket license was 2.5 % of advertising revenue for terrestrial radio stations, broadcast television networks, and cable networks. However, in the licensing agreement between radio broadcasters—represented by the Radio Music License Committee (RMLC)—for the period 2010–2016, the fee was set at a rate of 1.70 % of all revenue, including revenue derived from new media uses, while the rate for the ASCAP-Pandora license for the years 2011 through 2015 was at 1.85 % of revenue for every year of the license term.[12]

Mechanical licensing must be obtained from an entirely different agency and the licensing fees are statutory, that is, the fees are fixed by statute or law. At the date of writing, the fixed-rate or the cost of a mechanical license for the reproduction of a song is 9.1¢ per copy or $1.75 a minute of playing time whichever is greater for physical records and permanent digital songs. The royalty rate payable for each ringtone made and distributed is 24¢.[13] With the decline in sales of vinyl records,

---

[10]See Patry (2011, pp. 177–188) and Cardi (2007).

[11]Outside of the United States, a single agency may handle both performance and mechanical rights. See the PRS of Music organization in the United Kingdom: http://www.prsformusic.com/Pages/Rights.aspx.

[12]See the details here: *US vs. ASCAP & In Re Applications of RealNetworks, Inc., Yahoo! Inc.* (2010); *US vs. ASCAP & In re Petition of Pandora Media* (2014).

[13]Historical and current mechanical royalty rates under compulsory licensing for making and distributing records can be found here: (a) Historical rates: http://www.copyright.gov/carp/m200a.pdf and (b) Physical phonorecord deliveries, permanent digital downloads and ringtones; rates for interactive streaming and limited downloads and limited offerings, mixed service bundles, music bundles, paid locker services purchased content locker services: http://www.loc.gov/crb/motions/parties_motion_adopt_settlement_041112.pdf.

cassette tapes, and CDs, mechanical licenses have become less useful in favor of new technologies such as music subscription and streaming.

2.5.2 *PRO's Royalty Computation and Survey Methodologies*

These agencies can be administratively inefficient, corrupt and their incompetence can often lead to mal-investments as the only gatekeepers and bottlenecks in music licensing.[14] ASCAP's royalty payment system is a source of massive confusion and obfuscation, even to the society's own established members and staff, and some often view the process as "mystical" or "ephemeral" and their quarterly statements as though it is written in "secret code" because it is so incomprehensible.[15] Each PRO uses a different payment and obscure formula for calculating and distributing royalty payments to composers, songwriters, lyricists, and music publishers and the allocation process is often described as ineffective and inefficient. The formulas used are extremely complex and convoluted, and can have a substantial effect on a particular songwriter's current or future earnings when methodological changes are made to payment rules; changes that often benefit the status quo. It is almost impossible to cross-reference the PRO's collected musical performance data with the royalty payment data on members' statements, even using a detailed flowchart of the process. Furthermore, the proprietary algorithms used by some licensing agencies to compute royalty payments—outside of a regulatory framework—are never publicly or fully disclosed for auditing or transparency purposes. The PRO payment distribution process is hidden in accounting obscurity, and an area of research that few economists have examined, particularity the adoption of their often dubious concept of "multipliers." Songwriters and composers expect that the more often their music is performed, the more they will be paid in royalties.[16] There is no consistent method to ensure that there is a *fair and equitable* distribution of songwriters' royalty income across all PROs. Each PRO uses different monitoring services (Media Monitors, MediaGuide, RCS MediaBase and Nielsen) as well other sample survey sources, and which monitoring service's methodology is *scientifically* more superior to the others is the subject of debate in the industry. The same song and the same number of associated musical performances used in the same time period can often pay different amounts of royalty income depending on the PRO's computation methods and survey methodologies. Thus, it is often difficult for aspiring songwriters to determine which PRO will compensate them best in terms of both short-term and long-term financial solvency.[17]

---

[14]See Patry (2011, pp. 177–188) and Cardi (2007).

[15]See Pollock (2014, pp. 149–150).

[16]See Brabec and Brabec (2011, chapter 10, pp. 309–357) where the PRO payment process takes up an entire chapter.

[17]See Passman (2012, pp. 241–242), Wixen (2014, pp. 64–69).

Furthermore, SESAC is a for-profit organization that is not subjected to the restrictions of consent decrees, and therefore has more leeway in the way in which its royalty payment formula is administered. When it comes to the timely payment or distribution of royalties, some may engage in unscrupulous accounting and business practices. For example, on certain occasions, these societies withhold royalty distributions intended for members and affiliates for extended periods in order to take advantage of the "float" or working cash, that is, they collect interest payments for some interval between when a royalty distribution should be made to members' bank accounts and the actual day that the amount is deducted from the agency's bank balance.[18] The songwriters and composers of unregistered works—often the result of poor music publishing administration—that appear in the performance data collection processes are often not paid.

It was often impossible to monitor all musical performances played in the entire country, except in some cases where the music performance data were provided on cue sheets, prior to the era of digital fingerprinting. Hundreds of thousands of bars, restaurants, and other retail establishments were licensed but performance data on music use were never collected. The distribution of royalty payments to songwriters and composers was largely an art of approximation, substitution, and subjective judgment. Royalty payments to PRO members and affiliates were often based on an extrapolation from a relatively small nationwide statistical sample of musical performances. Radio and television musical performances were often used to correlate music use in bars, restaurants, and other retail locations. Songwriters and composers—whose musical compositions were performed but not captured in a statistical sample or survey—were often not paid.[19]

2.5.3 Scandal at ASCAP

PROs can be dangerous places for employees when royalty-payment anger boils over, particularly when they lag behind or are slow in adopting modern monitoring technologies that would change the benefits of the older status quo. Music was exploding all over the Internet—with teenagers being the driving force—but most of it were not the Tin Pan Alley, background or underscore variety. There was a shocking scandal at ASCAP—that is related to music that is not being captured in surveys or otherwise—that left employees terrified. Following allegations, a songwriter actually walked in and threatened to kill employees because he was convinced that his music was being performed and he wasn't being paid by ASCAP. The terrified receptionist and whoever happened to be in the area would have been

[18]See Patry (2011, pp. 177–188).

[19]See Patry (2011, pp. 177–188) and Cardi (2007).

the innocent victims had this man not been stopped.[20] Employees returning from their lunch break couldn't enter the building due to the police investigation. Some speculated that the incident reached the breaking point that it did because ASCAP's payment method was highly suspect to the songwriter (and this likely followed from industry accounts of labels not paying their artists), and the poor songwriter was probably repeatedly given the same tired and thread-bare excuse long used that unless his/her music was performed and captured in a survey or elsewhere they would not be paid royalties. The incident was an exception—and not all songwriters and composers are this extreme requiring such action to get paid their fair share of royalties—but it goes to show why the convoluted royalty payment and distribution system needs to be simplified and made more transparent so that songwriters can believe it is fair, accurate, efficient and they are compensated in a timely manner. Songwriters are expecting to be paid for every single performance of their music. Possible bomb threats requiring the entire evacuation of the office building were another workplace safety hazard for employees.[21]

2.5.4 Royalty Payments and Confidentiality Agreements

Before the widespread use of digital fingerprinting as a superior music performance monitoring system—a technology that some PROs were slow to implement because of the impact on (lower) royalty payments to status quo members as a result of an accurate count of all performances that could now be made, and the pool of royalty payments divided among a larger set of songwriters—the excuse was always made that members could not be paid because the performances of their music were not captured in the limited PRO surveys.

When royalty payments were made to songwriters and composers, they were hidden in confidentiality agreements—supposedly at the request of some songwriters themselves. This outdated practice serves to obfuscate the underlying economic reality of which types of musical performances are more heavily weighted than others (feature, theme, underscore, jingle, etc.); bonus and premium payments (the arbitrary decisions and what qualifies); who is getting paid (Tin Pan Alley versus contemporary writers whose music is being downloaded or purchased); how much they are paid (superstars versus every other writer); how often they are paid (theme songs from old TV shows still being broadcast may generate performances every quarter, while some songs are performed occasionally); and what is the platform type (dying terrestrial old-media that favors older writers' music and the status quo royalty payment system, or the Internet where the demand for music by younger

[20] ASCAP is not the only place that such dangerous incidents can occur. At AT&T the spouse of worker was let into the building and he attempted to kill her, but the gun jammed, saving her life and probably others as well.

[21] BMI's New York Office is now housed in the rebuilt 7 World Trade Center building, and, rightly or wrongly, it must be a daily reminder of what can occur.

songwriters is growing and there are millions more performances (streams) of a song).

The secrecy behind the non-disclosure of royalty payments to composers, writers, and music publishers prevents the proper economic valuation for what an individual musical performance may be worth across media platforms, and stymied the rapid development of new markets, business models, and technologies.

2.5.5 PRO Inefficiencies in Pricing and Royalty Payment Options

The issue of a flexible fixed-rate versus a-percentage-of-revenue formula in licensing fee agreements is always under review and the subject of rate court proceedings. There is always a fair of amount of skepticism as to whether a rate court or a copyright board can effectively determine the fair market value for a blanket license for all buyers and sellers in the absence of an honest price discovery mechanism from competition and market forces. The reason for this is simply due to the fact that there is not enough licensing fees and royalty distribution payment data made available for experts to compare prior years information and from there create the benchmarks and deflators for the price of a blanket license using the market's supply and demand dynamics. In robust years when the economy is strong, and advertising revenue is growing at a rate that exceeds price increases in licensing fees, music users lobby for a fixed-rate blanket licensing agreement with PROs so that revenue is adjusted and aligned with input costs.

In years in which there is a recession, like in 2008, and advertising revenue is declining, there is often a preference for a percentage-of-revenue formula in performance licensing agreements. For example, prior to 2008, the radio industry paid a flat-fee (instead of a percentage of revenue of formula) for a blanket license and the fee was later allocated among RMLC members, but as the 2008 financial crisis steadily worsened, the RMLC members now wanted to switch back to a percent of revenue formula as radio advertising revenue collapsed. Switching between a flat-fee and a percentage of revenue formula for a blanket license entailed another round of delays, lengthy court hearings, and costly litigation.[22] There was no flexible and adaptive PRO licensing system in place in which music users could decide whether a flat-fee or a percent of revenue formula made economic sense, and the formula enacted swiftly, smoothly, seamlessly and without costly court action. This was yet another of the PRO inefficiencies that the economic conditions associated with the decline in advertising revenue exposed in the PRO industry.

In addition, future changes to the Copyright Act might be more flexible and adaptive by incorporating the desire of some younger songwriters and composers

[22]See Oxenford (2009); *US vs ASCAP & In Re Application of the Cromwell Group Inc. and Affiliates et al* (2012); and *Section III: The RMLC-ASCAP License Agreement for the Period 2010–2016, US vs. ASCAP & In re Petition of Pandora Media* (2014, pp. 19–22).

who may want to avoid the complicated and convoluted royalty-payment rules and profit from their copyright ownership by being paid a fixed, up-front, lump-sum amount for the future value of their copyrights rather than wait around to collect tiny annual performance royalties.[23] PROs may claim that they are battling for the 500,000 songwriters, composers, and music publishers that are individual members of their organizations, but it is only a few songwriters along with music publishers who earn the lion's share of performance royalties.

The key point is that music users, songwriters, and composers want a flexible and adaptive licensing or royalty payment system in which they can choose the best licensing formula that suits their economic interests without the need for costly rate court litigation to switch between the two methods when a contractual period is over.

2.5.6 PRO Overhead and Administrative Costs

The overhead and profit margins skimmed off the top from the licensing fees collected by PROs have been a source of tension in the music industry and has led to an economic revolt by some music users, music supervisors, and music publishers. Some music publishers and music users have decided to bypass the PROS and negotiate their licensing agreements with music users as a way to lower the costs associated with performance rights licensing.[24] PRO overhead expenses, as a percentage of licensing revenue, are often obscenely high in the double digits. For example, in recent years, ASCAP's overhead expenses have varied from 17 % to 23 %, while the fees charged by BMI and SESAC are comparable but slightly lower than ASCAP's.

When high overhead costs (that often include the sunk costs associated with redundant, prestigious, and expensive corporate offices in high-rent districts in multiple locations that songwriters may not want to pay for, exorbitant legal fees charged by expert witnesses and outside counsel for lengthy litigation and the need to recover the amortized and mal-investment costs for long-delayed computer system upgrades) are deducted, the leftover portion of licensing fees reduces the amount of royalty income available to songwriters and composers.[25] Even though digitalization offers lower cost advantages and other efficiencies, these cost-savings have not led to lower licensing fees for some music users.

The PROs resistance to new technologies, new business models, institutional reform and other innovations became even more desperate, as the DMX case that we analyze below will reveal. The executives who built their careers on the old and outdated music licensing models fought tooth and nail to prevent new entrants from

[23]See Karp (2013).

[24]See Christman (2011, 2013b); Sisario (2011).

[25]See Patry (2011, pp. 177–188) and Cardi (2007).

entering the music industry. As the various industry players needed more and more revenue to sustain inefficient and obsolete operations; pay large salaries and bonuses to executives; amortize the sunk costs associated with infrastructure and IT system upgrades; recover litigation expenses; ward off new entrants and competitors; mask inadequate leadership and prevent internal rot, music piracy became the scapegoat for all ills in the industry. Anonymous "pirates" became the implacable enemies of the music industry.

In fact, it was consumers driving the process because there was no longer a "scarcity" in music. Digital music was now a commodity and efficiently distributed in unlimited quantities over the Internet by iTunes, YouTube and music streaming services for a small amount of money. In some cases, the music was free, if the users were willing to accept advertising-supported services. It was not just music, but the entire video programming libraries of broadcast and cable networks, movie libraries from film studios and electronic books by book publishers that were being made available for a subscription fee of just a few dollars a month.

In reality, it was the content creators—the songwriters, composers, musicians, lyricists, authors and others—who were suffering due to the inequitable distribution of royalty income and the steep overhead costs—including litigation and advocacy—of administering the blanket license—forcing some musicians to turn to touring and merchandising to offset the loss of income from mechanical and performance royalties. What is often not disclosed by these licensing agencies is that the distribution of royalty payments to individual songwriters and composers is highly skewed, that is, a few top songwriters and music publishers are earning the most money and all the rest receive just pennies.[26] This lack of transparency and public accounting of royalty payments are often powerful incentives to resist change and maintain the status quo in music licensing. In some cases, the leadership of the music licensing agencies has been in place for decades protecting their perks and benefits that could easily be skimmed off the top of collected licensing fees and the remaining (dwindling) pool of money is then distributed to copyright holders. Many of these executives suffered the least and very few have actually had to deal with a decline in income while remaining at these agencies, even as songwriters' incomes were evaporating as music was now a commodity and priced accordingly.

The PROs became fatalistic and demanded government action through their politically connected lobbyists because they thought that they were powerless to stop the music 'pirates' who were allegedly stealing music. Lobbying by special interests to preserve the benefits of the status quo is a large part of the reason why comprehensive reforms to the *Copyright Act* and consent decrees have been inefficient, difficult and poorly implemented over the years.

It became extremely challenging for legislators in the digital era to make new laws in medial usage because technology—particularly with the creation of mobile streaming apps for smart phones—was rapidly outpacing the rules and regulations

[26]See Pitt (2010, 2013, 2015).

even as they were being written.[27] Cynics have argued that many executives in the music industry assumed that "lost sales" from piracy could be easily recovered. The rationale was simple: *If* consumers weren't busy pirating content, they would be flocking to music stores to buy CDs, purchasing seats, merchandise and concession items at live concerts or listening to terrestrial radio to boost ratings and advertising revenue.

In point of fact, it was hard to quantify the real threats and opportunities that piracy and the disruption associated with digital technology presented—except for attorney fees—because some "pirates" eventually spent money on other music content, merchandise or concert tickets after discovering new music through piracy. Still, others may have downloaded the pirated content because it was readily or easily available, but they had no intention of purchasing anything because it was too expensive to obtain it legitimately.[28] The piracy argument would later strain credulity as technology; competition; innovation; economic and financial conditions; and consumer preferences would expose the structural problems in the music industry that led to the decline in revenue. Legitimate music and video services such as iTunes, Netflix, and Spotify would later demonstrate that some of the best methods to combat piracy—and its associated unmet consumer demand—was not copyright infringement lawsuits, but to use the right combination of price (singles versus bundles), aggregated inventory (combined music and video catalogs of copyright owners), technology (higher-quality streaming, smart phones, tablets and personal computers), and convenience (content available anytime or anyplace and binge-viewing).

2.5.7 Resigning from a PRO

An independent and centralized registry of song title data would help to solve a vexing problem associated with PRO membership or affiliation, and, that is, when a songwriter or composer has a strong desire to resign and join another PRO for whatever reason, usually for higher monetary compensation. The resignation process is a long one—that is built into the PROs licensing agreements—in which members or affiliates must give notice months (6–9 months that was recently shortened to 3–6 months for ASCAP)—in advance of a resignation, and some may find that the rules, regulations, and the process are so arduous that it may not be worth the effort, even though they may earn more elsewhere. Missing the specific cut-off dates or window for resigning could mean that a writer may

[27]See https://www.opensecrets.org/lobby/clientsum.php?id=D000000432 for the annual lobbying expenditures spent by PROs.

[28]See *RIAA Spent $64M to Win $1.4M From Pirates Between '06 and '08* available here: http://www.dailytech.com/RIAA+Spent+64M+to+Win+14M+From+Pirates+Between+06+and+08/article19034.htm.

have to wait a year or more for another opportunity to resign. There is always the fear among songwriters that if they leave a PRO they might miss payments, bonuses, premiums, and other incentives from prior months in the convoluted royalty payment process. Follow the dollar?—the "dollars" ought to be following the songwriters and composers. This is another roadblock put in place by incumbent PROs that prevents songwriters and composers from *easily* moving their catalogs to a different PRO, and new competitors from entering the industry, a priority for any future changes to consent decrees and the *Copyright Act*. The resignation process is not made that easy because PROs often fear that the best songs in their repertory, the ones that are performed frequently, would be migrating elsewhere to competitors. The PROs may have millions of registered songs and hundreds of thousands of songwriters in their repertories, but in any given quarter, it is only a small number of popular songwriters who are receiving the lion's share of royalties—and this can be a source of panic when members resign and the reason why there is no internal effort to change the current royalty distribution process. From its earliest founding, PROs were more or less set up to benefit the influential insiders (Tin Pan Alley writers and publishers) and were often exclusionary.

There are often complications when resigning that involve co-writers who may wish to remain; co-writers' PRO affiliation; publisher agreements, judicial claims (alimony, child support payments and collateral), the PRO blanket licensing agreements in place at the time with radio and television networks, and what ASCAP's says are "legally binding representations, warranties and covenants," whatever that jargon means. Resigning members must also agree to something called the *indemnification of ASCAP*. Members who have resigned from ASCAP must agree to "indemnify ASCAP (i.e., defend and hold ASCAP harmless) from and against certain claims arising out of that Member's resignation." It is almost too terrifying to think about under what circumstances should such a need arise. It sounds like resigning members might actually have to present the PRO with some sort of high risk insurance policy upon exit.

While songwriters and composers are limited to only one PRO membership or affiliation at a time, publishers may belong to more than one PRO, depending on song title registration. For example, a song may have two co-writers—one who is a member of ASCAP and the other an affiliate of BMI—but they may share the same music publisher. Each writer would receive a royalty check from their PRO, while the publisher would receive two checks, one from ASCAP and another one from BMI. From this vantage point, the music publisher gets a ton of performance and royalty payments data from across all PROs, asymmetrical information and intelligence that are not often available to songwriters and composers.

Some writers may find that they are unable to remove their songs in a timely fashion from a PRO's repertory because the songs are included in the blanket license sold by each PRO to radio and TV stations, and may not do so until the blanket license's contractual period ends. According to ASCAP's website, "when a Member resigns, a music user that is a party to a License-In-Effect will continue to have the right to perform publicly all musical works in the ASCAP Repertory, including works that are the subject of a Member resignation, for the term of the License-in-Effect."[29] The resignation process does not need to be so complicated since most radio and television networks obtain blanket licenses from all PROs to avoid infringement lawsuits, and it is just a matter of the money and the collected performances data following the songwriter or composer to a new PRO. The resignation process ought to be as simple as rolling over a 401K-type retirement plan.

Each PRO routinely collects the performance data of songwriters and composers who are not registered members or affiliates (but no royalty payments are made) in the normal course of performance data collection. The performance data are often used to analyze (otherwise called snooping) what a non-member/affiliate might have earned under the particular PRO's convoluted payment formula and the decision made whether it is economic to acquire that songwriter's catalog of songs. No such transparent information is available for songwriters and composers to determine whether it makes economic sense to switch from their current PRO to a different one, unless songwriters from different PRO compare their quarterly statements or a publisher is willing to share such information.

2.5.8 Reorganization, Restructuring, and Layoffs

As economic pressure mounted—from music users looking to lower their licensing expenses as advertising revenue declined and songwriters wanted increased royalty income as the demand for Internet music skyrocketed—for PROs to demonstrate efficiency and transparency, a panicky attempt was often made to give the appearance of lowering their obscenely high administration fees through rigorous cost controls, layoffs, restructuring, and other methods. Piracy was not compounding the economic problems of PROs (unlike the film industry) and it will have nothing to do with the eventual demise of PROs. The elephant in the boardroom turned out to be the music publishers who are their own members or affiliates. In most cases, the radio industry and broadcast and cable networks, signed multi-year licensing contracts whose fees could only be renegotiated when those contracts were up for renewal.

Industry observers have alleged that some copyright infringement lawsuits typically followed after the PROs lost a major court battle and they made a futile attempt to recoup the millions of dollars in litigation expenses by suing bars, restaurants, clubs, and others. After losing infringement lawsuits in court, it was also not uncommon for mass layoffs or some sort of restructuring to occur in yet another desperate attempt to lower PRO administration overhead expenses. Legal

[29]See *Compendium of ASCAP Rules and Regulations, and Policies Supplemental to the Articles of Association* that is available here http://www.ascap.com/~/media/files/pdf/members/governing-documents/compendium-of-ascap-rules-regulations.pdf, pp. 6–10.

staff, economic analysts, and others were often hired to conduct research for rate court proceedings and then later cruelly laid-off without the common decency of a moment's warning to some of those employees who had lost their jobs.

The layoffs were sometimes staggered in a such way that they attracted very little outside attention and may have violated the intent of some of the provisions of the *Worker Adjustment and Retraining Notification Act* (WARN), such as to provide written notices to some employees 60 calendar days in advance of plant closings and mass layoffs, and the size of the layoffs affecting at least fifty people at a single site of employment. Hypothetically for example, to avoid WARN requirements for a mass layoff, 30 people might be let-go in round one, instead of 50 so as not to trigger the WARN Act. After a series of layoffs, the cumulative effect was the same; a mass layoff over some time interval skirting the rules of WARN. This is yet another example of the unethical practices at some PROs, if these allegations are true. Even if the layoffs were legal, it raised questions about the fairness of the entire process and the poor treatment of employees. Some employees were given severance packages based mostly on their length of employment and other factors, plus additional payments for signing a termination agreement that imposed an intimidating gag order that prevented employees from speaking out.

To the displaced workers—a big part of the experienced workforce—in the 2009–2010 period, the situation appeared bizarre at one of these PROs. What was rather surprising (as highlighted in Table 4.2 on page 131 and Table 4.4 on page 133) was that, even though the PROs were apparently well-funded, with a modest reduction in licensing fees for some, they were already behaving as though the entire system of collecting licensing fees (and the gains from economies of scale associated with a natural monopolist) was completely broken down, judging from the mass layoffs and the internal state of panic that occurred before and after the year 2010. The bureaucratic and bitter infighting only worsened as new competitors, technology, market conditions and possible new laws exposed the ineffective leadership, tactical execution errors, inefficiencies and outdated processes. It was clear there was no advanced contingency planning in place for all of the developments that were occurring, even ones that were clearly expected or should have been expected.

During a massive reorganization of a PRO, there was a mad scramble to reduce and consolidate office space in one high-rent New York location, and workers were suddenly required to work from home, presumably to cut down on office expenses in preparation for the onslaught of competition. Many believed that it was all a clever stratagem to get rid of workers; the telecommuters were some of the first workers to lose their jobs and then followed closely by those workers that remained on-site. It was the classic maneuver, similar to AT&T, in which a rudderless, inefficient, and incumbent monopoly PRO was about to be pummeled by competition, innovation, and technology. AT&T's cost-cutting measures of eliminating layers of management were often portrayed as an attempt to become more nimble and better prepared to meet the digital onslaught. It would take years for the old AT&T to become "nimble" (which it never did) until its eventual demise. Interestingly enough, some of the senior executives responsible for the debacle—mal-investment, bloated corporate structure, a failure to conduct the proper due diligence on certain acquisitions, bureaucratic in-fighting, and a reliance on outside consultants for strategic thinking and their flavor-of-the-month ideas—were never really held accountable for their own mistakes. The transformational shift from analog to digital technologies—and with the rapid increase in speed and capacity and lowered costs for information processing—destroyed the old market structure.

Some managers had only prior work experience with the federal government—hardly an organization that you would expect to promote innovation, competition, and efficiency—and spent decades performing the same mundane task. Their knowledge (institutional memory) of arcane procedures would eventually be absorbed into modern information processing methods with a greater capacity for speed and accuracy. Some of these managers were often clueless in understanding the implications for future competition and new business models in the industry. It was an atmosphere of "survival mode" in which the managers conducting the lay-offs were worried that the laid-off workers were far more competent than the managers themselves and were a threat in exposing their incompetence, lack of leadership skills or other job-related insecurities such as boredom, burnout, and the fear of losing their jobs. It was the typical government bureaucracy mentality of hoarding job assignments and the fear that delegating assignments would be detrimental to their careers. Incidentally, PROs are often viewed in the same negative light as governmental agencies with their ability to tax the labor contributions of others and so the government bureaucracy mentality was apt.

As the financial squeeze from the dubious, relentless, and failed lawsuits became apparent later on, both songwriters and laid-off PRO employees ended up paying for the corporate mistakes and excessive risk taking with the loss of income, jobs, and homes. If one outside law firm failed in their quest for preserving the status quo or increasing fees, another law firm could be easily hired to repeat the same and often futile litigation cycle. Workers understood that during a downturn in business and economic cycles, layoffs were possible as input costs were realigned to match revenue, but in 2009, both ASCAP ($995 million) and BMI ($905 million) collected the most licensing fees in their entire history, an accomplishment that was well-publicized in the trade press and elsewhere. The experience of some workers revealed the extent to which the PROs had not prepared for competition, the adverse outcomes of the various court cases and other internal problems tied to the execution errors in capital projects. It called into question the managerial incompetence—that created the corporate bloat in the first place to justify their existence in some way or the other—of pinning the blame for risky decision-making on the laid-off workers. It was too late in the game to hire digital strategists when even the CEOs and in-house economists did not have a clue to where the music industry was headed. Even with a new organizational design, skeptics were wondering if the PROs would ever be efficient enough to offer weekly royalty payments, given the current processes that they have in place. It remains to be seen if any of the cost-savings from the layoffs or moving to a digital platform actually resulted in lower licensing fees for music users and higher royalty payment distributions to songwriters and composers. It is always a sign of good executive leadership when the best CEOs can plan for all possible contingencies in advance in order to minimize tactical errors and recover quickly from competitive threats and innovations.

2.6 Corporate Governance and the PRO Boardroom Panic

The trend of music publishers withdrawing digital rights from the PROs is a major contributing factor in the decline of PRO licensing fee income. With direct licensing, ASCAP and BMI were about to suffer the same fate as The Harry Fox Agency, now a mere third-party accounting administrator for small music publishers who were not able to negotiate their own licensing deals.

The panicked reaction by PROs to meet the demands of music publishers in the digital rights withdrawal movement is another illustrative example of how maximizing revenue for one set of members can be detrimental to another set of members. It is a cautionary tale of what exactly is the economic purpose of PROs and the diminished economic leverage of songwriters and composers as digitalization transforms the music industry. As court documents revealed, that on April 27, 2011, the ASCAP Board adopted a resolution to amend its Compendium to allow a publishing member to withdraw from ASCAP its rights to license music to new media outlets, while allowing ASCAP to retain the right to license those works to other outlets. ASCAP's knee-jerk response in its eagerness to change its bylaws to allow the partial withdrawal of digital rights and without a complete economic and financial assessment of the impact on songwriters' and composers' future income was not only damaging in the short-term (as reflected in bad corporate governance, flawed judgment, poor negotiating skills of songwriters and composers and the tarnished reputation of the board), but damaging in the long-term (cost burden shifted to songwriters and composer) to the value of music.[30]

ASCAP was too eager to change its bylaws to allow the partial withdrawal of digital rights without a complete economic and financial assessment of the impact on songwriters' and composers' future income, the actual creators of musical compositions. It was rather uncommon that six songwriter-members—of the 12 publisher-members and 12 writer-members board—abstained from the vote, but there was no vote in opposition. This was a repeat of a past and common ASCAP practice in which Tin Pan Alley publisher-members were the ones with undue influence and who benefited most from the system.[31]

Industry critics have often cited the conflicts of interest, corruption, outrageous snobbery, lack of diversity, lack of clearly-defined objective standards, lack of integrity and non-transparency among the governing bodies in the music industry that are often under the undue influence of a single member (music or magazine

---

[30]See *US vs. ASCAP & In re Petition of Pandora Media* (2014).

[31]The current list of the twenty-four ASCAP board members can be found in the 2013 Annual Report on page 4 and can be found here: http://www.ascap.com/about/annualreport.aspx.

publisher) and his or her cronies. These governing bodies are often described as being too homogeneous, that is, they are often populated with members with a similar status quo vision who are 'too old, too white, too male and too rich' and who may be detrimental to the careers of younger and popular artists. As a result, their subjective views on what is considered artistic excellence or merit can often mean the exclusion of certain highly-accomplished artists who may not fit the narrow mold and they may have to forfeit the significant financial benefits that may accrue from membership. Therefore, certain artists who may have an inclination to join these exclusive societies may be silenced from speaking out and punished in many ways if they do—such as not being nominated for a prestigious board seat, the failure to be inducted in a 'hall of fame' or denied the coveted cover on an industry magazine. In 2013, ASCAP's was no exception to the criticism; their board of directors was majority male with a single African-American female.[32]

Why had the abstentions occurred when clearly the, "[song]writers were concerned that to the extent that the major publishers pulled their significant resources out of ASCAP, the writers would have to shoulder a larger burden in paying for activities like licensing, advocacy, and litigation?"[33] The songwriters' abstentions were peculiar because it may have exposed the extent to which music publishers are more influential on PRO boards and the lack of songwriters' and composers' economic leverage in collecting societies that is commensurate with copyright ownership. This is, perhaps, where the perception originates that songwriters and composers and artists are not receiving the proper amount in royalty compensation. Sony/ATV's Chairman and CEO Martin Bandier—in a July 2014 letter to tens of thousands of Sony's songwriters—threatened to withdraw all rights from both ASCAP and BMI, "if it turns out that his appeal asking the rate courts to allow partial withdrawal of [digital rights] or if the US Dept. of Justice doesn't revise the consent decrees" in music publishers' favor.[34] BMI's response—as reported in the New York Times—to the letter should have raised troubling questions about its underlying economic reality, mismanagement and exposed the symptoms of a dysfunctional PRO licensing system devoted to a business model that is practically obsolete in the digital era. The economic impact on BMI's songwriter-affiliates by granting publishers such flexibility was never addressed in the report. BMI's General Counsel, presumably speaking on behalf of the PRO, suggested that the "Justice Department should give *publishers* the flexibility in how they use the rights agencies to license their music," in a similar response to ASCAP change in its bylaws to accommodate music publishers.[35]

[32]See *Jann Wenner Answers Rock and Roll Hall of Fame 'Too Male, Too White, Too Rich' Critics*, Billboard Magazine, April 10, 2015, https://www.billboard.com/articles/news/6531175/inside-rock-roll-hall-fame-induction-process-secrets-jann-wenner.

[33]See *US vs. ASCAP & In re Petition of Pandora Media* (2014, pp. 45–47).

[34]See Christman (2014b).

[35]See Sisario (2014d). Emphasis added.

This appeal by a music publisher for government action through coercive tactics and public threats to the incumbent PROs is a startling effrontery that may not only be considered inappropriate, but, perhaps, without a historical precedent in the public policy debate over music licensing. It adds to the public's perception of a grand conspiracy, cronyism, influence-peddling, greed, competitive restrictions and insider collusion to fix prices in music licensing. The PRO leadership were putting the interests of a few publisher-members first at the expense of songwriter-members, and the PRO and its employees who invested their time and talents. Where was the fiduciary responsibility to protect *all* members or affiliates? Where exactly were their "core values" that are often cited in puff pieces?

This conflict underscores the degree to which panicky PROs are being held captive to the self-serving and pecuniary needs of highly paid CEOs of major music publishers, and the way in which the adjustment process to the wave of digital innovations in music licensing has become highly and unnecessarily politicized. It is also reveals how songwriters—who are board members of PROs and who tend to focus on the artistic rather than on the commercial exploitation of music—can be silenced even when their income was being threatened. This raises serious doubts concerning the perverse corporate governance—the voting structure, model, oversight, control and business practices—involved in the makeup of PRO's board of directors. The intellectual property rights of some members are worth more than others could be a key take-away here.[36]

At first glance it appears as though publisher-members would have been able to increase their royalty payments with their digital withdrawals, while individual songwriter-members would be hurt immediately and collectively over the long-term. Yet, it appears that the music publishers' pleas might be groundless given the recent "all or nothing" court rulings and the outcome might be in serious doubt, despite the pleadings of PROs that the Department of Justice should permit music publishers the flexibility to determine how they want to use licensing agencies.[37]

---

[36]The conflict between PROs and their members or affiliates is often described as the *principal—agent problem* or *agency theory* in economic literature by Alchian and Demsetz (1996); Coase (1996); Eisenhardt (1989); Fama (1996); Putterman and Kroszner (1996); Rees (1985a,b); Williamson (1996).

In this model, the principals (copyright owners) hire agents (PROs) to manage their performance licensing rights, and economic problems occur when agents shirk their fiduciary responsibilities at the expense of some or all of the principals.

This is said to create agency costs such as when CEOs use their control to reward a select few insiders or reckless decision-making increases expenses, but not revenue and profits decline. The corporate discretion given to a CEO leads to agency costs because in some cases the principals are unable to measure and monitor the agent's performance.

However, agency theory is now being discredited for its lack of rigor and consistency by Dobbin and Jung (2010); Hirsch et al. (1990); Perrow (1986); Stout (2012) and perhaps should not be used in economic analysis.

[37]See *BMI vs. Pandora Media Inc.* (2013); Sisario (2014d); *US vs. ASCAP & In re Petition of Pandora Media* (2013, 2014).

2.7 How Maintaining the Status Quo Has Been Harmful

The transition from the old status quo to the emergence of a new technology paradigm—that has caused the reordering of an industry—means that reforms are often slow to occur because they undermine the power, egos, privileges, and influence accrued over time by the current leadership. Reforms face two significant obstacles. First, there is a strongly entrenched resistance to change perception among the status quo leadership as their absolute control begins to evaporate, and the ambitions of new leaders and exogenous forces take hold.

Second, there is often the sunk costs associated with the existing infrastructure that may have taken decades to build and executives used to climb the corporate ladder, and, in addition, the human and financial costs of new investments to consider. With all of these technological changes in the music industry destroying outdated business models, PROs and record labels used financial leverage, that is, they spent vast sums on often-dubious infringement and time-consuming lawsuits to resist change, deter infringers, and reinvent their organizations. In the process, the PROs, record labels, music publishers, television networks, and others demanded changes in copyright laws to protect their outdated business models from the new waves of industry competition and innovations. In an aggressive attempt to make PROs and record labels relevant in the digital age, industry lobbyists were often used to influence the political and economic outcome of changes in copyright law; weaken antitrust legislation to permit market concentration, roll-ups and consolidation; eliminate competitive products and services; create new performance rights, entitlement fees and revenue streams and prevent market innovations from reaching consumers.

As court documents reveal, in order to accommodate the massive new demands of music publishers and PROs for changes in music licensing, some of these lawsuits could have been easily consolidated and settled amicably by agreement much sooner if it were not for the purported desire of outside counsel hired by some PROs to maximize billable hours by over-staffing assignments and filing frivolous claims using erroneous interpretations of copyright laws.[38]

It was detrimental to the PRO industry, as we will discuss below, when ASCAP's attorneys ignored the real-world feedback and obvious warning signs in the DMX's rate court ruling in the BMI case that was announced on July 26, 2010.[39] It was difficult to comprehend why the attorneys and economists thought that they could easily explain away compelling evidence that did not fit with their flawed assumptions, theories and reality. As their options narrowed, ASCAP proceeded to trial with an identical direct licensing dispute with DMX, expecting a different outcome. The judge would later admonish ASCAP's attorneys for proceeding to

[38]The millions in annual lobbying expenditures spent by the various agencies and the number of lobbying firms that they hired can be found here: https://www.opensecrets.org.

[39]See *BMI vs. DMX* (2010).

trial with the knowledge of the outcome of the earlier BMI/DMX ruling because it appeared as though ASCAP's inflexible strategic thinkers failed to analyze the BMI/DMX ruling for similar issues, gaps or shortcomings, and the results used to revise their fundamental assumptions, amend or settle the fee dispute with DMX. This was profoundly embarrassing because it appeared to be borderline professional incompetence.[40] In these particular rulings and in subsequent rulings to follow, the justices attempted to balance current copyright law with the reality of the new digital marketplace and sent a clear signal that institutional reforms in the PRO industry were necessary.

In another example of an infringement lawsuit seeking new industry entitlement fees, a PRO argued that retail wireless communication companies required a public performance license for the downloading of ringtones, a digital musical composition that is heard when a customer receives an incoming call. In a summary judgment motion, the court ruled that "while it is undisputed that the act of reproducing and distributing a ringtone implicates the mechanical rights in a musical work created by the Copyright Act, the downloading of a musical file is not a public performance."[41] Similarly in a case involving Yahoo and RealNetworks, the court ruled that a "download of a digital file containing a musical work does not constitute a public performance of that work because the song is not audible to the user during the transfer. Only after the file has been saved on the user's hard drive can he listen to the song by playing it using a software program on his local computer."[42] While downloading a song does not require a public performance license from the PROs, some webcasting (non-interactive) and interactive music streaming-on-demand sites are required to have a public performance license when a user streams a song.

2.8 The Bruce Springsteen Case Study

It is even more embarrassing when the intrinsic merits of a PRO's copyright infringement litigation strategies are out of alignment with the creative, economic, and financial sensitivities of one of their own respective songwriters. The catastrophic risks and consequences of an ill-advised infringement lawsuit that ASCAP filed against a bar for the unauthorized use of its members' music—naming Bruce Springsteen as one of the plaintiffs in the lawsuit—couldn't be more of an illustrative paradox of PROs. The lawsuit exposed the adversarial relationships that exist between PROs and their affiliates or members, and demonstrates how PROs can hurt songwriters and composers, both individually in the short-term and collectively in the long-term. In fact, this adversarial relationship is common between the music content creators and the other agencies (record labels and music

[40]See *US vs ASCAP & In Re Capstar (DMX)* (2010).

[41]See *US vs. ASCAP & In Re Application of Cellco Partnership D/B/A Verizon Wireless* (2009).

[42]See *US vs. ASCAP & In Re Applications of RealNetworks, Inc., Yahoo! Inc.* (2010).

publishers) that are exploiting the value in songwriters' copyrights. Songwriters may have interests, demands, and attitudes that are different from PROs, record labels, and music publishers when it comes to copyright exploitation. You cannot assume that these conflicting interests will simply go away. How these differences and divisions are going to reconciled when copyright laws and consent decrees are revised will be a major challenge for the Copyright Office and the Department of Justice. Mr. Springsteen refused to get involved in the lawsuit and the media stunt backfired because of another round of negative publicity (for ASCAP) that ensued. Mr. Springsteen's representatives said in a statement that

> "Bruce Springsteen had no knowledge of this lawsuit, was not asked if he would participate as a named plaintiff and would not have agreed to do so if he had been asked. Upon learning of this lawsuit this morning, Bruce Springsteen's representatives demanded the immediate removal of his name from the lawsuit."[43]

What was good for ASCAP's corporate strategy, was not necessarily good for Mr. Springsteen and his loyal fan base of consumers who bought merchandise and tickets to concerts after hearing the music they loved played in a bar. This case demonstrates how out-of-touch with reality the executives at ASCAP were with interests and values of some members and the changing business models in the music industry. It is not hard to speculate why the artist might have reacted negatively to such an overzealous infringement lawsuit, particularly when the holistic income approach from an already successful singer-songwriter is factored in. Mr. Springsteen may also have wanted to avoid the interminable copyright infringement battles between PROs and other establishments that always created a negative consumer backlash.[44]

First, in the US media, Mr. Springsteen is often portrayed as a "workingman's musician," whether such a popular image is real or perceived. Second, the contribution of an individual and successful singer-songwriter is exploited by the PROs as though the individual artist represented the entire music industry in order to increase royalty revenue for the PROs. The adverse publicity (for bars) from such a stunt was designed to act as a deterrence to future infringers, and intimidate other bars to fall into line, pay up, or they themselves might be sued by an organization with lots of songwriters' money to squander on litigation. Finally, Table 2.4 shows that Mr. Springsteen's band was ranked number 7 on Pollstar's *Mid Year 2012 Top 100 North American Tours* and raked in $30 million dollars from successful touring alone during the first half of 2012. In all likelihood, Mr. Springsteen had a bigger

---

[43]Reported by: http://www.spinner.com/2010/02/04/bruce-springsteen-lawsuit-bar on 2/4/2010. As part of their copyright administration agreements with the PROs, songwriters and composers permit the PROs to file copyright lawsuits on their behalf. However, these lawsuits are often filed without the awareness of the songwriters or composers.

[44]See Bumiller (1996) for an account of another amusing and memorable public relations debacle for ASCAP when they attempted to sue the Girl Scouts of America for singing camp songs without a license. The recent bad press resulting from BMI's lawsuit against bars and restaurants for copyright infringement is documented here: Gardner (2013).

Table 2.4 *Pollstar's* top ten North American touring acts: mid year January 1, 2012–June 30, 2012

Rank	Artist	Gross revenue ($ millions)	Share (%) revenue ($)	Tickets sold
1	Cirque du Soleil	$78.50	20.47	703,793
2	Roger Waters	$61.90	16.14	575,544
3	Van Halen	$44.90	11.71	448,506
4	Kenny Chesney/Tim McGraw	$33.90	8.84	386,989
5	Lady Antebellum	$30.90	8.06	708,715
6	Drake	$30.20	7.87	514,660
7	Bruce Springsteen & the E Street Band	$30.00	7.82	328,483
8	Elton John	$26.00	6.78	229,580
9	Dave Matthews Band	$24.40	6.36	448,247
10	Radiohead	$22.80	5.95	394,668
	Total	$383.50	100.00	4,739,185

Source: Based on data from: *Pollstar*.
http://www.pollstarpro.com/files/charts2012/2012MidYearTop100NorthAmericanToursTours.pdf.

share of income from concert tours (a cut of ticket sales, lucrative merchandising, licensing and sponsorships) than he did from performance royalty in the first half of 2012.[45]

Most people listen to or "experience" music first before deciding on whether to purchase CDs, downloads or concert tickets. The patrons in the bar represented Mr. Springsteen's dedicated fan base who would probably purchase tickets and merchandise for one or more of his live concerts, something that ASCAP missed in their overzealous lawsuit. It was difficult to see how these types of infringement lawsuits were "building the careers or protecting the long-term interests" of some obscure, unknown, and new songwriters. This type of rhetoric is common among the PROs and used to justify their fiduciary obligations to songwriters and composers, and the significant amounts of licensing income that are often squandered on a grand scale on legal fees in some of their copyright lawsuits.[46]

For bars that decided not to seek an ASCAP license, this meant restricting music access, alienating core fans and preventing future fans from listening to Mr. Springsteen's and other songwriter's music.[47] The lawsuit reinforced two common industry economic fallacies of the PROs' litigation business model, a business model that no longer works when the costs versus the benefits are considered. First, large administration licensing fees (in the double digits) are often required to fund such dubious lawsuits, and the economic beneficiaries are mostly the copyright administrators, collecting agencies, outside legal counsel and expert witnesses. With each losing lawsuit that dramatically raised operating, overhead and administration costs, the PROs inefficiencies and incompetence are exposed and even more licensing fees are needed to sustain ongoing operations.

Second, copyrights cannot provide the necessary and *initial* economic incentive that cause songwriters and composers to create music in the first place. Copyrights ensure that works once created and successful can be protected from unauthorized use. Owning a portfolio of copyrights is not beneficial if songwriters and composers cannot pay their bills or have the time to create music because they are forced to work full-time at a different job.[48] Indeed, the PROs are only interested in a top few songwriters who are *already* successful superstars and receive the lion's share of royalty income, instead of struggling songwriters who are unable to make ends meet and never receive any performance royalty income.

---

[45]With the decline in royalty income from the sale of recorded music on CDs, live concerts and touring became a significant source of income for performers.

[46]It is also misleading language because it is record labels' and music publishers' responsibilities to worry about the career direction of their recording artists.

[47]PROs have no leverage over the selection of playlists on radio or the music used in television productions. As the radio industry consolidated into a few station owners and their ratings and financial problems (debt service, declining advertising revenue and profitability) mounted, radio stations began eliminating DJ staff and cutting their playlists to a few well-known artists that could boost ratings. The same music programs were used in different geographical markets with minor changes. New and unknown songwriters had little chance of hearing their music on the radio, and hence, earning performance royalty income.

[48]See Patry (2011, pp. 16–17).

The PROs are notorious for touting their hundreds of thousands of songwriters and composers and the millions of songs in their respective repertories in marketing material, yet the vast majority of the songwriters and composers never see a dime in performance royalty income because their music is never performed anywhere. In fact, bars, restaurants, and retail stores fall under the PRO's general licensing agreements and the music performance data were never collected before the digital era and the satellite delivery of music to retail outlets. This meant that songwriters were never paid, unless their music was registered, performed elsewhere on radio and television and captured in some other PRO performance data or statistical survey.

2.9 PROs Technical Expertise

As some of the economic advantages associated with economies of scale have begun to evaporate, PROs faced what is called, "the commoditization of scale," that is, digital technologies—such as open-source software distributors and cloud services—provide small competitors with access to the same resources of a larger corporation in which the latter may have benefited from economies of scale, scope and specialization in business processes such as processing billions of transactions each year. The proprietary technologies (complex and modern IT systems) that once provided scale-related advantages (including barriers to entry) are becoming increasingly cheaper (free in some cases), faster, reliable, and more ubiquitous, resulting in smaller bureaucracies.[49]

Open-source software is software in which the copyright holders have granted a license to the public to freely use, study, change, and distribute software with certain copyright restrictions to control the modification (the original source files must be highlighted and code changes explained) and distribution (the copyright holders are attributed and acknowledged). Open-source software—easy to copy and distribute remotely over the Internet; could handle unstructured data from the Internet and smart phones; and is inter-operable across a cluster of computer servers that provide reliable, scalable and distributed computing automation—became a threat to the PROs *technical expertise* in the collection and processing of billions of musical performances from radio stations, television networks, and the Internet that are now provided in an electronic format.

Inexpensive computer storage and servers; readily available open-source software (such as *Hadoop* and the *R* Statistical Language); and digital fingerprinting lowered the production costs for administering blanket licenses and eliminated a barrier to entry in PRO licensing. This meant that compiling, processing, and analyzing voluminous music performance data were not as cost prohibitive or

[49]See Mele (2013) and *The Commoditization of Scale* available here: http://blogs.hbr.org/2012/03/the-commoditization-of-scale.

complex as in the recent past for smaller firms with fewer employees and less bureaucracy. More importantly, however, the centralized and secretive control of compiling and processing music performance data was rapidly decentralized across many independent firms and organizations and no longer strictly in the hands of specialized experts at the PROs.

Open-source software distributors displaced commercial vendors that sold proprietary—sometimes referred to close-source—systems in which their source code was considered a trade secret and intellectual property laws were applied. The source of income for the owners of proprietary commercial IT systems depended on licensing fees generated from copyrights, patents, or trademarks. End-users of proprietary software were often restricted from modifying the original source code and were purchasing the right to use the software without actually owning it. This restriction had the effect of imposing a form of artificial scarcity on the product that once the first copy was made, the marginal cost of producing and distributing an additional copy was practically zero. Many of the independent firms freely distributing open-source software—like Cask, Hortonworks, Cloudera, and Palantir Technologies—are or were once technology start-ups whose innovations substantially increased competition. Most of their business models consist of supplying open-source software to business enterprises and collecting revenue from installation and technical support subscriptions; consulting; data center management; and software security services rather than proprietary licensing. The market for big data technology is expected to reach close to $42 billion by the year 2018 for these services with a sustainable business model.[50]

One of the primary reasons for collecting societies like ASCAP to be regulated as a natural monopoly had evaporated due to open-source distributors that made processing voluminous data cheaper and more efficient. It is one thing to build a state-of-the-art data processing facility when the basic software is free and easy to scale up, hardware prices are tumbling, and YouTube can easily process its own musical performances data by desktop, laptop, tablet, and smart phone media platforms, but the improvements are not reflected in lower royalty fees for music users or higher royalty payments for songwriters and composers. All that is needed is a centralized database with equal access to song registration data in which music users can match musical performances to copyright owners and thus eliminating many of the functions of licensing intermediaries like PROs.

In the past, it was just AT&T (as a natural monopoly) that provided telephony services and anyone that wanted telephone service had no other choice but to choose AT&T as their carrier. AT&T was eventually marginalized by the RBOCS, new competitors, cable operators, and wireless phone companies. Digital innovations produced an overlapping sequence of transformations across several industries and the net effect was always lowered production costs. As the telecom industry was transformed, many internal and external processes needed to be rebuilt because the focus was on marketing in a highly competitive environment. In today's

[50] See Lohr (2014).

music industry, music users must choose *all* three incumbent, monopoly PROs to provide performance clearance if they want to avoid being sued for copyright infringement. Some people whose prior work experience was mostly in government service and not in a competitive industry simply lacked the valuable insights and expertise needed for advising CEOs on strategic marketing (as acquisition, retention and loyalty marketing became important); sophisticated statistical analysis as new theories and concepts (marketing segmentation, Long Tail; voice-video-data-wireless bundles for example) emerged; upgrading computer systems to handle (new billing, new licensing); short-term and long-range planning and to prepare an organization for the eventual abolition of consent decrees. During the monopoly era, some had done the same mundane tasks (such as preparing court filings or providing expert testimony) and were a complete embarrassment when their court testimony revealed how unprepared they were for the onslaught of competition.

The processing of billions of domestic (intra-lata and inter-lata) and international calls (that required hundreds of interconnection agreements with foreign countries) was a daunting task even for telecom carriers' IT departments as competition took hold. However, it was surprising to the author that the processing of music performance data completely overwhelmed an IT department in which data processing was far less complex and voluminous than in the telecom industry where billing was done on a monthly basis.

Creating hourly web traffic reports by users; location; time of day; mapping IP addresses to locations, and predicting the likely purchasing behavior of consumers using historical Internet patterns and log files are now easily solved using open-source software. Furthermore, music users such as Google, Yahoo, Spotify, and others are now collecting precise music performance data on what digital song titles have been played, the artists featured, the frequency of songs downloaded, the duration of each song played, the number of users, interactive vs non-interactive users, performance type, the time of day and access platform used in real time. The PROs' outdated practice of collecting music performance data and then paying royalties several months later no longer makes sense. The implementation of such readily available software means that songwriters and composers can be paid closer to the actual time that their musical performances occurred on the radio, television, and Internet, perhaps on a weekly or monthly basis. In addition, in future revisions to the Copyright Act and consent decrees, *if* a statutory fixed-rate licensing fee—instead of a percentage of revenue calculation—for a musical performance is developed, some music users would be able to pay copyright holders directly without the intervention of intermediaries such as PROs, and thus eliminating another administrative inefficiency of PROs.

The natural monopoly that is said to exist in the PRO industry has been completely eroded because the modestly (low) fixed cost of production associated with compiling, collecting, and processing performance data have declined dramatically with the implementation of new technology. Most of the fixed capital costs that could be depreciated or amortized were associated with computer equipment and maintenance. This is about the only relatively fixed cost in a PRO that the author can think of, except for corporate leases that could only be changed when the contract-period was up for renewal. There were no music distribution networks, music production infrastructure or research and development laboratories. However, the glut of office space that appeared following the 2008 financial crisis meant that landlords were often accommodating to lease-holders to avoid protracted vacancies in their buildings. It was not the type of fixed costs in which a particular strategy could not be changed in a short period of time. For example, in oil drilling, oil rigs had to be structured before production could occur and companies had to be committed to both a strategy and an engineering technology. Therefore, it should be easy for new entrants to enter the PRO industry (or any industry for that matter) with such relatively low fixed costs, but with the PROs' market power, it is almost impossible without court intervention.

PRO costs are variable because most tasks are highly labor-intensive and based on a trivial number of head-counts to compile performance data for royalty payments and maintaining the data processing systems. Therefore, most PRO expenses are variable, unless labor input costs associated with attorneys and litigation are now considered fixed input costs that can be amortized and depreciated like capital equipment. It is a system with high variable costs that can be inefficient, depending on the corporate strategies involved in licensing, copyright infringement, and advocacy. It is not surprising, therefore, that labor-saving technologies are big threats to such organizations because no type of song production is involved and it is now easier to replicate what they do.

Unlike other businesses that make real products with a strong focus on sales, customers, and net profit, and may struggle as a going-concern, face a scarcity of resources or incur large debts for machinery investment, some PROs generate a surplus or revenue by skimming the top off of licensing fees collected for administering the blanket license. Most television and radio networks comply with copyright laws to avoid costly infringement lawsuits with occasional PRO audits conducted to determine what revenue should be included or excluded in the percent-of-revenue licensing fee formulas. In the case of a network with a music publishing subsidiary, the network pays for a performance blanket license, while a portion of the fees paid for in the blanket license is returned to the subsidiary and their songwriters and composers in the form of performance royalty payments. While the blanket license fee might remain constant for the duration of the licensing agreement, the quarterly performance royalty payments to publishers and songwriters may vary for a wide variety of reasons, including the convoluted royalty payment formulas. The net offsetting effect—in terms of an actual budget and a forecast—is therefore the amount that is skimmed off the top for administering the blanket license and the quarterly fluctuations in royalty payments to the network's publishing arm and its songwriters and composers. Invariably, these networks have more leverage than the tens of thousands of retail stores that fall under general licensing who are at a financial disadvantage because there is no offset to the blanket licensing fee and the music publisher is a well-connected insider.

It is only after a song has been created by a songwriter, registered by the music publisher and the music is performed in some media outlet with a blanket license that the PROs royalty payment process begins. Furthermore, new competitors and new entrants (like DMX) lowered the cost of obtaining a blanket licensing and that exposed the inefficiencies of monopoly PROs. Song output is still expanding and music performances are increasing across all Internet and mobile platforms. Not a single consumer has been inconvenienced by new entrants into the PRO industry, but still the cost of a blanket license kept rising.

2.10 Why Overhauling the Copyright Act Is Needed

Some songwriters, lyricists, and composers are not skilled at singing or they may have no desire to perform in public (like Diane Warren, Brian Holland, Eddie Holland and Lamont Dozier), therefore, vocalists (like Celine Dion) and background musicians are often hired to bring the songwriter's music to life. There are singers/songwriters (like Bruce Springsteen), who write and perform their own music. When a song is publicly performed on terrestrial radio, television, or elsewhere that is sung by a hired vocalist but written by a different songwriter and composer, it is only the credited songwriters, composers, and music publishers who are paid performance royalties by ASCAP, BMI, and SESAC under current copyright laws. The same is true for *cover versions* of a song in which there is a new recording or new interpretation of a previously released song that is performed by someone else other than the original vocalist. The exception to this rule is SoundExchange that pays digital performance royalties to vocalists and background musicians and is illustrated in Table 8.7, page 227.[51]

Economic and legal experts are beginning to question whether the weakened empirical and theoretical foundations—the old conventional wisdom—of the ubiquitous blanket licensing process reflect the economic reality of today's digital marketplace. The *Copyright Act* is now viewed as a complex set of outdated regulations that serve to protect the vested interests in music licensing from the intrusions of innovation, particularity when such innovations disrupt the long-established, corrupted, bloated, and crony bureaucracies of PROs, record labels, and music publishers.

These experts are struggling to reach a consensus on how the new business models and laws that are being developed in music licensing should better serve the hundreds of thousands of *individual* songwriters and composers. In reexamining the existing copyright laws that will be made even more difficult because—as

[51] See http://www.songwritershalloffame.org/exhibits/C183. Diane Warren is considered one of the more prolific songwriters in the US and who is relatively unknown to the general public. She has written songs that include several genres and have been performed by Elton John, Tina Turner, Barbra Streisand, Aretha Franklin, Roberta Flack, Roy Orbison, Patti LaBelle, 'N Sync, Gloria Estefan, Britney Spears, Christina Aguilera, Reba McEntire, Whitney Houston, Enrique Iglesias, Aerosmith, Ricky Martin, Faith Hill, Celine Dion, Mary J. Blige, and LeAnn Rimes. Brian Holland, Eddie Holland, and Lamont Dozier were the prolific songwriting trio who were partially responsible for the commercial success of Motown.

was shown earlier in the Bruce Springsteen case—different songwriters may have different values and diverse interests that are not always in harmony with PROs, record labels, and music publishers.

Therefore, new copyright laws must find the correct balance between corporate fiduciary responsibilities and the conflicting demands of songwriters, composers, and other musicians when their interests diverge. (In Table 5.2 on page 140, we review some of the barriers to entry in the music industry that were erected by PROs, record labels, and music publishers to limit price discovery and competition.) Furthermore, few scholarly articles have evaluated the effects of (a) direct licensing on individual songwriters and composers; (b) how should songwriters, composers, and other music content creators have their vested interests protected by both regulatory and contractual agreements, as the market value of their copyrights has increased during the digital era; (c) what is the economic purpose, advantages, and disadvantages of intermediaries, PROs, music publishers, and record labels, in the digital era; (d) are any of the alternative theories on the new legal copyright structure valid and (e) how should consumers be protected in the new digital era from relentless infringement lawsuits. At the date of writing, Congress were debating several bills in which a *public performance right for sound recordings* on terrestrial radio is included.[52] It is important to keep in mind that, "[a] right to the public performance of a sound recording is the right to control the performance of one recording of a performance of a song. By contrast, a right of public performance in a composition is the right to control the use of the underlying musical composition itself. The latter right has been long recognized; but the right of public performance of a sound recording is a relatively new phenomenon and is restricted to digital services."[53]

This legal jargon may sound arcane and practically indecipherable in what it all means, but to some copyright owners it is the difference of not being able to collect past and future royalties on the works that they own. It is this massive confusion (and added transaction costs) over the multiple rights—the sound recording and physical reproduction rights (spoken voice, singing or sound effects) and the performance rights embedded in the musical composition (the melody and lyrics)—that vary according to different federal and state copyright laws, and the multiple agencies that are collecting and distributing royalties in the digital era. Adding to all this confusion, is the fact that SoundExchange distributes performance royalties to vocalists, background musicians, and record labels for certain digital performances, while ASCAP, BMI, and SESAC are only collecting performance (melody and lyrics) royalties for songwriters, composers, and music publishers for mostly terrestrial broadcasts. The right of a public performance for sound recordings is being challenged in court by copyright owners in several states.

---

[52]See *H.R. 4079 Songwriter Equity Act of 2014* and available here: https://beta.congress.gov/bill/113th-congress/house-bill/4079.

[53]See *US vs. ASCAP & In re Petition of Pandora Media* (2014, p. 36).

> "The Federal Copyright Act exclusively governs rights attendant to works of authorship in many areas; however, it explicitly leaves certain segments of copyright law open to state regulation... When Congress passed the Federal Copyright Act in 1976, it carved out pre-1972 sound recordings as a limited area of copyright law unaffected by the new federal law and within the domain of the states: With respect to sound recordings fixed before February 15, 1972, any rights or remedies under the common law or statutes of any state shall not be annulled or limited by this title until February 15, 2067... Federal Copyright Act does not apply to those earlier recordings and explicitly allows states to continue to regulate them."[54]

In addition, the US Copyright Office had issued a *Music Licensing Study: Notice and Request for Public Comment* order as the first stage in conducting a study on the effectiveness of the existing methods in licensing music. The dilemma that the Copyright Office faced was familiar in copyright law enforcement: How to manage the conflict of interest between incumbent licensing agencies seeking to maintain the status quo, and songwriters who may been harmed by the current industry practices such as recoupment. In other words, there is an intense debate on how to distribute the spoils of music licensing revenue among songwriters, composers, record labels, music publishers and PRO administrators. Reading through some of the earlier comments that were submitted at the website, it was obvious that the discussion was dominated by the same powerful, special-interest groups with different competing agendas and the focus was on how the existing copyright laws should be re-written to protect the incumbent PRO, record label and music publishing outdated and failing business models that could no longer be sustained. They were hoping that the pending demise of some of these intermediary licensing agencies caused by digital technology, innovations, competition and consumer demand could somehow be reversed or stalled for an indefinite period. It was an attempt to change the copyright licensing system by retaining many of the perks that perpetually benefited the outdated status quo system. It appeared as though it was all a final effort to save the doomed status quo using the legislative process. The concern here is that future revisions to copyright laws and consent decrees might be limited to just these self-serving participants and may not include a broader cross-section of parties that may be impacted in the future. In order to "establish rates and terms that most clearly represent the rates and terms that would have been negotiated in the marketplace between a willing buyer and seller" there must be a transparent *price discovery* process where licensing fees, rates, terms, conditions and royalty payments are made public.[55]

The long-standing adversarial relationships among PROs, record labels and music publishers were evident and the participants were not united on what was in the best interests of songwriters and composers. For example, music publishers

[54]See *Flo & Eddie Inc. v. Sirius XM Radio Inc.* (2014); *Flo & Eddie Inc. v. Sirius XM Radio Inc. and DOES 1-10* (2014) for more on the allegations that Sirius XM committed common law copyright infringement by publicly performing Pre-1972 sound recordings.

[55]See Copyright Office (2014). Comments from the various stakeholders responding to the Notice can be found here: http://www.copyright.gov/docs/musiclicensingstudy/comments/Docket2014_3/.

wanted to eliminate compulsory licensing for the physical reproduction of copyrighted recorded music so they can negotiate their own, often secretive, licensing fees by bundling mechanical, performance and synchronization licensing into a single-fee type structure, but the record labels liked the current system for mechanical licensing where licensing fees are fixed by statute and their royalty revenue is not commingled with that of the music publisher. In addition, when a statutory fixed-rate licensing fee is used—as opposed to a percentage of revenue formula and the revenue streams are ill-defined, ambiguous, undisclosed, hidden or aggregated—the fixed-rate fee calculation is not an arbitrary, unilaterally determined, statistically manipulated or a deliberately confusing number.[56]

There is also a separate issue on how to evaluate dormant works in a publisher's catalog, that is, songs that are no longer being performed and sold at retail outlets, but are included in the financial valuation when song-catalogs are sold or purchased and in the value of a PRO's blanket license. Another fundamental question that should be addressed when the new copyright laws are written is how should the songwriters of dormant works share in the proceeds when a catalog is sold.[57]

2.11 Why Overhauling Consent Decrees Are Needed

The PROs' role of music licensing intermediaries is in a state of terminal decline and regulation is often used to prevent innovations from rapidly entering the industry. Lengthy and costly rate court litigation is often used as an economic barrier for some competitors. The PROs deliberately exploit the regulated and unregulated features of their consent decrees and copyright laws, depending on their own needs. The consent decrees' controlled-pricing for a blanket license by a rate court make it simpler and more cost-effective for the incumbent PROs to control the pricing for a blanket license. It is a "take it or leave it" pricing system for access to each PROs distinctive repertory of copyrighted musical compositions in which music users have no alternative if they want to avoid copyright infringement. This chicanery has allowed the PROs to raise licensing fees and all the while preventing new competitors and faster and better technologies from entering the industry that could lower the costs of licensing through efficient and transparent methods. In practice, the current consent decrees put new competitors at a cost disadvantage and this slows down the process of competition and innovation by maintaining the inefficient status quo. On the other hand, the largely unregulated distribution of performance royalty payments to songwriters, composers, and music publishers—months after their songs have been performed—is so convoluted that the same song with the same number of performances in the same period can earn different royalty amounts

---

[56]See Christman (2013a); Wixen (2014, p. 137) for more on the conflict between fixed-rate vs percentage of revenue formulas that can change over time.

[57]Dormant, as distinct from public domain works, which have lost their copyright protection.

depending on the computation methods used by the different PROs and the double-digit costs for administering the blanket license.

Consumers have decided that they prefer the convenience of music subscription services, that is, they no longer wish to own physical records, but prefer to have music reside on remote servers and interactive cloud services where any piece of music can be accessed at any time on a wide variety of media platforms. Unlike the decline in vinyl sales due to the introduction of CDs, record labels were able to raise prices and generate large profit margins, with every new innovation in digital music, whether downloads or streaming, record labels and music publishers have not been able to fully recover revenue from lost and cannibalized record and download sales.

Because streaming is not considered a sale nor a download, and streaming revenue has not been able to offset the decline in revenue from CDs and downloads, this has created an enormous conflict among songwriters, composers, recording artists, music publishers, record labels, PROs, and others on how streaming revenue will be collected, commissioned, and distributed. The decline in CD sales has led to the decline in mechanical royalties and has made the Harry Fox Agency mostly irrelevant. As a result, music publishers are also looking to have consent decrees modified and the process by which rate courts set blanket licensing fees eliminated so that they can negotiate higher direct licensing fees with music users. Of course, higher licensing fees often translate into higher operating costs for music users and those fees are passed on to consumers in the form of higher subscription prices.

As the major music publishers withdraw digital rights from PROs, direct licensing is a now a mortal threat to the survival of PROs.[58] Streaming services earn revenue from a combination of subscriber fees and advertising sales, depending on their business models. Given these revenue models and expenditures for the acquisition of music content (a major input cost for streaming services), most of these streaming services struggle to become profitable as we illustrate in Table 10.4 on page 258 and Table 10.5 on page 259. Music streaming services' subscription revenue is paltry when compared to the monthly subscription fees charged by broadcast cable operators for access to their content. The costs of music content licenses and litigation expenses strangle some of these nascent streaming services before most of them have had a chance to build critical mass in order to increase revenue.[59]

Furthermore, in the mad scramble to divvy up royalty income from streaming services, the different PRO payment formulas; contract agreements with licensees, organizational structures (for-profit and non-profit) and royalty collection amounts have led to a huge discrepancy placed on the value of a musical performance, depending on whether royalties are paid by terrestrial radio and television music users through a PRO or paid by new media streaming services such as Pandora, Spotify, and YouTube. All of these factors add to the growing schism on the fairness and equitable treatment of royalty compensation among PROs, record labels, music publishers, songwriters, composers, and judges overseeing ASCAP's and BMI's

[58] See Christman (2013a, 2014b); Sisario (2014d).

[59] See Robertson (2011).

consent decrees. Music publishers are now threatening to abandon PROs if their ultimatums for consent decree revisions are not met.[60]

It was reported that Rihanna's song *Diamonds* has had 52 million streams, but the four songwriters were only paid $78,000 or a minuscule $0.0015 per stream.[61] This gets to the heart of the dispute among PROs, music publishers, and the judges enforcing the various consent decrees on the value of songwriters' copyrights. What is the equivalence of 52 million streams on Pandora, YouTube, and Spotify versus 52 million performances on terrestrial radio and television for the same song under ASCAP's convoluted royalty payment system of station weight, use weight, strata multiplier and feature multiplier in which performances are translated into credits and each credit may be worth as much as $7.10 or more and BMI's multi-tiered bonus and current activity payment system? Another way of asking the same question is: How many streams does it take before copyright owners make the same amount of money from the same number of performances that are used in ASCAP's and BMI's royalty payment formulas when they distribute the nearly $2 billion a year to songwriters, composers, and music publishers?[62] In the industry's standard conversion metric, 1,500 streams or ten individual downloads is now considered the equivalent of one album sale. In 2014, out of a total of 257 million album sales, 106.5 million (41.44 %) were from downloads.[63]

This is a compelling case for price transparency in both the collection of licensing fees and the distribution of royalty payments to songwriters and composers that should be resolved in a revision to consent decrees and copyright laws for a fair and equitable distribution of royalty income. It is really the music creators who are the biggest losers in such an archaic system—that is not always equitable across old and new media—because songwriters must often worry about who is paying more for musical performances. In the DMX case, "market rates" were established by a rate court only after lengthy and costly rate court proceedings. In some cases, it made economic sense for small retail owners to pay for the cost of a blanket license because the benefit outweighed the financial risk of spending tens of thousands of dollars in litigation expenses that they couldn't recover from normal business operations. Rate court proceedings are often cited as one of the administrative inefficiencies of PROs and the reason why entirely new copyright regulations should be developed. The industry is slowing moving in the direction in which price discovery, choices and market rates are no longer determined by a rate court under consent decrees, but by the market itself determining the true value of copyrights.[64]

---

[60] See Christman (2014b); Sisario (2014d).

[61] See Christman (2014b).

[62] See *ASCAP Payment System* that is available here:http://www.ascap.com/members/payment/royalties.aspx.

[63] See *Music Downloads Plummet in U.S., but Sales of Vinyl Records and Streaming Surge*, Wall Street Journal, January 2, 2015, p. B2.

[64] See http://www.musicreports.com for more information on one such firm.

Songwriting is often a collaborative effort among lyricists, composers, and record producers, except for songwriters who write and perform the bulk of their own material. Therefore, it is not unusual for a single song to have as many as five or six credited songwriters who must then split the writer's 50 % share of performance royalties, which is often not that much unless the song is a mega-hit or an evergreen title that is performed repeatedly. In addition, the artists may have conducted their own song plugging on YouTube without the help of the record label or music publisher. The remaining 50 % share of performance royalties or NPS goes entirely to the music publisher who is performing fewer song-exploitation functions in the digital era. Today, some major music publishers are likely to focus more on synchronization licensing rather than on some of their previous functions such as song-plugging and royalty collection; however, they are still receiving the same royalty share as in the past for doing even less for songwriters and composers.[65] The royalty rate that PROs charge some radio and television music users for a blanket license can often influence the *net publisher's share* (NPS) of performance royalty income paid by PROs. This rate, set by a rate court, is often the chief source of tension between PROs and music publishers who feel the rate is too low when compared to rate that record labels receive for the sound recording rights of their copyrighted musical compositions. This is the disparity, more like a distortion in pricing, that is fueling the partial digital withdrawal rights movement in the music industry.[66]

NPS is the amount that is retained after the music publisher expenses are paid. It is used as one of the profitability measures in evaluating a music catalog, along with other income from mechanical and synchronization licensing.[67] There is said to be an inverse relationship between the NPS sales multiple and the expected rate of return when music catalogs are bought or sold. For example, a music catalog may be valued at ten times its average NPS, depending on prestige, evergreen hits, popular cover versions, favorable tax laws, Termination Rights, earnings from historical performances, and supply and demand dynamics. A catalog that sells for ten times its average NPS is said to have an annual rate of return of 1/10th, or a 10 % return on investment, all things being equal.[68]

It is a powerful myth in the music industry that PROs, music publishers, and record labels are there to maximize the income of *all* music content creators. It is a bit of fiction because there is a hidden set of complex issues that cannot be easily simplified, and it is one of the reasons why royalty payments are shrouded in

---

[65]See *BMG Chrysalis Exec On How To Attract a Major Publisher*, Music Connection Magazine, November 2014, p. 46 and accessed online: http://issuu.com/musicconnectionmagazine/docs/mcnov14.

[66]See *US vs. ASCAP & In re Petition of Pandora Media* (2014) for details on the withdrawal movement.

[67]ASCAP uses the 50 %/50 % for writers and publishers, while BMI uses a confusing 100 %/100 % convention.

[68]See Wixen (2014, pp. 31–32).

secrecy and buried in confidential agreements. The PROs are happy to report their licensing fee receipts and royalty payment distribution in the aggregate—creating the transient illusion that the money is evenly distributed among *all* songwriters in their registries—but ask for a statistical distribution of royalty payments broken down into the following bins, $0–25, $25–50 and over $100, and you will easily the highly skewed and dramatic payment histories of the top individual songwriters and music publishers who are reaping the most benefits under the current system in place. The reason for such a skew to the top songwriters lies in the convoluted payment formulas used in tabulating royalty payments. In such a system in which the top few are earning the lion's share of royalty income, there is a strong resistance to industry reforms.[69]

As a matter of fact, countless studies have shown that there is a "superstar effect" in which the majority of royalties end up in the pockets of a few songwriters and composers, and music publishers.[70] The vast majority of songwriters cannot support their livelihoods from performance royalties under the current system. The amount of resources spent on CEO's expensive pay packages, perks, stock options, and other incentives—subsidized by songwriters, composers, and recording artists—is scandalous, when you consider the pennies a month that some songwriters earn from sound recording and performance royalties. Over time, it is music executives who are handsomely rewarded—even when the risks associated with talent acquisition are considered—while some music creators are the biggest losers. Patry (2011, p. 183) suggests that compensation packages for the executives of licensing agencies should be made public annually and their term of office should be limited to 4 years. The reason is rather straightforward: There is often little or no managerial accountability when executives become so entrenched in maintaining the status quo and enamored in the perks and benefits in these PRO organizations that it is often rather difficult for stakeholders to dislodge them.

In June 2014, the US Department of Justice, Antitrust Division (DOJ) began a review to examine the operations and effectiveness of the various consent decrees governing ASCAP and BMI. In particular, the DOJ requested public commentary on several issues that we have listed in Table 2.5. In addition, the author has suggested several important questions to augment the narrowly focused and insufficient list of review questions from the DOJ's review process—and those are listed as items (h), (i), (j), (k), (l), (m), (n), (o), (p), and (q), respectively in Table 2.5—because other key PRO oversight and public accountability issues that are needed to remove the structural impediments to competition, innovation, productivity, and efficiency were excluded. In addition, a comprehensive and holistic policy-making for the future that puts the *individual* songwriter and composer first were also missing. The problem in music licensing is structural, and minor tweaking in copyright laws and consent decrees will not mitigate the problem in the slightest.

---

[69]See Brabec and Brabec (2011, p. 316) for ASCAP's and BMI's aggregate receipts and royalty distribution payments to members and affiliates for the years 1992–2009.

[70]See Newman (2005); Rosen (1981).

Table 2.5 Modified DOJ consent decree issues (June 2014): items (h)–(q) added

(a) Do the Consent Decrees continue to serve important competitive purposes today? Why or why not? Are there provisions that are no longer necessary to protect competition? Are there provisions that are ineffective in protecting competition?
(b) What, if any, modifications to the Consent Decrees would enhance competition and efficiency?
(c) Do differences between the two Consent Decrees adversely affect competition?
(d) How easy or difficult is it to acquire in a useful format the contents of ASCAP's or BMI's repertory? How, if at all, does the current degree of repertory transparency impact competition? Are modifications of the transparency requirements in the Consent Decrees warranted, and if so, why?
(e) Should the Consent Decrees be modified to allow rights holders to permit ASCAP or BMI to license their performance rights to some music users but not others? If such partial or limited grants of licensing rights to ASCAP and BMI are allowed, should there be limits on how such grants are structured?
(f) Should the rate-making function currently performed by the rate court be changed to a system of mandatory arbitration? What procedures should be considered to expedite resolution of fee disputes? When should the payment of interim fees begin and how should they be set?
(g) Should the Consent Decrees be modified to permit rights holders to grant ASCAP and BMI rights in addition to "rights of public performance"?

(h) Are inefficient intermediaries like PROs still needed in the music industry to protect the outdated business models of the incumbents?
(i) What is the cost to consumers when music users like Pandora are forced to raise subscription prices when the cost of music licensing increases?
(j) How should the bundling or aggregation of mechanical, performance and synchronization licensing be handled to make sure that songwriters' royalties are not arbitrarily reduced and monies are paid *directly* to copyright holders such as songwriters and composers?
(k) Should a simplified, statutory fixed-rate music *performance* license with *direct* payments to copyright holders be included in revisions to the Copyright Act and Consent Decrees?
(l) Should performance royalty (distribution) payments to songwriters, composers and music publishers be publicly disclosed in a timely fashion to allow for accounting transparency and auditing?
(m) Should the repertories, song-title registration, copyright owners and royalty payment data from ASCAP, BMI, and SESAC be combined into a single, centralized, and comprehensive registry with *equal access* to all licensees and competitors in order to create an efficient and transparent music licensing process?
(n) What changes are necessary in the Consent Decrees to permit new PROs into the music licensing industry?
(o) Is the conventional 50/50 basis for allocating performance royalties between music publishers and songwriters still valid as the traditional relationship between music publishers and singer/songwriters has changed to where musicians are now assuming some of the roles of the music publisher?
(p) How should royalty payments to songwriters and composers be equalized across all PROs, new and old media without the fear of price-fixing, insider collusion or other antitrust problems?
(q) How should valuable data intelligence and marketing insights collected by PROs and music service providers be shared with recording artists, songwriters, composers, and others?

Source: Modified from the list found here:
http://www.justice.gov/atr/cases/ascap-bmi-decree-review.html.

There are often vast differences in the corporate purpose of maximizing revenue and the desire of individual songwriters and composers to maximize income. The changes to copyright laws and consent decrees cannot ignore the adverse impact that these changes may have on consumers, employees, music users, songwriters and the economy as a whole.[71] The consent decrees cannot be fully scraped until the Economic Demands and Structural Barriers to Entry in the Music Industry described in Chap. 5, Table 5.2 on page 140 are addressed.

2.12 Statutory Fixed-Rate Licensing for a Musical Performance

Revised copyright laws and consent decrees should not focus myopically on the self-serving ambitions of corporate managers at the expense of consumers, innovation, competition, investment, and the vested interests of *individual* songwriters, composers, authors, lyricists, vocalists, and musicians who are the actual creators of music content. It may be heretical to suggest but the time may have come to consider whether there should be a simplified accounting and statutory fixed-rate licensing requirement for each musical performance just like there is for mechanical licensing that includes streaming services. But, the collection, distribution, and direct payments to individual copyright holders written into law to protect music content creators from recoupment and those who may not wish to bargain over licensing fees.[72]

Despite its many flaws, mechanical licensing rates set by the Copyright Board serve an important function in music licensing by *visibly* setting market-pricing signals for the copyright clearance in sound recordings, a pricing mechanism that is missing for the performance and synchronization rights. It is similar to bench-mark interest rates (the price of money) in which borrowers and lenders can calculate the costs of a loan or the feasibility of a project can be determined by the discounted cash flow method.

Due to the statutory prohibition on factoring sound recording rates in setting a rate for a license for the public performance of a musical work, rate courts may not take the rates set by the CRB into account in determining the fair market rate for a public performance license.[73] However, performance or airplay tracking using *digital fingerprinting* has now made it easier and cheaper to track each individual

---

[71]Price (2011) believes that PROs and other intermediaries may no longer be needed in the digital era and the issue of the ultimate cost of higher licensing fees on listeners was raised by Sisario (2014a).

[72]See Copyright Royalty Board (2012) for the recent settlement that has been reached to set the complicated royalty rates and terms under Section 115 of the *Copyright Act* for distributing physical and digital phonorecords.

[73]See *US vs. ASCAP & In re Petition of Pandora Media* (2014, p. 212).

musical performance or airplay of a song because each digital audio file has its own unique signal or fingerprint with the metadata embedded in the file. (We discuss digital fingerprinting in Sect. 5.7 on page 152.) Therefore, a simplified, accounting and statutory fixed-rate licensing for a musical performance can now be implemented following the changes in consent decrees and copyright laws as one of the possible alternatives in the pricing of performance rights licensing. A simplified, accounting and statutory fixed-rate licensing requirement for musical performances with *direct* payment to each copyright owner would accomplish the following three objectives in creating a functioning pricing mechanism for music licensing.

2.13 Elimination of PRO Convoluted Payment Formulas

A statutory fixed-rate licensing requirement for musical performances eliminates the convoluted performance royalty payment rules that arbitrarily make a distinction between types of musical performances (feature, theme song, underscore, jingles, and promos) and the specific weights given to each type of performance that vary by PRO. Each PRO uses a different weighting system to unilaterally determine the value of a musical performance and the weighting system is changed periodically. Therefore, a musical composition can be weighted on the type and duration of a musical performance; whether the song is used on small or large radio and television stations and the time of day the song is used. In addition, bonus and premium payments are paid to songwriters and publishers for their contributions to the success of highly rated television shows using another arbitrarily set threshold that can be statistically manipulated.[74]

2.13.1 *Elimination of Price-Fixing and Collusion Concerns*

It has been argued that setting up a uniform royalty payment and distribution system across all PROs would (probably) entail price-fixing or collusion under various antitrust laws and this is the reason for the different royalty payment and distribution methods used across PROs. The different payment methods increase the overhead costs of administering the blanket license. When there is no public accountability and transparency, PROs administrative expenses can be easily manipulated to hide mal-investments, litigation expenses, cost overruns, expensive real estate, and other inefficiencies that are built into the double-digit percentage that is lopped off the top of the fees that are collected for administering blanket licenses. Countless and intrusive man-hours are wasted looking externally for all the places where music is performed in order to justify an increase in licensing fees before a rate

[74]See Brabec and Brabec (2011, pp. 309–357) for the payment formulas used by all three PROs.

court judge, rather than looking internally to root out inefficiencies that would lower the cost of a blanket license for music users. A statutory fixed-rate licensing requirement for musical performances would make the royalty collection process much easier by simplifying (or eliminating) the collection function of music publishers and PROs. For example, there is no reason why Google cannot collect digital performance data from its YouTube website—if and when a statutory fixed-rate licensing requirement for musical performances is developed—and make direct payments to individual copyright holders on a timely basis, eliminating the need for intermediaries like ASCAP, BMI, and SoundExchange and lowering the cost of copyright administration.

It is not entirely clear why some PRO overhead expenses are *still* in the double-digits percentage when the production costs of processing music performance and song registration data have declined significantly due to the increased use of technology and the industry has gone through rounds of massive layoffs, restructurings, and office closures. The real reason may be that PROs have no desire to make the music licensing process more efficient and transparent if that meant lowering the cost of obtaining a blanket license for music users. Lowering the cost of a blanket license also meant that the songwriters and composers who earned the lion's share of licensing fees would also see a reduction in performance royalties and executives might not earn their large bonuses. This is how inefficiencies in the systems are used to protect the status quo. It is often new entrants and product innovators, like DMX, that root out the inefficiencies associated with monopolists, changing the structure of the industry.

PRO administrative expenses remain a mystery because there is a huge variation in what financial, accounting, operating, and music performance data are made public and the true costs (inefficiencies) of administering blanket licenses remain hidden. For example, ASCAP issues a detailed annual financial statement to its members, while BMI and SESAC do not. However, there is no or very little data reported on which songs were paid the most in royalties; the number of performances associated with each paid song; how many and how much each individual songwriter, composer, and music publisher were paid; and what is in the compensation, perks, and benefit packages of executives. This type of secrecy is what fuels the perception that without transparency and public accountability, there is often corruption within these organizations. ASCAP uses a January–December fiscal year, while BMI's year runs from July 1 of 1 year to June 30 of the following year and so a one-to-one comparison is difficult.[75] This concern about price-fixing and collusion would be eliminated with a statutory fixed-rate for a musical performance and provide more PRO transparency.

---

[75]See Brabec and Brabec (2011, p. 316). Table 4.3 takes a selective look at ASCAP's 2011 Annual Report. The full report is found here: www.ascap.com/about/~/media/Files/Pdf/.../annual-reports/annual_2011.pdf.

2.13.2 Elimination of Secretive and Confidential Licensing Agreements

One of the central issues in the revisions of both the Copyright Act and consent decrees is how should the bundling of mechanical, performance and synchronization licensing be handled to make sure that songwriters' royalties are not arbitrarily reduced, royalties are paid *directly* to copyright holders and there is no imbalance of power or price discrimination in licensing transactions. When bundled licensing agreements for all music clearances are negotiated separately between individual music publishers and music users and subject to confidentially agreements, there is no honest price discovery. Therefore, determining the price for each specific license through supply and demand factors cannot be done. It may be costly, inefficient, and unfair for songwriters and composers to gain access to the terms and conditions in these confidential licensing agreements and may make the enforcement of contracts difficult. A statutory fixed-rate for a musical performance would increase price discovery for a blanket license because all the relevant pricing information in a transaction would be known to all negotiating parties. This would eliminate attempts by PROs, record labels, and music publishers to engage in price discrimination—that is, to charge different music users difference prices for licenses based on the leverage that may be associated with size, insider deals or other factors. A metering mechanism for enforcing a statutory fixed-rate for a musical performance can be developed for any new revisions to consent decrees or copyright laws. More importantly, however, a statutory fixed-rate for a musical performance would control the fluctuation in the price for a blanket license, simplify business planning and forecasting, and stabilize the cost structure and cash flow of music users.

2.13.3 Drawback of Statutory Rates

There is always a drawback when statutory rates (compulsory licenses) are involved in the music licensing process in terms of setting a reasonable rate at which a willing buyer and a willing seller would agree to in a regular market transaction, and who gains and who loses when a rate increase (or possible rate decrease) occurs. For example, if a rate increase is granted to, say, the record labels or PROs (who believe rates should always go up), the rate increase is coming from the operating budgets of music users (like Pandora who believe that rates should always be headed down) who may already be financially strapped under the burden of licensing costs. On the other hand, more money is flowing to PROs, record labels, songwriters, composers, musicians, and music publishers. The reverse would happen if there is a rate decrease.

All of these factors can have an impact on how much a songwriter or composer is paid and these payments can vary by performance quarter. Music content creators are likely to have different interests, different time frames and diverse attitudes toward how they want to be compensated for their musical creations, therefore, the old one-dimensional approach used by PROs, record labels, and music publishers may not be realistic in the digital future.

Perhaps, the Copyright Office will use the occasion to actually broaden the bargaining leverage of *individual* songwriters and composers whose musical creations will live on, and not protect the current intermediaries who may not even be around in a decade or so. The new copyright laws should have some flexibility to accommodate the likely mergers and other consolidations that will occur in the future so that it is *individual* songwriters and composes who are reaping the largest and direct economic benefits from the exploitation of their musical creations.

2.13.4 Independent and Central Registry for Song Titles

All of the PROs established traditions and vested interests were slowly being stripped away by new technology, new market conditions, and new competitors. PROs have no tangible assets of their own: There are no physical manufacturing facilities or music distribution networks that can be sold. PROs, like music publishers, are simply licensing houses where there is no creative activity, but they are valuable because they are able to put money in the pockets of songwriters and composers.[76]

To say that "We Create Music" in PRO marketing material is just puffery and a gimmick because PRO organizations are not involved in the actual song creative process of their members or affiliates and in the risky financial side of song and talent acquisition, production, recording, publishing and distribution of record labels and music publishers. PROs are merely licensing agencies that play no role in the song and artist development functions of a producer, record label, and music publisher. In other words, PROs never decide which songs are going to be recorded and distributed. PROs may permit third-parties to use their premises—the building adds a certain amount of cachet with long lines of potential songwriters queuing up in the lobby area on occasions—for paid workshops on songwriting. It is misleading to the participants because they often believe that they might actually strike a record deal, and it is more of a shameless exploitation of these naive and ill-informed songwriters. A serious songwriter would never submit a demo to a PRO because they do not handle such material and submissions, and it would not be effective. The most a PRO would do is to refer a potential songwriter to one of their member-publishers; a rare exception and considered unsolicited material. Record labels would not want to be in the position of being sued by an artist who claims that their music was stolen and used by the record label.

[76]See Patry (2011, p. 21). Occasionally, the PROs hold workshops for potential songwriters where established songwriters explain the songwriting process.

PROs license music only *after* a song has been created and registered. Furthermore, even if a song is registered, but not performed anywhere, the songwriter or composer is not paid. The short-term focus of PROs then becomes who is the "hottest songwriter" of the (fleeting) moment based on airplay popularity. PRO "market share" is then computed by looking at *Billboard's* tabulation of the songwriters and composers whose musical compositions (often performed by a well-known vocalist and not by the songwriters or composers themselves) made it into the top ten or such listings. Royalty bonuses and premiums are often paid for these chart-topping songs at the expense of other songwriters and composers. This raises an important question, and, that is, should these contemporary "hot songwriters" be paid the same as songwriters who may not have written a hit song in decades (but who fill up the board seats at PROs)? The copyright owners of dormant works are not compensated even though their works are included in the cumulative total of the songs available in PRO repertories and it is the foundation for the "value" in a blanket license.[77]

The PROs *knowledge base* or central registry consists mainly of their proprietary databases associated with the copyright ownership of a song (that is, who owns what on a song with multiple copyright holders and their allocated share of ownership); the payment methods in which performance licensing fees are allocated; and the historical earnings or royalty payment allocation data for songwriters, composers, and music publishers. This is the intangible know-how that PROs have built up over time—along with direct payments to songwriters, composers and music publishers that is not co-mingled—and is the source of their licensing proficiency. In other words, PRO assets are mostly a bunch of computer servers with song registration, licensing fees collected, compiled music performances and royalty payment history data that should be made public.

Due to the asymmetrical information available to licensees, and the shocking revelations revealed during rate court litigation, there is an unnecessary (and costly) pricing arbitrage in music licensing. Therefore, PRO licensing data that should be made available on an independent and equal access basis in a central registry to everyone seeking a music license so that a freely functioning pricing mechanism for musical performances can be developed based on the law of supply and demand. The effect would shed light on the mysterious inner workings of how performance royalties are calculated; why licensing costs continue to soar; and why PRO's bloated administration costs are totally out of whack as modern data processing costs have declined. It has been suggested that a "comprehensive, centralized database for locating rights-holders and facilitating licensing agreements is a necessary precondition for creating an efficient and transparent worldwide music marketplace."[78] Song or title registration data—including digital fingerprints and metadata for each version of a song—in a central and publicly available database

[77] *Billboard Magazine* is one of the important trade journals in the music industry.

[78] See Silver (2012) where the challenges and costs faced by several organizations that are trying to establish such a global music registry are discussed.

will make it much easier for potential music users to quickly locate copyright owners and their contact information.

There are now independent firms that have accumulated the same copyright ownership data and specialized knowledge that are contained in PRO databases or registries. The data on copyright ownership were obtained directly from music publishers and records labels, and cover virtually all of the tens of millions of songs and recordings that are commercially significant. The data can be used to negotiate direct licenses between music publishers and music users. In the process, PROs are bypassed and market rates are established for the use of music. In other words, the diminishing proprietary value in a PRO's database has now become an "open-source" in itself. However, this process is not as efficient as it should be because of the litigation expenses associated with rate court proceedings are required to overcome the *regulatory barriers* before some licensing costs are reduced.

2.14 Why Reforms Often Fail

Reforms become bogged down in mostly irrelevant rhetoric—such as piracy—because it is a convenient scapegoat for those in power who failed to capitalize on innovations and consumer preferences in the industry, or innovations were selectively restrained to maintain the status quo. Consumers were no longer interested in purchasing songs bundled or aggregated (mostly unwanted fillers) and over-priced on a CD that was the old music industry business model prior to Apple's iTunes innovation. Apple's model aggregated the contents of record labels' repertories and simplified the purchasing of single digital downloads, while at the same time exposing the inefficiencies—unprofitable business model using minimum advertised-price (MAP) policies—of music sales. Now, consumers have decided that they may not want to own music at all, but prefer to subscribe to music streaming services such as satellite radio, Pandora and Spotify and have those services available on-demand on smart phones, laptops, iPads, and computers.[79]

It is often the case that there is no real desire for meaningful reforms and the reforms are not always successful because the few who are earning dramatic returns or benefit from the perks are the ones who will likely want to perpetuate the existing status quo, keep the current inefficient processes or bureaucracies in place and centralize control over the entire licensing process. There is often only a token support for limited innovations, transparency, real solutions or industry reforms until it becomes apparent that such changes threaten or disrupt the status quo and the vested interests of insiders.

PROs and major music publishers control the licensing process through their considerable market power and as a result their inefficient operations can be profitable in maintaining the status quo if change meant creating new business

[79] See Christman (2008).

models that benefits mostly consumers. Allegations of unethical business practices, asymmetrical information, insiders making changes to PRO bylaws and behind-the-scenes collusion between music publishers and PROs are now being reported.[80] In reviewing ASCAP's leadership from 1914 to the present, the list reads like a much older generation of writers and publishers—the special interests who are heavily invested in and benefits from the current-status quo-royalty system.[81] Internal change is unlikely to occur rapidly—giving a different set of younger writers and publishers a more influential voice—if it is going to alter the royal payments that these members are receiving. Many of the today's popular and influential songwriters, composers, and self-publishers—that are writing and selling the millions of digital songs listed in Table 2.1 on 59—are not even on the governing boards of some of these PROs, further increasing the strong internal resistance to disruptive technological change.

It is only when consumers abandon the old business models because they are offered better prices, service, quality, and technology elsewhere, and revenue streams dry up that there is a clamor for change, but there is no unified approach to solving the industry problems among the licensing agencies. There is usually very little agreement among PROs, record labels, and music publishers on how the current and complex system of music licensing should be revised after decades of government regulation (consent decrees) and a patchwork of federal laws governing copyright that have not kept up with the rapid pace of digital downloads and music streaming in the industry. It is very difficult to satisfy all the competing parties (and egos) in the rapidly evolving but fragmented music market because there is a vested interest by some in maintaining the status quo, while others are against certain aspects of the status quo.

Ordinarily, the same licensing organizations that you would expect to be on the same side of an issue are often the ones competing against each other in a rather hilarious zero-sum game. Record labels taking a larger share of streaming revenue pie only reduces the finite amount of revenue for music publishers and others. For example, it has been reported that Pandora paid 49 % of its revenue, or about $313 million, to record companies, but only 4 %, or about $26 million, to publishers for a total of $339 million in 2013. In other words, Pandora paid about 12 times more in licensing fees to record labels than it paid to music publishers, the two sides of the same copyrighted song. These record labels may be also subsidiaries of the major music publishers and it highlights the difference in the sound recording and music publishing copyrights embedded in the same song in today's outdated copyrighted laws.[82] This difference in multiple rights and multiple licensing agencies creates conflicts and frustration among PROs, music publishers, and record labels over the discrepancy in badly allocating licensing fees.

---

[80]See Christman (2014a).

[81]See Appendix A, *ASCAP Leadership Through The Years* in Pollock (2014, pp. 189–195).

[82]See Sisario (2014c).

Record labels benefit from Pandora's higher licensing fees and the direct payments may be subjected to recoupment, while it is songwriters and composers who are negatively impacted by recoupment, asymmetrical information and other industry practices, particularly when performance, mechanical and synchronization licenses are aggregated and the contents of the licensing agreements cannot be disclosed due to confidentiality agreements between the licensing parties. Songwriters and composers are often not aware of the revenue generated by publishers and record labels from such licensing agreements because there is no public and accessible directories of song licensing and transactions information.[83] (We discuss in Chap. 8, Sect. 8.2 on page 228 how songwriters are negatively impacted by licensing agreements.)

On the other hand, music publishers—who are dependent on performance royalties—that are split on a 50/50 basis with songwriters and composers and there is no co-mingling of performance royalty payments between songwriters and music publishers—allege that performance licensing fees set at a lower rate by a rate court judge may not reflect the market value of music licensing, given the way in which music licensing fees for the sound recording may differ from the fees for a performance blanket license. Increasingly, music publishers are looking to bypass PROs and negotiate their own direct licensing deals for higher licensing fees with streaming services, bypassing PROs altogether. This illustrates why there is no unified approach in solving the problems in the music industry when publishers and record labels are competing against each other for higher licensing fees. The problem may be just an internal accounting issue because the record labels are sometimes subsidiaries of the major music publishers: It is just a matter of how the royalty pie is allocated among licensing agencies without even an afterthought to the impact on songwriters and composers.

The system is, therefore, structured to reward a few at the top rather than focusing on changing the existing leadership when necessary or on an equitable distribution of income to all songwriters and composers, while fueling the "expectations myth" of the many who will earn just pennies. This is particularly true for performance royalty income because it is often the only source of income for songwriters and composers whose musical compositions are no longer sold in stores—but are still being performed on radio, television and the Internet—and it is not subjected to recoupment. To make matters worse, these composers must often wait for months after their music was performed to collect their royalties. For example, if their music was performed in the first quarter of a calendar year, some songwriters may not receive performance royalty payments until the fourth quarter or even later in some cases and that can be a hardship for some writers without a string of popular hits or reserve income.

With the widespread use of YouTube for music discovery and distribution, and independent publishers like Kobalt, the traditional roles that music publishers played in popularizing music changed dramatically because singers/songwriters were

[83]See Christman (2014b); Sisario (2014b).

writing, recording, popularizing, and distributing their own music. Yet, there is still the conventional 50/50 basis split between a songwriter and a music publisher for performance royalties, a convention that contributes to the difficulty and confusion in the collection, licensing and allocation of royalties. The singer/songwriter, who is also a self-publisher, is still getting 100 % of the proceeds but it comes with two payments and two separate checks. Wixen (2014, pp. 11–13) concludes that if such atavistic conventions didn't exist, music publishing would be less complicated, required less math and logic, and songwriters could do a lot more for themselves.[84]

References

Alchian, A. and Demsetz, H. (1996). Production, information costs and economic organization. In Putterman, L. and Kroszner, R., editors, *The Economic Nature of the Firm: A Reader*, chapter 14, pages 193–216. Cambridge University Press, Cambridge, United Kingdom, second edition.

Anderson, C. (2008). *The Long Tail: Why the Future of Business Is Selling Less of More*. Hyperion, New York, NY.

Bacharach, B. (2014). 'What the Songwriting World Needs Now'. *Wall Street Journal*, page A11. January 23, accessed online: http://search.proquest.com/docview/1491047402?accountid=35927.

Blacc, A. (2014). 'Streaming Services Need to Pay Songwriters Fairly'. *Wired*. November 14, accessed online: http://www.wired.com/2014/11/aloe-blacc-pay-songwriters.

BMI vs. DMX (2010). No: 08 Civ. 216 (LLS), S.D.N.Y. July 26, accessed online: http://www.leagle.com/decision/In%20FDCO%2020100727985.xml/BROADCAST%20MUSIC,%20INC.%20v.%20DMX,%20INC , pp. 1–33.

BMI vs. Pandora Media Inc. (2013). No: 13-cv-04037 (LLS), S.D.N.Y. December, accessed online: http://docs.justia.com/cases/federal/district-courts/new-york/nysdce/1:1964cv03787/58544/61/0.pdf?1387564284, pp. 1–14.

Brabec, J. and Brabec, T. (2011). *Music, Money and Success: The Insider's Guide To Making Money In The Music Industry*. Schirmer Trade Books-Music Sales, New York, NY.

Bumiller, E. (1996). ASCAP Asks Royalties From Girl Scouts, and Regrets It. *New York Times*. December 17, accessed online: http://www.nytimes.com/1996/12/17/nyregion/ascap-asks-royalties-from-girl-scouts-and-regrets-it.html?pagewanted=all&src=pm.

Cardi, W. J. (2007). Über-middleman: Reshaping the broken landscape of copyright music. *Iowa Law Review*, 92:835–890.

Christensen, C. (1997). *The Innovators Dilemma: When New Technologies Cause Great Firms to Fail*. Harvard Business School Press.

Christman, E. (2008). 'Cashing In'. *Billboard Magazine*, 120:26–28. October 25 issue, accessed online: Academic Search Premier, EBSCOhost accession number: 34888428.

Christman, E. (2011). 'Sirius' Direct-Licensing Efforts Come Under Attack From Recording Academy, AFTRA'. *Billboard Magazine*. October 27 issue, accessed online: http://www.billboard.biz, story:1005445642.

Christman, E. (2013a). 'Copying The Left'. *Billboard Magazine*, 125:12. June 29 issue, accessed online: Academic Search Premier, EBSCOhost, accession number: 88430185.

[84]It may be in the interest of songwriters and composers to have a quarterly statistical distribution of royalty payments reported to make sure that there is transparency in PRO agencies.

Christman, E. (2013b). 'Universal Music Publishing Plots Exit From ASCAP, BMI'. *Billboard Magazine*. February 7 issue, accessed online: http://www.billboard.com/biz/articles/news/publishing/1537554/universal-music-publishing-plots-exit-from-ascap-bmi.

Christman, E. (2014a). 'Dept. of Justice Sends Doc Requests, Investigating UMPG, Sony/ATV, BMI and ASCAP Over Possible 'Coordination''. *Billboard Magazine*. July 13, accessed online: http://www.billboard.com/biz/articles/news/publishing/6157513/dept-of-justice-sends-doc-requests-investigating-umpg-sonyatv.

Christman, E. (2014b). 'Sony/ATV's Martin Bandier Repeats Warning to ASCAP, BMI'. *Billboard Magazine*. July 11, accessed online: http://www.billboard.com/biz/articles/news/publishing/6157469/sonyatvs-martin-bandier-repeats-warning-to-ascap-bmi.

Christman, E. (2014c). 'The Digital Decline: What's Behind the First Downturn of the iTunes Era? And Can Streaming Save the Day?'. *Billboard Magazine*. January 18 issue, pp. 34–36.

Coase, R. (1996). The Nature of the Firm. In Putterman, L. and Kroszner, R., editors, *The Economic Nature of the Firm: A Reader*, chapter 7, pages 89–104. Cambridge University Press, Cambridge, United Kingdom, second edition.

Copyright Office (2014). *Music Licensing Study: Notice and Request for Public Comment, No. 201403*, Federal Register, Vol. 78, No. 51. May, accessed online: http://www.copyright.gov/fedreg/2014/79fr14739.pdf, pp. 14739–14743.

Copyright Royalty Board (2012). *Adjustment or Determination of Compulsory License Rates for Making and Distributing Phonorecords: Motion to Adopt Settlement, Docket No. 2011-3 CRB Phonorecords II*. April, accessed online: http://www.loc.gov/crb/motions/parties_motion_adopt_settlement_041112.pdf, pp. 1–33.

DiLorenzo, T. (1996). The myth of natural monopoly. *Review of Austrian Economics*, 9(2):43–58.

Dobbin, F. and Jung, J. (2010). The misapplication of Mr. Michael Jensen: How agency theory brought down the economy and why it might again. In Lounsbury, M. and Hirsch, P. M., editors, *Markets on Trial: The Economic Sociology of the U.S. Financial Crisis: Part B*, volume 30 of *Research in the Sociology of Organizations*, pages 29–64. Emerald Group Publishing Limited.

Eisenhardt, K. (1989). Agency theory: An assessment and review. *Academy of Management Review*, 14(1):57–74.

Fama, E. (1996). Agency problems and the theory of the firm. In Putterman, L. and Kroszner, R., editors, *The Economic Nature of the Firm: A Reader*, chapter 22, pages 302–314. Cambridge University Press, Cambridge, United Kingdom, second edition.

Flo & Eddie Inc. v. Sirius XM Radio Inc. (2014). No: CV 13-5693 PSG (RZx), C.D.C.A. September 14, accessed online: http://www.soundexchange.com/wp-content/uploads/2014/09/Flo-Eddie-v.-Sirius-XM-Order-on-MSJ.pdf, pp. 1–15.

Flo & Eddie Inc. v. Sirius XM Radio Inc. and DOES 1-10 (2014). No: 13 Civ. 5784 (CM), S.D.N.Y. November 14, accessed online: www.soundexchange.com/wp-content/uploads/2014/11/2014-11-14-Order-on-Summary-Judgment-Flo-and-Eddie-v-Sirius-XM-SDNY.pdf, pp. 1–40.

Gardner, E. (2013). BMI Freaks Out Over TMZ Copyright Story. *Hollywood Reporter*. June 6, accessed online: http://www.hollywoodreporter.com/thr-esq/bmi-freaks-tmz-copyright-story-564170.

Hirsch, P., Friedman, R., and Koza, P. (1990). Collaboration or paradigm shift?: Caveat emptor and the risk of romance with economic models for strategy and policy research. *Organization Science*, 1(1):87–97.

Karp, H. (2013). Reaping profits from soundtracks. *Wall Street Journal*, page B6. December 16 2013, accessed online: http://search.proquest.com/docview/1468227178?accountid=35927.

Lepore, J. (2014). 'The Disruption Machine: What the Gospel of Innovation Gets Wrong'. *New Yorker Magazine*. June 23 issue, accessed online: http://www.newyorker.com/magazine/2014/06/23/the-disruption-machine.

Lohr, S. (2014). 'In Big Data, Shepherding Each Client Comes First'. *New York Times*. December 15, p. B1.

Mele, N. (2013). 'The End Of Big Business'. *Billboard Magazine*, 125:17. June 1 issue, accessed online: Academic Search Premier, EBSCOhost, accession number: 87933600.

Newman, M. (2005). Power Laws, Pareto Distributions and Zipfs Law. *Contemporary Physics*, 46(5):323–351.

Oxenford, D. (2009). 'ASCAP and BMI – Another Royalty Battle for Broadcasters? *Broadcast Law Blog*. October 3, accessed online: http://www.broadcastlawblog.com/2009/10/articles/ascap-and-bmi-another-royalty-battle-for-broadcasters.

Page, W. and Garland, E. (2009). The Long Tail of P2P. *Economic Insight*. Published by PRS, UK and accessed online: http://www.prsformusic.com/creators/news/research/Documents/The%20long%20tail%20of%20P2P%20v9.pdf.

Passman, D. (2012). *All You Need To Know About The Music Business*. Simon & Schuster, eighth edition.

Patry, W. (2011). *How To Fix Copyright*. Oxford University Press, New York.

Perrow, C. (1986). *Complex Organizations: A Critical Essay*. Random House.

Pitt, I. L. (2010). *Economic Analysis of Music Copyright: Income, Media and Performances*. Springer, New York. Available online: http://www.amazon.com/Economic-Analysis-Music-Copyright-Performances/dp/1441963170/ref=sr_1_1?s=books&ie=UTF8&qid=1417266944&sr=1-1&keywords=economic+analysis+of+music+copyright.

Pitt, I. L. (2013). Power laws and skew distributions: An application and analysis of performance royalty income. *Forthcoming: Journal of Income Distribution*.

Pitt, I. L. (2015). The Growth and Decay of ASCAP 1914–2014: Innovation, Disruption and Deregulation. *Working Paper*.

Pollock, B. (2014). *A Friend in the Music Business: The ASCAP Story*. Hal Leonard Books.

Price, J. (2011). 'Why Everyone But The Artist and The Music Fan is Doomed'. *Blog. TuneCore.com*. November 22, accessed online: http://blog.tunecore.com/2011/11/why-everyone-but-the-artist-and-the-music-fan-is-doomed.html.

Putterman, L. and Kroszner, R., editors (1996). *The Economic Nature of the Firm: A Reader*. Cambridge University Press, Cambridge, United Kingdom, second edition.

Rees, R. (1985a). The Theory of Principal and Agent–Part I. *Bulletin of Economic Research*, 37(1):3–26.

Rees, R. (1985b). The Theory of Principal and Agent–Part II. *Bulletin of Economic Research*, 37(2):75–97.

Robertson, M. (2011). 'Why Spotify can never be profitable: The secret demands of record labels'. *GigaOm.com*. accessed online: http://gigaom.com/2011/12/11/why-spotify-can-never-be-profitable-the-secret-demands-of-record-labels.

Rosen, S. (1981). The economics of superstars. *American Economic Review*, 71:845–858.

Silver, J. (2012). 'In Pursuit of a Global Music Registry'. *Future of Music.org*. June 27, accessed online: http://futureofmusic.org/blog/2012/06/27/pursuit-global-music-registry.

Sisario, B. (2011). 'Sirius's Move to Bypass a Royalty Payment Clearinghouse Causes an Uproar'. *New York Times*. November 7, accessed online: http://www.nytimes.com/2011/11/07/business/media/siriuss-move-to-bypass-royalty-agency-causes-uproar.html?_r=1&pagewanted=print.

Sisario, B. (2014a). 'Justice Department Plans to Begin a Review of Music Licensing Rules'. *NYTimes.com*. June 4, accessed online: http://www.nytimes.com/2014/06/04/business/media/justice-department-is-said-to-plan-a-review-of-music-licensing-rules.html?_r=0.

Sisario, B. (2014b). 'Music Industry Officals Agree on Need for Licensing Rule Changes, but Little Else'. *New York Times*. June 11, p. B3.

Sisario, B. (2014c). 'Pandora Suit May Upend Century-Old Royalty Plan'. *NYTimes.com*. February 13, accessed online: http://www.nytimes.com/2014/02/14/business/media/pandora-suit-may-upend-century-old-royalty-plan.html?_r=0.

Sisario, B. (2014d). 'Sony Threatens to Bypass Licensers in Royalties Battle'. *New York Times*. July 11, p. B2.

Stout, L. (2012). *The Shareholder Value Myth: How Putting Shareholders First Harms Investors, Corporations, and the Public*. Berrett-Koehler.

US vs. ASCAP & In Re Application of Cellco Partnership D/B/A Verizon Wireless (2009). No: 09 Civ. 7074 (DLC), S.D.N.Y. October 14, accessed online: www.eff.org%2Ffiles%2Ffilenode%2FUS_v_ASCAP%2FASCAP%2520v%2520Verizon%2520Order.pdf, pp. 1–34.

US vs ASCAP & In Re Application of the Cromwell Group Inc. and Affiliates et al (2012). No: 10 CV 5210 DLC MHD, S.D.N.Y. January 30, accessed online: www.ascap.com/~/media/files/pdf/licensing/.../final%20order.pdf.

US vs. ASCAP & In Re Applications of RealNetworks, Inc., Yahoo! Inc. (2010). Nos: 09-0539-cv (L), 09-0542-cv (con), 09-0666-cv (xap), 09-0692-cv (xap), 09-1572-cv (xap), US Court of Appeals, 2d Cir. September 28, accessed online: http://caselaw.findlaw.com/us-2nd-circuit/1539469.html, pp. 1–49.

US vs. ASCAP & In Re Capstar (DMX) (2010). No: 09 Civ. 7069 (DLC), S.D.N.Y. December 1, accessed online: http://www.leagle.com/decision/In%20FDCO%2020101209735 , pp. 1–87.

US vs. ASCAP & In re Petition of Pandora Media (2013). No: 1:12-cv-08035-DLC, 41 Civ. 1395 (DLC), S.D.N.Y. October, accessed online: http://www.digitalmusicnews.com/uploads/77/9f/.../pandoravascap.pdf, pp. 1–30.

US vs. ASCAP & In re Petition of Pandora Media (2014). Nos: 12 Civ. 8035 (DLC), 41 Civ. 1395 (DLC), S.D.N.Y. March 14, accessed online: http://www.business.cch.com/ipld/PandoraUSASCAP031414.pdf, pp. 1–136.

Williamson, O. (1996). The governance of contractual relationships. In Putterman, L. and Kroszner, R., editors, *The Economic Nature of the Firm: A Reader*, chapter 9, pages 125–135. Cambridge University Press, Cambridge, United Kingdom, second edition.

Wixen, R. (2014). *The Plain & Simple Guide to Music Publishing*. Hal Leonard, third edition.

Chapter 3
Copyright Law and Natural Monopolies

Copyright laws protect copyright holders such as songwriters and composers against copyright infringement or the unauthorized use of songs. US copyright laws recognize songwriters' musical creations as a "property right" and its use requires permission as well as compensation.[1] The most valuable part of a song can be found in the copyright protection laws that apply when music is transcribed in some sort of fixed form such as a recording on tape, sheet music, or lead sheet.[2] "Copyright laws arose out of eighteenth-century markets and technologies, the most important characteristic of which was artificial scarcity.

Artificial scarcity was created by a small number of gatekeepers, by relatively high barriers to entry, and by analog limitations on unauthorized copying."[3] "Copyright law was the commodity concern of publishers and other distributors who acted in a dual gatekeeper role: first as the gatekeeper of who would be published, and second as the gatekeeper of price and other access issues affecting the public."[4] Before the digital age began, it took a "fair amount of capital and labor to mass produce and distribute books, recorded music and many other works. Unlicensed users needed access to expensive duplication equipment and very visible distribution mechanisms (book stores, video stores, retail locations) to sell infringing or knock-off goods."[5]

With the introduction of the Internet and other digital innovations, there was a certain amount of "technological ignorance" among music publishing executives who may have planted the seeds of their own self-destruction. Most of these

---

[1]See Brabec and Brabec (2011, p. 310).

[2]See *Copyright Act* (2011); *Digital Millennium Copyright Act* (1998); Koenigsberg (2002); Korman and Koenigsberg (1986); Krasilovsky and Shemel (2007).

[3]See Patry (2011, p. 2).

[4]See Patry (2011, p. 38).

[5]See Downes (2011); Patry (2011, p.38).

I.L. Pitt, *Direct Licensing and the Music Industry*,
DOI 10.1007/978-3-319-17653-6_3

older music executives were accustomed to selling physical disks based on analog technologies. Their corporate cultures were built on the earlier incarnations of their corporate beginnings in the 1920s as manufacturers of phonographs that were later combined with radio. For example, EMI started out as the Gramophone Company; RCA was the Victor Talking Machine Company; Columbia Records was the Graphophone Company; and Decca was the Decca Phonograph Company.[6] Perhaps, this is why music executives believed that digital music was a fad that would soon fade away and devoted limited financial and human resources, if any, to creating new business models. Sometimes even when a lot of resources are thrown at a new technology, it doesn't necessarily mean it will survive. Rupert Murdoch's $580 million purchase of MySpace could not save the entity. Perhaps, the desire for a faster return on investment (ROI) for investors—with a greater emphasis on positive cash flow, and a steady growth in revenues and earnings rather than the user experience—meant that MySpace could not be monetized fast enough to meet such corporate objectives. The product life cycle of MySpace was brief and its audience found more compelling reasons to switch to new social networks such as Facebook and Twitter.

3.1 Copyright Law

In the United States, copyright protection lasts for the lifetime of the songwriter (or the last surviving co-writer) plus 70 years for songs created after 1978. Pre-1978 copyrighted songs are granted a total of ninety-five years of copyright protection.[7] Figure 3.1 describes the current US copyright law process for musical works in which there are two distinct copyright parts of a song: the musical composition and the sound (master) recording. For example, the figure shows a copyrighted song broken down into its copyrighted components; what the copyrights cover; the various copyright owners; royalty income derived from copyright licensing; the collection or licensing agencies for each component; and the various music users who license the copyrighted song. It is worth noting that a single song has multiple copyrights attached to it and multiple copyright owners as well. As a result, this may entail separate and complicated licensing contracts for songwriters, composers, and musicians, one with a record label (the master recording) and one with a music publisher (publishing rights). In addition to royalty income from copyright laws, singers/songwriters also earn income from sheet music, touring, merchandising, sponsorships, and endorsements.

A copyrighted song is broken down into a musical composition (generally the lyrics and the melody) and a sound recording, the actual audio portion of

[6] See Murphy (2014, pp. 392–347); Morgan (2014).

[7] See Krasilovsky and Shemel (2007) and Peter Hirtle's table on copyright terms and conditions here: http://copyright.cornell.edu/resources/publicdomain.cfm.

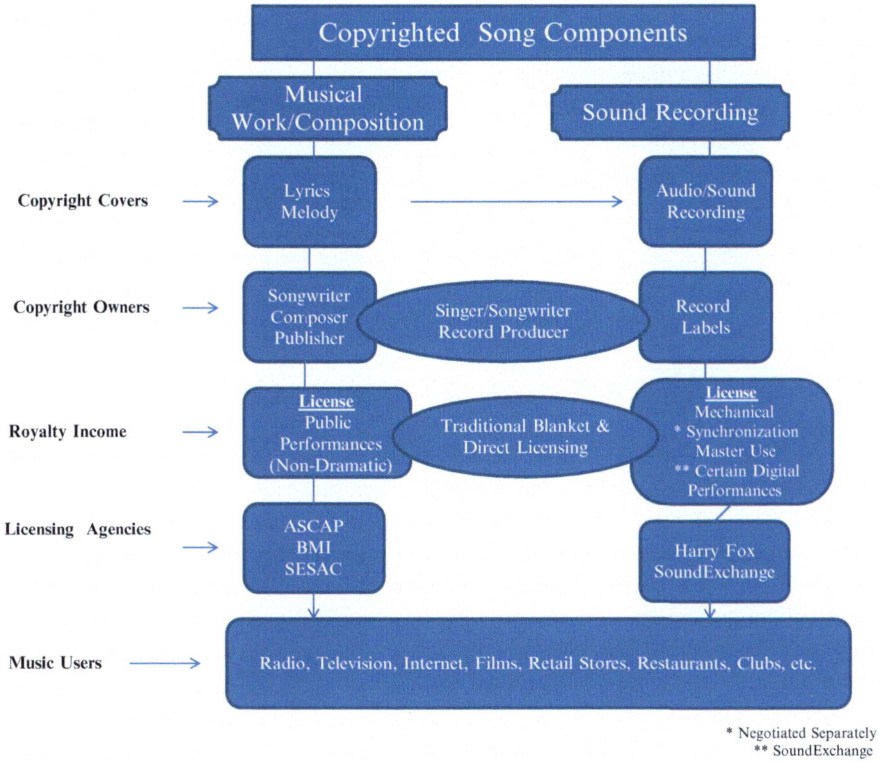

Fig. 3.1 US copyright law music process: multiple rights and multiple administrators

the song. Songwriters, lyricists, composers, vocalists, music publishers, record producers, and record labels can all share in the copyright ownership of a song. The songwriter/producer, in addition to helping polish a song, can also contribute his/her song writing talent to ensure the success of a song.[8] The sources of royalty income for a songwriter will vary depending on how the various music users decide on using a song. Multiple collecting agencies (PROs and the Harry Fox Agency) record labels and music publishers are involved in clearing the copyrights for the use of a particular song. There is the concern that with a multiplicity of copyrights and a corresponding set of licensing agencies requiring copyright clearances often create economic conditions that discourage the licensing of music for innovative use and stifle the success of new music technologies not only in the digital era, but also throughout the past century.[9] Some PROs refer to their songwriters, composers, and music publishers as members, while others use the term affiliates, depending

[8] See Pitt (2010, pp. 81–92).

[9] See Cardi (2007); Patry (2011).

on the manner in which the organization was incorporated. Performing Rights or Performance Rights are also used interchangeably. A songwriter is also considered a composer or the author of a musical composition.

There has been a widespread discussion on whether the primary purpose or objective of copyright laws should be to reward copyright holders or to promote the "progress of science and useful arts."[10] According to Lunney (2001), "copyright signifies a system of protection designed and intended primarily to serve the public interest in the creation and dissemination of creative works, rather than the private interest of enriching those who create and disseminate such works."

3.2 Natural Monopoly

Baumol (1982) defined a natural monopoly as the case where a single firm can produce output in a particular market at a lower average cost than two or more competitors, or the case in which competitors might avoid entry into a market due to profitability concerns or predatory measures by the incumbent monopolist. Telephone companies and electrical power generation utilities were once considered natural monopolies, and subjected to various types of regulation. In the case of telephone companies, the relatively high fixed cost structure once consisted of running telephone cables from a local switch in a central office to a customer's premise, and then to buried cables along railroad tracks to other switches for interstate and long distance traffic. Duplicating switches and getting the legal right-of-way clearance to bury additional cables would have been a significant barrier to entry for any competitor looking to compete with the old AT&T (Ma Bell).

Eventually with US Justice Department lawsuits, microwave technology, wireless phones, high-speed fiber optic cables and cable television companies, the AT&T monopoly was broken up and the industry became competitive. The cost of long distance telephony services dropped dramatically with the added competition brought on by technological change and innovation. Today, the distinction between local and long distance calls hardly matters since it costs about the same to call a neighbor in New York, as it is to call a friend in London. The old AT&T hardly exists today as stiff competition from cable companies and the Regional Bell Operating Companies eventually forced its demise, and its remains gobbled up by its sibling, SBC and re-branded the new AT&T.[11]

With the introduction of fiber optic cable and wireless technology, both the price difference and distance between a local and a long distance (including international) call no longer mattered, and AT&T (a former monopolist) tried to reinvent itself. Of course, fiber optics, coaxial cable, and wireless technology meant new competition and economic growth as cable and wireless companies competed with incumbent

---

[10] See Boldrin and Levine (2009).

[11] See Cairncross (1997); Cauley (2008); Kearney (1999).

phone companies. Some consumers liked the idea of "bundling," that is, having their voice, video, and data services provided by a single company on a single bill, even though in some cases pricing transparency was problematic. The problem occurred when cable companies lumped all services into one price that made it difficult for customers to determine what they were paying for each individual service.

Prior to the digital age, the rationale behind the natural monopoly regulation of PROs, instead of a competitive system, was that a single collective agency reduced the transaction costs of publicly performing copyrighted musical compositions for both individual music users and copyright holders. It was often impractical, time-consuming, laborious, and non-economical for individual users of musical compositions to contact individual copyright holders to obtain copyright clearance for millions of copyrighted musical works. The blanket and per-program licenses became the preferred method for administering copyright licensing without consideration for alternative forms of licensing. By centralizing the collective copyright administration of musical compositions, it was often argued that collective administration promoted the most efficient method for licensing music users, monitoring the public performance of music, enforcing copyright laws, and making timely distribution of royalty payments to copyright holders.

Due to the economic efficiency of the blanket license to lower the transaction costs for hundreds of thousands of individual music users seeking to avoid contacting millions of copyright holders for a music clearance license, it was alleged that copyright collection agencies were a "natural monopoly." This was probably true from a historical point of view when the cost of contacting every single copyright owner for music clearance would have been cost prohibitive, but it is being challenged in the digital era with the use of direct licensing agreements and independent registries of copyright ownership. Accordingly, ASCAP and BMI are regulated by a series of consent decrees after several antitrust lawsuits.[12]

Sobel (1983) provides an excellent economic analysis of the traditional blanket license, and for the sake of brevity, we do not repeat that exposition here. However, some of Sobel's economic ideas for retaining the blanket license are no longer valid in the digital era. For example, one of the biggest *profit* centers (the sound-track division) for record labels is synchronization rights, the licensing of master recordings of *individual* musical compositions to film and television production companies, and to new music services such as iTunes, Spotify, and Pandora.[13] Synchronization generated $13.9 billion in worldwide revenue for the years 2006–2011 as shown in Table 3.1.

[12]See DiLorenzo (1996) for his overview of natural monopolies. He concludes that, '[t]he theory of natural monopoly is also a-historical. There is no evidence of the "natural monopoly" story ever having been carried out—of one producer achieving lower long-run average total costs than every-one else in the industry and thereby establishing a permanent monopoly.'

[13]As described in an interview in Gordon (2011, pp. 304–315). The interviewee makes the distinction between income and profits from CD sales, which are not the same.

Table 3.1 Worldwide synchronization revenue 2006–2011

Year	Revenue ($ billions)	Percent (%)
2006	$2.1	15.11
2007	2.2	15.83
2008	2.3	16.55
2009	2.4	17.27
2010	2.4	17.27
2011	2.5	17.99
Total 2006–2011	$13.9	

Source: Based on data from: http://www.grabstats.com/statcategorymain.aspx?StatCatID=9.

Due to the diminishing roles of royalty collection; the discovery of artists with an established and loyal fan-base on YouTube; and music sales and distribution methods driven by social media, the Internet and mass merchants like Walmart in the digital era, synchronization is now one of the few major functions of music publishers in the exploitation of music. Each year the major music publishers negotiate hundreds of synchronization licenses with third parties for the millions of master recordings in the repertories that they already own for the use in films, television, the Internet, advertising and video games. The music publisher will then split the revenue from synchronization licensing with songwriters and composers, depending on the terms in their publishing contracts.

While the income from CD sales is important to the record labels, the final product is not often the [initial] CD sales for some songs, but the six-figure movie licensing deal in which the expense for a synchronization license is virtually close to zero, leaving a 100 % profit margin for the publisher.[14]

In other words, the labels often invest in new artists to recoup the research and development costs of building a catalog through CD sales so that they can someday license music for $1,000 to the penny. To do this, the record labels spend money on creating and promoting new records and hits.[15] In addition, a single song—with great lyrics, great melody, great singer, great production—when combined in a memorable scene or a background/foreground setting in a film can electrify the audience and ignite their emotional senses much more so than pure dialogue could achieve. A single song in a single movie scene could generate the incremental sale of millions of additional CDs and billions in revenue as movie fans try to recapture the emotional experience of the film by purchasing the motion picture sound-track.[16] Indeed, this is one of the unique characteristics of music publishing in which a small number of successful song-titles (and artists) generate most of the revenue,

[14]The publishers' expenses would probably include the minor costs of repackaging the music content of their catalogs and some marketing expenses.

[15]See Gordon (2011, pp. 304–315).

[16]Celine Dion's theme song, *My Heart Will Go On*, from the movie *Titanic* is one such example of the commercial success of a song-title used in a movie.

the so-called superstar effect. For example, from the box-office success of a film, a small number of revenue generating titles must then offset the declining sales of once-popular artists or cover the losses of the vast majority of titles released by the record labels that did not attain commercial success.

3.3 Multiple Licensing Agencies and Multiple Rights

In the United States, there are multiple music licensing agencies with separate agencies for performances rights and mechanical rights. In other countries, both performance and mechanical rights music are licensed by a single agency. Regardless of the country, each agency is often described as a natural monopoly. The right to perform copyrighted musical compositions in public places is collectively administered by Performing Rights Organizations (PROs) such as ASCAP, BMI, SESAC, and SoundExchange on behalf of individual copyright holders such as composers, lyricists, and music publishers. The Harry Fox Agency handles mechanical rights licensing.

ASCAP and BMI are the two largest, dominant, and incumbent PROs in the business of licensing public performance rights on behalf of their 1,035,000 copyright holders, the songwriters, composers, and music publishers, as shown in Table 3.2. Together, these two PROs control sixteen million unique copyrighted musical compositions that cannot be licensed elsewhere. SESAC is a distant third in terms of both affiliates and copyrighted song titles in its repertory.

From a music user perspective, there is virtually no competition among the PRO agencies since they each represent different songwriters and composers, and their repertories are separate and distinct. Music users—such as radio stations, television networks, Internet sites and other businesses—must obtain a blanket license from all three PROs if they want to avoid infringement lawsuits. Songwriters can only belong to one PRO at a time. Occasionally, an important songwriter may be persuaded to resign from one PRO organization and join another for some sort of lucrative compensation (loans, advances, and earnings guarantee against future

Table 3.2 PRO membership and repertory 2013

PRO	Members/ Affiliates	Member share (%)	Copyrighted titles in repertory	Incorporation status	Regulatory constraints
ASCAP	435,000	41	8,500,000	Non-profit	Consent decree
BMI	600,000	56	7,500,000	For-profit[a]	Consent decree
SESAC	30,000	3	250,000–400,000	For-profit	None
Total	1,065,000				

Source: Based on data from *RMLC v. SESAC* (2013, pp. 4–5).
[a]A for-profit that operates as a non-profit. BMI's operating expenses are a portion of collected licensing fees, similar to ASCAP's method.

royalty payments). This compensation is often based on that individual songwriter's catalog of copyrighted songs that may make a difference in the sale of blanket licenses to music users and on the known level of previous royalty income from musical performances. ASCAP and BMI are more or less duopolies that must be policed to constrain their inherent market power. A district rate court has observed that, "ASCAP's ability to collectively license the non-exclusive performing rights of its 400,000 members' musical compositions gives the organization market power when negotiating with music users. ASCAP's exercise of this market power has been constantly monitored by the US Department of Justice for anti-competitive behavior since 1941."[17]

Both ASCAP and BMI have been sued over the years for alleged market power violations under the *Sherman Antitrust Act.* As a result, ASCAP and BMI are governed by *consent decrees* that are intended to limit the duopoly nature or market power of these agencies, foster a more competitive industry, and promote growth and development in the industry. The operative provisions in the BMI consent decree are identical to the provisions in the ASCAP consent decree. Under the consent decrees, there is a mechanism in place called a *rate court* in which a US District Court has direct oversight of PRO's anti-competitive and predatory conduct, and the ability to settle legal claims and licensing fee disputes between the PROs and music users.[18]

SESAC is the smallest of the three PROs in the United States. Unlike ASCAP and BMI and the legal restrictions placed on the two leading PROs, SESAC has never been subjected to a consent decree. A consent decree is an important mechanism that is often used to challenge unfair pricing, antitrust issues, and contractual disputes associated with granting a blanket license for non-dramatic musical performances. However, "in the years leading up to 2008, SESAC's latitude to set the terms of music licenses was otherwise limited: first by a series of industry-wide agreements it negotiated with the television broadcast industry; later, for the period April 2005 through December 31, 2007, by a contractual duty that bound SESAC to arbitrate its disputes with licensee stations. Since January 2008, however, SESAC's range of motion has no longer been thus inhibited. SESAC has been free unilaterally to set the terms on which it will issue licenses to perform the music of its more than 20,000 affiliated composers."[19]

[17]See *US vs. ASCAP & In Re Capstar (DMX)* (2010). Unfortunately, this monitoring does not include the quarterly reporting of *Code of Federal Regulations* (CFR) financial data (income statements, balance sheets, and chart of accounts), executive compensation data, membership income data, operating data, and musical performances data that would make transparency easier for outside auditing groups. At a minimum, the amount of money spent on internal and external legal expenses broken down in finer detail should be made public so that songwriters could have an idea how these resources are utilized.

[18]The latest updated version of ASCAP's consent decree, sometimes referred to as the *Second Amended Final Judgment (AFJ2)*, can be found here: AFJ2 (2001). *BMI vs. DMX* (2010); *US vs. ASCAP & In Re Capstar (DMX)* (2010) are examples of recent rate court decisions that settled fee disputes.

[19]See *Meredith Corp. v. SESAC LLC* (2014, p. 2).

Even though it is a distant third and is not constrained by a consent decree, SESAC is not immune from the same anti-competitive, monopoly power, and direct licensing challenges to the traditional blanket license that have affected the larger two PROs. Court documents and press reports reveal that a court is set to determine whether SESAC "engaged in an overall anti-competitive course of conduct designed to eliminate meaningful competition to its blanket license when a small percentage of SESAC members—less than 1 % of its 20,000 members—who appear to get the largest advances from the PRO and signed supplemental agreements with the organization. The supplemental agreements give the affiliates an advance or an otherwise guaranteed amount of money, sometimes well over $1 million a year; and in exchange for that they agree not to license their music directly or face large monetary penalties."[20]

Furthermore, it has been alleged that SESAC has used various techniques to limit the access of local television stations to alternative or less expensive sources of performance rights. These techniques include: (a) removing the incentive for a station to acquire a direct license by offering no fee credit against the cost of its blanket license for music the licensee has separately acquired from the copyright owners making its per-program license (PPL) economically non-viable by revising the formula by which the cost for that license is calculated so that it invariably exceeds the cost of the blanket license; (b) promising its key affiliates—composers whose music is so ubiquitous that a station effectively cannot avoid—large upfront payments, and in return requiring these affiliates to enter into supplemental agreements that effectively bar them from offering direct licenses; (c) threatening to withhold access to any part of its repertory; and (d) refusing to disclose the full contents of its repertory to impede stations from making independent licensing arrangements.[21]

Technological change and innovation often provide the means for competition, lower costs and reducing some of the intrinsic inefficiencies inherent in monopolies.[22] As Scherer (1984) found, it is often smaller firms or external forces that seek to introduce major innovations to challenge the dominance of the incumbent monopolist, and introduce an industry transformation to the benefit of consumers. In the AT&T case, it was MCI using microwave technology and its 'friends and family' pricing plan to enter the long distance market. In the airline industry, it was small start-up Southwest Airlines using short haul markets and standardized equipment—the Boeing 737—to challenge American Airlines. Just like MCI and Southwest, DMX would later challenge and disrupt the outmoded status quo in music licensing with the use of its direct licensing business model.

---

[20]See Christman (2014a).

[21]See *Meredith Corp. v. SESAC LLC* (2014); *RMLC v. SESAC* (2013) for additional details on lawsuits concerning SESAC's licensing practices and federal antitrust laws.

[22]See Laffont and Tirole (1993); Schap (1985).

References

AFJ2 (2001). *Second Amended Final Judgment, US vs. ASCAP Civ. No.* 41 − 1395, S.D.N.Y. June, available online: http://www.ascap.com/~/media/Files/Pdf/members/governing-documents/ascapafj2.ashx, pp. 1–19.

Baumol, W. (1982). Contestable markets: An uprising in theory of industry structure. *American Economic Review*, 72:1–15.

BMI vs. DMX (2010). No: 08 Civ. 216 (LLS), S.D.N.Y. July 26, accessed online: http://www.leagle.com/decision/In%20FDCO%2020100727985.xml/BROADCAST%20MUSIC,%20INC.%20v.%20DMX,%20INC , pp. 1–33.

Boldrin, M. and Levine, D. (2009). Does intellectual monopoly help innovation? *Review of Law & Economics*, 5(3):991–1024.

Brabec, J. and Brabec, T. (2011). *Music, Money and Success: The Insider's Guide To Making Money In The Music Industry*. Schirmer Trade Books-Music Sales, New York, NY.

Cairncross, F. (1997). *The Death of Distance*. Harvard Business School Press.

Cardi, W. J. (2007). Über-middleman: Reshaping the broken landscape of copyright music. *Iowa Law Review*, 92:835–890.

Cauley, L. (2008). *End of the Line: The Rise and Fall of AT&T*. Free Press.

Christman, E. (2014a). 'SESAC Facing New Anti-Trust Legal Challenge'. *Billboard.com*. March 14, accessed online: http://www.billboard.com/biz/articles/news/publishing/5937426/sesac-facing-new-anti-trust-legal-challenge.

Copyright Act (2011). Copyright Law of the United States, United States Copyright Office, Library of Congress, Washington, DC, Circular 92. December, accessed online: http://www.copyright.gov/title17/circ92.pdf.

Digital Millennium Copyright Act (1998). U.S. Copyright Office Summary, United States Copyright Office, Library of Congress, Washington, DC. December, accessed online: http://www.copyright.gov/legislation/dmca.pdf.

DiLorenzo, T. (1996). The myth of natural monopoly. *Review of Austrian Economics*, 9(2):43–58.

Downes, L. (2011). 'Leahy's Protect IP Act: Why Internet Content Wars Will Never End'. *Forbes Magazine*. May 16, accessed online: http://www.forbes.com.

Gordon, S. (2011). *The Future of the Music Business*. Hal Leonard, Milwaukee, WI, third edition.

Kearney, J. (1999). From the fall of the Bell System to the Telecommunications Act: Regulation of telecommunications under Judge Greene. *Marquette University Law School Faculty Publications*, pages 1395–1472. Paper 505, accessed online: http://scholarship.law.marquette.edu/facpub/505, pp. 1395–1472.

Koenigsberg, I. (2002). *Performing Rights In Music And Performing Rights Organizations, Revisited*. White and Case, LLP, New York, NY.

Korman, B. and Koenigsberg, I. (1986). Performing Rights in Music and Performing Rights Organizations. *Journal of the Copyright Society of the USA*, 33(4):332–367.

Krasilovsky, M. W. and Shemel, S. (2007). *The Business of Music: The Definitive Guide to the Business and Legal Issues of the Music Industry*. Watson-Guptill Publications, New York, tenth edition.

Laffont, J. and Tirole, J. (1993). *A Theory of Incentives in Procurement and Regulation*. MIT Press.

Lunney, G. (2001). The death of copyright: Digital technology, private copying, and the Digital Millennium Copyright Act. *Virginia Law Review*, 87(5):813–920.

Meredith Corp. v. SESAC LLC (2014). No: 09 Civ. 9177 (PAE), S.D.N.Y. March 3, accessed online: http://tvmlc.com/wp-content/uploads/2012/07/3_6_14-Court-Process-Decision.pdf, pp. 1–69.

Morgan, B. (2014). 'History of the Record Industry, 1877 - 1920s: Part One: From Invention to Industry'. *Medium.com*. Accessed online: https://medium.com/@Vinylmint/history-of-the-record-industry-1877-1920s-48deacb4c4c3.

Murphy, G. (2014). *Cowboys and Indies: The Epic History of the Record Industry*. St. Martin's Press.

Patry, W. (2011). *How To Fix Copyright*. Oxford University Press, New York.
Pitt, I. L. (2010). *Economic Analysis of Music Copyright: Income, Media and Performances*. Springer, New York. Available online: http://www.amazon.com/Economic-Analysis-Music-Copyright-Performances/dp/1441963170/ref=sr_1_1?s=books&ie=UTF8&qid=1417266944&sr=1-1&keywords=economic+analysis+of+music+copyright.
RMLC v. SESAC (2013). No: 12-cv-5807, E.D.P.A. December 20, accessed online: http://www.fhhlaw.com/RMLC%20v%20SESAC%20injunc%20decision.PDF, pp. 1–40.
Schap, D. (1985). X-inefficiency in a rent-seeking society: A graphical analysis. *Quarterly Review of Economics and Business*, 25:19–27.
Scherer, F. M. (1984). *Innovation and Growth: Schumpeterian Perspectives*. MIT Press.
Sobel, L. (1983). The music business and the Sherman Act: An analysis of the economic realities of blanket licensing. *Loyola of Los Angeles Entertainment Law Journal*, 3:1–44. available at: http://digitalcommons.lmu.edu/elr/vol3/iss1/1.
US vs. ASCAP & In Re Capstar (DMX) (2010). No: 09 Civ. 7069 (DLC), S.D.N.Y. December 1, accessed online: http://www.leagle.com/decision/In%20FDCO%2020101209735, pp. 1–87.

Chapter 4
Traditional Blanket License

The blanket license allows music users the immediate use of all musical compositions and provides greater flexibility in the unlimited choice of the works in a PRO's repertory. This system proved beneficial for some small music users and copyright owners who wanted to avoid the one-on-one transaction costs of negotiating the clearance rights for the entire repertory of a PRO. The blanket license also provides protection in the form of a government appeal over licensing fee disputes.[1]

DMX challenged the transactional efficiency of the traditional blanket and prevailed in court. The reason was simple. "Contracting instruments that enhance transactional efficiency such as the [traditional] blanket license are sometimes seen as anti-competitive restrictions that compel each user to make an 'all or nothing' choice that may force acceptance of a full license contract in place of a less inclusive alternative that a user may actually prefer."[2] The traditional blanket license is not the only alternative way to license music and has been the subject of antitrust litigation for decades. One reason for the duration and complexity of the litigation has been the difficulty of economists, attorneys, judges, and others in determining the net effect of these unique [licensing] arrangements associated with the blanket license.[3] The courts are increasingly adopting a more competitive framework for regulating the PROs. It is unfortunate, but not entirely surprising, that other blanket licensing options were not made available sooner.

The current economic literature in music licensing has focused mainly on the desirability and PRO administrative efficiency of the traditional old media

---

[1]See Patry (2011, p. 181).

[2]See the analysis of Einhorn (2006); Einhorn and Kurlantzick (2003) for more here. This "all or nothing" blanket license—as the only viable option for local television stations to obtain the performance rights to the music of SESAC's affiliates—is featured prominently in the *Meredith Corp. v. SESAC LLC* (2014) lawsuit.

[3]See Nye (2000); Sobel (1983).

I.L. Pitt, *Direct Licensing and the Music Industry*,
DOI 10.1007/978-3-319-17653-6_4

Table 4.1 Selected types of music licensing

License type	Rights granted
Performance (Public & Non-Dramatic)	Right to use live or recorded music on terrestrial radio & television, cable TV, digital radio & television, retail outlets, the Internet, and other venues
Mechanical	Right to reproduce & distribute physical products such as CDs, cassettes, digital downloads, etc.
Synchronization	Right to use songs that combine music with a moving image such as audio/visuals in films & commercials

blanket license, even though it may not be economically efficient and in some ways anti-competitive for music users in the digital age. Many of these studies involved compulsory licensing, the monopoly powers granted to music creators and performing rights organizations over the licensing of music content, and the disputes involved in the enforcement of both civil and criminal penalties for the unauthorized use of music associated with the traditional blanket license.[4]

There are many types of licensing agreements between songwriters, and those in the business of exploiting music for income opportunities. Performance (blanket), mechanical (master recording) and synchronization licenses are the most common music licenses required for using copyrighted music.[5] Table 4.1 describes the most prevalent licenses and how they are used by music users, film studios, and video production companies. The focus of this monograph is primarily on the performance rights aspects of music licensing.

4.1 Dramatic and Non-Dramatic Public Performances

Copyright owners, the members and affiliates of PROs, grant the PROs a *non-exclusive* right to license the public performance right to their musical compositions. Performing (or Performance) Rights Organizations in turn collect (non-dramatic) performance royalty payments (licensing fees) from music users such as television stations, radio stations, Internet companies, bars, restaurants, clubs, retail stores, etc. when the copyright owners' musical compositions are "performed" in those venues. ASCAP, BMI, SESAC, and SoundExchange are the four separate, distinct, and incumbent PROs representing different songwriters, composers, lyricists, publishers, record labels, musicians, and other copyright holders. Each organization licenses only the copyrighted works of its own respective affiliates or members. In the past, obtaining a blanket license from a PRO made economic sense since

[4]See Allen Consulting Group (2003); Besen et al. (1992); Jain (2008); Liebowitz and Margolis (2009); Nye (2000); Sobel (1983).

[5]See Brabec and Brabec (2011, pp. 397–427).

it avoided the time-consuming task of a music user having to contact hundreds of thousands of copyright holders in order to gain access to the millions of works in the respective repertories.

4.1.1 Dramatic Performances

A *dramatic performance* is a song that is used in a live theater production, musical, ballet or opera with elaborate sets, scenery, and paid admission. The copyright owners of musical compositions and production companies negotiate dramatic rights separately from non-dramatic performance, mechanical and synchronizations licensing. Playwrights face some of the same creative, royalty, and financial issues that are familiar to songwriters and composers. Playwrights must create the *scripts* for dramatic theater productions—linking the music of composers and lyricists with themes, plots, characters, dialogue or dance numbers, the essential content for any show. Dramatic productions cannot succeed unless there are producers willing to finance a show and they are able to recoup their investment; and there is a (for-profit or non-profit) theater for the show's production. Just like in the music industry, Broadway producers and artist directors can be risk-averse. They may be reluctant to stage a play if the playwright is unknown, or there are no stars as cast members with previous track records of selling tickets and filling seats. There are exceptions such as *The Lion King*—an adaption of an animated film—that has maintained a run of 17 years that is due to its pricing strategies; movie tie-in; simple storyline; spectacular scenery; family-oriented themes that would appeal to an international audience; has no big-name stars; and has been produced by Disney Theatrical Productions, a unit of Disney Studios that also includes Disney Music Group. The production features music by Elton John and lyrics by Tim Rice.

In general, a playwright's income is often based on a commission paid by theater owners for new scripts, and royalties based on a percent of revenue from the box office receipts during dramatic performances. Unlike others on the artistic team and in some cases, a playwright may not be paid for what is called "pre-production activities" such as casting calls and rehearsals. Just like songwriters and composers, a playwright's income can vary depending on whether he or she has a hit show or whether a show is in current production. Hit shows, such as the *Lion King* with a long On-and-Off Broadway run, can earn a playwright millions of dollars.

It has been reported that *The Lion King* has grossed over $6.2 billion in worldwide sales from stage productions (excluding revenue from the sales of posters, CDs, other merchandise, film and licensing fees) in the 17 years since its debut, making it the most successful work in any media in entertainment history. The *The Lion King* is said to have benefited from what is called premium or "dynamic pricing." Dynamic pricing involves the use of computer generated algorithms for flexible and competitive pricing based on increasing or decreasing ticket prices for certain seats depending on current market supply and demand factors. Dynamic pricing is a common practice in several industries such as hotels (cost of rooms depending on time of the day and demand); airlines (day of the week, time of day, and number of days before a flight considerations); sports (opponents and outdoor stadiums in which weather may be a factor); and retail (matching competitors' pricing or geographic pricing variations). Unlike other shows that may charge more for tickets, the average ticket price for *The Lion King* was $128, while the highest price $197.50, an attempt to keep prices below $200 to boost demand.[6] However, the reality for playwrights is similar to songwriters and composers, that is, most struggle to make a living, most cannot live off royalties, and most often supplement their incomes with other jobs like writing scripts for television.[7]

4.1.2 Non-Dramatic Performances

A *non-dramatic public performance* can be a song played on cable and broadcast television networks, the radio, in bars, restaurants, hotels, and other venues with the exception of the home. Musical compositions, though considered dramatic in the context of their original theater, are generally under the non-dramatic right when performed individually on television or radio.[8] Licensed musical compositions are used in a variety of ways, and can include: (a) *feature* performance of a song used in part or in whole in a variety show; (b) *theme* music used to open and close a program; (c) *background or foreground* music that is neither the theme nor a feature performance used to create a mood in certain scene settings or the music heard in retail outlets that enhance purchasing or ambiance; (d) memorable *jingles* used in commercials to brand particular products or services or (e) *promotional* spots used to promote upcoming shows to increase viewers or listeners.[9]

When songwriters, composers, and lyricists join a performing rights organization such as ASCAP, BMI, or SESAC, it is generally understood that it does not involve the transfer of copyright ownership. The PROs are only allowed *non-exclusive* rights to the songs in their repertory. When a songwriter/composer or copyright holder signs a non-exclusive agreement with a particular PRO, he or she is not prohibited from seeking similar licensing agreements with other organizations once the contractual terms of the PRO membership or affiliation are over. A songwriter/composer can belong to only one PRO at a time, while music publishers can belong to multiple PROs depending on a particular song title registration.

In a typical licensing fee agreement with ASCAP, BMI, or SESAC, a music user after paying the required royalty licensing fees is issued a *blanket license* to perform

[6]See "*The Lion King*' musical breaks box office record with $6.2 billion worldwide': http://www.nydailynews.com/entertainment/theater-arts/lion-king-musical-breaks-box-office-record-6-2-billion-worldwide-article-1.1948400, September 22, 2014.

[7]See London et al. (2009) for their analysis of the financial problems facing playwrights.

[8]See Brabec and Brabec (2011, p. 311).

[9]See Pitt (2010).

the musical works in the PRO's repertory for the period specified in the agreement. There is also a *per-program* blanket license that is used by local television stations or radio stations whose main programming consists of sports or talk shows in which they pay a variable fee only for the actual music used in their programs. Both forms of licensing are allowed under the terms of the consent decrees signed by ASCAP and BMI. In both forms of licensing, blanket or per program, the music user is allowed unlimited use of all the musical compositions in the respective repertories of each PRO. The musical compositions can be performed as frequently as music programming demands.

4.2 PRO Licensing Fees

Licensing fees collected from music users represent the single largest revenue income stream for PROs and a significant input cost for some music users. Table 4.2 shows the licensing revenue growth rates for the years 2005–2010 for the two leading PROs in the United States. In 2010, ASCAP and BMI collected $1.852 billion in licensing fee revenue from various music users, a slight decrease of $48 million or 2.59 % over the previous year. The year-over-year decline in PRO revenue has been partially attributed to the shift in advertising dollars away from their biggest source of income—terrestrial radio and television—to online media marketing and mobile devices. After PRO administration costs are deducted, the remaining revenue is then distributed to the copyright holders as performance royalty income, months after the actual performance of their musical compositions.

Table 4.2 Growth in PRO licensing revenue 2005–2010 in ($MM)

PRO	2010	2009	2008	2007	2006	2005	Average 2005–2010
ASCAP	$935[a]	$995	$933	$863	$785	$749	$877
Y/Y Change	−$60	$62	$70	$78	$36	$50	$39
Y/Y Change (%)	−6.42	6.23	7.50	9.04	4.59	6.68	4.60
BMI	$917	$905	$901	$839	$780	$728	$845
Y/Y Change	$12	$4	$62	$59	$52	$55	$41
Y/Y Change (%)	1.31	0.44	6.88	7.03	6.67	7.55	4.98
Total	$1,852	$1,900	$1,834	$1,702	$1,565	$1,477	$1,722
Y/Y Change	−$48	$66	$132	$137	$88	$105	$80
Y/Y Change (%)	−2.59	3.47	7.20	8.05	5.62	7.11	4.81

[a]This figure is from ASCAP's Press Release:
http://www.ascap.com/press/2011/0331_Financial_Results.aspx.
ASCAP's 2011 annual report cites the number as $931,770.
BMI's 2011 revenue were not available at the time of writing.

Competition among the PROs is rare because each PRO controls the musical compositions in its own repertory and licenses only the works of its members or affiliates. Therefore, in order for music users to have the proper copyright clearance for virtually all the copyrighted music in the world, they must obtain costly licenses from all performance rights organizations, including foreign markets. As a result, PROs have a significant degree of bargaining leverage because they control a substantial number of popular songs in their respective repertories, as was shown previously in Table 3.2 on page 121. Recent rate court rulings, to be discussed below, have begun to set licensing fees using competitive industry benchmarks. Similarly, the often-secretive economic demands and other potential barriers to entry for a new PRO would be extremely high because a new entrant would lack access to existing popular songs, and the long-term licensing contracts between copyright holders and the PROs might prevent entry.

Table 4.3 shows the industry sources of ASCAP's licensing fees in 2011. It is worth noting that approximately 35 % of their licensing fees came from foreign sources, indicating that the demand and the performance of US copyrighted music are coming from markets outside of the United States. Foreign collecting societies license the works of US PROs, collect foreign licensing fees, and remit those fees to US PROs with reciprocal licensing agreements. Similarly, US PROs act on behalf of foreign collecting societies when their licensed music is performed in the United States. ASCAP's domestic music users accounted for 65 % of total licensing fees, with the radio industry as the largest domestic contributor. Most of ASCAP's 2011 domestic revenue came from old media terrestrial industries, and a mere 2.43 % of licensing revenue came from what ASCAP calls "new media." Old media industries, such as radio, are still an important format for some songwriters who are trying to reach a narrower mainstream audience.

Table 4.4 shows the estimated global revenues of the 200 royalty collecting societies around the world that are members of the International Confederation of Societies of Authors and Composers (CISAC). Global licensing revenue was

Table 4.3 ASCAP's revenue by industry segments 2011 in ($000)

Source	2011	Share (%)
Foreign royalties	$347,061	35.31
Radio	$227,581	23.16
Cable	$170,203	17.32
Television	$105,876	10.77
General licensing	$100,528	10.23
New media	$23,929	2.43
Symphonic & Concert	$5,897	0.60
Other	$1,710	0.17
Total	$982,785	
Domestic only	$635,724	64.69
Foreign royalties	$347,061	35.31

Source: Based on selected data from www.ascap.com/about/~/media/Files/Pdf/.../annual-reports/annual_2011.pdf.

Table 4.4 2010 Estimates of global royalty licensing fees by region and rights in (€000)

Region	Performance	Mechanical	Other	Total	Share by region (%)
Europe	€3,364,268	€876,124	€360,326	€4,600,719	60.97
North America	1,058,424	275,635	113,361	1,447,421	19.18
Asia Pacific	841,557	219,159	90,134	1,150,850	15.25
Latin America Caribbean	221,142	57,590	23,685	302,417	4.01
Africa	32,242	8,397	3,453	44,092	0.58
Total	€5,517,633	€1,436,904	€590,960	€7,545,498	
Shares by rights (%)	73.12	19.04	7.83		

Source: Based on data from Patissier (2012).

estimated in the range of €7.5 billion, and this was reported to be a record year despite the prevailing economic conditions. The €7.5 billion figure represented a 5.5 % increase over 2009 with growth recorded in every region of the world. CISAC's European and North American regions accounted for close to 80 % of all performance, mechanical and other royalty revenue in 2010.[10]

Many of the manual, labor-intensive, and time-consuming transaction costs—such as song title registration, copyright ownership, the collection of music performance data, royalty payment transfers, indemnification from infringement lawsuits, expensive rate court litigation and access to new musical works—once associated with the natural monopoly concept and clever PRO marketing schemes, have been destroyed by the Internet. For example, DMX used Music Reports Inc. (MRI), a company specialized in high-volume music license administration to assist in the design and implementation of its direct licensing program according to the documentation in *US vs. ASCAP & In Re Capstar (DMX)* (2010). By developing its own independent central registry of copyright holders' data (such as who owns what, where, and for how long), MRI became an alternative and competitor to the PROs, and has shown that negotiating directly with copyright holders is no longer the logistical and financial hurdle of the past. Innovators such as DMX, MRI, TuneCore, Last.fm, and others are now challenging the duopoly system of having the two major incumbent PROs that provide the bulk of performance rights copyright licensing. The original rationale in copyright licensing, based on the economic concept of a "natural monopoly" as more efficient may no longer be valid in the digital era.[11] It is likely in the near future that incumbent PROs will no longer be afforded such natural monopoly protection, particularly when it inhibits innovation and competition in the music licensing industry. Digital technology, among other technological changes, has become a key driver behind the transformation of the PRO industry into a more competitive market.

---

[10] See Patissier (2012). The reporting of PRO licensing data is often primitive. Important licensing fees and royalty payments price deflators and other valuable statistical tools are often missing from these compiled industry reports, adding to the lack of transparency in music licensing.

[11] See the extensive discussion in Boldrin and Levine (2009); Einhorn (2006); Katz (2005, 2006).

References

Allen Consulting Group (2003). Economic perspectives on copyright law. Research Paper ISBN 1 876692 05 7, Centre for Copyright Studies Ltd, Strawberry Hills NSW 2012, Australia. The Centre is funded by Copyright Agency Limited, a copyright collecting society in Australia.

Besen, S., Kirby, S., and Salop, S. (1992). An economic analysis of copyright collectives. *Virginia Law Review*, 78(1):383–411. Symposium on the Law and Economics of Intellectual Property.

Boldrin, M. and Levine, D. (2009). Does intellectual monopoly help innovation? *Review of Law & Economics*, 5(3):991–1024.

Brabec, J. and Brabec, T. (2011). *Music, Money and Success: The Insider's Guide To Making Money In The Music Industry*. Schirmer Trade Books-Music Sales, New York, NY.

Einhorn, M. (2006). Transactions costs and administered markets: License contracts for music performance rights. *Review of Economic Research on Copyright Issues*, 3(1):61–74.

Einhorn, M. and Kurlantzick, L. (2003). Traffic jam on the music highway: Is it a reproduction or a performance? *Review of Network Economics*, 2(1):10–28.

Jain, S. (2008). Digital piracy: A competitive analysis. *Marketing Science*, 27(4):610–626.

Katz, A. (2005). The potential demise of another natural monopoly: Rethinking the collective administration of performing rights. *Journal of Competition Law and Economics*, 1(3): 541–593.

Katz, A. (2006). The potential demise of another natural monopoly: New technologies and the administration of performing rights. *Journal of Competition Law and Economics*, 2(2): 245–284.

Liebowitz, S. and Margolis, S. (2009). Bundles of joy: The ubiquity and efficiency of bundles in new technology markets. *Journal of Competition Law and Economics*, 5(1):1–47.

London, T., Pesner, B., Voss, Z. G., and Mingovits, V. (2009). *Outrageous Fortune: The Life and Times of the New American Play*. Theatre Development Fund.

Meredith Corp. v. SESAC LLC (2014). No: 09 Civ. 9177 (PAE), S.D.N.Y. March 3, accessed online: http://tvmlc.com/wp-content/uploads/2012/07/3_6_14-Court-Process-Decision.pdf, pp. 1–69.

Nye, W. (2000). Some economic issues in licensing of music performance rights: Controversies in recent ASCAP-BMI litigation. *Journal of Media Economics*, 13(1):15–25.

Patissier, F. (2012). Global economic survey of the royalties collected by the CISAC member authors' societies in 2010. Technical Report COM12-0093, CISAC (International Confederation of Societies of Authors and Composers). Accessed online: http://www.cisac.org/CisacPortal/initConsultDoc.do?idDoc=22951.

Patry, W. (2011). *How To Fix Copyright*. Oxford University Press, New York.

Pitt, I. L. (2010). Superstar effects on royalty income in a performance rights organization. *Journal of Cultural Economics*, 34(3):219–236.

Sobel, L. (1983). The music business and the Sherman Act: An analysis of the economic realities of blanket licensing. *Loyola of Los Angeles Entertainment Law Journal*, 3:1–44. available at: http://digitalcommons.lmu.edu/elr/vol3/iss1/1.

US vs. ASCAP & In Re Capstar (DMX) (2010). No: 09 Civ. 7069 (DLC), S.D.N.Y. December 1, accessed online: http://www.leagle.com/decision/In%20FDCO%2020101209735, pp. 1–87.

Chapter 5
Direct Licensing as an Alternative to the Traditional Blanket License

The digital world is embracing alternative forms for the licensing of musical compositions, and in the process reducing the barriers to entry for competitors looking to bring innovative new services to the marketplace at a lower cost to retailers and consumers. Direct licensing is the latest example of the gradual shift away from the traditional blanket license. Researchers are now beginning to analyze the economic, political, and legal aspects of directly licensing music to determine whether it is a better and desirable solution for music licensing. Copyright holders have the choice of using a traditional PRO, direct licensing or a combination of both, depending on which choice maximizes economic value. For music users, direct licensing offers greater efficiency, simplicity, and transparency, while lowering some administrative costs.

In the digital sphere, there is a demand for the "direct licensing" of musical compositions as an alternative to the traditional blanket license. With a direct license, music users negotiate a separate agreement directly with music publishers, record labels, and other copyright holders for the use of their works eliminating the costly middle layer of performing rights organizations (PROs) and mechanical rights agencies. Direct licensing was never an issue due to the fact that digital streaming of music was not a threat to the incumbent players' controlled distribution system until recently. Direct or source licensing, an alternate form of the traditional blanket licensing agreement, was used mainly by some broadcasters. These broadcasters negotiated a direct license with copyright owners to acquire the performing rights to their music. In addition, those same broadcasters negotiated a source license with production companies and other music distributors who had already negotiated and secured the performing rights from the copyright owners of music used in television programming.[1] Direct or source licensing essentially eliminates one of

[1] See Passman (2000, pp. 237–238).

I.L. Pitt, *Direct Licensing and the Music Industry*,
DOI 10.1007/978-3-319-17653-6_5

the principal functions of PROs by excluding them from negotiating the fees paid for the use of copyrighted music in their respective repertories. By eliminating (and bypassing altogether), the negotiating function of PROs, direct or source licensing also eliminates the principal source of revenue for PROs.

It is often very difficult to access the type of economic information that is needed for the economic study of PROs and record labels because there is no transparency.[2] It is only when information, as in the DMX rate court proceedings, is made public that economists get an illuminating glimpse into the Byzantine music licensing process. In December of 2010, DMX, Inc., a background/foreground music competitor won a major licensing fee ruling that innovated the way music is licensed in the PRO industry. By developing its direct license, DMX fundamentally changed the business models, competition, and the pricing structure of performance rights licensing as we discuss below.

It was the power to exclude competition that permitted the monopolist PROs to charge licensing fees way above a market or competitively derived rate that became the central focus of the lawsuits in which the anti-competitive business practices of American society of composers, authors and publishers (ASCAP) and BMI were found to be outside the bounds of antitrust law. The entire DMX rate court process was tedious and a significant of amount of money was spent on litigation. Although for DMX, it was the same issue of obtaining a direct license from both ASCAP and BMI, it was necessary to file two separate lawsuits because there are different judges monitoring ASCAP's and BMI's consent decrees. DMX's victory came at the cost of considerable legal expenses, including those of expert witnesses. The district court judges found there was sufficient evidence of the economic power of the dominant PROs in their ability to control the pricing of licensed copyrighted music and/or exclude competition after reviewing the testimony (that appeared improvised and not terribly effective) and statistical analysis of the PRO's economists and expert witnesses in DMX's antitrust complaints.

Both ASCAP and BMI appealed the district court decisions, and on June 13, 2012, the United States Court of Appeals for the Second Circuit affirmed the two lower trial court victories DMX obtained against ASCAP and BMI for the direct licensing of music. The Second Circuit Court found that the licensing fees set by the district rate courts were reasonable for the following four reasons. First, ASCAP and BMI were reasonably compensated for the use of their services by the fees set in the rate court proceedings.

Second, the annual $25 per-location royalty pool was a reasonable benchmark because it met the four standards of a benchmark: A comparable right, similar parties, similar economic circumstances and the rates were set in a sufficiently competitive market. Third, the rate courts were not erroneous in treating the advance paid by DMX to Sony as a cost of entry into the market.

---

[2]See Robertson (2011); Towse (2008).

Table 5.1 Industry leaders in background/foreground music 2010

Company	Locations	Share (%)
Trusonic	11,487	3.44
Music choice	34,988	10.48
PlayNetwork	49,110	14.71
DMX	95,000	28.46
Muzak	143,222	42.91
Total	333,807	

Source: Based on data from US vs. ASCAP & In Re Capstar (DMX) (2010).

Finally, in the evolving commercial music market, incorporating direct licensing into existing licensing fee structures fostered fair pricing and competition, thereby advancing the purpose of ASCAP's and BMI's consent decrees.[3]

Background (BG) music is the pre-programmed music heard playing softly in elevators in office buildings or other commercial spaces such as hotels and restaurants. Foreground (FG) music is the loud music often heard in fashionable clothing stores or other retail outlets that cater to young "hip" shoppers. Table 5.1 shows the five leading background/foreground (BG/FG) music providers and their share of retail locations. In 2010, DMX was the second largest music supplier in terms of the number of locations that carried its programming. In the copyright rate court proceeding (lawsuit) against the ASCAP, US District Court of New York ruled in DMX's favor by setting DMX's adjustable blanket license fee for the 95,000 retail locations it served. Furthermore, the December lower court ruling was similar to a July 2010 case (in a different rate court proceeding) in which DMX prevailed against BMI, an ASCAP rival in the industry.[4]

These court rulings were significant because DMX re-defined copyright music licensing as administered by the two leading incumbent performance rights agencies in the United States. The court rulings may have signaled that there is a need for further flexibility in adapting the traditional blanket licensing process to meet a changing competitive market and modern technology.

5.1 Competitiveness and Economic Barriers to Entry

Patry (2011, p. 29) observes that, "in any commodity business, the most benefits flow to gatekeepers because gatekeepers have the most leverage in contracts for the purchase and sale of the commodity." "By permitting fewer works into the

[3]See BMI vs. DMX, ASCAP vs. THP CAPSTAR (2012). It is no wonder that the public view the PROs as having one foot in the grave and the wounds are largely self-inflicted when technology and competition diminishes the intermediate role of incumbent PROs. This is a classic example of the Innovator's Dilemma.

[4]See BMI vs. DMX (2010); US vs. ASCAP & In Re Capstar (DMX) (2010) for the court rulings and the law review article of both cases by Olson (2012).

market and by controlling the distribution channels to the market, gatekeepers minimize competition and create artificial scarcity in order to drive up demand for those works they do publish, thereby permitting them to charge monopoly prices. The combination of gatekeeper role and the enforcement mechanisms provided by copyright laws make it possible to avoid the common economic fate of falling prices that occurs when competitors enter the same market."[5]

In a PRO context, "superstar commodities" take the form of *evergreen libraries*, that is, perennially popular song-titles played over and over on the radio or television earning performance royalty income for the copyright holders (songwriters and music publishers) and licensing fees for the PROs. Some songs, compositions, and recording artists long considered passé or dated can become popular again when a particular song is used in a successful film or advertising commercial. In the case of music, each new generation of technology affords a new opportunity for record labels and music publishers to profit from reselling music to consumers; music that the consumers may already own in the older and dated music format.[6] For example, many consumers repurchased music on a CD format (at prices higher than that of vinyl) when they already owned the vinyl copy, or they repurchased digital music they owned on a CD in order to use an iPod. In other words, each new music technology extinguishes the older technology as that technology reached the end of its natural product life cycle and consumers switched to the newer products or innovations. The decline in some music revenues from the older technologies, therefore, had nothing to do with piracy issues.

DMX developed a new and innovative direct license called a "music composition catalog license" (MCCL) in which it created a licensing pool or central registry of individual copyright owners (music publishers and recording labels) and then negotiated a separate blanket licensing agreement with those licensing agencies for the use of their copyrighted music. DMX's innovative license created a direct challenge to the music copyright gatekeepers because it provided the bargaining power needed to change the entrenched monopoly practices of the PROs.

As revealed in court documents, numerous economic demands, obstacles, and structural barriers to entry—that impeded competition, innovation, productivity, and efficiency—were put in place by the major incumbent PROs that made DMX's efforts to obtain a blanket license with a carve-out difficult. In addition, the court documents revealed that many of the advantages associated with incumbent PROs were no longer sustainable in a digital environment. By virtue of their market control over the music licensing process, the PROs attempted to prevent an innovation from reaching the market using ethically questionable methods.[7] The gatekeepers' obstacles and economic power included some of the following practices: (a) offer-

[5]See Patry (2011, pp. 82–83). The music publisher can also be described as just another music licensing agency whose role is to exploit revenue opportunities from copyrighted music.

[6]See Grant and Wood (2004, p. 43–92).

[7]See BMI vs. DMX (2010); US vs. ASCAP & In Re Capstar (DMX) (2010).

ing the entrenched traditional blanket/per program license without a carve-out; (b) multi-year litigation with expensive expert witnesses to settle licensing fee disputes; (c) insider collusion among PRO and publishing CEOs; (d) substantial and guaranteed short-term and long-term financial assistance (advance) payments by PROs to music publishers and songwriters; (e) unreasonable licensing fee proposals by the PROs; (f) restrictions to per segment licenses; (g) refusals to renew MCCLs; and (h) most favored nation (MFN) clauses.

We summarize the many disadvantages associated with the economic roadblocks put in place by both the PROs, record labels and music publishers to limit competition in the music industry as discussed in various rate court proceedings that were made public, as well other sources in Table 5.2.[8] According to the rate court documents, ASCAP and BMI tried their best to prevent the major publishers from entering direct licensing agreements with DMX. The court noted that under ASCAP's consent decree, the *Second Amended Final Judgment*, ASCAP is restrained from "[l]imiting, restricting, or interfering with the right of any member to issue, directly or through an agent other than a performance rights organization, non-exclusive licenses to music users for rights of public performance."[9] For example, ASCAP's alternative fee proposal for DMX's direct license with a carve-out was rejected by the court because it required DMX to bear the full cost of its MCCL program, in addition to an annual administrative fee of $25,000. Simply put, the lower district court concluded that ASCAP's fee proposal was designed to convince DMX to discontinue its direct license program by making its implementation inequitable for DMX. Furthermore, ASCAP members who did not enter into a direct licensing agreement with DMX could expect a windfall or surplus income.

The reason for the windfall is that "ASCAP is entitled to and does withhold payments from those members who enter into direct licensing agreements." The withheld money is then distributed as surplus income to other members because "no member is entitled to be paid twice, both by ASCAP and DMX for the same licensing rights." It is estimated that the members' windfall could include up to a "40 % premium above the royalty payments they would otherwise receive from ASCAP. By increasing the surplus income to publishers whose works are performed by DMX, but have not entered in direct licenses with DMX, ASCAP provided even less of an incentive for publishers to join the DMX program." Publishers now had to weigh the costs versus the benefits of a 40 % premium from ASCAP or the revenue stream from DMX's licensing pool.

---

[8]See BMI vs. DMX (2010); Cardi (2007); Christman (2014b); Meredith Corp. v. SESAC LLC (2014); Patry (2011); RMLC v. SESAC (2013); Robertson (2011); US vs. ASCAP & In Re Capstar (DMX) (2010).

[9]See AFJ2 (2001); BMI vs. DMX (2010); US vs. ASCAP & In Re Capstar (DMX) (2010).

Table 5.2 Economic demands and structural barriers to entry in the music industry

Economic demands	Terms	Disadvantages	Selected demands faced by DMX
Entrenched PRO licensing	Only blanket or per-program available No carve-outs permitted until now	With PRO market power it is, "take it or leave" it for music users	Required litigation to obtain an AFBL or direct license
General deal structure	Pay the largest of: (A) Pro-rata share of min. of \$X/sub. (B) Per-play costs at \$Y per play (C) Z % of total company revenue (D) Flat Fee	Labels & PROs de facto set retail prices which limit the ability of music service to develop ancillary revenue streams	ASCAP used different Form licenses for retail and non-retail BG/FG locations License fee varies from per location to % of music service "gross billings" ASCAP abandons flat fee when it no longer benefits for a different method of calculating an annual fee Organic growth beyond a certain percentage required additional fees
Equity stake	Labels get partial ownership of the company	Labels get to set the price of the service and they also get partial ownership	–
Insider collusion	PROs prevent major publishers from signing direct licenses due to strong affiliation	Music users unable to secure rights to certain popular catalogs	Independent publishers willing to sign MCCLs only after major publishers' deals[b]
Boycotts	Music users denied the right to use music in agencies' repertories	Alternative music sources required, if available	DMX's restricted use of ASCAP's and BMI's repertory
Up-front payments	Large amounts of cash payments are necessary	May stifle innovation in services & business models	Sony's MCCL included a recoupable \$2.7 million[a] "non-returnable/non-refundable" advance
Detailed reporting	Labels make additional demands such as overall market share reports, unrelated to payments to artists	The labels effectively offload their business analysis and the cost of such analysis onto the music services	BMI required monthly reporting, but the court permitted quarterly accounting DMX promised publishers more detailed reporting of music performances than they received from PROs
Data normalization	Some labels provide their data in different formats	No standard method or format for referencing artists, tracks, and albums It is the responsibility of the music services	Initial overhead costs for administering AFBL may be borne by one party

Publishing deals	Deals require both record label & publisher approval	Services may have the rights to stream from labels, but unable to get the publisher rights May have unknown copyright holders	Unidentified works split using PRO share of DMX's performances Refusals by labels to renew MCCLs
Most favored nation	This could be a form of collusion since each label gets the best terms that other labels negotiate One label provides low-cost terms knowing others will demand higher rates, then benefits from the higher rates	This constricts the ability to work out unique contractual terms and further limits business models	The MFN clause in DMX's MCCL requires the same royalty rate for all publishers BMI offered Universal $1.875 million to prevent a direct licensing agreement with DMX
Non-disclosure asymmetrical information	Strict language prohibiting music services from revealing payments to labels Labels receive payments for all entitled parties	Disclosing licensing terms could jeopardize or invalidate license deal Music services cannot reveal payments to songwriters One party has more or better information than others	DMX can reveal the Sony MCCL agreement, but terms & advance are confidential
Publisher/Label mergers	Completely new or different negotiation terms	Substantial catalogs can be pulled to force a renegotiation	–
Artist holdouts	Denial of access to new albums	Holdouts until massive royalties or advances are paid	–
Litigation	Rate court settles party disputes	Resources tied up in lengthy & costly legal proceedings as new competitors & technologies emerge Costs often exceed benefits	Increased operating costs as competitors[c] replaced BG/FG music providers by using iPods to create playlists Retailers using their own storage devices to create playlists Competition from Internet-based commercial streaming services Increased competition affects DMX's rates and revenue

[a]This is a significant cost of entry. The court noted that there is little to no likelihood that DMX would recoup its $2.7 million advance from its $25 per location royalty rate even by increasing the percentage of music use from the Sony catalog, an MCCL extension through September 2012 or increasing revenue by securing more locations.
[b]The four major music publishers controlled approx. Eighty percent of the market in 2010 and in 2007 only Sony had signed with DMX.
[c]New competitors include Activaire, Audiostiles, Gray V & Music Styling.
Sources: Based on data from BMI vs. DMX (2010); Robertson (2011); US vs. ASCAP & In Re Capstar (DMX) (2010).

Table 5.3 DMX growth in direct licensing deals 2006–2010

	2006	2007	2008	2009	2010[a]
Signed agreements	65	50	150	300	250
Cumulative		115	265	565	815

Source: Based on data from US vs. ASCAP & In Re Capstar (DMX) (2010).
[a]As of September 2010.

In a blatant attempt at insider collusion and a violation of its consent decree, "ASCAP's John LoFrumento actively tried to discourage the CEOs of Universal and Sony from entering into MCCL agreements." "Universal Music decided not to enter a direct license agreement with DMX only after being offered $1.875 million in guarantees from BMI." Recall that music publishers are members or affiliates of both ASCAP and BMI. In addition, these same publishers are board members that govern those PRO organizations. Failing to prevent some publishers from signing direct licenses with DMX, BMI demanded refunds of royalty payments made to some publishers during their direct license period with DMX if they renewed their direct licenses with DMX. The typical term for an MCCL lasts about 3 years. Perhaps, sensing the direction of music licensing in 2011 and innovative business models by independent labels like Kobalt, Sony was the only major music publisher that entered into an MCCL agreement with DMX. The MFN clause in the DMX's MCCL agreements requires that the same formula and the per-location rate used to calculate royalty payments are used for all publishers.

More recently, it has been reported that the Department of Justice was investigating the alleged "coordination" or collusion among ASCAP, BMI, Sony/ATV Music Publishing, and Universal Music Publishing Group following allegations made by Pandora during its rate court trial that "the major music publishers and the PROs were working together to make changes to ASCAP and BMI by-laws that would allow for partial withdrawals, yielding higher performance royalty rates for all music publishers."[10]

The MCCL is essentially an adjustable fee blanket (AFB) license with "carve-outs" for the licensing fees already paid by members of DMX's licensing pool. Table 5.3 shows the growth trajectory of DMX's direct licensing deals, from 65 signed agreements in 2006 to 815 by September of 2010. The courts later agreed with DMX's argument that the blanket licensing fees it pays to ASCAP and BMI should be reduced accordingly to reflect the licensing fees already paid to the copyright holders in its licensing pool. In ruling in favor of DMX, the courts recognized that both ASCAP and BMI abused their monopoly powers and tried to prevent an innovation from reaching the market with their anti-competitive licensing rates.

[10]See Christman (2014a).

5.2 Simplicity in Pricing

Liebowitz and Margolis (2009) have argued that when "a carve-out occurs, it is necessary to determine how much the blanket license payment should be reduced to account for those songs that are negotiated outside the blanket license and there is no obvious way to do this." In addition, "relying principally on the testimony of its expert economist, ASCAP contended that they cannot be required to issue a blanket license with a carve-out because no willing seller would ever offer such an license."[11] However, the rate court and DMX found a way to compute a "per-location" blanket fee with a carve-out using a simple formula:[12]

$$\text{Per-Location Fee} = \text{FF} + (\text{UMF} \times (\%)\ \text{Share Licensed by PRO}),$$

where FF is a floor fee or minimum that DMX pays for a PRO license even if all the music DMX performs are from its direct licensing pool. The floor fee is designed to compensate the PROs for the [economic] value they create in administering the blanket license. UMF is the unbundled music fee, which is the value of the performance rights for a PRO music performed by DMX or its licensees. The UMF is calculated using an industry per-location benchmark that is adjusted for DMX's mechanical and performance licensing mix.

To give DMX a discount for its MCCL program, the UMF is multiplied by the share of DMX performances of PROs licensed music. DMX provided actual marketplace rates for music performance rights when licensed in individual transactions with music publishers in its licensing pool. These rates proved to be significantly lower than the fee levels sought by ASCAP and BMI under their prevailing blanket license fee structures. Table 5.4 shows the PRO share of music content used in DMX's UMF calculations. DMX's customers used 48 % of the works controlled by ASCAP and 40 % of the music compositions in BMI's repertory. Under the MCCL agreements, music publishers have granted DMX several rights in their musical compositions in exchange for a pro-rata share of the $25 per location royalty pool. Like ASCAP, DMX estimates that approximately 10 % of its royalty pool is attributable to the grant of mechanical rights as opposed to the public performance right. Thus, "the royalty pool for public performance rights is limited to $22.50 per location."[13]

"The $22.50 figure is further adjusted to reflect ASCAP's share of total performances on the DMX network. DMX concluded that 48 % of its customer's performances were of works owned or controlled by ASCAP members. Consequently, DMX proposed that the unbundled music fee should be $10.74 per location.

[11] See US vs. ASCAP & In Re Capstar (DMX) (2010).

[12] See BMI vs. DMX (2010); US vs. ASCAP & In Re Capstar (DMX) (2010).

[13] See US vs. ASCAP & In Re Capstar (DMX) (2010).

This measurement includes all of ASCAP's music, whether DMX obtained a direct license for the music."[14]

$$\text{Licensing Fee} = \text{FF} + \text{UMG}$$
$$\$13.74 = (\$3) + (\$10.74)$$

For example in ASCAP's rate court settlement shown in Table 5.4, DMX's licensing fee is computed as follows $3 in floor fee (FF) and $10.74 in unbundled music fee (UMF) for a total of $13.74 per location.

In setting direct licensing fees, the courts recognized BMI's and ASCAP's inefficiencies by noting that in their desire for monopoly pricing (pricing way above the marginal cost) in a controlled market, the PROs rarely, if ever, *lowered* licensing fees, reduced access to copyrighted works and often raised the costs and barriers of doing business for music users with their pricing policies. Technology lowered the PROs' production costs, there were mass layoffs and office closings and yet none of these activities appeared to have had the intended effect of lowering the costs of music users in obtaining a performance blanket license. Both ASCAP and BMI's pricing were truly disconnected from the costs in a competitive marketplace.

5.3 Competition Lowers Transaction Costs

In the case of firms operating in a competitive environment and a difficult economy, there is always a concern about survival and the need to reduce costs in order to be more efficient and profitable in the marketplace. After emerging out of bankruptcy, DMX sought to reduce the transaction costs associated with the licensing of performance rights in the commercial music services (CMS) industry by seeking to lower the royalty rates charged by ASCAP and BMI. Those rates were not reflective of the competitive CMS industry facing difficult economic challenges, product substitutions, and other technological issues.

ASCAP's direct license fee proposal, which was rejected by the court, reduced DMX's license fees by the annual fixed amount paid to its direct licensors. The ASCAP fee proposal did not allow for reduced payments based on the proportion of music used from the ASCAP catalog. DMX would have to absorb the cost of its MCCL program, and ASCAP's blanket license fees and administration costs. The court concluded that DMX could only reduce its public performance licensing fees by reducing the number of its direct licenses or by canceling ASCAP's blanket license altogether and relying solely on its directly licensed music that would have limited the marketing potential and revenue of the music service.[15] DMX's pricing structure for the unbundled music fee paid to music publishers in the MCCL pool

[14] See US vs. ASCAP & In Re Capstar (DMX) (2010).

[15] See US vs. ASCAP & In Re Capstar (DMX) (2010).

Table 5.4 DMX music use share and fee settlement 2010

PRO	Share (%)	Proposed fee	Settlement	Diff.	Change (%)
ASCAP	48	$49.00	$13.74	$35.26	72
BMI	40	$41.81	$18.91	$22.90	55
Total		$90.81	$32.65	$58.16	64

Source: Based on data from BMI vs. DMX (2010); US vs. ASCAP & In Re Capstar (DMX) (2010).

was straightforward and open. In the case of ASCAP, "DMX calculated a floor fee of $3 per location. This represented the combination of $2.14 for BG/FG music service specific expenses and $0.86 in allocated general overhead expenses. Both of these numbers were derived from ASCAP's own records and the allocation methodology of ASCAP expenses associated with the BG/FG industry."[16]

DMX identified the appropriate benchmark for the unbundled music fee as the rate paid to those music publishers who have joined DMX's direct license program. In its price discovery, DMX's own market data were used in determining "reasonable" licensing fees in both ASCAP's and BMI's rate court proceedings. Both rate courts adopted DMX's pricing proposals for an AFB license in which credit was granted for the direct licenses secured by DMX in its licensing pool. As Table 5.4 shows the rate court rulings set the background music blanket fee for DMX at significantly lower rates than those proposed by the two dominant incumbent PROs. Instead of paying the PRO industry rate of $90.81 per location that ASCAP and BMI demanded, DMX lowered its music licensing costs through its MCCL agreements to $32.65, a 64 % reduction. DMX was able to reduce its costs through direct licensing. In both lower court cases, the courts found ASCAP and BMI's pricing to be anti-competitive. In other words, both ASCAP and BMI were using their relative market power to charge more for music licensing than the competitive pricing obtained by DMX. It is worth emphasizing that it was only direct competition (economic rivalry) from DMX, aided by the antitrust rulings that compelled the two dominant PROs in the market to lower the cost of obtaining a license.[17]

5.4 Flexibility

"The MCCL provides DMX with a broader scope of rights than it would otherwise receive under an ASCAP or BMI public performance license agreement."[18] One key feature of DMX's MCCL is that *both* the performance and mechanical rights are

[16]See US vs. ASCAP & In Re Capstar (DMX) (2010).

[17]SESAC is a distant third in terms of affiliates, copyrighted songs and market share, but their repertory may not be as negligible as they are often treated in the industry.

[18]See US vs. ASCAP & In Re Capstar (DMX) (2010).

granted to DMX at the same time adding flexibility and efficiency to the licensing process. "The MCCL provides DMX not only with the right to publicly perform musical works in the publisher's catalog [normally obtained from ASCAP, BMI and SESAC], it also grants DMX a non-exclusive right to reproduce, distribute, and edit such works to eliminate offensive lyrics that customers may find objectionable (a mechanical right that would be obtained from the Harry fox agency (HFA))."[19] This flexibility further lowered the administration, transaction, and marketing costs for DMX by reducing the number of intermediaries (PROs and the HFA) involved in copyright administration.

5.5 Drawback of MCCL Upfront Payments and Recoupment

There are two major problems with directly licensing music and both concern music publishers/record labels control over royalty payments and disbursement that could badly hurt recording artists and songwriters if songwriters and composers are not protected in future changes to consent decrees and the *Copyright Act.* The first problem is the upfront advance payments—sometimes referred to as unallocated advances that are not tied to a particular song or songs—made by music users such as Pandora and DMX to music publishers and record labels in exchange for granting a license to play the songs in their respective catalogs. Although the rate courts were not erroneous in treating the $2.7 million advance payment made by DMX to Sony as a cost of entry into the market, the payment may have had a negative impact on the income of songwriters and composers because of the co-mingling of royalty payments. Co-mingling of performance royalty payments is not an issue with PROs such as ASCAP and BMI because their songwriters and music publishers are paid *directly* using a 50/50 split of collected licensing fees after a deduction for administration costs. Gordon (2014) writes that it is doubtful whether Sony's writers received any portion of the DMX advance paymemt because publishers generally do not have to share such monies with their songwriters and composers for the following reason:

> 'Individual music publishing contracts vary depending on the bargaining power of individual writers or the negotiating skills of their lawyers (among other reasons), but almost all agreements have a provision similar to this one: "In no event shall composer be entitled to share in any advance payments, guarantee payments or minimum royalty payments which Publisher may receive in connection with any sub publishing agreement, collection agreement, licensing agreement or other agreements… "The rationale for this clause is that if a publisher secures an advance for all of its songs it should not have to share that money with each songwriter. But the clause did not contemplate direct licenses by publishers for performing rights… However, if publishers are allowed to enter into direct licenses, this clause would allow the advances to fall into publishers' coffer."

[19]See US vs. ASCAP & In Re Capstar (DMX) (2010).

More recently, it was reported that in a confidential licensing contract between Sony and Spotify that was leaked to the media, Sony received advances totaling $42.5 million and $9 million in advertising credits, which it was free to resell at a profit. It was unclear whether artists, songwriters, or publishers were going to share in the revenue.[20]

The second problem is that of advance payments made by a music publisher or record label to an artist that is subjected to recoupment. Recoupment is the music industry practice of recovering the advance (initial upfront record label investment), recording, video production, promotion, marketing, tour support, equipment and other expenses associated with a song from the recording artist's royalty income. Advances can often leave a recording artist, even a successful one, owing hundreds of thousands of dollars to a record label. In general, the artists are paid only after the record labels have recovered these expenses (which may take years before it is repaid), and most artists may never achieve the level of record sales required to repay those expenses. Cash advances work more as a "loan" (and with it, there is long-term financial and debt implications) to the singer-songwriter, may involve terms of exclusivity, and the record label keeps the artist's royalties until the advance is repaid.[21]

Recoupable expenses can affect both new and established artists. For example, if recoupable expenses and multiple reductions are $10,000 and the royalty rate is $1 per record sold, and the artist only sold 9,000 units of records worth $9,000, the account is said to be in *deficit* and the label is owed $1,000. The artist would not have earned any royalties from the recording label. Yet the record label would have earned the wholesale cost multiplied by 9,000. The publisher could then recoup the remaining $1,000 from the proceeds of direct licensing, or past and future albums in what is called *cross-collateralization* of a deal. While substantial sums of money may have been generated from record sales for established artists, a tremendous amount of money (that cannot all be recovered from royalties) is often spent on recording and video production, ultra-expensive touring costs for live performances, a large entourage of personal assistants, poor financial and management advice and personal habits that are all contributing factors to why so many established artists file for bankruptcy protection. Songwriters may sometimes switch to other music publishers, but their past recordings may remain with the original publisher.[22]

For some artists waiting for a breakthrough to occur in their chosen field, the emotional and often romanticized image of the artist starving for the love of art, the so-called starving artist comes to mind. Whether it is voluntary or involuntary, these are the artists whose prospects of future financial reward or broad recognition have gone unfulfilled. However, without income and other financial resources from their musical creations needed to make them excel, these struggling musicians are

---

[20]See *Spotify's Video Play*, Billboard Magazine, May 30, 2015, p. 16.

[21]See Passman (2012, pp. 83–87).

[22]See Passman (2009, pp. 79–83).

often forced to consider temporary and other non-musical careers in the services' sector (as bartenders, waiters, secretaries, etc.) to pay their bills further diminishing their musical aspirations. In some cases, advances are *non-returnable* which means that if an artist does not sell enough records, the record label absorbs the risk. The non-returnable aspect is significant in another financial aspect for the songwriter: It means that advances are taxable income when received by the songwriter as opposed to when they are recouped.[23] On the other hand, a songwriter's income derived from performance royalties is generally not recoupable from advances and other recording royalties because PROs payments are made directly to the songwriter. Indeed, this is one of the advantages of being a member or affiliate of a PRO because music publishers/record labels have no control over the songwriter's or composer's share of performance royalties that could be used for recoupment purposes. PRO royalty payments are made following song title registration and the collection of performance data. For some songwriters and composers, this may be the only income that they would ever receive from their copyright ownership due to the industry's recoupment practices.

In the past, most of the fixed capital investment costs—and a significant barrier to entry, not just for struggling musicians but other artists such as those in film, theater and the visual arts as well—of producing a record, including the advance, marketing and promotions costs, were sunk upfront in producing the first physical copy. It may have taken years before the capital costs were recovered from vinyl records, CD sales, or other copyright exploitation. Indeed, the old business model consisted of a few recording artists with major hits subsidizing the majority of other artists who feared poorly in record sales.[24] With digital recordings, the costs of printing up booklets, manufacturing CDs, packaging and product shipment were eliminated, yet some of these costs in older recording contracts were still being recouped by the record labels for digital distribution and delivery.[25]

---

[23]See Passman (2009, pp. 79–83), Jefferson (2010).

[24]See *Economic Characteristics of Music Production*, Pitt (2010a, pp. 9–14) and Grant and Wood (2004, pp. 43–92).

[25]See Thall (2006, pp.17–21).

See also these readily available online articles.

RIAA Accounting: Why Even Major Label Musicians Rarely Make Money From Album Sales here: http://www.techdirt.com/articles/20100712/23482610186.shtml.

Wixen (2014, pp. 152–153) discuses why auditing a record company is necessary.

In addition, the following two online articles contain separate links to court documents filed by singers Brad Paisley, Kelly Clarkson, Carrie Underwood, and others in their lawsuits on allegations that Sony Music has been systematically robbing them of millions of dollars in royalties.

See *Bombshell "American Idol" Lawsuit Claims Sony Stiffs Carrie Underwood, Kelly Clarkson (Exclusive)* that is available here:

http://www.hollywoodreporter.com/thr-esq/bombshell-american-idol-lawsuit-claims-681625.

The link to the Clarkson court document (*19 Recordings Limited vs Sony Entertainment*) appears here:

http://www.hollywoodreporter.com/sites/default/files/custom/Documents/ESQ/American_Idol_Clarkson.pdf.

5.6 Limitations of PRO Sample Survey Methodologies

Historically, the PROs relied on statistical sampling techniques to obtain a universal count of musical performances on thousands of radio stations and avoid the enormous expense of obtaining a national count of *all* performances. This was the issue in 1941 when ASCAP boycotted radio stations to extract higher licensing fees based on audience size after US Federal Courts ruled that radio stations could play records they had purchased. The court rulings cleared the way for the modern radio format of disc jockeys playing records. Back then the national association of broadcasters (NAB) claimed that they had no clear means to accurately quantify the audience size of their radio station members in the United States.[26]

Critics have long complained that there is little or no transparency when it comes to the way in which PROs monitor and track music performances. Holden (2001) writes, "further, and perhaps even more significant, is the *unpublished nature* of the substance and functions of PRO samples, surveys and other monitoring methodologies. In a digital age, how statistically accurate are the methods employed by our PROs? What percentage of American music broadcasts are actually monitored and paid, and what percentage is ignored? As it is, no such reports are available to members and affiliates of America's PRO's. Simply put—we know very little about the statistical effectiveness of music performance administration in the United States."[27] Hutchinson (1999) in a speech cites several reasons for the industry old practice of paying artists months or sometimes years after a performance. "It is a lot easier to sit back and earn interest on the float of money that PROs hold than to pay it out quickly and accurately, and continental societies believe they can keep their members' loyalty by the use of social and cultural deductions from Anglo-American royalties to line the pockets of their own members." Cash versus the accrual system of accounting is often exploited for the advantage of PRO administration, and not necessarily for the benefit of their members and affiliates.

Country Superstar Brad Paisley Sony Music Stole $10 Million From Me! appears here: http://radaronline.com/exclusives/2014/04/brad-paisley-lawsuit-sony-music-10-million-dollars/.
The link to the Paisley court document (*Brad Paisley vs Sony Entertainment*) in a PDF format appears here: http://amradaronline.files.wordpress.com/2014/04/pasileybb.pdf.
In particular, the Paisley court document contains an extensive list of accounting items necessary for conducting an audit of the record label royalty payment process.
The author has not seen disputed-earnings lawsuits similar to ones mentioned above in which well-known songwriters or composers have sued their PROs for alleged fraud, intentional malfeasance, corruption, theft, conflict of interests, and underpayment of royalties—when such an audit is justifiable—and those lawsuits received national attention in the trade press.
Perhaps, some of the PRO lawsuits were settled privately and the details of these "convenient mistakes" were not made public, or songwriters may not have exercised their right to an audit, pursuant to licensing agreements, if such an agreement existed.
It is not uncommon for PROs to audit the books of music users in their pursuit of royalty revenue.

[26]See Murphy (2014, pp. 74–76).

[27]Emphasis added.

With the widespread use of digital fingerprinting, it is now possible to get a 100 % census of all musical performances. There is no longer the need to rely on a flawed statistical sampling survey methodology, extrapolations from surveys, elaborate weighting formulas and generally dubious "economic multipliers" that only provide a partial, limited, arbitrary or untimely count of musical performances. Unlike the banking industry's money multipliers—in which the transmission process between bank reserves and the money supply in credit creation that varies with economic and financial conditions is fully understood and studied—it is often difficult to understand the velocity conditions associated with PRO's economic multipliers. How exactly did these opaque multipliers vary when there were quarterly fluctuations (lags in performance data collection and song title registrations, changes in music users' programming schedules and disputes over royalty payment) in musical performances or changes in the depleted amount of money in a royalty pool available for distribution? The material effects of inflated gains or losses on songwriters' royalty income with the use of these multipliers—when compared to alternative methods—have not been properly assessed by independent and competent economists and the results published in peer-reviewed academic journals.

Limited sample surveys often miss the unexpected and abrupt changes in radio formats such as when stations change ownership, or when television networks preempt regularly scheduled programming for entertainment specials, news events and natural disasters that do not appear in program listings. In addition, the sudden death of a popular singer/songwriter (like Michael Jackson) results in an upsurge in musical performances on radio and television of the songwriter's works that are not immediately captured in limited surveys. Even if the upsurge is later captured, invariably, the increased performances shrink the royalty pool of available funds for distribution so that other songwriters who would have been paid more in the period would now receive less income. All of which can often result in huge fluctuations in quarterly royalty payments and the source of bitter complaints by copyright holders, even as shown in Table 4.2 on page 131 that there was a steady growth in PRO licensing fees over time, except for 2010.

The huge fluctuations (over and under payments to copyright holders) in quarterly payments, even when known musical performances were held constant, often lead to budgeting problems and other royalty disputes for copyright holders such as television networks (Univision and Disney to cite just two) with their own music publishing divisions. These networks employ their own songwriters and composers and they are featured prominently in the networks' daily music programming schedule. The networks have an excellent idea of the amount of money paid for a blanket license (a percentage of their revenue), and the amount the publishing division and their songwriters and composers ought to be receiving in performance royalties based on their internally known number of musical performances in a period and on historical royalty payments. Roughly, the networks conduct a crosscheck in which their publishing subsidiaries expect to receive performance royalties at a minimum somewhere near the amount paid in blanket licensing fees less PRO overhead expenses. These networks would be the first ones to notice anomalies in accounting, royalty computation and the steep rise in PRO overhead expenses, and are in the position of seeking a complete forensic, managerial, and accounting audit of PRO practices.

Overpaying one set of copyright holders—due to accounting errors and manipulated multiplier effects in payment formulas—shrinks the pool of available royalty payments and that means that other copyright holders may be underpaid in a given period. Clawing back overpayments to copyright holders is wrought with the danger of exposing accounting practices because the copyright holders find it incredulous that a licensing agency in business for decades can make such critical accounting errors and it could remain undetected. The threats of litigation and a *forensic audit* when clawback claims are made are usually enough to quickly settle such embarrassing situations. It was also not uncommon for struggling songwriters and composers to seek short-term financial assistance (an *advance* from the PROs) against future royalty income to offset the decrease in royalty income from inadvertent, irregular or unintentional accounting errors due to the convoluted payment formulas. Accounting errors that could easily be spotted by well-trained, in-house statisticians conducting periodical reviews, and proper managerial and accounting audits conducted to validate the methodology used in the computation of royalty payments. For example, ASCAP uses a sample survey of 60,000 h of taped 6-h radio segments that are combined with MediaGuide's detected airplay data and other measures to determine radio performances as outlined in ASCAP's *Survey and Distribution System: Rules & Policies.*[28] Given the thousands of radio stations, some have questioned whether such a sample is truly reflective of radio performances, given the sample bias that may exist. Large (urban and popular) radio stations that pay more in licensing revenue to ASCAP are weighted more heavily than smaller stations, and are invariably sampled more often than other stations. This system favors the songwriters and composers who get heavy airplay in ASCAP's survey sample, and benefits the established and already successful songwriters. For example, at ASCAP, performances that occurred in April–June of 2011, publishers were not paid until December 2011, while writers were paid in January of 2012, 6 months or more after a performance.[29] The income potential from performance royalties for struggling niche songwriters is diminished if stations playing their music are excluded from the surveys.[30]

As was shown previously in Table 4.3 on page 132, ASCAP collected $118,420,000 in general licensing fees in 2010 and you can be sure that the same retail outlets required blanket licenses from BMI and SESAC for the use of music from their respective repertoires. General licensing is the licensing of retail outlets, bars, restaurants, and other venues in which licensing fees are collected, but the PROs never obtain music performance data. These retail outlets were considered

[28]See http://www.ascap.com/~/media/Files/Pdf/members/payment/drd.ashx.

[29]http://www.ascap.com/members/payment/payment.aspx.

[30]Many recording artists and copyright holders are now calling for changes in the anachronistic legislation and policies in the various consent decrees to make sure that all music users are monitored by a digital fingerprinting service to eliminate the flawed sample surveys.

non-surveyed and royalty income was allocated using the same formulas for radio, television, and other surveyed media. National chain stores with thousands of retail outlets across the country often vary their BG/FG musical selections depending on the geography, local market tastes, and demographics of their customers. Using television and radio proxies to allocate general licensing fees is often inaccurate in fairly capturing music use and it benefits popular songwriters whose music is performed on radio and television. The cost savings from not having to collect musical performance data from tens of thousands of bar, restaurants, hotels, and retail outlets should have been a significant factor in lowering the cost of obtaining a direct license with a carve-out.

5.7 Digital Fingerprinting, Transparency and Efficiency

Performance or airplay tracking using *digital fingerprinting* has now made it easier and cheaper to track performances or airplay. Digital fingerprinting has also significantly reduced the costs of collecting the billions and billions of music performances and identifying song titles. Digital fingerprinting has also eroded one of the original rationales for granting PROs a natural monopoly: The manual process of collecting song title registration, performance data, matching song titles to copyright holders and computing royalty payments. It is worth noting here that under the traditional blanket license (excluding the per-program license) issued by ASCAP and BMI, it is ASCAP's and BMI's responsibility to monitor and keep track of music performances and usage, not the music users. In the past, this was often a huge undertaking and the means to survey hundreds of thousands retail outlets would have been cost prohibitive.

All digital audio files have their own unique signal or fingerprint, and DMX utilizes this feature to track performances via its off-premise DBS transmissions. It is here that DMX exploited the inefficiencies of the incumbent PROs' distribution and royalty allocation process in its model. The same technology can be used to monitor signals transmitted from terrestrial radio, satellite radio, television stations, and cable networks or the Internet to track distribution platforms and sales, and identify music use content. In terms of accuracy, it is easier and more efficient to use digital fingerprinting technology to identify millions of song titles and songwriters. DMX provides music programming to its retail customers through either an "off-premise" or an "on-premise" delivery system. The off-premise delivery system involves the transmission of music to the customer premise using direct broadcast satellite (DBS) technology. The on-premise delivery service involves a proprietary playback device installed at the customer's premise that is updated through a CD, DVD, or network connection.[31]

[31] See US vs. ASCAP & In Re Capstar (DMX) (2010).

As part of its MCCL, DMX reports to BMI the identity of each piece of music broadcast over its off-premise channels, and the songs sent to its on-premise equipment.[32] This is a huge cost saving for the PROs in which they do not have to monitor each DMX retail location for BG/FG music performances. Furthermore, DMX provides an accurate count of performance data at its retail outlets, and there is no longer the need to use radio and television performances and fee data to allocate royalty payments for general licensing purposes. New firms like BigChampagne monitor social network sites and include such music performance data in their metrics. BigChampagne[33] is another independent media measurement firm for external performance data that can be used to augment PRO performance data collected from mostly television cue sheets and radio station logs that often exclude music performed elsewhere.

A digital fingerprint is a unique international standard recording code (ISRC) that is encoded at the mastering stage of the recording with tags or metadata descriptors such as song title, recording artists, songwriters, composers, record label, music publisher, genre, version and other bits of descriptive data. All of the information that PROs use to match performances to song title registrations is new being embedded in a digital fingerprint and this eliminates another PRO inefficiency. The digital fingerprint and its associated metadata descriptors remain with an individual recorded track forever, regardless of changes in ownership. Each recorded variation (the jazzy version, for example) of the same track can have its own unique digital fingerprint. When consumers purchase a single song instead of a full-length album or a single article instead of an entire newspaper, the basic unit of content consumption is now referred to as the "atomic unit of consumption."[34] Therefore, a digital fingerprint to a song can be used as an atomic unit of consumption in which the metadata could include royalty rates for mechanical, performance and synchronization in place at the time and with periodic rate changes to be included at a later date.

The immediate benefits of digital fingerprinting—from the metadata that travels with a digital file that is not music itself—are apparent. First, digital fingerprinting reduces human error in the time-consuming process of tracing song title identification, particularly when unknown or unregistered works are collected in various statistical samples conducted by the PROs. Royalty payments, in most cases, are never paid for unregistered song titles even when performed as a part of a broadcast. Second, digital fingerprinting provides access to performance data that was not readily available outside of PROs. This is useful for developing an audit trail to verify discrepancies that may occur with the use of statistical sampling techniques and deliberately confusing "economic multipliers" as discussed above. Finally, digital fingerprinting speeds up the processing of performance data. This makes it easier for copyrights holders to be paid sooner and closer to actual performance dates.

---

[32]See BMI vs. DMX (2010).

[33]BigChampagne is owned by Live Nation Entertainment.

[34]See Patry (2011).

5.8 Publishers and Music Users Bypassing PROs

Music publishers were in the process of partially withdrawing digital rights from ASCAP and BMI, pending changes to the various consent decrees signed by ASCAP and BMI. In turn, music publishers would negotiate direct licensing agreements with music users and thus force music users to pay higher licensing fees than the ones charged by the PROs for a blanket license.[35] The digital withdrawal rights movement is controversial because it allows publishers to withdraw the digital rights to licensed works in a PRO's repertory for a class of new media users such as Pandora, Spotify, and YouTube, while permitting the remaining musical compositions in PRO's repertories to be licensed to traditional (old) media users such as radio and television. However, in separate rate court rulings, the two judges who preside over ASCAP's and BMI's consent decrees have indicated that the consent decrees may not permit the partial withdrawal of music copyrights by music publishers in order to negotiate higher licensing fees with other music services. In other words, music publishers must withdraw *all* musical works or nothing at all. The music publishers' withdrawal movement bypassing PROs, whether whole or in part, is now being seen as the beginning of the end of performing rights organizations.[36]

The motivation to do direct deals is driven by the increasingly antiquated Copyright Act, the licensing fees charged by PROs to administer performance rights on behalf of music publishers, the disparity (more like a distortion) between rates for the sound recording and performance rights, and the desire to ensure that songwriters are fairly compensated for their creative output based on transparent market rates. In addition, by removing the middle layer of PROs, music publishers can lower the substantial administration fee, estimated around 11–13 % of collected licensing revenue, that the PROs charge to cover their overhead and administrative expenses.[37]

It is generally believed (by music publishers) that ASCAP and BMI, which operate under consent decrees and compulsory licensing may be hamstrung in getting a market rate from music services like Pandora. However, a recent court ruling suggests that

[35]See *Scope of Digital Rights Withdrawal* at http://www.bmi.com/licensing/entry/drw.

[36]See BMI vs. Pandora Media Inc. (2013); Christman (2013a, 2014c); Sisario (2014); US vs. ASCAP & In re Petition of Pandora Media (2013); and *Section VI: The April 2011 ASCAP Compendium Modification*, and *Section VII: Second Compendium Modification in December 2012: the "Standard Services" Agreement* in US vs. ASCAP & In re Petition of Pandora Media (2014) for more analysis on the recent rate court rulings on the matter.

[37]See Brabec and Brabec (2011, p. 316), Christman (2013b).

> the CRB decided that the market for sound recording rights was materially different from the market for the public performance rights to musical compositions, and set rates for compulsory license fees for sound recordings at rates many times higher than the prevailing rates for the licensing of the public performance of the compositions. Consequently, Pandora pays over half of its revenue to record companies for their sound recording rights, and only approximately 4 % to the PROs for the public performance rights to their songs. "The disparity between rates for the public performance of compositions versus sound recordings does not exist for most of ASCAP's revenue streams since, as just explained, the need to acquire sound recording licenses only applies to services who conduct digital audio transmissions. Thus, there is no disparity at all when it comes to most of ASCAP's business, including its general licensing program and its licensing of cable TV, broadcast TV, and terrestrial radio. Because only new media music services must acquire sound recording licenses, the PROs end up receiving far more money from public performance rights license fees for compositions than do the record companies from public performance license fees for sound recordings."[38]

As summarized in Table 5.5 before the adverse court rulings on digital withdrawals, *Billboard Magazine* reported that Universal was to license its entire repertoire directly to streaming service Last.fm, sidestepping its previous arrangement with PPL, the collection agency in the United Kingdom. Sony granted DMX the performance and mechanical rights to its repertory, with certain exceptions. EMI was expected to withdraw certain performance rights previously represented by ASCAP in order to bundle its performance, mechanical and synchronization rights in a move to streamline licensing for digital music service providers. Some music users would not have been able to obtain a blanket license from ASCAP and may have had to obtain a direct license from EMI for the use of its repertory. Universal Music Publishing and BMG Chrysalis had notified ASCAP and BMI that they were no longer going to rely on the two performance rights organizations to negotiate digital performance licenses and royalty rates for music users. At the end of 2014, most of the major music publishers were expected to have withdrawn all of their digital rights from ASCAP and BMI. However, PROs were expected to still handle some of the performing rights administration functions other than licensing negotiations on behalf of some music publishers for a fee, that is less than the 11–13 % of revenue that the PROs typically charge for copyright administration.[39] At the time of writing, digital withdrawals were placed on hold, pending court action.[40]

In a yet another industry article on direct licensing, *Billboard Magazine* reported that SiriusXM, a digital music service, was attempting to directly license music from record labels, bypassing SoundExchange, a PRO. SoundExchange handles

---

[38]See US vs. ASCAP & In re Petition of Pandora Media (2014, pp. 38–39).

[39]See Christman (2011a); Christman et al. (2013); Smirke (2011); US vs. ASCAP & In Re Capstar (DMX) (2010). In 2012, following regulatory approval, EMI's music publishing and record label assets were acquired by Sony and Universal, respectively.

[40]See BMI vs. Pandora Media Inc. (2013); US vs. ASCAP & In re Petition of Pandora Media (2013, 2014).

Table 5.5 Selected music publishers direct licensing deals: expected year of digital withdrawal rights from PROs[a]

Publisher	Deal	ASCAP year	BMI year
Universal[b]	Will no longer rely on ASCAP and BMI to negotiate digital performance licenses and royalty rates	2013	2014
	Licenses Last.Fm directly for all tiers of service		
EMI	Bundles performance, mechanical and synchronization to streamline licensing for digital music service providers	2013	2013
	Direct licensing deal with Pandora		
Sony	Grants DMX performance and mechanical rights to entire Sony repertory, except for the Neil Diamond catalog	2013	2013
	Directly licenses music to Pandora		
BMG Chrysalis	Negotiated the option to withhold its digital performance rights from ASCAP and BMI, but undecided on its direct deal strategy	2013	2014
Warner/Chappell	Expects to withdraw all digital rights from PROs	2014	2014
Kobalt	Expects to withdraw all digital rights from PROs	2013	2014
All publishers (Who opt-in.)	Grants YouTube a direct license for synchronization rights[c] for musical works with videos posted by YouTube		
	Performance rights are not included	–	–

[a]Adverse court rulings have prevented the partial withdrawal of digital rights.
[b]At the time of writing when Universal Music was in the process of acquiring EMI's record label operations, while Sony was in the process of purchasing EMI's music publishing division, subject to a regulatory review.
[c]The HFA is the *license administrator*. See http://www.youtubelicenseoffer.com.

the performance rights for sound recordings, and as such collects performance royalties on behalf of record labels, musicians, and vocalists for certain digital audio performances on the Internet, and on satellite radio and television broadcasts. Recall from Fig. 3.1 on page 117 that ASCAP, BMI, and SESAC are collecting performance royalties only for songwriters, composers and publishers. For example, in moving to directly license *masters* (recordings), SiriusXM was seeking expanded licenses to add more music functionality such as allowing subscribers to record blocks of programming; to rewind and fast forward programming segments and cache music on local devices and applications. These added capabilities were to make sure that SiriusXM retained its customers base to compete with music services like Spotify and cloud-based music services.[41]

[41]See Christman (2011c).

New cloud services offered by music streaming services and others are now coming to market, and consumers may be willing to pay storage fees for unlimited access to their stored music. Consumers can create their own playlists and access them on multiple platforms. In one potential business model, music licensing fees are to be recovered from a paid subscription to cloud services using digital fingerprint information. It is expected that within a new regulatory framework songwriters can be paid fairly and directly by the music services without intermediaries such as PROs and record labels.

References

AFJ2 (2001). *Second Amended Final Judgment, US vs. ASCAP Civ. No.* 41 – 1395, S.D.N.Y. June, available online: http://www.ascap.com/~/media/Files/Pdf/members/governing-documents/ascapafj2.ashx, pp. 1–19.

BMI vs. DMX (2010). No: 08 Civ. 216 (LLS), S.D.N.Y. July 26, accessed online: http://www.leagle.com/decision/In%20FDCO%2020100727985.xml/BROADCAST%20MUSIC,%20INC.%20v.%20DMX,%20INC, pp. 1–33.

BMI vs. DMX, ASCAP vs. THP CAPSTAR (2012). No:10-3429-cv, 11-127-cv., US Court of Appeals, 2nd Cir. June, accessed online: http://www.ca2.uscourts.gov/decisions, pp. 1–47.

BMI vs. Pandora Media Inc. (2013). No: 13-cv-04037 (LLS), S.D.N.Y. December, accessed online: http://docs.justia.com/cases/federal/district-courts/new-york/nysdce/1:1964cv03787/58544/61/0.pdf?1387564284, pp. 1–14.

Brabec, J. and Brabec, T. (2011). *Music, Money and Success: The Insider's Guide To Making Money In The Music Industry*. Schirmer Trade Books-Music Sales, New York, NY.

Cardi, W. J. (2007). Über-middleman: Reshaping the broken landscape of copyright music. *Iowa Law Review*, 92:835–890.

Christman, E. (2011a). 'EMI Music Publishing Taking Over Licensing Digital Rights From ASCAP'. *Billboard Magazine*. May 3 issue, accessed online: http://www.billboard.biz, story:1005167992.

Christman, E. (2011b). 'Sirius' Direct-Licensing Efforts Come Under Attack From Recording Academy, AFTRA'. *Billboard Magazine*. October 27 issue, accessed online: http://www.billboard.biz, story:1005445642.

Christman, E. (2011c). 'SiriusXM Attempting to License Directly From Labels'. *Billboard Magazine*. August 11 issue, accessed online: http://www.billboard.biz, story:1005312752.

Christman, E. (2013a). 'Pandora Ruling Has Far-Reaching Implications For U.S. Publishing Industry'. *Billboard.com*. December 23, accessed online: http://www.billboard.com/biz/articles/news/publishing/5847835/pandora-ruling-has-far-reaching-implications-for-us-publishing.

Christman, E. (2013b). 'Universal Music Publishing Plots Exit From ASCAP, BMI'. *Billboard Magazine*. February 7 issue, accessed online: http://www.billboard.com/biz/articles/news/publishing/1537554/universal-music-publishing-plots-exit-from-ascap-bmi.

Christman, E. (2014a). 'Dept. of Justice Sends Doc Requests, Investigating UMPG, Sony/ATV, BMI and ASCAP Over Possible 'Coordination''. *Billboard Magazine*. July 13, accessed online: http://www.billboard.com/biz/articles/news/publishing/6157513/dept-of-justice-sends-doc-requests-investigating-umpg-sonyatv.

Christman, E. (2014b). 'SESAC Facing New Anti-Trust Legal Challenge'. *Billboard.com*. March 14, accessed online: http://www.billboard.com/biz/articles/news/publishing/5937426/sesac-facing-new-anti-trust-legal-challenge.

Christman, E. (2014c). 'Sony/ATV's Martin Bandier Repeats Warning to ASCAP, BMI'. *Billboard Magazine*. July 11, accessed online: http://www.billboard.com/biz/articles/news/publishing/6157469/sonyatvs-martin-bandier-repeats-warning-to-ascap-bmi.

Christman, E., Pham, A., and Peoples, G. (2013). 'Special Report: The Pandora Wars'. *Billboard Magazine*. August 10 issue. pp. 20–25.

Gordon, S. (2014). Direct Licensing Controversy: Will Publishers Be Able To License Public Performing Rights To Digital Music Services Directly (Instead of through the PROs) and What Are the Consequences for Songwriters? *Future of the Music Business*. May 27, accessed online: http://www.futureofthemusicbusiness.biz/2014/05/direct-licensing-controversy-will.html.

Grant, P. and Wood, C. (2004). *Blockbusters And Trade Wars: Popular Culture In A Globalized World*. Douglas and McIntyre, Vancouver, BC.

Holden, M. (2001). Where's the beef?: PRO policies and the non-disclosure of music usage in America. *Film Music Magazine*. April 11, accessed online: http://www.filmmusicmag.com/?p=644.

Hutchinson, J. (1999). Can collecting societies survive beyond the digital frontier? *Film Music Magazine*. January 11, accessed online: http://www.filmmusicmag.com/?p=647.

Jefferson, C. (2010). 'The Music Industry's Funny Money: The Great Divide: Who Is Getting Paid (And How Much) In The Music Industry'. *TheRoot.com*. July 6, accessed online: http://www.theroot.com/views/how-much-do-you-musicians-really-make?page=0,0&GT1=38002.

Liebowitz, S. and Margolis, S. (2009). Bundles of joy: The ubiquity and efficiency of bundles in new technology markets. *Journal of Competition Law and Economics*, 5(1):1–47.

Meredith Corp. v. SESAC LLC (2014). No: 09 Civ. 9177 (PAE), S.D.N.Y. March 3, accessed online: http://tvmlc.com/wp-content/uploads/2012/07/3_6_14-Court-Process-Decision.pdf, pp. 1–69.

Murphy, G. (2014). *Cowboys and Indies: The Epic History of the Record Industry*. St. Martin's Press.

Olson, C. (2012). Changing tides in music licensing? BMI vs. DMX & In Re THP. *Northwestern J. Technology & Intellectual Property*, 10(3):277–293. Accessed online: http://scholarlycommons.law.northwestern.edu/njtip/vol10/iss3/8note.

Passman, D. (2000). *All You Need To Know About The Music Business*. Simon & Schuster, fourth edition.

Passman, D. (2009). *All You Need To Know About The Music Business*. Simon & Schuster, seventh edition.

Passman, D. (2012). *All You Need To Know About The Music Business*. Simon & Schuster, eighth edition.

Patry, W. (2011). *How To Fix Copyright*. Oxford University Press, New York.

Pitt, I. L. (2010a). *Economic Analysis of Music Copyright: Income, Media and Performances*. Springer, New York. Available online: http://www.amazon.com/Economic-Analysis-Music-Copyright-Performances/dp/1441963170/ref=sr_1_1?s=books&ie=UTF8&qid=1417266944&sr=1-1&keywords=economic+analysis+of+music+copyright.

RMLC v. SESAC (2013). No: 12-cv-5807, E.D.P.A. December 20, accessed online: http://www.fhhlaw.com/RMLC%20v%20SESAC%20injunc%20decision.PDF, pp. 1–40.

Robertson, M. (2011). 'Why Spotify can never be profitable: The secret demands of record labels'. *GigaOm.com*. accessed online: http://gigaom.com/2011/12/11/why-spotify-can-never-be-profitable-the-secret-demands-of-record-labels.

Sisario, B. (2014). 'Sony Threatens to Bypass Licensers in Royalties Battle'. *New York Times*. July 11, p. B2.

Smirke, R. (2011). 'Universal Music Strikes Direct Licensing Deal With Last.fm'. *Billboard Magazine*. July 15, issue, accessed online: http://www.billboard.biz, story:1005279482.

Thall, P. (2006). *What They Will Never Tell You About the Music Business: The Myths, the Secrets, and the Lies (& a Few Truths)*. Billboard Books.

Towse, R. (2008). Why has cultural economics ignored copyright? *Journal of Cultural Economics*, 32:243–259.

US vs. ASCAP & In Re Capstar (DMX) (2010). No: 09 Civ. 7069 (DLC), S.D.N.Y. December 1, accessed online: http://www.leagle.com/decision/In%20FDCO%2020101209735, pp. 1–87.

US vs. ASCAP & In re Petition of Pandora Media (2013). No: 1:12-cv-08035-DLC, 41 Civ. 1395 (DLC), S.D.N.Y. October, accessed online: http://www.digitalmusicnews.com/uploads/77/9f/.../pandoravascap.pdf, pp. 1–30.

US vs. ASCAP & In re Petition of Pandora Media (2014). Nos: 12 Civ. 8035 (DLC), 41 Civ. 1395 (DLC), S.D.N.Y. March 14, accessed online: http://www.business.cch.com/ipld/PandoraUSASCAP031414.pdf, pp. 1–136.

Wixen, R. (2014). *The Plain & Simple Guide to Music Publishing*. Hal Leonard, third edition.

Chapter 6
Conclusion

Music is now an "information good" that must be experienced, and for the most part, is no longer distributed as a physical product. Music is now marketed as an on-demand or subscription service. The Internet has destroyed the analog business models of many intermediary players in the music industry, even though some players are still clinging to the old way of doing business in a digital world. In what some are calling it the next generation of database or "viral" marketing, many artists are now establishing direct marketing relationships with their fans through social media platforms such as Facebook, YouTube, Twitter, and online fan clubs to sell music, merchandise, concert tickets, and release video content.

Today's technologies provide an interconnected digital-media access across a wide variety of electronic platforms. The rapid decline in the price of music performance data collection and storage technologies made it cheaper and easier to collect and store indefinitely the vast amount of music performance data needed for computing royalty payments, doing away with one of the reasons for granting PROs their alleged monopoly status.

Unlike the old analog world, consumers now have many choices in which to listen to music such as using a computer or the Internet, watching television, purchasing a DVD, downloading a song from iTunes or using a mobile phone. Unfortunately, intellectual property laws from an earlier era have not evolved fast enough to reflect the different set of technological choices available to today's consumers that accommodate the flexibility of digital media, even with constant changing and updating of the Copyright Act. Patry (2011, p. 74) suggests that what is needed is a moratorium on new laws, a "fit-for-purpose" review of outdated copyright laws and the entire Copyright Act rewritten from scratch to reflect modern markets and rapid technological change.

The DMX rate court proceedings exposed the major flaws, incomplete and misleading information, dysfunctional licensing, and price distortion process in obtaining a blanket license. The music rights collecting agencies tried to prevent an innovation in the music industry through higher licensing (transaction) costs.

I.L. Pitt, *Direct Licensing and the Music Industry*,
DOI 10.1007/978-3-319-17653-6_6

ASCAP and BMI miscalculated in holding out for higher blanket licensing fees and placed roadblocks to prevent DMX from obtaining a direct license with a carve-out, and ironically revealed the music market's price-discovery process when there is no transparency and an open market. ASCAP's and BMI's roadblocks are strikingly illustrative of an industry in chaotic transition where "those who rely for their profits on inefficiencies in the exchange of information between creators and their audiences (and collaborators) will fight the revolutionary and uncontrollable transformation of their industries with every cent of rent-seeking capital at their disposal."[1] Without the use of Music Report's data and their independent song title registry, DMX would have lacked real pricing data and that could have resulted in unprofitable decisions.

DMX developed a direct licensing program (MCCL), an industry pricing benchmark and per-location pricing formula that provide greater transparency, accountability, efficiency, and access to market data that were previously unavailable. DMX prevailed because the various court rulings found ASCAP's and BMI's fees to be "unreasonable, extraordinary aggressive and strongly anti-competitive."[2] The PRO policy of making royalty payments 7–9 months (or longer in some cases) after the original airdate of a performance and a lengthy accounting schedule maybe some of the anachronisms that may soon fade away in the digital environment. The new music industry models now include transparent bookkeeping; auditing; online access to performance data and a faster royalty payment schedule. Without the free flow of accounting, financial and economic data, that are often buried in confidentiality agreements, it is hard to tell whether the PRO/record label's behavior is only self-serving or in the best interests of the songwriter.

The free flow of information is likely to curb some of the excesses—such as distorted pricing—that we have seen in the music industry. The salaries of superstars in sports-entertainment are often made public, yet the superstars' incomes from performance rights are never revealed by PROs. It is not hard to see why these contracts are cloaked in confidentially agreements, as it would embarrass some of the 1,035,000 copyright holders that ASCAP and BMI often boast about in marketing material. Pitt (2010, 2013) found that it is a small number of composers, songwriters, and publishers who received the lion's share of performance royalty income, royalty income is concentrated on a relatively few already successful songwriters and PRO administration often focused on that small subset of songwriters.

It was not only PRO economic demands that made obtaining a blanket license uneconomical for some music users, but the [un]economic demands by record labels as well. These economic demands are significant barriers to entry for music services and they all appear to have an adverse effect on songwriters' income. The economic demands—as barriers to entry in the music industry—should now be considered in a new regulatory framework that promotes competition, efficiency, transparency, and the free exchange of information in contractual relationships. It is often the

[1] See Downes (2011).

[2] See *US vs. ASCAP & In Re Capstar (DMX)* (2010).

songwriter/composer whose potential income is diminished when he or she does not have complete access to the information contained in record labels' licensing deals or how that information is often distorted when reported.

Songwriters and record labels face the challenges of fairly allocating the pool of money generated from direct licensing, getting songwriters paid, and giving consumers access to the creative works of the songwriters. Songwriters and composers should also be concerned as to whether they are fairly compensated when PRO administrative costs are in the double digits, and resources are squandered on administrative overhead, including dubious lawsuits. In 2009, ASCAP allocated 10.82 % of its revenue from the background music services industry toward administration and general overhead expenses,[3] while SoundExchange's administration costs amounted to 6.7 % in 2010.[4] The double-digit deductions for administrative expenses in administering the blanket license is another reason why copyright holders are looking for licensing alternatives in which the money saved from such costs can be shared with copyright owners and increase their income.

The court rulings in the DMX cases have irrevocably changed the blanket licensing process by exposing the inefficiencies of the incumbent PROs and the complexities of the music licensing system. PROs must now offer an adjustable blanket license with a carve-out and music users are free to negotiate directly with copyright owners for the use of their musical works. Furthermore, the rate court decisions have set a new carve-out precedent in music licensing that recognized the power of market innovation, competition, and the limitations of the traditional blanket license issued by the collective copyright licensing agencies. These decisions may help to fulfill the government's (antitrust) intent of the consent decrees of maintaining reasonable licensing fees, fostering competition, transparency, innovation and reining in the inherent pricing and market power of incumbent PROs. The regulatory licensing mechanism in place today is slowly moving in the right direction in terms of remaking copyright law to match current markets with today's technologies in a world that the PROs are no longer able to control.[5] The new changes in copyright law that may not protect some old media business models and the status quo that are no longer viable in the digital era.

There is the possibility of entry of a new PRO by an Apple/Google/Facebook merger replacing some of the current relationships among songwriters, PROs, music publishers, music users, and consumers. In any event, the diminishing and intermediate role of PROs may not be relevant to some of the future creators of digital music who will benefit from today's innovations, market adjustments, and the efficient distribution of content.

At his blog site, the founder and CEO of TuneCore, observes that with so many intermediaries involved in royalty distribution, "the digital age has rendered the

---

[3]See *US vs. ASCAP & In Re Capstar (DMX)* (2010).

[4]See Sisario (2011).

[5]See also the suggestions by Cardi (2007); Patry (2011) for reforming the PROs and fixing copyright laws in general.

digital part of what ASCAP and other entities do moot and a thing of the past. These organizations are not needed to track sales in iTunes or video streams in YouTube, and yet they are fighting and litigating to try to keep songwriters' money going to themselves to stick in their pockets. They do not really give a damn that 98 % of the world's songwriters do not get their cut of the money owed to them. The only thing keeping them propped up is that there are artists who do not understand how much money they are owed and where it is."[6]

Indeed, innovators, like TuneCore and MRI, are changing the market structure of the music industry by causing a shift in market share from incumbents that may result in the inevitable demise of some record labels, music publishers and PROs.

There is still the need for a longitudinal study—a pooled time-series, cross section analysis—to determine the lifetime value of a songwriter's performance copyrights (or a single piece of intellectual property) that includes the dormant, old and new compositions using the registered works and historical payment data to songwriters and publishers housed in PRO databases. In future changes to the Copyright Act, some younger songwriters and composers might want to be paid an upfront lump sum amount for the future value of their copyrights, and payment history data in PRO databases can be used in developing such models. One complicating factor in such a longitudinal study is how to adjust the model when not just heteroscedasticity and autocorrelation may occur simultaneously, but skewness errors as well in a pooled time series cross sectional model.[7]

References

Cardi, W. J. (2007). Über-middleman: Reshaping the broken landscape of copyright music. *Iowa Law Review*, 92:835–890.

Downes, L. (2011). 'Leahy's Protect IP Act: Why Internet Content Wars Will Never End'. *Forbes Magazine*. May 16, accessed online: http://www.forbes.com.

Patry, W. (2011). *How To Fix Copyright*. Oxford University Press, New York.

Pitt, I. L. (2010). Superstar effects on royalty income in a performance rights organization. *Journal of Cultural Economics*, 34(3):219–236.

Pitt, I. L. (2013). Power laws and skew distributions: An application and analysis of performance royalty income. *Forthcoming: Journal of Income Distribution.*

Price, J. (2011). 'Why Everyone But The Artist and The Music Fan is Doomed'. *Blog.TuneCore.com*. November 22, accessed online: http://blog.tunecore.com/2011/11/why-everyone-but-the-artist-and-the-music-fan-is-doomed.html.

[6]See Price (2011). See also the extensive examples of new music business models (digital retail, subscription, artist-to-fan, licensing, project funding and webcasting) and how labels, artists and songwriters are paid here: http://futureofmusic.org/sites/default/files/FMCnewbusinessmodels12.pdf.

[7]See Pitt (2010, 2013); Xie et al. (2009) for suggestions.

Sisario, B. (2011). 'Sirius's Move to Bypass a Royalty Payment Clearinghouse Causes an Uproar'. *New York Times*. November 7, accessed online: http://www.nytimes.com/2011/11/07/business/media/siriuss-move-to-bypass-royalty-agency-causes-uproar.html?_r=1&pagewanted=print.

US vs. ASCAP & In Re Capstar (DMX) (2010). No: 09 Civ. 7069 (DLC), S.D.N.Y. December 1, accessed online: http://www.leagle.com/decision/In%20FDCO%2020101209735, pp. 1–87.

Xie, F.-C., Lin, J.-G., and Wei, B.-C. (2009). Diagnostics for skew-normal nonlinear regression models with AR(1) errors. *Computational Statistics and Data Analysis*, 53:4403–4416.

Part II
Why Putting Music Content Creators First Is Important

Chapter 7
Introduction

In Part I of this monograph, we examined the role that direct licensing played in making the music industry more competitive by eliminating the inefficiencies associated with copyright administration. The first part focused on the role played by performing rights organizations (PROs) in preventing direct licensing from reaching the market by imposing higher licensing fees and other transaction costs on DMX, a music user. The actions of the PROs illustrated a music industry in transition with the development of alternative licensing and business models.

In Part II of the monograph, we focus on the music publisher and the role direct licensing and competition may play in the changing business models in the music industry that will benefit copyright holders such as songwriters. In addition, we speculate on a potential new entrant into the music industry as the result of a merger of several key players that should make the industry more competitive for copyright administration. The merger model may occur because consumers are demanding new music platforms and copyright holders are looking to exploit changes in new markets and technologies.

The old record label strategy of creating single hits (in the teenage market) to drive radio airplay and then increase the marketing and promotion for the sale of an entire album (adults market) became obsolete as music consumption, social habits, and purchasing behaviors changed in the digital transformation of the music industry. Strong radio airplay was no longer the only driving force for breaking new acts. The new business models that are replacing the old analog, legacy or traditional publishing models all have highly beneficial advantages for individual music creators who are adapting to the digital era. Patry (2011, pp. 144–145)—in his book on how to fix the broken copyright system—discusses the following examples of the advantages of the various new models. First, digital technologies have redefined the function and scope of distributing music. Digital distribution eliminates some of the behind-the-scenes work and overhead administration costs (such as talent acquisition, marketing, promotion, copyright licensing, and royalty collection) of music publishers and record labels. There is no longer a central

I.L. Pitt, *Direct Licensing and the Music Industry*,
DOI 10.1007/978-3-319-17653-6_7

gatekeeper (music publisher or record label) controlling independent music creators (songwriters and composers). Digital music is distributed across a variety of multiple-access platforms (computer, Internet, or mobile phone). Digital distribution has lowered the retail pricing of music. Digital distribution has changed the music consumption patterns of consumers by not forcing them to buy an entire album when they prefer just a few songs.

Second, there is no longer the need for aspiring songwriters and composers to negotiate away the copyrights to their creations in exchange for a record label contract with all of the recoupment drawbacks.

Third, the *means of music production* in creating a professional quality demo CD is now within the financial reach of singers/songwriters who in the past may have relied on expensive recording studio facilities. Music creators can be their own background studio musicians with the help of music production software, manufacturers of physical copies of CDs if needed, distributors on a wide variety of mobile and Internet platforms.

Finally, independent songwriters can become their own web-based retailers. They can promote their music through websites and social networks and in the process obtain valuable demographic and geographic data on their music fans for marketing and touring purposes. For example, many singers/songwriters and independent artists can create a *demo recording* of their songs in a home studio (or use a professional demo service), and release it on YouTube where they can connect directly with fans. Music creators using YouTube as a distribution platform have a direct way of reaching their potential audiences without the middle layer of music publishers, PROs, record labels, studios or radio and TV stations.

Still in the midst of all these changes, musicians still hope to be "discovered" by record industry talent scouts—who peruse the Internet looking for new talent—because record labels can often help them to accomplish goals that they could not achieve on their own. Internet websites are now one of the primary means for music industry talent scouts to listen to new music without the need to spend countless hours in nightclubs and bars. Record labels may only be willing to invest resources in potential artists who may have already built a successful following on the Internet. Recording artists hope that the widespread exposure to their music on YouTube maximizes their royalty income, while record labels and music publishers are hoping to maximize their return on investment in recording artists.

7.1 Role of Technology and Its Creative Destruction

The many consumer electronic devices and digital services that have reshaped the entertainment industry in recent years are shown in Table 7.1. As a result of the conversion from vacuum tubes to solid state devices—such as the transistor and later integrated circuit and microprocessors—computers were no longer the costly systems owned by large institutions such as corporations, universities, and government agencies. By the 1990s, the increases in productivity were due to the

Table 7.1 Product displacement and changing consumer demand

Legacy products & services	Displacement & new formats
Sheet music	Recorded music
Phonograph	Commercial radio
Eight-track tape	Cassette tape
Cassette tape	Compact-disk
Compact disk	MP3 players and iPods
Landline phone	Wireless network. Smart phones with music, instant messaging & web access
DSL-lines	High-speed fiber optic internet
Home personal computer	Laptop computer
Laptop & net book computers	Tablet computers & smart phones
Record-label studio	Auto-tune software, VoiceLive play and digital multi-track home recording equipment
Brick and mortar storefronts	Internet-only websites
Napster and Kazaa	Torrent sites and cloud services
Digital downloads	Streaming
Video stores	Netflix
Terrestrial radio & MTV	Internet & satellite radio and YouTube
Bundled cable networks	Stand-alone networks
Printed and audio books	E-books
Complete editions of newspapers and magazines	Individual digital articles on social network sites and blogs
Local and national classified advertising	Craigslist, a free provider

lower cost of microprocessor-based PC hardware, inexpensive and easily deployable networked workstations, file servers, and Intel's microprocessors. The PC was heavily mass produced and expanded its presence in homes and small businesses. Concurrent with the changes in Table 7.1—in terms of increased reliability, interactivity, and productivity; and decreased cost, size and power consumption—the market for mainframe computers (IBM) evolved into minicomputers (DEC), then micro or personal computers (Microsoft), the Internet (Amazon, Google and Facebook), and finally the smart phone (Apple and Samsung). Several of the pioneering computer companies that first built minicomputers and PCs are now extinct or have evolved into the makers of "servers" and other computer-related equipment. More importantly, however, the table illustrates the cyclical nature of the music industry that has been constantly evolving since its inception. Yet with all of these technological changes the music industry is still not extinct.

In some parts of the music business, obsolete formats were replaced by new technology. The new sounds and new ideas introduced by the new formats created new business models in which the music industry flourished and this pattern is repeated several times over. As these and many other new exogenous product innovations became popular due to increasing consumer demand, market share shifted from incumbent industry players to new entrants, and forever changed the entertainment industry's structure. Although one might expect significant new technologies to be endogenous (and hence proprietary) in the music industry, several important technological innovations in music recording were, in fact, largely exogenous product inventions by firms outside the industry.[1] As digital platforms became more ubiquitous, some of the technical barriers to entry in e-commerce were being dismantled and prices (margins) began to fall, yet there is still a strong desire to cling to unsustainable business models that are obsolete. The Internet has long displaced physical record stores, landline phones, and CD players, and one can imagine that physical books, newspapers, magazines, and bookstores are next.

7.2 The Human Cost of Technology

There is also a human downside to the all of the digital technologies that we are discussing here in terms of efficiency and optimization. Although the growth in progress, revenue and profits may have occurred with the widespread use of technology, efficiency and optimization have meant that the livelihoods of many workers are destroyed, jobs are consolidated and rendered redundant, and employers than once employed thousands are now employing just a few hundred workers. Expensive labor has been outsourced to Third-World nations or on-site labor has been replaced with a computer. Moreover, many of the jobs that were once performed by humans are now being performed by computers, particularly work that requires mental and cognitive abilities.

The ratio of jobs destroyed to the number of jobs created has been climbing in information technology and this has created a protracted level of unemployment—for the skilled and the unskilled—that has probably led to a decline in incomes and the standard of living for some workers. Moreover, some displaced workers with narrow skill sets were not only rendered unemployable, but obsolete as well because their jobs will never be recovered.

For some displaced workers, this meant that they had to "reinvent" themselves and some were caught in a trap in which they were too old—relative to labor force participation—to start over, but were too young to retire. Some Internet-only firms have a higher market capitalization than some old-world companies, yet they employ just a few thousand workers. The smart phone has become the dominant device and the media platform of choice for the information processing needs of consumers that were previously done elsewhere.

[1] See Alexander (1994).

Consumers are already configuring themselves around a new economy based on the Internet and the trend is new apps—or the development of computer software applications to perform the functions of mundane everyday tasks—and new designs with incremental changes in speed, storage, and processing power.[2]

7.2.1 Displacement of Musicologists

Prior to digital fingerprinting, the PROs used a system of tape recordings of actual broadcasts from across the country to monitor musical performances, radio formats, and other data. This was the process or the monitoring technology that was in place for decades.

PROs employed musicologists—housed in a stuffy warehouse of cubicles, and armed with headphones and tape recorders—to decipher musical performances (melody and lyrics) in order to retrieve the names of songwriters and composers from the musical compositions captured in sample surveys. This was a daunting task because the musicologists had to be able to recognize the millions of tunes in the repertories of the PROs. This was the equivalent of a taxi driver having to know the locations of every street address in the United States, something that a global positioning system (GPS) has solved very nicely. With the use of humans for such labor-intensive activities, there were bound to be errors and mistakes caused by daily fatigue, unfamiliarity with new music, and other factors. The accuracy of such a monitoring system was always a cause for anger among struggling songwriters and composers.

If a songwriter's music was performed, but not captured in a sample survey, they were not paid performance royalties, and the sample survey provided a ready-made excuse made by PROs for the non-payment of royalties. Similarly, if the work was captured in such a survey, but it was unregistered, the songwriter may not have been paid. This would be the equivalent of a factory worker not being paid because his/her hours were not captured on a time-card or it was captured late. The sample survey is still in use today and has been augmented by digital fingerprinting firms such as MediaGuide.

Table 7.2 shows a list of the popular song identification software that eliminated the need for certain types of musicologists at PROs. Some of the apps have distinctive features such as being able to identify a song just by humming or knowing a few lyrics and in some apps they can do both. The widespread use of digital fingerprinting has eliminated one of the important reasons for granting PROs their status as a natural monopoly: Song titles, composers, songwriters, and lyricists identification are no longer as labor intensive as in the past.

---

[2]The debate on whether technological advances in aggregate create more jobs than they destroy is discussed in *The Digital Storm*, Chapter 8, Galbraith (2014, pp. 129–147), Cyert and Mowery (1987), Leontief (1983), and Brynjolfsson and McAfee (2014).

Table 7.2 Song titles and lyrics identification software

App	Features	Cost
Shazam	Instant song identification integrated with Facebook, Twitter, Spotify, and Pandora	Free
Soundhound	Song identification by singing a tune	Free
Hound	Song identification by naming the artists	Free
musiXmatch	Song search based on lyrics	Free
Spotsearch	Lyrics search integrated with Spotify and YouTube	Free
TrackID	Track identification on Sony devices	Free
Google play	Recognizes music and songs playing around you	Free

7.3 Boom, Bust and Rebirth in the Music Industry

It is uncanny in circa 1920 and illustrated in the brief but extended quotation below, we see some of the same music executives' extremely suspicious reaction to new technology that are *still* contemporaneous today.[3] For example, the following issues were common then: (a) litigation to hamper economic growth (patent lawsuits, copyright infringement, and licensing fees disputes); (b) economic business cycles (The Great Depression, currency turmoil and massive national debt); (c) marketing segments and demographics (rural versus urban areas, luxurious versus economical music entertainment, and youth versus adults); (d) consumer-driven demand for new technology (recorded music, telephones, electricity, and automobiles); (e) loss of virtual monopoly (market for laterally cut recording discs opened to mass competition and the decline in price for classical and operatic records); (f) recording artists' royalty income disputes (exorbitant flat fees changed to percentage-based royalties with a guaranteed minimum annual income and superstars receiving the most generous deals); (g) new innovations (the threat of hundreds of radio stations with new entertainment and information and news formats); (h) alternative and independent record labels (Black Swan record label started targeting the African American market and other ethnic groups with a crossover appeal); (i) sociological shifts (the South to North migration of African Americans to cities such as New York's Harlem and Chicago, rejection of the Victorian era's values and ideals of femininity and tastes in classical music, marching bands and vaudeville, and the end of The Great War); (j) new trends (faster and louder dance music other than the tango and foxtrot in night clubs); (k) new musical genres or niche music (jazz, blues, ragtime, country, folk, and ethnic music); (l) new music distribution networks (records sold at newsstands, Pullman porters peddling copies at whistle stops, and door to door salesmen); (m) *subversive pirates* of the airwaves (excited teenage *boys* or *amateurs*—a lucrative market for early radio equipment as *ham-radio*

[3]See Morgan (2014) in which he documents one of the first and relatively unknown crashes in music sales in the music industry.

traffic exploded—with an "addiction to radio" who disrupted maritime shipping communications with foul language and pranks); and (n) decline in record sales (as consumers switched to radio networks).[4]

"When commercial radio began in 1920, the sound reception was mostly fuzzy and not very good. It improved a lot over the next few years, however, and record companies were furious about this business of people getting music piped into their homes for free. Many listeners, though, believed radios would quickly make phonographs and the whole record industry obsolete. Why pay 50 cents or $1 (equivalent to at least $10–$20 today) per song when you can get non-stop music for free? Also, with radio, you didn't have to get up after each song to change the side, not to mention crank up the phonograph for each song. Plus, music on the radio never wore out—there were no scratches or ticks as there were on your old records. And by 1924 or so, the sound quality of most radios was better than that of most phonographs.

Much like the lawsuits major labels initially reacted to digital file-sharing with, record companies in the 1920s tried to prevent records from being played on the radio, even though stations at the time preferred broadcasting live musicians (as records played on the air resulted in mediocre sound quality.) They certainly could not stop the growth of radio, however, and after accepting this reality, they focused on innovation to improve records and record players. After all, some listeners would always want the option of putting on whatever music they want, rather than listen to the choices of a radio station.

And so, starting in the early 20s, the record companies and phonograph makers introduced several important innovations. First, they made more models which ran on electricity, so people didn't have to wind up the device for each song. In 1925, Victor introduced what they called "orthophonic" sound, which meant the music was recorded electrically, with the new electric microphones and amplifiers, instead of acoustically as was the case before. The new "electric" sound (quickly adopted by most of the other labels) was much clearer, and was closer to the sound people heard on radios. Also, for the first time ever, the fainter instruments, such as keyboards, guitars, the lower bass notes and higher high notes were audible (partly because soft instruments could now be "microphonally amplified" through the new "loud-speakers.") Instruments such as drums also appeared on records for the first time, presumably because before that a drummer would drown out the other sounds. In short, the noticeable improvement in sound helped turn sales around. Shortly after this "electric sound" revolution, record sales for the top songs of the day surpassed sales of sheet music for those same songs for the first time ever.

By the end of the roaring 20s, radio-and-phonograph combinations were being sold as one unit. Obviously both mediums found a way to complement each other; although records were still never played on air, it never hurt a major star's record sales to perform their hits live on the radio. Aside from that, the booming economy, the increased purchasing power of the middle class, the new consumer youth (those "flappers" and their fur-coat wearing boyfriends), and the ever-increasing popularity of jazz all helped fuel huge record sales by the end of the decade.

But as with everything else, the Great Depression changed all of that. The downturn in the record industry was by far the worst in its history (far worse, in fact, than the losses of today's majors.) Total annual record sales dropped from about a hundred million in 1927 to just six million in 1932. Radio, which from the beginning was driven mostly by advertising (which tends to stay stable in hard times) was less badly hit.

A major shakeup in the record industry followed. Nearly all of the smaller, independent labels disappeared almost overnight. RCA, a major radio manufacturer, bought the venerable Victor Records, in what was probably the first instance of media "convergence." (Many

[4]See also Murphy (2014, pp. 1–56).

people pointed out this precedent back when AOL bought Time-Warner, i.e. that the new media was buying up the old. After AOL's stock collapsed, however, it became more like the old propping up the new, and Time-Warner just recently dropped AOL from its name.)" *Source*: ©Morgan (2014) and used with permission.

As radio was introduced in 1922, the decades-old phonograph industry would shrink dramatically to within 6 % of its former size—record sales went from $104 million in 1927 to $6 million in 1932—sending the record industry into its first and serious prolonged recession that lasted about 20 years, including the Great Depression and World War II.

KDKA, the first commercial radio station, had begun broadcasting in 1920, and within two years there were 200 more stations. By 1925, the radio audience numbered fifty million. In 1926 NBC lined up the first coast-to-coast network with 19 stations. By 1938, it had 110, and 80 percent of the country could tune in to the same show if it so desired. The Depression accelerated radio purchases, since music was free once the hardware was paid for; there were fifteen million radios in the United States in 1931 and fifty million in 1939. Nationwide shows meant national tours, and bands moved to New York to be near the center of the radio business. Radio flexed its power in other ways, buying up record companies to make sure it had plenty of material just as film companies were doing the same thing with music publishing. So the Radio Corporation of America (RCA) bought ARC (which included Columbia, Okeh, Vocalion, and Brunswick).[5]

Radio broadcasting of musical performances worsened the job opportunities for live performers and musicians, but it also gave rise to new jobs as the industry developed and matured. Stores that sold phonographs now sold radio equipment as the business models changed. Other businesses would replace the phonograph industry and some would last for the next 90 years until the digital revolution made them irrelevant, just like some PROs.

Around the same period, RadioShack, the electronics retailer, was founded to capitalize and profit from the growing interest in radio electronics by amateur and ham-radio enthusiasts and do-it-yourself (DIY) consumers who liked to build electronic gadgets. RadioShack was the store where the ham and ship radio operators in the early 1920s bought their radio equipment and the company was able to exploit this growing market segment for technology enthusiasts in search of the latest gadgets. RadioShack was the early pioneer in selling electronic and component parts—such as diodes, transistors, circuit boards, batteries, cables, and connectors—that could be used to build new things like radios, computers, and other devices, and to also repair broken televisions and other gadgets. After close to a century in business, RadioShack—now re-branded as "The Shack" after dropping "Radio" from its name—was struggling to reinvent itself in 2014. At the time of writing, the company's stock price was less than a dollar and was in danger of being de-listed on the New York Stock Exchange. The retailer has been unable to capitalize on the shift to wireless and Internet technologies such as the smart

[5]See McNally (2014, pp. 198–199) for more on the facts and figures of early radio. This book is a historical account of the contributions of African-Americans to the evolution of music in the United States and contains an extended music bibliography.

phone that has cannibalized sales in its inventory for several reasons. First, smart phones with built-in features such as digital cameras, GPS equipment, wireless connectors, answering machines, tape recorders, and calculators eroded the sale of these individual items at many stores.

Second, the significant drop in prices for certain televisions, computers, wireless phones and other gadgets and their complicated designs with fewer parts, fewer defects and continuous improvement meant that it was cheaper to replace these gadgets with newer ones than to repair them, diminishing the market for spare parts and repair-type stores.

Third, physical locations and store fronts could not match the convenience of ordering equipment from online retailers such as Amazon at any time of the day, further eroded Radio Shack's relevance to consumers. RadioShack once had about 7,000 retail locations, but in 2014 was down to about 4,000 stores and was looking to close around 200 under-performing stores a year over the next few years, if they did not run out of cash sooner. Best Buy and Walmart and other big-box retailers, important anchor stores at shopping malls, would soon capture the bulk of electronic sales.

Finally, RadioShack "suffered from poor, often overpaid leadership, which could not focus on a single plan and then was left grasping for a rescue strategy." Several new business models and other concepts failed as their original mission was increasingly becoming obsolete.[6]

In ASCAP's early days, the members who benefited most from the system were the founders and their brethren, the theater and Tin Pan Alley writers of Broadway.[7] ASCAP was celebrating its 100th anniversary in 2014 and its future looked grim with the digital "Sword of Damocles" dangling precariously over its head. The Harry Fox Agency has already fallen by the wayside.

7.3.1 ASCAP's Disastrous Boycott of 1941

In the 1940s, the music industry experienced two general strikes—the first by ASCAP and second by the American Federation of Musicians—over royalty payments that would have significant long-term financial and damaging reputational consequences for PROs, songwriters, composers, musicians, record labels, and music publishers. In the first strike in 1941, ASCAP—now a powerful lobby, music licensing gatekeeper and soon to be part of a price-controlling cartel—led a boycott of radio over its insistence that radio stations should pay increased licensing fees relative to their audience size. Radio stations were blocked from playing the music of established Tin Pan Alley songwriters—such as Irving Berlin, Cole Porter, and Johnny Mercer—in ASCAP's repertory. Ironically, this seminal event that lasted a

---

[6]See Harris (2014) and Solomon (2014).

[7]Pollock (2014, pp. 22–23).

few months and sought to increase royalty payments (a reported staggering demand of 7.5 % of the networks' *gross* income) for ASCAP's charter members would mark the beginning of the end for the stranglehold that Tin Pan Alley songwriters and publishers held in the music industry. The boycott was devastating to the livelihoods of songwriters, composers, and musicians because most music was performed live on the radio in those days. Not only did the 1,250,000 songs in ASCAP's repertory vanish from the broadcast airways, but the income from performance royalties for many band leaders, songwriters, and composers disappeared as well. This prompted Mercer Ellington—who was a BMI affiliate and whose father, Duke Ellington, was a member of ASCAP—to join his father's orchestra and compose some of the most enduring standards from that era.

In response to ASCAP's disastrous boycott and looking to the future, BMI found public domain and other alternative non-ASCAP music for the boycotted radio stations in (African-American, rural and foreign) genres such as jazz, blues, country, and folk music—genres in which the snobby ASCAP gatekeepers had long shunned; music that was distinct from ASCAP's repertory and were not played on the radio networks; and often ignored by the major music publishers as well. The Tin Pan Alley cultural gatekeepers'—many of whom had lived in the United States for less than an entire generation and heavily influenced by European composers, customs and norms—narrow biases on what music *they* considered to be in good taste, prestigious, artistic, sophisticated, superior or creative for the entire American population were about to be tested. It was patently offensive, repulsive, and demeaning to many Americans for the likes of Al Jolson (a member of ASCAP) to perform—what is now considered *standards* in the Great American Songbook—in black-face. The grotesque caricatures and stereotypes of African-Americans were harmful when a more dignified approach to introducing jazz to a white audience could have been handled in a different manner.

BMI's competitive entry at the time introduced a wider range of musical compositions by an even broader set of indigenous American songwriters, and in the process exposed Americans to a richer variety of music, not particularly suited for either Broadway or Hollywood movies. Songwriters and composers were now able to take economic advantage of a new media platform, the radio, as the barriers to entry came tumbling down. Music publishers (and their subjective notions of what they considered artistic excellence) would no longer determine which one or two songs were to become hits. New record labels, like Capitol, were formed to cater to this new, eclectic variety of music, songwriters and consumers. ASCAP in later years would embrace some of these jazz composers, but only after years of pleading their cause due to ASCAP's selectivity, arrogance, racism, and cultural snobbery. As these alternative genres—non-ASCAP affiliated music outside of Tin Pan Alley music publishers—received more airplay, the genres became widely popular with several of the musical compositions reaching the number one spot on the charts, further weakening ASCAP's monopoly and increasing BMI's market share. Long after ASCAP's disastrous boycott ended, these musical genres would endure.[8] BMI's effort was far from noble because it was only after a number of years that songwriters and composers were allowed to become affiliates of BMI, with the implicit assumption that the music-publisher affiliates would then equitably distribute royalty payments to songwriters and composers, presumably those payments were subject to recoupment and other shady practices that were harmful to songwriters.[9]

7.3.2 Ferdinand "Jelly Roll" Morton Case Study

By the 1930s, ASCAP was collecting about $10 million annually in royalty licensing fees, the equivalent of $135 million in 2014 dollars. Songwriters were often not made aware of the process for registering song titles to collect performance royalties in the early days as radio flourished—a registration function normally performed by the music publisher in which the percent of copyright ownership between songwriter(s)/composer(s) and publisher should have been listed—and, therefore, they had little or no idea about the large amounts of money that were collected by PROs for the distribution as performance royalties to music publishers and a select-few songwriters and composers of the Tin Pan Alley variety. This was yet another way that many songwriters, including many African-American music pioneers, were cheated out of their rightful share of music royalties. The PROs had the same restrictive and discriminatory policies and the country-club mentality of exclusion, a disgusting and shameful stain on the memory of the geniuses that created modern American music and died penniless. Performance royalty income was often the only source of income for songwriters and composers when sheet music and sound recording sales dried up.

Prolific composer and jazz pioneer, Ferdinand "Jelly Roll" Morton (1890–1941), wasn't allowed to join ASCAP until 1939, 3 years before his death in 1941. Mr. Morton was previously rejected by ASCAP during his most successful years because "all applicants had to be proposed and seconded by a member of ASCAP," a considerable hurdle to overcome in two important ways in order to be paid performance royalties for his own music.

First, "ASCAP's exclusionary policies kept out many worthy applicants. By limiting membership, the organization ensured that those already in ASCAP got a bigger cut of radio revenues."[10]

Second, "The bitter truth was that Walter Melrose [Mr. Morton's publisher] had belonged to ASCAP since 1927, records show. Melrose was collecting ASCAP publisher royalties and author royalties—for lyrics he added to tunes by Morton and

---

[8] See Stanley (2014, pp. xviii–xx).

[9] See Pollock (2014, pp. 41–42).

[10] See Reich and Gaines (1999a). A detailed treatment of Mr. Morton's innovation and his injustices can be found in Reich and Gaines (2003).

others—*13 years before Morton received a dime*."[11] The lack of transparent and public accounting practices for the distribution of royalty payments to individual members and affiliates have been the cornerstone of PROs from the beginning. The *Copyright Act* was only useful to the chartered members of ASCAP as long as they benefited. This was quite shocking for an organization known for litigating for higher licensing fees in its early founding. How was it possible to overlook the economic and legal protection granted to all composers, authors, and songwriters in the *Copyright Act* when in the early days songwriters couldn't even join in order to collect their royalties? Today, it is easy to join any PROs (resigning to join another PRO is an entirely different matter), but the PROs are only too willing to adapt to changes desired by influential music-publisher members or affiliates at the expense of songwriters. This is one of the flaws in the current *Copyright Act* in which it is left up to PROs subjective and arbitrary judgment to determine how songwriters and composers are to be compensated for the performance rights to their music.

Mr. Morton probably received no performance royalties for the previous decades when he was denied admittance to a PRO and his works were performed and captured in a PRO survey. And to add insult to injury, highly accomplished composers like Mr. Morton had to start at the bottom of ASCAP's arbitrary new-member hierarchy and classification system when they were finally allowed to join that "exclusive" society. ASCAP placed Mr. Morton into their lowest class-designated royalty system that paid the least amount, even though it was not unusual for ASCAP's Writers' Classification Committee to place special new members (Jay Livingston and Ray Evans!) in advanced classes based on their perceived "value" to ASCAP. At the time Mr. Morton was only expecting to receive $120 a year (that is $30 a quarter) from ASCAP in performance royalties—based on an arbitrary classification rather than performances of his music—while top ASCAP songwriters, such as Cole Porter and Irving Berlin, were reportedly paid $15,000 a year in performance royalties, further evidence of the skewness in performance royalty payments.[12]

What it took to reach an advanced class with the other ASCAP's noted songwriters would probably devolve into wild and humorous conspiracy theories surrounding ASCAP's Writers' Classification Committee. Clinging to the status quo mentality to make sure that a select few got the lion's share of royalties—as newer members' music began eclipsing those of the fading Tin Pan Alley composers and whose music is now mostly background and underscores—still permeates the current convoluted royalty payment system.

Table 7.3 highlights ASCAP's undemocratic and unfair payment formula that was in place for decades—a somewhat dubious improvement over the previous complicated classification system that ranked members into 13 separate classes ranging from AAA to 4 based on the number of songs written, sales and hits over the

[11] Reich and Gaines (1999a). Emphasis added.

[12] See Yagoda (2015, pp. 41–43 and pp. 98–100), Reich and Gaines (1999a), and Reich and Gaines (1999b).

Table 7.3 ASCAP's quarterly royalty payment formula 1929–1952

Category	Amount
Class A	$2,000
Class B	$1,000
Class C	$500
Class D	$250

Source: Yagoda (2015, pp. 41–43).

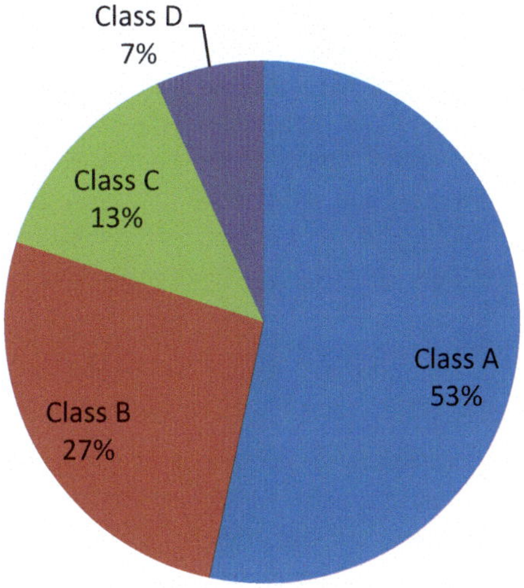

Fig. 7.1 ASCAP's skewed royalty payments 1929–1952

course of the songwriter's career. Royalty payments were then made on this arbitrary classification system. It was all rather dubious because the royalty payments were based on subjective, arbitrary and irrelevant factors rather than on the frequency of radio performances or airplay. This version of their convoluted payment system was eventually scrapped in 1952.[13]

Figure 7.1 illustrates in graphical form the highly skewed nature of performance royalty payments—the so-called superstar effect—that is, the top-tier songwriters in Class A were making almost eight times more than the songwriters in Class D as far back as 1929, a familiar skewed pattern even today and one of the reasons why there is all this secrecy surrounding royalty payments. It would be illustrative if statistical distributions of royalty payments made to songwriters and composers by all PROs were made public on a routine basis, something that a revision to the various consent decrees should be addressing.

In Mr. Morton's case, it is hard to imagine that the well-known pianist could not be located and paid for his works, even though his publisher was being paid by ASCAP. It is not clear if ASCAP rectified this unseemly situation with the

[13]See Yagoda (2015, pp. 41–43).

heirs to Mr. Morton's estate. This is the reason why when ASCAP gets on Capitol Hill to claim they are fighting for all songwriters and composers and pleading for changes in copyright laws and consent decrees, they are routinely mocked by musicians as being completely phony, given ASCAP's notorious past reputation of being "a closed-door organization who were only interested in a limited group of songwriters/composers and a limited kind of music." The Society was once instrumental in institutionalizing a royalty payment system that valued "prestige" over innovation for the benefit of Tin Pan Alley musicians and was unfair and unjust to many African-American composers. Even with various modifications and improvements over the years, the convoluted payment formulas are still a major source of complaints by composers, lyricists, and songwriters when their unregistered works are performed but they are not paid, or there is wide fluctuations in payments. Today, BMI and ASCAP make separate and direct payments to songwriters and publishers, and those payments are longer co-mingled. However, the individual payment history to songwriters, composers, and publishers is still secret and hidden in confidentiality agreements.

7.3.3 Musician's Union Strike

Responding to ASCAP's settlement with the radio networks that benefited mostly songwriters and the way in which their royalties were collected, the American Federation of Musicians (AFM)—the musician's union—led a second strike in 1942 against record companies—which at the time were synonymous with radio corporations like RCA and CBS—in which the union sought royalty compensation; retirement and death benefits and collective bargaining rights for the thousands of musicians (instrumentalists) who continued to lose work because of new recording technologies. Unemployment of musicians was a major concern for the musician's union due to technology displacing its members, and the economic dislocations associated with World War I, The Great Depression and World War II. For example, in 1927—with the release of the first "talkie," The Jazz Singer—orchestras in movie theaters were displaced when technology permitted the synchronizing of music with pictures for the movies. "Within 3 years, 22,000 theater jobs for musicians who accompanied silent movies were lost, while only a few hundred jobs for musicians performing on soundtracks were created by the new technology." During the strike, union members were banned from recording and no new records could be made. In addition, shellac, an essential component in phonograph records, was in short supply due to the war. The war also made touring difficult for big bands, further crippling this music genre. The record companies soon realized that the strike did not apply to solo vocalists—just musicians—and to fill the void, they put together vocal groups who sang a capella backing behind stars such as the Tommy Dorsey's Band Frank Sinatra. When the musician's union finally settled the strike, the popularity of the big bands had been largely eclipsed by solo vocalists, and new independent record labels had established themselves as competitors to the major labels. Decca—an independent label that had no backlog of previously recorded music—signed with AFM in 1943 and in 1944 had fifteen of the seventeen number one hits on the Billboard list. In Decca's wake, smaller labels like Commodore, Blue Note, and Savoy also signed with the AFM.[14]

Frank Sinatra's success as a lead singer—who was no longer secondary to a big-band—would usher in the era of the so-called bobby-soxers; screaming and *subversive* teenage girls worshiping a singing idol. Other vocalists would soon leave the big bands to start solo careers as singers. It was just a matter of time before subversive teenage boys and girls would unleash their considerable economic power in the music industry to broaden what music was to be considered mainstream, and this would persist into the digital era. Teenagers as a group were not going to be told what music they should listen to and enjoy. It appeared as though rock music now described as "jungle music" when combined with "teen spirit" was a recipe for anarchy in America. The FBI was even called in to investigate whether song lyrics were having some sort of subliminal effect on teenagers causing delinquency.

7.3.4 The Demise of Tin Pan Alley

Tin Pan Alley gatekeepers were in their death throes—as their balance of power shifted—caused in part by the disastrous ASCAP boycott, portable radios, new recording technologies (33½ and 45 rpm formats extinguished the traditional 78), a new dominant form of music and the end of World War II. Figure 7.2 shows that from a peak in the 1920's of 432 new musicals, Broadway shows began a precipitous decline to 220 shows in the 1930's, 147 in the 1940'sand 119 in the 1950's, a trend that continues to today with an average of 37 production a year for all shows between 1984 and 2014.[15]

ASCAP—their complicated rules for membership and the contempt for other popular genres heavily influenced by African-Americans and country and western songwriters—was now in a state of denial because their stable of songwriters were no longer in demand and the world was no longer centered around show writers. The music industry was about to undergo another seismic, long-term economic shift in which the record labels' sound recording role (such as using payola to control what was played on the radio) became more prominent than the music publisher's (that relied mostly on performance and synchronization royalties with the introduction of television), and the vocalist/performer (like Elvis Presley) become more important than the songwriter or composer in the sale of music. Yet another seismic shift would occur with the distribution of music over the Internet in later years.

---

[14]See Stanley (2014, pp. xviii–xx), McNally (2014, p. 243) and AFM History 1896–2009: http://www.afm.org/about/history.

[15]See Yagoda (2015, p. 215) and *Broadway Season Statistics*, http://www.broadwayleague.com/index.php?url_identifier=season-by-season-stats-1.

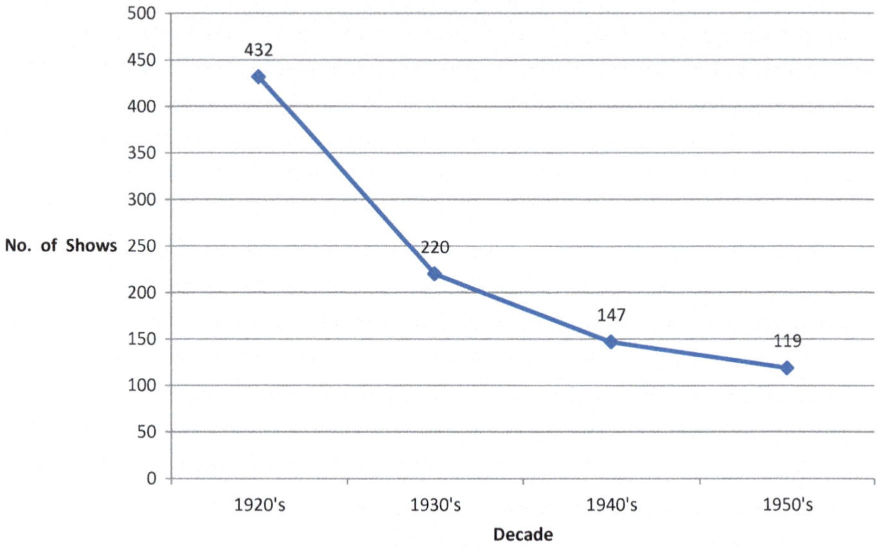

Fig. 7.2 Decline of broadway musicals 1920s–1950s

Rock and roll was not a fading music fad, and would later banish the traditional roles and musical style of Tin Pan Alley songwriters for good. Rhythm and blues and rock and roll had peaked the imagination of teenagers and new songwriters were now catering to this marketing segment. The Great American Songbook would now be relegated to occasional performances on PBS Specials during "pledge week," and every Christmas ASCAP got to tout the number of its Tin Pan Alley songwriters that made the seasonal top ten list, including Irving Berlin's *White Christmas*, in a press release. America's taste in popular music was evolving over time and the pattern was not always consistent. This evolution would be documented by Billboard Magazine which began to publish charts of bestselling sound recordings and radio airplay. The music market today is segmented into jazz, rock, rap, pop, soul, gospel, hip-hop, R&B, dance, country, folk, classical, alternative, and Latin music genres in which some are overlapping. The number of songs by genre and year that made it into the top 100, for example, showed the ebb and flow of America's musical tastes.

To ASCAP's members, early radio—the latest technological and disruptive innovation in music distribution that soon make business models obsolete—was described as a mixed blessing. After years in which publishers were the gatekeepers and primary promoters of songs and songwriters, radio had the power to instantly make or a break a song. Obscure songs that languished in a publisher's catalog could now become hits, due to radio exposure. Publishers became concerned that overexposure of a song on the radio would cause sheet music sales to plummet and they were correct.[16] As consumer demand for radios and recorded music increased dramatically (along with mechanical and performance royalties), the sale of sheet music (a source of revenue for music publishers) and pianos declined in a familiar life cycle pattern. World War II and radio would eventually kill off big-band music. World War II was a contributing factor that led to the demise of big-band music because many musicians were drafted into military service and shipped overseas, forcing clubs and other venues to close. Gasoline rationing made long-distance travel difficult and amusement taxes added to admission prices for movies and the theater only made financial matters worse for the remaining band leaders.

Disc jockeys, playing records on the radio, would soon displace live on-air music on most radio stations because it costs less to employ a DJ with a stack of records than a live band. This new radio format or the shift from live music to records played by a DJ on the radio led to the decline of big-band music. The decline in big-band radio broadcasts also had a dramatic effect on Broadway and the songwriters who wrote for those shows. Radio with live broadcasts by big bands often played current Broadway hits, and the radio broadcasts generated publicity and attendance for those shows. As records replaced live big-band music, this vital strand of publicity was lost.[17]

Playing records on the radio was the beginning of the phenomenon in which radio airplay was used to create and generate the sale of hit songs, increase ratings, increase listeners, and in the process generate radio advertising revenue. Teenagers' listening and buying habits—influenced by the disc jockeys on the radio and jukeboxes in retail outlets—would help to revive the stagnant record industry with their music purchases. In 1948, the transistor was invented, making radio portable. Other inventions such as the car radio and Sony's Walkman would later expand the reach of radio and become the obsession of teenagers. As Napster and MP3 devices became popular around 1999, even as CD sales were still booming, the status quo in the music industry would become irretrievable altered once again by (a) new taste in dance music (manufactured groups like Backstreet Boys, Britney Spears and 'N Sync); (b) new genre (Deejay-mixed compilations and house music); (c) electronic music created in home studios; (d) new technologies (iPod); (e) innovators (Apple); (f) competition (Best Buy and Walmart); (g) over-leveraged and rapidly shrinking music publishers; and (h) demographic and cultural changes (teen-pop market and adult electronic music). File sharing devices, apart from being freely available, enabled consumers to easily assemble their own playlists of individual songs that they wanted. The latest "subversive action" in music history was now hidden on the Internet, usually among college students, and away from retail stores.[18] It is the same pattern that will repeat itself over and over as new technologies were introduced. It is with a great sigh of relief that the music industry has survived its

---

[16]See Pollock (2014, p. 35).

[17]See Stanley (2014, pp. xviii–xx).

[18]See Murphy (2014, pp. 339–347).

near-death' experience for close to a century because some music executives were adept at spotting emerging trends and capitalizing on them.[19]

In 2001, Apple would spot this trend and began marketing its iPod, an MP3 player, with the remarkable storage capacity of 5 GB at the time. Later generations of iPods became portable media centers with added features such as a video player, photo viewer, and 160 GB hard drive. All of the features of the iPod were later combined with a wireless phone and an Internet connection that became the ubiquitous smart phone, the Apple iPhone. Between 2003 and 2011, Apple is reported to have sold more than "300 million iPods and 10 billion songs via its iTunes Store. The big picture in music sales soon became clear: As more iPods and iPhone devices were sold, more music was being bought by consumers."[20] Apple's growth as a major music-licensed distributor that pooled the repertories of *all* the major music publishers only worsened the commodity-pricing economics of music publishing. The major music publishers are now down to three with the merger of Sony and BMG, and parts of EMI that were sold to Sony and Universal.[21]

Old media analog devices have been replaced by faster, better, and cheaper digital devices and services. In the new Internet environment, music content creators such as songwriters (including independent songwriters), lyricists, and composers have an entirely new platform to create and distribute music content. It is now easier to track music use on radio, television, and the Internet. Digital fingerprinting of song titles—used in creating play-lists and cue sheets—provides real-time performance data such as the media platform, frequency and locations in which a distinct song is played, data that were not easily available before the Internet.

The new digital technologies have many advantages and disadvantages as shown in Table 7.4. Digital technology has provided a mass communication system with multiple access platforms such as radio, television, Internet, smart phone, iPod, iPad, and tablet computers. With the increases use of smart phones, digital music has expanded dramatically with more people listening to more music in more places than ever. "Internet radio allows millions of listeners to select virtually any conceivable genre of music, from classic rock, to disco, to movie soundtracks, to

[19] See also Murphy (2014, pp. 1–46) for his historical account of the boom and bust time period in the record industry. In interesting anecdotes that we mentioned earlier, Murphy reveals on page 43 that due to the high cost radio equipment, there was an upsurge in pay-phone vandalism in 1920 all across America because teenagers were ripping out the receivers in phone booths on a massive scale to use as parts to make headphones. By the end of 1922, there were 20,300 radio stations licensed and of that amount, 15,780 belonged to amateurs, many of whom were youngsters clogging up the airwaves with music. Murphy also describes on page 46, ASCAP's early lawsuit for copyright infringement against Bamberger & Company (now Macy's), a department store and owners of WOR, a radio station in New Jersey. ASCAP's disastrous boycott of radio stations in 1941 is described on pages 74–76. The book is quite fascinating with an emphasis on the boom and bust and rebirth of the music industry, but it does not contain footnotes and the bibliography is rather scant.

[20] See Murphy (2014, p. 347).

[21] See Sisario (2012a) and Christman (2014).

Table 7.4 Advantages and disadvantages of new digital technology

Advantages	Disadvantages
True mass communications systems with multiple access	Fragmented consumer market with different tastes
More people listening to music in more places	One size does not fit all
Efficient music distribution systems with a virtual supply chain	How to monetize the demand for such music? Industry in chaotic transformation
Increased digital sales	CD sales are declining due to end of the product cycle
Increased economies of scale and scope	Consumers reluctant to pay for music downloads Use of illegal file sharing services
Unlimited inventory (supply) on demand	A low margin business
Declining transaction costs of administering blanket licenses	Duopoly of incumbent PROs

classical, to jazz, to Mediterranean, to 1940s oldies, to contemporary country, to seasonal, and many more. These listeners are exposed to artists they would not otherwise hear, providing a tremendous promotional benefit to recording artists andincreased music sales."[22]

7.4 Product Life Cycle Patterns in Music

In a way, the Sony Walkman—first introduced in 1979 that made music portable and convenient for consumers—can be considered a crude version of today's iPods that allow users to store thousands of songs and to listen to music wherever they traveled. The tectonic shift in control that would forever change the music industry now had a beginning and a familiar product life cycle pattern: Music industry sales volume and revenue for music on cassette tapes would soar—while the sale of vinyl records would begin its rapid decline—as consumers replaced the same music on cassettes that they already owned on vinyl disks. The product life cycle in music often mirrors the natural life cycle of the economy and demographic trends in general so that in recessions consumers spend less on discretionary item and in boom periods they may spend more. Online shopping culture using smart phones replaced some of the shopping done at malls and that forced the demise of some brick-and-mortar stores. With the introduction of Sony's Discman and its improved technological features—such as convenience, superior sound quality, smaller size when compared to vinyl records and scratch resistance—the global conversion to music CDs began and the sale of music on cassette tapes plummeted and higher prices could be charged

[22]See Stockment (2009) for a review of the economic impact of royalty rates on Internet radio.

for music on CDs. High CDs prices would later force structural changes in music pricing, publishing and distribution that Apple would later exploit.

When the CD market took hold, it did so rapidly with big-box and discount retailers such as Walmart, Best Buy, and Target became major music distribution networks. The industry got rid of vinyl LPs (long playing records) and replaced them with CDs at twice the price. The record labels became profitable due to catalog sales. About 45 % of the record labels' revenue were to due to consumers repurchasing their favorite music on CDs at 60–80 % higher prices.[23] The high prices of music CDs—that fell over time—with just one or two hits would later create a consumer revolt as the Internet took hold. Walmart and Best Buy were able to aggressively undercut established record chains—forcing their demise—because they sold products other than music that could make up for smaller margins in CD sales. In 1996, Walmart and Best Buy sold 154 million compact disks alone. With Walmart and Best Buy accounting for approximately 65 % of the CD sales market, Tower Records and Musicland, the older record chains, could no longer compete on just music.[24] In addition, record label profitability had a negative impact on recording artists' royalty payments. Hidden in the recording artists' contracts were clauses that royalties could be reduced by 20 % for any new technology. For example, if an artist was getting a dollar in royalty payments on an album, the payment was now reduced to eighty cents for a CD. In some cases, another 25 % was taken off for packaging deductions, which meant that the artist ending up with just 55 cents.[25] As Napster and other file sharing technology took hold in 2000, retail CD sales began to plummet. Apart from the issue of piracy, file-sharing services allowed the pubic to get the one song that they wanted. The same pattern would be repeated as digital music sales increased rapidly, the demand for music on physical disks such as CDs steadily declined. However, digital music sales required a different adjustment for music industry executives than the introduction of cassette tapes and CDs because entire music catalogs could be digitized and distributed over the Internet in a matter of seconds. In an interesting paradox for music executives, as the sales of CDs continued its rapid decline, the demand for digital music on the Internet platform exploded. The massive restructuring, music supply concentration, buyouts and mergers in music publishing caused by the crash in CD sales had begun.[26]

Patry (2011, pp. 142–143) attributes the decline in vinyl, cassette and CDs sales—not so much to copyright infringement, intellectual property rights ownership and piracy issues as often cited by copyright owners in legal matters—but to the natural end to the product life cycle of vinyl records, cassettes, CDs, and DVDs. Indeed, many other stand-alone product lines—landlines, music players, cameras, calculators, stopwatches, alarm clocks, computing, video gaming, and even TV/entertainment viewing—are now fully incorporated into a single electronic

[23]See Murphy (2014, pp. 339–347).

[24]See Murphy (2014, pp. 339–347).

[25]See Murphy (2014, pp. 339–347).

[26]See Murphy (2014, pp. 339–347), Sisario (2012a), Sisario (2012b), and Christman (2013).

device such as a smart phone or a tablet and manufactured by fewer and fewer competitors. In other words, these product lines and the associated revenue have disappeared, but consumers are still purchasing the consolidated products in a single device at prices that are often less than a single stand-alone product. As CD sales declined, music publishers began looking at other revenue streams such as the so-called 360 deal (the holistic or unified approach) to maximize revenue. A 360 deal is an income-related agreement in which artists and record labels share income not just from publishing, mechanical and performance rights licensing, but encompasses touring, fan club, merchandising, image licensing, sponsorships, and endorsements revenue-sharing deals. With a 360 deal, all of the artist's rights are now considered potential revenue streams or *unified rights* that can be managed by a single entity.

7.5 Music Piracy

Piracy—the illegal downloading or sharing of copyrighted music, television shows, films, video games, e-books, and computer software using file sharing platforms—became the scapegoat for some, if not all, of the music industry-wide structural changes in technology, innovation, consumer preferences, music genres, economic conditions, risky investment choices, and the spree of mergers and acquisitions made by PROs, record labels, radio stations, and concert promoters.

The music piracy issue reached patently absurd heights when the decline in concert attendance, half empty arenas, and weak ticket sales for live concerts were blamed not on consumers stealing tickets, but on "consumers stealing music." Apparently, consumer outrage at the fundamentals of concert ticket pricing and skyrocketing ticket prices—that included the cost of admission, VIP packages and scalping of the tickets themselves, service and order processing fees, parking costs, facility charges, concession prices, and other convenience add-ons—was not seen as one of the major issues in the decline of concert attendance. For example, a single $20 lawn ticket could cost nearly $50 when a "facility charge" ($12), "convenience charge" ($10.05), "order processing fee" ($5.20), and "TicketFast Delivery," i.e., print-at-home ticketing ($2.50) fee were added. Consumers were soon asking where are the laws to protect them from such predatory practices.[27]

For the major music publishers, it was not so much piracy—including illegally manufactured or copied music CDs—that contributed to their economic problems. Their loss of market share and revenue were due, in part, to the rise of independent music labels who did not inherit the overhead and pre-Internet legacy costs of the major music publishers; failure to keep pace with technology advances that allow for a full replication of a mixing studio in a musician's home; the lower costs of music distribution using the YouTube platform; the end of the product life cycle of vinyl and CDs; and the introduction of Apple's iPhone and iTunes that turned piracy

[27]See Budnick and Baron (2012, pp. x–xi).

into a legitimate market. With these developments, the barriers to entry in the music industry and the role of the major music publishers acting as music gatekeepers quickly evaporated. The limited number of songs and artists in their individual repertories meant that record labels could not produce a product like iTunes that included the content of all music publishers' catalogs. The digital generation's *subversive teenagers* were hardly going to wait around patiently for the labels to decide on business models, content access, content selection, timing, competitive pricing, media platform, distributors, and other factors that they labels could control. Fortunately, Apple's iTunes emergedwith its innovative model that ended the piracy stalemate between frustrated teenagers and record labels, much to the benefit of both sides.

The spurious platitudes of the PROs that the file sharing of music was responsible for their economic problems is just plain ludicrous, to put it politely. Recall that songwriters and composers are only paid performance royalties if their music is performed on radio, television, and new media, and those performances are captured and used in the PROs payment formulas. It is rather embarrassing when the PROs could not articulate, even if music was illegally downloaded, *how* file sharing affected the programming choices or airplay of music on radio and television stations, song title registration or performance royalty payments. Did radio stations stop playing songs that were illegally downloaded and this meant fewer performances and therefore less performance income for songwriters and composers?

7.6 Role of Litigation in the Music Industry

Hidden behind the innovations and new technological products and services in the entertainment industry were tens of thousands of copyright infringement lawsuits in which the record labels, music publishers, and the motion picture studios fought consumer electronics manufacturers, new technological advancement and consumers as the traditional music business model was replaced by something new. The adversarial relationship among PROs, record labels, and music publishers grew even louder and stronger as they reacted to the sweeping changes in digital music delivery. The incumbents could not agree on an equitable royalty payment system for all songwriters and composers, and on the necessary revisions that were needed in copyright laws for a new era, even as Apple, Twitter, Facebook, and Google became the dominant players in different market segments. The copyright infringement lawsuits were, typically, filed as a violation of the authorized copy and distribution rights granted to copyright holders under the Copyright Act or the Digital Millennium Copyright Act (DMCA).[28] The lawsuits were filed with a short-term goal of wanting to preserve the unsustainable status quo.

In most cases, the new technologies threatened to diminish or eliminate the leverage (and financial rewards) that the music industry's executives obtained from

[28]See *Copyright Act* (2011) and *Digital Millennium Copyright Act* (1998).

their exclusive relationships with distribution networks such as radio stations, record stores, and movie theaters, and the restrictive use of their music and film repertories. Instead of finding ways to compete directly with the new technology, the industry's business strategy was costly and time-consuming litigation. For example, the motion picture industry once opposed the VCR, pre-recorded films on videocassettes and the home taping and time-shifting of television programming—even though consumers found the VCR technology appealing—because it was believed that the VCR would cannibalize movie theater ticket sales. Eventually new VCR business models and new firms emerged, and the home entertainment segment became a multi-billion-dollar market in videotape and DVD sales and rentals. This model occurred only after interminable copyright lawsuits and the 1984 US Supreme Court ruling in the "Betamax" case that the home recording of copyrighted programming for the purpose of time-shifting is not copyright infringement, but is legitimate fair use.[29]

The music industry's other failed attempts to stop the unauthorized playing, storing, copying, and distribution of online music and films included the following initiatives: The secure digital music initiative (SDMI) and the "rootkit disaster."[30] Under the SDMI, electronics manufacturers, security technology firms, ISPs, and others were asked to include computer and CD burner software that prevented the transmission and downloading of content that was not authorized by content owners. This would become a financial problem for Sony Music and its parent company because the parent company was one of the leading manufacturers of digital devices (computers, blank optical disks, and CD players) used to record and copy music, while Sony Music was a record label that sold millions of recorded music on CDs.[31]

In the rootkit disaster, Sony BMG Music embedded copyright protection software on CD releases, but the rootkit software contained security vulnerabilities that allowed malware, worms, and viruses to attack and destroy computers. Thousands of consumers filed class action lawsuits against Sony BMG and the company ended up settling the lawsuits for untold millions.[32]

Recently, the music and entertainment industries were successful in winning two landmark copyright infringement lawsuits (*A&M Records Inc. vs. Napster, Inc and MGM vs. Grokster*)[33] against file sharing technologies that would later turn out to

[29]See the analysis of the landmark Betamax court case also known as *Sony Corp. of Am. vs. Universal City Studios, Inc., 464 US 417 (1984)* in Samuelson (2006). Blockbuster Video became one of the pioneers in movie and video rental services and would later file for bankruptcy as it became difficult to compete with the digital offerings of Netflix movie-streaming services, DVR recorders on cable set-top boxes and cloud services that provide simultaneous access to multiple platforms such as smart phones, televisions, computers, and tablets.

[30]See the discussion in Gordon (2011, pp. 119–126).

[31]See Gordon (2011, pp. 119–126).

[32]See Gordon (2011, pp. 119–126).

[33]See also Langenderfer and Cook (2001) and *MGM vs. Grokster*, US Court of Appeals for the Ninth Circuit, Case No. 04-480, argued March 29, 2005 and decided June 27, 2005 for additional details.

be pyrrhic victories for the record labels because the big wins turned into bitter losses. Even with their court victories and the demise of earlier renditions of file sharing sites such as Napster, the music industry was still unable to stomp out the file sharing of music using the Internet. A new generation of other file sharing sites such as Kazaa, and more recently, torrent sites soon cropped up to become the primary means for today's "subversives" (teenage college students) to trade music, movies, e-books, and software online. Torrent-networking sites became popular for several reasons, and among them are the fast download speed of large media files to millions of private users worldwide; the code is open-source, advertising-free, and generally adware or spyware-free; and the distribution system is decentralized among users, multiple sources and software programs. In other words, the MPAA and the RIAA are having trouble figuring out how to monetize (legalize) unlicensed content on file-sharing sites when there is no apparent single entity that is profiting from torrent success. Torrent sites are also being used by a growing number of individuals and institutions to distribute their own or licensed material.

The record labels were unsuccessful in launching their own alternative digital platforms such as MusicNet (Warner, EMI and BMG) and Pressplay (Sony and Universal). MusicNet and Pressplay were failures because neither allowed the downloading of music, neither allowed consumers to transfer music to other devices, each service offered music only from their own limited repertories, and restrictions placed by major recording artists meant their music was unavailable for either service.[34] In April 2013, Viacom lost its most recent legal battle seeking a $1 billion from Google/YouTube for alleged copyright infringement when users uploaded and posted unauthorized video clips from Viacom's shows. The court's decision shielded YouTube from copyright infringement claims by a safe-harbor provision in the Digital Millennium Copyright Act.[35]

By 2008, the RIAA stopped filing individual infringement lawsuits for the following reasons. The RIAA's dubious and short-term legal strategy of suing individual file-sharers—based on the mistaken assumption that piracy was the only root cause of music industry problems—was proven to be expensive and ineffective, further alienating consumers who contributing to ancillary industry revenue such as live concert tickets and merchandise and migrating to other media platforms. Piracy was used to camouflage the failures to adjust to the changing market, structural and cyclical conditions in the music industry. The PROs would soon join the piracy-bandwagon even though it is not entirely clear how piracy affected background and foreground musical performances on the radio and television.

Second, the lawsuits were more or less smoke screens that generated negative publicity because 12-year-old children and consumers who did not own computers and even dead people were sued for obscene amounts. The "victories" in winning certain copyright infringement lawsuits came at a high cost (huge legal bills that

[34]See Gordon (2011, pp. 125–126).

[35]The court's decision can be found here: *Viacom International, Inc. v. YouTube, Inc.* (2013).

benefited mostly attorneys) and did not end piracy, but delayed the long-term process for dealing with the financial consequences of digitalization.

The third reason is that of the 30,000 cases filed (and 18,000 people sued), the lawsuits had little impact on combating free file sharing and were quietly settled. Private BitTorrent sites, private intranets, Wi-Fi networks, instant messaging systems, hidden IP addresses and other ways were often used to avoid getting caught using peer-to-peer (P2P) networks, furthering increasing the humiliating defeat of industry efforts at the hands of computer hackers.

Finally, the lawsuits did not result in increased CD sales (if that was the intent) because consumers demanded other digital choices.[36]

With the failure to stop the alleged illegal file sharing, copying and the distribution of music on P2P networks through the costly litigation process, the record labels turned to other methods—for educating the public that copyright holders needed to be compensated for the use of their creative works—such as the automated take-down procedure for search engines and "The Copyright Alert System" for ISPs that make it harder to search and obtain alleged pirated copyrighted content over the Internet. For example, copyright holders, such as movie studio owners, have asked search engines to remove movie and TV-show links (URLs) that may contain alleged copyrighted infringement material from its public indexed search results using take-down notices under the *Digital Millennium Copyright Act* (1998).[37] Under the Copyright Alert System, that is "meant to educate rather than punish, and direct (users) to legal alternatives," Internet users who illegally share music, movies or television shows online could soon receive five or six "strikes" (warning notices) from their Internet service providers for unauthorized downloads. Failure to respond to the warnings would result in the Internet provider taking more drastic measures such as a temporary reduction in Internet speed or bandwidth; a temporary downgrade or bandwidth cap in Internet service tier; a black-out period when service was made unavailable; or redirection to a landing page for a set period of time, until a subscriber contacts the ISP or until the subscriber completes an online copyright education program.[38]

The new policy is already dead on arrival because there are many sophisticated ways to remain anonymous and disguise an IP address to thwart such policies, public wireless connections (hotspots) will not be monitored and each ISP is responsible for implementing and policing their own system.

---

[36]See Gordon (2011, pp. 135–150), and Fogarty (2008). Various industry associations typically filed these lawsuits on behalf of their members. For example, the Recording Industry Association of America (RIAA) is the trade group that represents the major record labels. The National Music Publishers' Association (NMPA) represents all the major music publishers. The Motion Picture Association of America (MPAA) members are owners of the motion picture studios.

[37]See *RIAA Set For Historic 10,000,000th Google URL Takedown* at http://www.torrentfreak.com/riaa-set-for-historic-10000000th-google-url-takedown-130204/.

[38]See http://www.copyrightinformation.org/the-copyright-alert-system.

7.7 The Broken Terrestrial Broadcast Advertising Model

For the incumbent PROs, their internal cash-flow problems, rate court litigation and incompetent management more focused on maintaining the status quo in some cases added to the crisis afflicting the PRO industry. The PROs external problems stemmed, in part, from the broken old-media-terrestrial broadcast-advertising model and the disruption caused by mobile and digital media. Terrestrial radio stations now faced stiff competition from alternative technologies such as Internet radio. The old broadcast media model in which the same standardized message was served to a (passive) mass audience on a single platform changed dramatically with digital marketing and advertising.[39]

The radio and television broadcast audience became fragmented and scattered into bits and pieces across a vast network of sites (Facebook, Twitter, Google, Netflix, Spotify, and YouTube) and platforms (computer desktops, laptops, tablets, and mobile devices) that could be easily monitored to optimize digital advertising goals based on location, time of day, digital activity, and other variables. Furthermore, it became extremely difficult to engage consumers who were already strongly resistant to advertising messaging across radio, television, online and social media marketing segments.

As terrestrial broadcast audiences dwindled year over year—because viewers switched to alternative web-based video programming and direct streaming services to their television sets or mobile platforms—advertising revenue followed this inexorable shift from radio and television and its mass audience approach to targeted online advertising, including mobile devices. Furthermore, even as their share of broadcast audience dwindled, the price of advertising continued to skyrocket on broadcast television. The price of advertising remained high because of the same issues that we have been discussing: predatory behavior; preserving the status quo; active resistance to industry reform; cartels; inefficiencies; secrecy; scarcity; out-of-date business models; intermediaries; a lack of transparency; barriers to entry; control of information and price discovery.

TV networks often act like a cartel. They create the illusion of scarcity using the so-called up-front buying season in which TV airtime is sold in blocks of 30-s units. The purpose of the cartel is to put a floor under some price—whether it is the cost of a blanket license or advertising rates—and permit the high-cost incumbents' business models to remain in place. The television up-front buying season is the period that lasts for about only 4 days in May in which the majority of broadcast advertising airtime available on TV networks are sold in advance to advertisers through their media buyers, usually without transparency on how advertising prices

[39]See Passman (2012, pp. 242–243).

and rates are determined.[40] The networks create the illusion of scarcity in order to keep the price of their inventory high by withholding some inventory until later in the year, making their airtime even more scarce and more expensive for latecomers. During the up-front season, the big media buying agencies pool billions of dollars of their clients [large national advertisers] money to cut up-front deals, in hopes of driving down the aggregate price through sheer volume.' Even with all that spending and the leverage that comes from such purchases made over decades, "advertisers never really know the "true" price of any 30-s slot. Via their media-buying agencies, they must cut their deals with networks without knowing what other advertisers are paying." Advertisers who do not participate in these "upfronts" face a severe disadvantage later in the season when all the good airtime is sold to national advertisers with large advertising budgets.[41]

The up-front system hurts new advertisers with smaller budgets because they lack the leverage of large national advertisers, and they do not know how deep the long-term discounts are that other buyers are getting on the same airtime. Several television online trading exchanges that were developed by Google, Wal-mart, Microsoft, and Spot Runner for selling advertising airtime closed because the networks failed to provide significant inventory to sell or they offered their worst niche inventory on obscure cable networks. Perhaps, if buying airtime was "done instead via an online trading exchange, someone might ask the awkward question of why media agencies exist at all?" "The inefficiencies are built in for a reason: Networks aren't about to make their own market more efficient if that would mean lower prices for buyers."[42] It is the same inefficiency issue when it comes to music licensing. There is no single medium of exchange, automated auction platform or an equal-access central registry of song title registrations, copyrights ownership, licensing fees and royalty payment history data which would enable music users and copyright holders to determine the reference price for various music licenses through the dynamic market forces of supply and demand.

The advertising industry was transformed—more or less to a degree of personalization—with the use of digital technology that customized and narrowed advertising messaging to individual consumers based on personal demographic information, Internet surfing behavior or purchasing habits obtained from smart phone usage, credit card purchases, and other online data collected by firms such as Google, Twitter, and Facebook. "Big Data" from the network of sites and the

---

[40] See Edwards (2013).

[41] See Edwards (2013).

[42] See Edwards (2013).

various platforms could now be combined into a single source to form individual profiles of advertisers' marketing segments.[43]

With the declining audience for terrestrial radio and television broadcasts due to online streaming services, social media and other choices, ratings suffered and advertisers balked at paying more in advertising dollars to reach fewer and fewer viewers or listeners when they could easily target consumers with relevant ads distributed on mobile devices using Big Data analysis. This led major advertisers, such as car manufacturers and consumer products companies, to demand advertising spending discounts through their media buyers. These discounts led to decreased advertising revenue for radio and broadcast television networks, and therefore reduced licensing fees for PROs. Music users (and their corporate owners) also balked at paying huge performance royalties (based on a percentage of advertising revenue) and looked for ways to reduce the costs of music performance licensing.

7.8 The Collapse of Advertising Revenue in 2008

The housing and mortgage bubble collapse and stock market crash in 2008 only added to the sharp decline in advertising revenue for radio and television stations as well as newspapers and magazines. This meant that PRO licensing fees based on a percentage of advertising revenue were also collapsing as existing licensing agreements expired in 2008, 2009, 2010, and beyond.Some of this lost advertising revenue would never be recovered when licensing agreements with broadcasters were later renewed. Personal consumption spending dried up as consumers were no longer able to extract mortgage equity withdrawals (MEW) from their artificially inflated homes to fund their unsustainable lifestyles that were in turn fueling radio and television advertising and cash flow needed for servicing the enormous amount of debt that had built up in the industry from serial mergers and acquisitions. This led to the collapse in housing and automobile sales, and decreased radio and television advertising among auto dealers, home builders, building supplies retailers, restaurants and bars: The primary beneficiaries of the bubble-induced consumer demand based on borrowed money and the heaviest advertisers on radio and television. There was now a mad scramble in the music industry to adjust operating costs to revised revenue projections.

In 2009, when its radio industry's blanket licensing agreement was up for renewal, the RMLC immediately demanded lower PRO licensing fees to reflect

[43]Big Data refers to voluminous streams (in terms of variety, scale, size, amount and form) of individual personal information collected from "clickstreams" or online browsing behavior, Internet Protocol (IP) addresses, mobile phone usage, social networks, blogs, online shopping patterns, and other electronic means.

Table 7.5 Revenue distribution of the top 10 radio station-owners 2008

Owner	2008 Est. revenue ($b)	Share (%)	Stations	Share (%)
Clear channel	$2.92	37.34	845	45.48
CBS radio	$1.59	20.33	130	7.00
Citadel	$0.72	9.21	205	11.03
Cumulus	$0.52	6.65	305	16.42
Entercom	$0.47	6.01	112	6.03
Cox radio	$0.45	5.75	85	4.57
Univision	$0.41	5.24	72	3.88
Radio one	$0.27	3.45	52	2.80
Bonneville	$0.25	3.2	28	1.56
Emmis	$0.22	2.81	23	1.24
Total top 10	$7.82		1,858	

Sources: Based on U.S. revenue data from Wall Street Journal, 12/21/2009, p. B3.
Station-Owner data based on licensed data from: www.bia.com.

this new reality, and this was soon followed by other music users as well.[44] Highly leveraged radio-station owners such as Clear Channel Communications—with 845 stations at the time as shown in Table 7.5—saw advertising revenue evaporate, even as competition from Internet radio increased. The truncated data in Table 7.5, ranked by revenue, illustrates the large dynamic range from the largest to the smallest radio station-owners in the Top Ten Ranking in terms of revenue and the number of radio stations owned. A percentage of the station-owner revenue pays for the radio blanket licenses. Cumulatively, three radio station-owners (Clear Channel, CBS Radio and Citadel) accounted for 66.88 % of revenue and 63.51 % of commercial radio stations listed in the top ten in 2008.[45]

Weak demand for tickets to live sporting and music entertainment events (in which ticket prices became an issue), the continued decline in CD sales, the migration of advertising spending from terrestrial radio and television to the Internet, and new radio competitors such as Spotify and Pandora with alternative technologies exposed the permanent and structural changes that were occurring in the industry. Table 7.6 shows the dramatic migration of advertising dollars to digital media, including smart phones and tablets, and away from older platforms such as print (over a century old), terrestrial radio (close to a century old), and other forms of advertising spending, as digital technologies transformed the entire advertising market by providing greater efficiency, productivity, transparency, and accountability. The table shows the estimated $43 billion in total digital advertising in 2013 that far

[44]See *Section III: The RMLC-ASCAP License Agreement for the Period 2010–2016, US vs. ASCAP & In re Petition of Pandora Media* (2014, pp. 19–22).

[45]As of September 16, 2014, Clear Channel was re-branded as iHeartMedia to incorporate a growing digital trend into its identity.

Table 7.6 Estimated total advertising revenue by media 2012–2013: revenue in $Billions

Media platform	2012 rev. ($)	2012 share (%)	2013 rev. ($)	2013 share (%)	Y/Y change (%)
Television	$64.53B	39.10	$66.37B	38.80	2.85
Digital	$32.51	19.70	$33.35	19.50	2.60
Mobile	$4.29	2.60	$9.75	5.70	127.23
Digital & Mobile	$36.80	22.30	$43.10	25.20	17.13
Print	$34.16	20.70	$32.50	19.00	−4.86
Radio	$15.35	9.30	$15.22	8.90	−0.81
Other	$14.19	8.60	$13.86	8.10	−2.38
Total	$165.03		$171.05		3.65

Source: Based on July 2, 2014 data from: http://www.emarketer.com/Article/Total-US-Ad-Spending-See-Largest-Increase-Since-2004/1010982.

exceeds advertising revenue for the shrinking radio industry, one of major sources of licensing fees for PROs, music publishers, songwriters, and composers. Without the growth in radio revenue and the digital withdrawal movement, the economic prospects for incumbent PROs looked grim and foreboding.

Mobile advertising, that includes smart phones and tablets, the fastest growing area in advertising sales, is being driven by consumers spending more time on their tablets and smart phones (about 2 h and 51 min per day in 2014), and the smart phones' location capabilities in which marketers can target shoppers within the radius of a particular store. By the end of 2014, mobile advertising is expected to generate 10 % of all media spending, surpassing print and radio for the first time to become the third-largest individual media platform behind television and some other platforms. The growth in mobile advertising is occurring despite the tiny banner ads on smart phones that consumers find annoying; questions about effectiveness of mobile advertising; challenges in measuring audience size (just like ASCAP's boycott issue in 1940 in radio audience measurement) and problems determining how to allocate spending across smart phones and tablets.[46]

The recession in 2008 would reveal the true structural changes and powerful realities in the music industry (and the broader economy in general) that the inflated piracy issue, even if it were measurable, had long obscured. Minor adjustments to consent decrees, insignificant tweaks to copyright laws, and lengthy litigation were only going delay the inevitable cyclical and structural changes and reforms that the efficiencies and increased productivity from digital technologies were causing in the music industry. Digital technologies were not merely transitory, but were structural and permanent. The difference between the crash of the music industry in the 1920s—following the introduction of radio and The Great Depression—and

[46]See Perlberg (2014) and *Total US Ad Spending to See Largest Increase Since 2004: Mobile advertising leads growth; will surpass radio, magazines and newspapers this year* at http://www.emarketer.com/Article/Total-US-Ad-Spending-See-Largest-Increase-Since-2004/1010982.

the 2008 Great Recession is only a matter on the order of magnitude. The structural dynamics are about the same because personal consumption that was fueled by debt had come to an abrupt end.[47]

7.9 The Paradigm Shift in Music Sales

With the launch of Apple's iTunes music service in 2003, the economics of the music industry experienced an inevitable paradigm shift because consumers preferred an entirely different listening experience and new companies were created to meet this demand. As discount retailers like Walmart, Target, and Best Buy began to dominate the retail industry following the demise of independent music specialty retailers, music sales suffered from the old music-pricing system that focused on album sales. Retailers had no control over pricing, packaging, or discounting because the record labels were allowed to set retail prices for physical records with their stringent minimum advertised-price (MAP) policies. MAP policies were controversial in the industry and the four major music publishers and a number of retailers were investigated by the Federal Trade Commission for price-fixing. MAP policies were eventually abolished after the parties involved signed consent decrees.[48]

The introduction of the Apple's iPhone in 2007 that incorporated the music player of the iPod, wireless Internet capabilities, and other features affected more than the music industry because consumers switched to smart phones and abandoned home-based telephone landlines and desktop computers. Younger consumers liked the reliability, practicality, portability, economics, and cultural aspects of having a mobile phone with music and thousands of apps. The smart phone (and its mobile utility) has been used to provide permanent access to all media platforms by consolidating several devices—such as a (water-resistant) wireless phone, music player, (underwater and video) camera, computer, e-reader, heart-rate monitor, and GPS equipment—into a single, complex, and miniaturized electronic device. The smart phone made the product life cycle of landline phones, desktop computers, digital cameras, MP3 players, and GPS devices obsolete. The smart phone technology is unique because it combines two aspects of product marketing—that are usually handled as distinct marketing segments—that have always baffled marketing experts: how to fulfill an existing consumer need and how to create a need or demand for a product or service that has not existed before that consumers would find indispensable? Fulfilling an existing need is far simpler than creating a need that did not exist before because the latter requires shrewd consumer persuasion and some amount of serendipity—perhaps using celebrity endorsers, well-connected business

---

[47]See Morgan (2014) and Murphy (2014) for their comparisons of the two periods.

[48]See Christman (2008).

partners and prominent product placement in video synchronization—and some of these products are not always successful even after years and millions are spent developing prototypes.

The smart phone fulfilled an existing need that made life easier and more convenient for placing phone calls on the go, but it also created a communications need that did not exist before for immediate access to the Internet, a camera, bill payment, check deposits, music, video, games, email, text messages, and social media platforms using a single device. The conspicuous, glossy, bulky, gaudy and expensive headphones—that are essentially speakers for the head and an aspirational status symbol for teenagers—marketed by Beats Music is a similar product to a smart phone in that it fulfilled a need that existed and also created a need that never existed before. The sharp decline in record sales left music executives looking for products other than records to monetize, and Beats' headphones with noise-canceling technology were born.[49]

A new dominant music format, a new business model in music sales and the legal market for digital downloads emerged in the industry—which the record labels never envisioned or were able to achieve on an individual basis—creating something of a crisis. The downloading of music and the sale of music over the Internet were not a fad that would soon fade away. Practically overnight, the old business model of selling entire albums or CDs (with maybe one or two hits) that needed distribution through a network of physical retail channels and required massive radio promotion became a model of selling a succession of singles at $0.99 a song as the sales of Apple's iPods skyrocketed due to consumer demand. Consumers were now creating their own albums with their own carefully selected singles that were stored on their smart phones. Music subscription services later emerged that created customized playlists based on subscribers' listening patterns. New apps by companies to personalize playlists went even further by matching music to a subscriber's daily activities such as moods swings, working, studying, home entertaining, shopping, exercising, or even weather conditions.

Apple would set up its own point-of-sale system, and physical distribution networks (such as Tower Records) could no longer compete with digital retailers. Today, the iTunes Music Store has evolved to sell more than just music, and other items for sale include TV shows, movies, e-books, and apps.[50]

With simplified pricing of digital music, some of the complicated methods used in the pricing of physical records such as cassettes and CDs and in the computation of royalties were eliminated. In the process, consumers were no longer forced to buy entire albums with fillers and soon this began to eat into retail sales of recorded music. Digital music could be created instantly to meet consumer demand and there was no need for retailers to stock inventory. For example, artists were only paid

---

[49]See Biddle (2013). On May 8, 2014, the *Financial Times* reported that Apple Inc. were in negotiations with Beats Music to purchase the company for US $3.2 billion.

[50]Although the iPod and MP3 players are both music players, the iPod is a specific brand of an MP3 player made by Apple that has a unique set of design features that utilize the software.

for each physical record that was "sold" and on a percentage basis of a cassette's or CD's wholesale price. Therefore, "special campaign free goods," "promotion copies," "return privilege," "reserves," and "90 % of net sales" were all discounted from the quantities sold or the suggested retail list price (SRLP) of a record that was used in the computation of royalties and further reduced payments to artists.[51]

Once again, music fans were recreating (getting rid of vinyl records and CDs) their personal music libraries, but were now only interested in selecting and purchasing the songs that they liked or wanted. Music fans were no longer interested in purchasing complete albums created by the record labels with only one or two hit songs and the additional songs were mostly "fillers" that they didn't want, worsening the crisis created by free file sharing for music distributors. In other words, consumers were paying $15.99 for one or two hit songs on a CD and it made no economic sense to continue to package or bundle songs that consumers did not need in order to justify the "value" in the sale of a CD. For the record companies, instead of making $8 wholesale for every $15.99 CD sold, they made $0.70 for every $0.99 download.

The record labels assumed that they had duped Apple into overpaying for the licensing rights to their repertories by obtaining a 70 % margin rather than the traditional 50 % gross margin that was the industry standard at the time. However, the volume of digital sales, even today, could not offset the declining sales of physical CDs.[52] As profit margins declined—offset by increases in performance and synchronization revenue—from about three-to-four dollars a CD to pennies for a single download, income plummeted by more than 50 % in the industry. The record labels no longer had the larger cash reserves to devote to artist development. Without big budgets to create promotional music videos, the importance of MTV to break new acts and sell records would diminish as well. This precipitated the inexorable shift to social media (YouTube, Facebook, Twitter) and other platforms where artists could be discovered without the help of record labels or other promoters.[53]

By 2012, Apple became the most profitable technology company—in a highly competitive industry—from selling devices that played music and not the music content itself.[54] There were also 20 million paying global subscribers to subscription music services and they accounted for a 10 % share of total digital music revenue. However, in early 2014, the sale of digital downloads, including albums and tracks, began its own decline in the short life cycle of music delivery in the digital era. The decline in digital sales was attributed to the increase in consumer interest and preference for both ad-supported and paid subscription music streaming services.

---

[51]See Passman (2012, pp. 74–82).

[52]See Gordon (2011, pp. 125–126).

[53]See Gordon (2011, pp. 153–160). One such platform was the broadcast television program, *American Idol* (and the other imitators) that created more impressions than the traditional radio format of breaking new artists.

[54]See Gordon (2011, pp. 125–126).

Table 7.7 Global digital revenue 2009–2012: US $Billions and percent change

Year	2009	2010	2011	2012
Rev$B	$4.70	$4.80	$5.10	$5.60
Y/Y Change (%)	9.30 %	2.13 %	6.25 %	9.80 %

Source: Based on data from IFPI Digital Music Report 2013, pp. 5–6.

In addition, it appeared that streaming was offsetting the decline in digital sales revenue, but it was not large enough to offset the decline in physical products such as CDs.[55]

Patry (2011, p. 144) calls this pattern of music publishers, record labels, and PROs challenging every new technology that comes along as an existential threat, squandering valuable time and resources on costly litigation and their initial reluctance to embrace digital methods of music distribution and newer industry business models, and then profiting from the new business opportunities over time, the defining relationship of gatekeepers to copyright law in which they are forced to adapt to a world they could no longer control.

Table 7.7 illustrates why the entire music industry could have been better off if the alleged existential threat from online digital music and piracy issues were resolved much sooner and the new digital business models and music services adapted much faster. Global digital sales in 2012 were estimated at $5.6 billion, and now account for around 34 % of total recording industry revenue. After more than a decade or more of costly copyright infringement litigation, it is now somewhat incredible to believe that in 2013—as digital sales have grown more than significantly enough to offset plummeting CD sales—that the music industry would announce that it "has adapted to the Internet world, learned how to meet the needs of consumers, monetized the digital marketplace and digital music drives innovation."[56] Although consumers are using smart phones to listen to their favorite music, purchase music, watch music videos, send photos, and stay connected with friends through text messaging, telephone calls, and social networks such as Facebook, the market in terms of demographics—such as age and income—is fragmented. The fact that music consumers, particularly young consumers, mostly grew up with the Internet and digital technologies means that "more than media companies, these consumers appreciate the potential of this new market, and expect service offerings and prices instantly to reflect it. When the industry hesitates, resists, and delays, users take matters into their own hands, empowered by increasingly disruptive technologies."[57]

---

[55]See Christman (2014).

[56]See International Federation of the Phonographic industry (IFPI), Digital Music Report 2013, pages 5–6, accessed online at http://www.ifpi.org/content/library/DMR2013.pdf and Vermeulen (2014).

[57]See Downes (2011).

Table 7.8 Price discounts to increase demand for new devices

Device	Original price	Discounted price	Difference	Change (%)
iPhone 5 16 GB	$189.97	$127.00	$62.97	33.15
iPhone 4S 16 GB	$89.97	$47.00	$42.97	47.76
iPad 16 GB	$499.00	$399.00	$100.00	20.04

As of December 15, 2012 for the base model iPhones and excludes monthly recurring voice, text and data fees.
The 32 and 64 GB versions of the iPhone cost considerably more.

With every new introduction or premium variant of an existing product in its life cycle, consumers flock to the latest version, product or service. Economic demand increases until the inevitable brick wall of market saturation or cannibalization at various price-points result in an unsustainable growth curve. Demand for the product (and complimentary product lines) falls off rapidly at a given price point because there is no compelling reason to upgrade as frequently as before. Retail price discounting and marketing promotions (two-for-the-price-of-one offers) begin in order to bolster demand and that further erodes profit margins. Smart phones are typically upgraded on a much faster replacement cycle than tablet computers. Smart phones—with screens larger than those of tablets—often cannibalize the demand for smaller tablets. In the Internet era, the latest new version of a product is often viewed as a marketing fad because of the modest incremental changes in features and functions when the new variants are unveiled. Meanwhile, the older product lines are still functional in terms of performance and the quality of the included software. The difference between the old and new variants of smart phones is often based on their new internal specifications, display resolution and the chassis (physical design) material. For example, it was reported in December 2012 that a few weeks after its introduction, Walmart stores began heavily discounting Apple's products at thousands of its retail outlets. Other retailers such as Best Buy, Target, and RadioShack were also considering matching Walmart's offer. The need to discount mobile devices is partially due to the short product life cycle of these devices, just a few months in some cases.

This short life cycle means that customers sometimes fear that they may be unwittingly buying a product that may be obsolete in just a few months' time. Just the rumored announcement of a pending release or even the predictable availability of a premium new variant of the old device can cause the device to become obsolete and send sales plummeting.[58] Table 7.8 shows the discounting and cannibalization that often occur in the smart phone market. For example, Apple's flagship product at the time, the iPhone 5, was discounted by 33.15 % from the original price of $189.97. Apple's iPad, a complimentary product line to the iPhone, was discounted as well. The most likely reasons for a steep price-cut a few weeks

[58]See *Walmart selling Apple's iPhone 5 at big discount*: http://www.reuters.com/article/2012/12/15/us-apple-walmart-iphone-discount-idUSBRE8BD1D120121215.

after its introduction were that: (a) the product failed to meet sales projections at the original selling price during the crucial Christmas shopping season; (b) customers were probably hesitant to purchase the device with the knowledge of leaks and rumors that a new variant might be unveiled in a short period; and (c) most people who wanted a smart phone probably already owned one.

From the perspective of Apple, the former product and price leader in smart phones and iPads in the US, the economic implications for Apple's weak (and over-estimated) demand, are apparent from Walmart-type mass market discounting for price-sensitive consumers: commodity pricing, cannibalization, decelerating revenue growth, declining profit margins, increasing competition, and market saturation. In an attempt to increase the company's penetration into "emerging markets" (geographical locations outside the US) and newer market segments in the US, lower-margin and cheaper products are becoming a bigger percentage of Apple's revenue. The price-value tradeoff of any product or service in the Internet-shopping age has to be reasonable before consumers consider a purchase or the next innovation.

7.10 The Future of Terrestrial Radio

Terrestrial radio, particularly AM/FM radio, is frequently perceived in the music industry as having a less than certain future among young consumers who listen to music in the automobile through an in-dash app or a smart phone connected via Bluetooth to the car's audio system. Consumers can easily stream music from their favorite streaming music service, Internet or satellite radio station through a smart phone that is connected to the car's electronic system. In 2013, analysts were predicting that AM/FM radios will be eliminated from car dashboards by two US automotive companies within 2 years and by all car makers within 5 years. New car technology would allow drivers and passengers to access the same features such as music, navigation, apps and services that they already have on their smart phones.[59]

Indeed, smart phone technology integrated into a new car's electronic audio system means that the days of listening to AM and FM stations and music on physical media such as cassettes and CDs while driving are just about over. More people are listening to audio on digital devices, and growth and momentum in both revenue and listeners appear to be digital-only listening. Smart phones, MP3 players, tablets, and laptops—connected to new cars with USB ports or wireless Bluetooth capabilities—provide drivers and passenger with the capabilities to listen to audio files, using voice-activated commands, features, and functions. The voice-activated features make it easier to perform functions like getting directions, making phone calls, and selecting music while safely operating the vehicle. In addition, new cars now come equipped with satellite radio—usually free with a trial subscription for a set period and then annual payments may be required—which allows the car to

[59]See Peoples (2013).

receive digital signals from local radio stations. The net effects of the smart phone use in the automobile are that it has further eroded the sale of music on CDs that were played in the car and diminished the competitive advantage once enjoyed by traditional radio broadcasting on AM/FM radio stations. The recent radio industry consolidation left many station-owners unable to service their enormous corporate debt as advertising revenue declined due to weak economic conditions in 2008, or advertisers switched their advertising dollars to other media such as the Internet.

7.11 The Future of Broadcast and Cable Television

MTV—surpassed by YouTube—was no longer as music intensive as in the past and their programming shifted from a steady dose of music-intensive videos to unscripted reality shows with much less musical performances, similar to other shows on other networks. The "music" in Music Television (MTV) was now secondary to the network's programming aimed at the shifting tastes and behaviors of its core audience of younger viewers. Music-based competition shows like *American Idol* replaced music-intensive video programming on broadcast networks. After a decade, this genre began a steep decline in ratings due in part to massive imitation and overexposure. As television ratings declined, the business model of music-competition programming—producing "hit singers" who could sell records, concert tickets and merchandise—was no longer viable because later winners did not meet with the same commercial success as previous winners.[60]

Internet streaming services such as Netflix, Amazon, and Hulu have disrupted the traditional broadcast and cable television content-and-distribution business models by making their programming available to subscribers over the Internet and on mobile devices; reshaped the way that consumers watch television; and transformed the economics of the older TV business model that depended on advertising. In general, some of these new Internet video and television streaming services distribute their programming content in an advertising-free environment and on an efficient, reliable, and easy-to-use digital multi-platform service, including tablets, smart phones, and TV sets. The expansion of these services into international markets is now easier and cheaper on digital platforms. Streaming services that do not produce their own programming are now licensing content from established television and movie studios. The content selection and availability at each streaming site are constantly changing due to the nature of licensing deals. In the process, these services have transformed the way in which some people watch television by turning television programming into an on-demand service that is available whenever and wherever they want and were cheaper than a cable or satellite package. The shift to video streaming was made possible by the new technologies that became ubiquitous and were able to handle the downloading of large files associated with television and movie videos and the large capacity in cloud storage.

[60]See Chozick (2013) and Carter (2014).

Netflix's new streaming business model quietly evolved from its DVD rental business that has been mostly abandoned. Netflix's innovative business model of distributing its own original video programming (*House of Cards* and *Orange is the New Black*) as well as licensed content from third parties demonstrated that it was profitable to bypass the traditional broadcast and cable distribution networks to stream on-demand video programming over the Internet, and consumers were willing to pay to unbundle their cable services. A significant amount of video streaming programming from Netfliix, Hulu, and Amazon Prime is from popular, current television programming in which consumers have the ability to watch several consecutive episodes of the same TV show in one sitting—in the so-called *binge-viewing* or *binge-watching* practice. With binge-watching on streaming services, there are no disruptive commercials selling products and services and this appears to be one of the most appealing features of video streaming services.[61] Unlike traditional television, consumers were interested in Netflix's business model because their programming has no paid advertising, and so there is no competition with traditional broadcast networks for advertising dollars and ratings. More importantly, Netflix is able to directly connect with customers, collect and analyze lucrative viewer data—such as the millions of plays per day (tracked by the number of rewinds, fast-forwards, and pauses in a movie); billions of hours of streaming video watched during a given period; subscribers' ratings of programming; millions of movie searches per day; Geo-location data; viewing device or platform information; metadata from third parties such as Nielsen; and social media data from Facebook and Twitter—that incumbents broadcast networks are lacking.[62]

In response to these new entrants, the traditional broadcast and cable (incumbent) networks are changing their business models by adding stand-alone Internet streaming services that target a new generation of viewers who watch television shows and movies on the Internet. HBO—a premium cable network that requires a basic cable subscription—and CBS—a traditional broadcast network with paid advertising—both announced plans to start new digital subscription video services that will augment their (status quo) business models to retain existing viewers and subscriber's fees. In HBO's case subscribers to their stand-alone streaming service will not have to buy a cable package. These services will offer thousands of episodes from current and previous seasons on an on-demand basis, including the streaming of live events.[63]

---

[61]See *How to Overcome a Binge-Watching Addiction: The key to the cure? Understanding how TV scripts and your willpower work*, Wall Street Journal, September 26, 2014 and available online: http://www.wsj.com/articles/how-to-overcome-a-binge-watching-addiction-1411748602. Binge-watching has apparently become "addictive" for some consumers and it probably means that these consumers may be leaving advertising supported networks for good.

[62]See *Netflix analyzes a lot of data about your viewing habits* that is available here: https://www.gigaom.com/2012/06/14/netflix-analyzes-a-lot-of-data-about-your-viewing-habits.

[63]See Carr (2014b).

Table 7.9 Cord-cutting households (in 000's): quarterly Y/Y change 2013–2014

Households	Q3 2013	Q3 2014	Change	Change (%)
Broadcast only	11,183	12,167	984	8.80
Wired cable	56,123	52,986	−3,137	−5.59
Satellite	35,110	34,723	−387	−1.10

Source: Based on data from: *The Total Audience Report: December 2014*, The Nielsen Company, p. 17.

These video streaming service are popular with consumers for a variety of reasons. Younger broadband users have never been subscribers to traditional cable and satellite television and are often described as *Cord-Nevers*. Some existing customers may be paying for a bundle of cable networks that they never watch and are interested in the option of purchasing cable as an à la carte service, that is, individual networks that can be purchased based on consumers picking and choosing what they like rather than a fixed bundle of channels. *Cord-Cutters*—interested in lowering their monthly costs for paid television—are dropping cable and satellite services altogether.

Table 7.9 shows the *what* that has been happening in the pay-TV industry, including wired cable and satellite services. These services lost more than 3.5 million households because customers have been "cutting the cord" and dropping pay-TV subscriptions for alternative entertainment, causing the deterioration of traditional TV viewers on advertising-supported networks. The number of households without pay television services increased by 984,000, as streaming services have begun to cannibalize the time consumers spend watching traditional television.

Table 7.10 shows the economic reasons of *why* cord-nevers, existing subscribers and cord-cutters are flocking to Internet video streaming services: Streaming services like Netflix and Hula cost substantially less than the annual subscription fees for bundled cable services—even if consumers subscribed to more than one service—giving the consumer another choice in selecting their own individual video programs at a lower cost.

Individual video content owners could face some of the similar problems that music publishers encountered when Apple's iTunes transformed music licensing by unbundling the music album that allowed consumers to purchase singles to create their own distinctive albums. Besides the technical, operational, infrastructure and media platform issues that come from unbundling cable networks, individual broadcast video streaming services may be limited by their own back-catalog, which is probably only a small percentage of content that is available. Consumers would have to pay additional fees for access to the content of other popular networks. In addition, all streaming providers could face the same content acquisition costs and cost structure when acquiring alternative content from a limited number of suppliers.

Table 7.10 Annual costs of digital and bundled cable services

Service	Type	Annual cost
CBS all access	Video	$71.88
Hulu plus	Video	$95.88
Netflix	Video	$95.88
Amazon prime	Music, video, books & storage	$99.00
New York times	Newspaper digital version	$105.00
YouTube music key	Video and music	$119.88[a]
Billboard	Magazine digital version	$119.88
Spotify (Premium)	Music	$119.88
Audible books	Books digital version	$179.40
HBO	Premium cable	$180.00[b]
Average bundled cable		$772.92[c]

Sources: Price data from company websites
[a]YouTube's ad-free and paid music subscription service with more extensive access to music, high-quality audio, the ability to store videos offline and links to other Google music services after promotional period.
[b]Estimated prices based on the current monthly subscription fee included in the fees paid by consumers for cable or satellite services. Service is expected to start in 2015.
[c]Expanded Basic Cable Service. *Report on Average Rates for Cable Programming Service and Equipment* (5/16/2014), available here: http://www.fcc.gov/encyclopedia/media-bureau-reports-industry.

7.12 The Future of Films

Video consumption and viewing patterns have changed, and consumers are no longer tied to a television set or an appointed hour to watch particular programs as on-demand streaming services have become ubiquitous. Music is an inherent feature in most films, but unlike music—that is divided into its musical composition and sound recording components that could be exploited separately—films cannot be divided into such consumptive elements for exploitation. One entity may own or control all of the distribution rights to a film, and the goal is to maximize revenue through its various *distribution windows*.

The digital upheaval in the film industry occurred at a much slower pace than in the music industry because downloading times and the technology to do so were inhibiting factors given the large files sizes associated with video-based content. The film industry avoided some of the issues that paralyzed the music industry and contained the damage because they were able to observe the innovations of iTunes, Netflix and the impact of peer-to-peer file sharing that had no geographical boundaries. Internet technologies, computer devices, on-demand services, and new distribution platforms have all undermined the traditional revenue system in films, and transformed the business models in the film industry.

Following the standard industry practice, film revenues were often based on *distribution windows*, that is, after a film's theatrical release, the film is then licensed to broadcast television, pay-per-view (PPV), cable television, airlines, hotels, home video, and other outlets at discrete time intervals with exclusive nor non-exclusive rights, which may sometimes overlap. Ancillary revenue from video games and merchandising was also added to the mix. However, with streaming technologies and new digital platforms, there have been new shifts in the distribution window patterns in which some producers release films on VOD, and all other key platforms simultaneously with their theatrical release, thus, compressing the discrete time intervals or sales cycle for a film's exploitation. Online pioneers such as Amazon, Hulu, NetFlix, and YouTube have all launched video production and development companies and are no longer relying on just licensing content from other producers.[64]

Long-form video content, such as movies, is vulnerable to the same threats that the broadcast, book publishing and music industries are facing, including what is the appropriate distribution window for Internet access.

> Despite technological changes, the turf of windows, being the lifeblood of certain businesses, tends to be defended at all costs by those who are threatened. What no one questions today, however, is that the increased variety of windows is creating more competition than ever before, and as a corollary leading to the compression of windows, acceleration of revenues (with most film now staying in theaters only a handful of weeks), and greater risk.[65]

The compression of distribution windows, online distribution, and films staying in domestic theaters for only a few weeks are actually accelerating the losses for movie chains who are dependent on blockbuster hits to sustain other underperforming releases. Movie chains are facing the same cyclical and structural threats that music retailers such as Tower Records faced before its demise: YouTube, smart phones, illegal torrents file-sharing websites, and on-demand streaming services. Profitability is now based on the first few weeks of a movie in theaters and before it is released to other viewing outlets.

For the top five movie theater chains in North America, American moviegoers in the 12 to 24 age category declined by 15 % for the first 9 months in 2014. Revenue from ticket sales is expected to decline by 4 % to $10.5 billion at year end 2014. With the drop in theater attendance, we can see the decline in profitability for the top five major chains as shown in Table 7.11. The reason for the decline in revenue and profitability is partially based on consumer alternatives such as on-demand streaming movies from Netflix that are viewed in the home.

---

[64]See Ulin (2014a, pp. 35–55) and also Ulin (2014b) where he discusses the impact of Netflix, Hulu, Amazon, YouTube, and cord-cutters in the film industry.

[65]See Ulin (2014a, pp. 42–43).

Table 7.11 Profits of top five North American theater chains: first 9 months of each year ($m)

Chain	2013	2014	Change
Regal cinemas	$133.6	$58.9	−74.7
Cinemark theaters	132.9	145.3	12.4
AMC theaters	84.8	34.3	−50.5
Cineplex (Canadian$)	63.4	44.2	−19.2
Carmike cinemas	1.9	−6.7	−8.6
Total	416.6	276	−140.6

Source: Based on data from: Barnes (2014).

7.13 The Future in Book Publishing

Digital technologies are changing the way books are written, published, marketed, sold, and read. Print on-demand is the now the preferred model for some publishers in which e-books are made available online first, followed closely by soft/hardcover books that is printed based on customer requests. Digital technologies have enabled the self-publishing of books—by both novice and established writers—without the need to own a printing press and distribution can occur online. Some books are now available in both printed and digital formats, and consumers can decide which format to purchase. The digital transformation of printed books into an electronic format has changed the book publishing business model with the surge in e-book sales.

The economic advantages of selling e-books—just like selling digital music—are that only the first digital copy is needed, there is no need for printing, inventory, warehouses and physical distribution, the marginal cost of reproducing additional e-book copies is small and e-books are never out of print. E-books serve the same function as printed books in terms of the advancement, preservation, and transmittal of ideas between writers and readers. However, e-books are more convenient for the downloading of an instant copy; portability and storage of scores of titles on a single e-reader, smart phone, computer or tablet; and interactive reading (the reader can click through to websites from the e-book itself). They can also provide writers and publishers with data-driven decision making on what books are sold and read, and valuable insights on the type of consumers purchasing books. E-book readers can also network with other like-minded people for book (fiction and non-fiction) discussions on the many public forums on the Internet.

Just like digital technology was seen as a threat to the status quo in the music industry, the popularity of e-books and the improved design of e-reader devices have raised similar issues in the book publishing industry such as: (a) e-book piracy; (b) e-book competitive pricing model—agency versus wholesale; (c) the top major book publishers and Apple forming a cartel to raise prices; (d) antitrust price-fixing litigation; (e) digital royalty rates for authors; (f) end-user licensing restrictions; (g) Most Favored Nations clauses; (h) restrictive consent decrees; (i) transparency in promotional lists; (j) contract disputes among distributors, writers and publishers; (k) insider collusion and conspiracies; (l) cannibalization of hardback books sales

Table 7.12 Book publishing standard royalty rates by format

Format	Royalty rate (%)[a]
Paperback	7.5
Mass market	8–10
Hardcover	15
E-books	25

Source: Based on data from: Publishers Weekly, December 9, 2013, pp. 5–6.
[a]These royalty rates may not include academic publications.

from lending libraries; (m) negative revenue growth in certain book segments; (n) plummeting sale of physical books; (o) the demise of Borders book stores and independent booksellers; and (p) the sensitive nature of the percentage of revenue that now comes from Amazon sales.[66] As shown in Table 7.12, at the time of writing, the royalty rate for paperbacks—which were once the cheaper alternative to hardcover editions of a book—was 7.5 %; one-half the rate for hardcovers. E-books were the cheapest alternative to both hardcovers and paperbacks and the royalty rate paid to authors was around 25 %; the largest for any format in book publishing. Authors and agents have been demanding that the digital rate of 25 % should be raised higher as the demand and profits for e-books are now increasing in the industry.[67]

The standard royalty rates in Table 7.12 may not include some academic publications, even though print on-demand and digital distribution through Amazon have reduced the production and distribution costs for all publishers. Older electronic editions are never out of print. Newer editions or editorial changes and corrections are just a matter of uploading a new digital copy. However, the price of educational material, including college textbooks, has remained high due in part to the labor-intensive process of creating such material; the limited market for some publications; instructors receiving free desk-copies and other instructional material from the publisher for adopting a text for classroom use; and the cost of text books are sometimes buried in the repayment schedule of student loans. Wikipedia has made educational material freely available on the Internet and cannibalized the

---

[66]The details on the related lawsuits against Apple and the five book publishers for fixing the prices of certain e-books in violation of the *Sherman Antitrust Act* are discussed here: *State of Texas vs Penguin Group & In Re: Electronic Books Antitrust Litigation* (2014).
Judge Denise Cote—presiding in the Apple/book publishers antitrust case—is the same judge who is enforcing ASCAP's consent decree. She is the author of many of the ASCAP-related court opinions and orders cited in this book.
See also *The Piracy Problem: What can YA publishers and authors do to get more readers to buy books instead of illegally downloading them?*, Publishers Weekly, July 21, 2014. p. 20.

[67]See *Checking in on the Digital Royalty Debate*, Publishers Weekly, December 9, 2013, pp. 5–6.

physical and digital sales of encyclopedias. Low-cost textbook start-ups attempting to enter the publishing industry have often been sued over copyright infringement claims.

Academic publishers, like music publishers, are able to aggregate or bundle several e-books or journals in their back catalogs as "consortium packages" that are sold to libraries, universities, and other institutions on a subscription basis. End-users at the subscribing institutions are able to download digital copies of e-books, in part or in whole, depending on the terms in the institution's licensing agreements.[68]

The royalty payments to academic authors from consortium package downloads may be treated differently from print on-demand orders or physical copies at some academic publishers in which the author is paid a percentage of net income (list price minus discounts and taxes) received by the publisher. In a typical academic publishing agreement, authors are paid royalties for consortium packages based on a formula that includes the total revenue from print sales of all titles in a package and the total revenue from consortium sales. Each individual author then receives what is referred to an "uplift" in the industry, that is, their share of royalty payments is based on the ratio of print sales and consortium revenue in the package and the total of each individual author's royalty payments. For example as shown in Table 7.13, if total print sales (all titles) included in the package are $10 million, and total consortium sales are $7 million, then each individual title receives a 70 % uplift. If the royalties for an individual academic title was $350, then an additional $245 would be paid to the author for consortium royalties. Titles with multiple authors would share the uplift amount.

E-books can cost less than printed versions, except in the case of licensing agreements with publishers on simultaneous usage, online reading, downloading, printing, inter-library loans or metering associated with lending libraries.[69] With the purchase of selected e-book titles, the bookseller may include other e-books in the same genre for free. Some e-books can also be read free online. E-books appear to have cannibalized the sale of audio-books due to price and the limited selection of titles. Table 7.14 shows the ranking by appearances of the top e-book publishers for

Table 7.13 Royalty calculation for an individual title in consortium sales

Total print sales (all titles)	$10 million
Total consortium sales	$7 million
Uplift (%) ($7m ÷ $10m)	70 %
Paid royalties on an individual title	$350
Author(s) uplift on title ($350 × 70 %)	$245

[68] See http://www.worldcat.org for a listing of the 72,000 libraries and lending institutions for physical and e-books.

[69] What are to become of physical lending libraries that were once the repository for printed books and displaced librarians are just some of the secondary effects of the digital revolution that remain unanswered.
The books will probably be stored at inaccessible off-site locations that may take days to retrieve.

Table 7.14 Top six e-book publishers first half 2014: ranked by appearances on bestsellers lists

Rank	Publisher	Appearances	Appearances share (%)	No. 1 bestsellers
1	Penguin random house	250	40.00	7
2	HarperCollins	156	24.96	12
3	Hachette	78	12.48	3
4	Amazon	60	9.60	2
5	Simon & Schuster	28	4.48	0
6	Self-published	25	4.00	1
7	Scholastic	8	1.28	0
8	Harlequin	4	0.64	0
9	Macmillan	4	0.64	0
10	Others	12	1.92	0
Total		625		25

Source: Based on data from: http://www.digitalbookworld.com/2014/ebook-publisher-power-rankings-top-publishers-of-2014-so-far.

the first half of 2014, and it is worth noting the accomplishment of self-publishers—and their ability to spread new ideas—at number six in the rankings with one title making it to the number one spot on the list. Self-publishers, as a group, are attracting hoards of readers and were ranked above publishers such as Macmillan, W.W. Norton, B&H Books, Houghton-Mifflin-Harcourt, and others who made the bestseller's list with fewer appearances but did not make to the number one spot.

Amazon is one of the most successful Internet-only retailers that has displaced many local and big-box physical retailers and in the process created an upheaval in retailing. Retailers have had to adapt to the speed and convenience that digital innovations such as the smart phone brought to shopping, even though in certain categories consumers had to wait a day or two for delivery. It is in the delay in product delivery of items such as food and medicine that some believe that Amazon may be vulnerable to competitive forces and may face its own disruption.[70] Amazon earns billions in revenue a year on worldwide sales—revenue that exceeds its next 12 competitors combined—but its business model (high sales volume growth and low profit margins) is always questioned because there is no consistency in its profitability.[71]

Amazon—with its own self-publishing platform and e-reader device, the Kindle–is responsible for close to a 30 % share of the physical book market and more

[70]See *Amazon Not as Unstoppable as It Might Appear*, New York Times, December 18, 2014, p. B1.

[71]See Anders (2013).

than 60 % of e-books sold in the United States.[72] This has drawn criticism from writers and other book publishers who have alleged that Amazon's market power dominance is based on the ability to delay the shipping times (free 2-day vs 2–3 weeks delivery) for certain book orders; elimination of discounts or raising prices; refusing pre-publication orders; steering customers to other publishers; and deceptive sales practices such as the difficulty in finding some physical books at their website.[73]

Amazon's market power is different from the PRO's in a distinct way. The PROs market power is based on monopoly pricing as a *dominant seller*, that is, the ability to raise prices or keep prices high, while Amazon's market dominance is allegedly based on monopsony pricing. In monopsony (or buyer's monopoly) pricing, a *dominant buyer* controls a large proportion of the market and drives down the wholesale price of an item in selected markets or segments. In general, a single company with monopsony power is not viewed as illegal in an antitrust sense because buying power often translates into lower retail prices for consumers.[74] For example, Walmart is said to function as a monopsony in certain market segments and that is the reason for its "everyday low prices" that benefit consumers.

Amazon has been accused of squeezing other book publishers on its platform by demanding a larger share or margins on the price of books, essentially driving down the price that it pays to acquire books, by dictating terms to its suppliers who have no choice but to agree to the terms. Supposedly, it is authors and publishers who are hurt—lower publishers' profits, and royalties and advances paid to authors—by Amazon's power to kill the *buzz* associated with a book and prevent it from making it on to a bestseller's list.

At the heart of the dispute is the issue of the pricing and discounting of e-books, just like it was in the music industry. Best Buy and Walmart were able to deeply discount music—even below record label prices—because they sold an array of other products that could offset music discounts, and that eventually caused the demise of independent music distributors like Tower Records. Amazon has been accused of applying the same pricing and discounting tactics with book publishers. Furthermore, Amazon not only sells e-books, but is in control of one of the most popular e-book reading/distribution devices, the Kindle. Table 7.15 shows the ease with which it is possible for independent authors to self-publish a print book or

[72]See http://www.apub.com/about.
Amazon has also developed a traditional publishing organization, which is similar to the "legacy" publishers, and consists of 14 imprints.

[73]See Gapper (2014).
In early November 2014, it appeared as though Amazon had settled the E-book and print sales pricing dispute with major publishers Simon & Schuster and Hachette.
See also *Amazon Versus Hachette: The Whole Story*: http://www.publishersweekly.com/pw/by-topic/industry-news/bookselling/article/63304-amazon-versus-hachette-the-whole-story.html, Publishers Weekly, November 2014, for a regularly updated series of articles on the dispute and its resolutions.

[74]See Gapper (2014).

Table 7.15 Self-publisher costs to print and distribute a book at Amazon

Line item	Price	Percentage (%)	Distribution terms
Sales channel	$3.60	40.00	Varies by sales channel and trim size
Fixed charge	$0.85	9.44	Varies by page count and page color
Per page charge	$2.20	24.44	Varies by page count if over a set limit
Total per book	$6.65		On-demand orders & shipping costs
Royalty rate	$2.34	26.00	
List price	$9.00		A 184-page book printed in black and white

Source: Based on data from: https://www.createspace.com/Products/Book/Royalties.jsp.

Table 7.16 Wholesale versus agency model in pricing

Wholesale model	Agency model
Publishers sell to retailers for a fixed price	Publishers set the price
Retailer sets the price for customers	Retailers get a commission for distribution
Retailer can discount to meet supply & demand	Retailers cannot offer discounts
Example: Traditional 50/50 Margin	*Example: Electronic 70/30 Margin*
Book publisher sets the price at 50 % of retail	Publishers set the price of books and distributors, like Amazon or Apple, receive a 30 % commission
Music CDs selling for $15.99 at retail would wholesale at $8	Music downloads are priced at $0.99 each and record labels get $0.70

Sources: Based on data from:

1. http://www.publishingtrendsetter.com/industryinsight/simple-explanation-agency-model.
2. Gordon (2011, pp. 119–126).

e-book on Amazon's publishing platform. Close to 74 % of the $9 price of a self-published book goes to Amazon to cover the costs of printing on-demand copies, electronic distribution, and shipping. The remaining 26 % is retained by the author as a royalty payment.[75]

The pricing of digital music singles and e-books follow a similar pattern and it appears as though the same margin pricing formula is being used in both industries. Incidentally, the same pricing problems and antitrust issues seem to have occurred in both industries. In the book industry, the *Agency Model* and *Wholesale Model* are used to price books as illustrated in Table 7.16; and technically the same is used in the music industry, even though the term "agency model" is not popular in the music industry. Amazon employs the wholesale model for the e-books they sell, while Apple uses the agency system by letting publishers set their own prices.

[75]There are many other e-book publishers and a list can be found here: *Which E-Book Publisher Is Right for You,?* Publishers Weekly, February, 14, 2014 and accessed online http://www.publishersweekly.com/pw/by-topic/authors/pw-select/article/61059-pw-select-february-2014-which-e-book-publisher-is-right-for-you.html.

Book publishers margins are about 70 % for e-books rather than the 50 % split they make with the traditional wholesale model. Perhaps, Apple wanted to standardize pricing and licensing agreements for both music and e-books that are available on its platform. The agency model is more appealing to book publishers because they earn a higher margin on each book.

In 2010, five book publishers decided that they would do business with Amazon only if Amazon adopted the agency pricing model that Apple was using. This would become part of another price-fixing scandal involving the pricing of electronic books in which Apple and the five books publishers colluded to artificially increase the price of e-books by letting publishers set the prices. The Department of Justice and several states filed lawsuits for antitrust violations. The end result is that some publishers settled the lawsuit and agreed to consent decrees with the usual court supervision restrictions, while others decided to fight the lawsuit. The case is still pending following a court ruling that Apple conspired to restrain trade in violation of Sect. 7.1 of the *Sherman Act* and relevant state statutes, and the court is in the process of imposing penalties against Apple. If all of this sounds familiar, it is because it is a replay of the same music publishing MAP price-fixing scandal that we discussed on page 199. Indeed, the publishers were attempting to keep prices high in a market in which they were rapidly losing control to new competitors. [76]

With Amazon's market dominance in e-book and hardback sales, control of the Kindle and its discounting ability, the publishers fear that eventually Amazon will become the only retail outlet for the purchase of print and digital books, and that will eventually drive them out of the market. It is not clear what happens to Apple's e-book platform in such a scenario. Presumably, after the competitors—including Apple—are driven out, Amazon will be able to raise prices, if consumers decided that they all want to purchase books online and not at a physical location. Borders, a major bookseller, has already met its demise. Ironically, Border's demise occurred after they began merchandising CD music—just as music sales were moving to Apple's iTunes—and after outsourcing its online sales operation to Amazon—a direct competitor. Barnes and Noble's e-reader, the Nook, has been struggling to compete with Amazon's Kindle and Apple's iPad, amid sluggish book sales and store closings.

Despite the market dominance allegations, Amazon has been a profitable partner to publishers (bringing innovation to a business of custom and practice) by

---

[76]See Christman (2008), *State of Texas vs Penguin Group & In Re: Electronic Books Antitrust Litigation* (2014), McKinney (2014), and Streitfeld (2014);
What Is the Agency Model for E-books?—Your Burning Questions Answered, available here: http://publishingtrendsetter.com/industryinsight/simple-explanation-agency-model;
Will the Agency Model Survive? Hachette, Amazon and the future of agency pricing, Publishers Weekly, May 19, 2014. p. 6; and
Endgame: With a final order issued, the Apple e-book price-fixing case is winding down—what happens now?, Publishers Weekly, September 9, 2013, pp. 5–6. and
Hyatt, M. (2010), *Why Do E-books Cost So Much? A Publisher's Perspective*, November 2, accessed online: http://michaelhyatt.com/why-do-ebooks-cost-so-much.html.

expanding reading and access to books; Amazon is the publishers' best account; Amazon offers tremendous volume with no returns (of unsold books); pre-ordering on Amazon helps put books on the bestseller lists on day one; and e-books margins remain high (offsetting the loss on hardback books).[77]

Consumers are the beneficiaries of monopsony in this case because Amazon has kept retail book pricing systemically low (at least in the short run and compared to Apple) to reinforce it market dominance, customer loyalty and customer service. Consumers are hurt when a title they request on Amazon is not made available (but it might be available on iTunes at a higher price), if deceptive sales practices are used.

The competitive response by music publishers to new entrants has been to merge and the music industry now has only three major music publishers. Likewise, book publishers are also consolidating and getting bigger. Recently, Penguin merged with Random House and HarperCollins bought Harlequin, one of the biggest independent book publishers.[78]

Amazon has essentially transformed the book publishing industry in the same way that Apple's iTunes content aggregation model transformed digital music online retailing, that is, they made it easier, convenient, and more affordable to legally own e-books from all the major and independent publishers. More importantly, however, demand and revenue are growing in the e-book market that is offsetting the purchase of physical and audio books.

7.14 The Future of Newspapers and Magazines

Digital technologies have undermined the outdated business models that are keeping traditional news media organizations afloat, raising the possibility that these institutions that have been around for more than a century may not survive—just like the incumbent PROs. The traditional newspaper publishers, journalists, and editors are no longer the official gatekeepers of national, foreign, and local news; business news; cultural news and criticism; editorials and opinion columns; sports and obituaries; lifestyle features; and science news—in which their particular biases, nuances, filters and propaganda were prominently featured in articles. Furthermore, in each of the individual news categories mentioned above, there are now several online competitors in each one that are making it difficult for legacy publishers to sustain themselves.

As consumers began to receive their news and information from online sources in an electronic format, digital technologies eliminated the formidable barriers to entry—such as printing presses, delivery trucks, delivery routes, and newsstands—in the newspaper industry. Social media sites, blogs, and search engines have

---

[77]See Gapper (2014).

[78]See Gapper (2014).

transformed journalism in the same way that Amazon and Apple revolutionized e-book publishing and music distribution, respectively, by providing news access to hundreds of millions of their users with on-demand, (free) individual digital articles rather than complete editions of newspapers and magazines. Blogs, short for weblogs, are individual websites that usually cover a single subject and the more technical ones are written and edited by a subject matter expert skilled in the area. Blogs have replicated most of the essential functions of newspapers and magazines, and some are free to use. Blogs, like, self-publishers of e-books, have broadened the marketplace of ideas by allowing ordinary people to publish articles online with very few restrictions and often with more depth and breadth of print newspapers. Some bloggers may not have to worry about the reaction from some advertisers when they publish unpopular material. Some technical blogs assume that their readers are well-versed in a subject area and do not have to water down material for the lowest common denominator like newspapers often do. Some blogs allow users to post critical commentary and reviews of articles in real-time and in virtually an unlimited space that is similar to letters-to-the-editors sections that you might find in newspapers. As a result, journalism's business model has changed to one in which some consumers preferred individual digital articles instead of bundled editions with numerous other articles or "filler" material found in newspapers and magazines—just like consumers that preferred the single music download instead of a CD packed with one or only two good songs or individual or à la carte cable networks. In addition, *Indeed.com*, *Craigslist*, *Linkedin* and other aggregators in online classified advertising and professional networking destroyed the source of revenue (up to one-third in some cases) for local and national newspapers by providing the means for anyone to post job-wanted ads on their websites, in some cases for free.

In September 2014, Facebook's *Daily Active Users* (DAUs) were 864 million out of an estimated 1.35 billion worldwide *Monthly Active Users* (MAUs), about 20 % of the world's population—putting the social network site in a category where they can reach an audience that is far larger than the combined total of newspapers, TV and radio, a major consideration for advertisers.[79] Sophisticated algorithms and data mining have replaced the traditional role of news editors in determining news content of users on social networks and it often varies by geographical locations. Facebook is now the number one source of traffic for digital publishers, and they are able to collect massive amounts of statistical data on the reader's experience, preferences and devices used. Facebook and Google are able to target online advertising—based on demographics, users' profiles, location, spending habits, browsing habits and other factors—and in the process they offer advertisers the possibility of advertising spending that are more relevant to the consumers who may be only interested in what they are selling. As a result of the amount of traffic generated and the algorithms used to determine stories that are timely and interesting to Facebook's users, the profitability of a news site is determined by the referral

[79]See *Facebook Reports Third Quarter 2014 Results* that is available here: http://www.finance.yahoo.com/news/facebook-reports-third-quarter-2014-200100790.html.

traffic and how well it performs on Facebook's *News Feed*. With increased traffic to a news organization's website, the publisher hopes to increase its advertising rates or convert some of the readers to paid subscribers. There is now growing tension between newspaper publishers and Facebook because the publishers are wary of Facebook's leverage, influence, economic clout, and control over their content.[80]

References

Alexander, P. (1994). New technology and market structure: Evidence from the music recording industry. *Journal of Cultural Economics*, 18:113–123.

Anders, G. (2013). 'No Stores? No Salesmen? No Profit? No Problem for Amazon'. *MIT Technology Review*. November 7, accessed online: http://www.technologyreview.com/news/520801/no-stores-no-salesmen-no-profit-no-problem-for-amazon.

Barnes, B. (2014). 'After a Tumultuous Year, Hollywood Looks to 2015'. *New York Times*. December 22, p. B1.

Biddle, S. (2013). 'Beat By Dre: The Exclusive Inside Story of How Monster Lost the World'. *Gizmodo.com*. Febuary 7, accessed online: http://gizmodo.com/5981823/beat-by-dre-the-inside-story-of-how-monster-lost-the-world.

Brynjolfsson, E. and McAfee, A. (2014). *The Second Machine Age: Work, Progress, and Prosperity in a Time of Brilliant Technologies*. W. W. Norton.

Budnick, D. and Baron, J. (2012). *Ticket Masters: The Rise of the Concert Industry and How the Public Got Scalped*. Penguin Group.

Carr, D. (2014a). 'Facebook Offers Life Raft, But Publishers Are Wary'. *New York Times*. October 27, p. B1.

Carr, D. (2014b). 'The Stream Finally Cracks The Dam of Cable TV'. *New York Times*. October 20, p. B1.

Carter, B. (2014). 'Overextended, Music TV Shows Fade'. *New York Times*. May 12. p. B1.

Chozick, A. (2013). Longing to Stay Wanted, MTV Turns Its Attention to Younger Viewers. *New York Times*. June 17. p. B4.

Christman, E. (2008). 'Cashing In'. *Billboard Magazine*, 120:26–28. October 25 issue, accessed online: Academic Search Premier, EBSCOhost accession number: 34888428.

Christman, E. (2013). 'Universal Music Publishing Plots Exit From ASCAP, BMI'. *Billboard Magazine*. February 7 issue, accessed online: http://www.billboard.com/biz/articles/news/publishing/1537554/universal-music-publishing-plots-exit-from-ascap-bmi.

Christman, E. (2014). 'The Digital Decline: What's Behind the First Downturn of the iTunes Era? And Can Streaming Save the Day?'. *Billboard Magazine*. January 18 issue, pp. 34–36.

Copyright Act (2011). Copyright Law of the United States, United States Copyright Office, Library of Congress, Washington, DC, Circular 92. December, accessed online: http://www.copyright.gov/title17/circ92.pdf.

Cyert, R. and Mowery, D., editors (1987). *Technology and Employment: Innovation and Growth in the U.S. Economy*. National Academy Press, Dulles, VA. Accessed online: http://www.nap.edu/catalog.php?record_id=1004.

Digital Millennium Copyright Act (1998). U.S. Copyright Office Summary, United States Copyright Office, Library of Congress, Washington, DC. December, accessed online: http://www.copyright.gov/legislation/dmca.pdf.

[80]See Kaiser (2014), Somaiya (2014), and Carr (2014a) for more on the issues involved in the digital transformation of the newspapers industry.

Downes, L. (2011). 'Leahy's Protect IP Act: Why Internet Content Wars Will Never End'. *Forbes Magazine*. May 16, accessed online: http://www.forbes.com.

Edwards, J. (2013). 'A Secret Cartel Keeps The Dying Broadcast TV Industry Afloat'. *BusinessInsider.com*. May 14, acccessed online: http://www.businessinsider.com/inside-the-madness-of-tv-upfronts-2013-5.

Fogarty, P. (2008). Major record labels and the RIAA: Dinosaurs in a digital age? *Houston Business and Tax Law Journal*, 9:140–173.

Galbraith, J. (2014). *The End of Normal: The Great Crisis and the Future of Growth*. Simon and Schuster.

Gapper, J. (2014). 'Publishers must become giants to take on Amazon'. *Financial Times*. May 28, accessed online: http://www.ft.com/cms/s/0/ab87b634-e5ad-11e3-aeef-00144feabdc0.html#axzz3GipACAWa.

Gordon, S. (2011). *The Future of the Music Business*. Hal Leonard, Milwaukee, WI, third edition.

Harris, E. (2014). 'RadioShack: In Need of Rewiring'. *New York Times*. August 20, p. B1.

Kaiser, R. (2014). *'The Bad News about the News'*. The Brookings Institute. October 16, accessed online: http://www.brookings.edu/research/essays/2014/bad-news#.

Langenderfer, J. and Cook, D. L. (2001). Copyright Polices and Issues Raised by A&M Records vs. Napster: "The Shot Heard 'Round the World" or "Not with a Bang but a Whimper?". *Journal of Public Policy and Marketing*, 20(2):280–288.

Leontief, W. (1983). National perspective: The definitions of problems and opportunities. In *The Long-Term Impact of Technology on Employment and Unemployment*, pages 3–7. National Academy of Engineering, Washington, DC. Accessed online: books.google.com/books?id=hS0rAAAAYAAJ.

McKinney, K. (2014). 'Book revenues are up – but without e-books, they'd be plummeting'. *Vox.com*. June 2014, accessed online: http://www.vox.com/2014/6/27/5849354/e-books-will-save-the-publishing-industry.

McNally, D. (2014). *On Highway 61: Music, Race and the Evolution of Cultural Freedom*. Counterpoint.

Morgan, B. (2014). 'History of the Record Industry, 1877–1920s: Part One: From Invention to Industry'. *Medium.com*. Accessed online: https://medium.com/@Vinylmint/history-of-the-record-industry-1877-1920s-48deacb4c4c3.

Murphy, G. (2014). *Cowboys and Indies: The Epic History of the Record Industry*. St. Martin's Press.

Passman, D. (2012). *All You Need To Know About The Music Business*. Simon & Schuster, eighth edition.

Patry, W. (2011). *How To Fix Copyright*. Oxford University Press, New York.

Peoples, G. (2013). 'AM/FM:Not Dead Yet'. *Billboard Magazine*. June 1 issue, accessed online without illustrations: https://web.ebscohost.com, accessed number: 87933587.

Perlberg, S. (2014). 'Mobile Ads Breach Historic Barrier: Spending to Reach People on Their Devices This Year Will Eclipse Radio, Print'. *Wall Street Journal*. July 22, p. B1.

Pollock, B. (2014). *A Friend in the Music Business: The ASCAP Story*. Hal Leonard Books.

Reich, H. and Gaines, W. (1999a). 'Down And Out In New York: Depression-era America Was Dancing To Jelly Roll Morton's Tunes And Someone Was Getting Rich Off Them. It Wasn't Him'. *Chicago Tribune*. December 13, accessed online: http://articles.chicagotribune.com/1999-12-13/news/9912130109_1_jelly-roll-morton-letters-jazz.

Reich, H. and Gaines, W. (1999b). 'The Great Jazz Swindle: Jelly Roll Morton Helped Invent Jazz In America. Then, He Was Cheated And Discarded By The Industry He Ignited.'. *Chicago Tribune*. December 12, accessed online: http://articles.chicagotribune.com/1999-12-12/news/9912120442_1_music-industry-french-quarter-apartment-ferdinand-jelly-roll-morton.

Reich, H. and Gaines, W. (2003). *Jelly's Blues: The Life, Music, and Redemption of Jelly Roll Morton*. Da Capo Press.

Samuelson, P. (2006). The generativity of Sony vs. Universal: The intellectual property legacy of Justice Stevens. *Fordam Law Review*, 74:101–145. Accessed online: http://people.ischool.berkeley.edu/~pam/papers/Sony%20legacy%20FLR.pdf.

Sisario, B. (2012a). 'Sony Closes Its Acquisition of EMI Music Publishing'. *NYTimes.com*. June 29, accessed online: http://mediadecoder.blogs.nytimes.com/2012/06/29/passing-final-hurdle-sonys-deal-for-emi-publishing-is-approved-by-u-s/.

Sisario, B. (2012b). 'U.S. and European Regulators Approve Universal's Purchase of EMI'. *NYTimes.com*. September 21, accessed online: http://www.nytimes.com/2012/09/22/business/global/universal-takeover-of-emi-music-is-approved.html.

Solomon, S. (2014). 'For RadioShack, a Long History of Misses and Missteps. *New York Times*. September 17, p. B5.

Somaiya, R. (2014). 'The News, À La Carte—Using Algorithms, Facebook is Changing The Way Its Users Consume Journalism'. *New York Times*. October 27, p. B1.

Stanley, B. (2014). *Yeah! Yeah! Yeah!—The Story of Pop Music: From Bill Haley to Beyoncé*. W. W. Norton & Company, first edition.

State of Texas vs Penguin Group & In Re: Electronic Books Antitrust Litigation (2014). No. 1:11-MD-02293-(DLC), S.D.N.Y. June 5, accessed online: blogs.reuters.com/alison-frankel/files/2014/.../ebooks-cote6.5opinion.pdf, pp 1–45.

Stockment, A. (2009). Internet radio: The case for a technology neutral royalty standard. *Virginia Law Review*, 95(8):2129–2179.

Streitfeld, D. (2014). 'Writers Who Support Amazon Speak Out on Dispute With Hachette'. *New York Times*. October 13, p. B6.

Ulin, J. (2014a). *The Business of Media Distribution: Monetizing Film, TV, and Video Content in an Online World*. Focal Press, second edition.

Ulin, J. (2014b). Internet Distribution and a New Paradigm: On-Demand and Multi-Screen Access, Cord-Cutting, Online Originals, Cloud Applications, Social Media, and More. In *The Business of Media Distribution: Monetizing Film, TV, and Video Content in an Online World*, chapter 7, pages 361–444. Focal Press, second edition.

US vs. ASCAP & In re Petition of Pandora Media (2014). Nos: 12 Civ. 8035 (DLC), 41 Civ. 1395 (DLC), S.D.N.Y. March 14, accessed online: http://www.business.cch.com/ipld/PandoraUSASCAP031414.pdf, pp. 1–136.

Vermeulen, F. (2014). 'How Removing Copy Protection Increased Record Companies' Music Sales'. *Forbes.com*. January 27, accessed online: http://www.forbes.com/sites/freekvermeulen/2014/01/27/how-removing-copy-protection-increased-record-companies-music-sales/.

Viacom International, Inc. v. YouTube, Inc. (2013). No:1:07-cv-02103-LLS, S.D.N.Y. April, accessed online: https://www.eff.org/sites/default/files/yt2013opinion_copy.pdf, pp. 1–24.

Yagoda, B. (2015). *The B Side: The Death of Tin Pan Alley and the Rebirth of the Great American Song*. Riverhead Books, NY.

Chapter 8
Roles of Publishers, Record Labels, and Producers

The traditional music publisher roles of evaluating promising songwriters and composers; persuading vocalists to record acquired music; marketing songs to radio and music television disc jockeys; negotiating synchronization rights for television and movie music; and collecting royalties payments have changed with the advent of digital technologies. The distinction between a music publisher and a record label can be confusing because the terms are often used interchangeably. To complicate matters further, the record labels can be subsidiaries of the major publisher, and the record label may perform some of the functions of a publisher as shown in Tables 8.1 and 8.2.

Table 8.3 shows the music publishing industry structure ranked by song titles at year-end 2011 by *Billboard Magazine*. The top four major music publishers at the time were EMI, Universal, Sony, and Warner with other independent publishers such as Kobalt Music rounding out the top 10. Invariably, the top four major publishers controlled most of the music industry due to size, and they represented most of the top recording artists in their catalogs. Without the Internet, most musicians would find it difficult to get their music distributed on digital platforms such as iTunes and Spotify without access to the major recording labels.[1]

With almost 80 % of the recorded music market controlled by the four largest music publishers in 2010, artists were often forced to submit to unfavorable and exclusive terms; bargain away their copyrights; locked into copyright ownership for 35 years; and simply not paid in a timely manner. Indeed, many artists had hoped that the Internet would break the big labels' stranglehold on the industry.[2] Table 8.4

[1]See Sisario (2012b,c). With the regulatory approval of the sale of EMI's record label assets to Universal and its music publishing assets to Sony, the music industry now shrinks to just three majors, more or less an oligopoly structure.

[2]See Bach (2004).

I.L. Pitt, *Direct Licensing and the Music Industry*,
DOI 10.1007/978-3-319-17653-6_8

Table 8.1 Major music publishers and record label subsidiaries

Music publisher	Record labels and distributors
Universal music	Interscope, Island/Def Jam, Capitol, Republic records Universal music, Verve and Show dog
Sony	Columbia, RCA, Epic, Arista, Legacy, Sony music, Masterworks, Vested in culture and provident
Warner/Chappell	Atlantic, Parlophone, Rhino, Warner music Alternative distribution alliance and WEA

Table 8.2 Selected roles of music publishers, record labels and producers: majors and independents

Entity	Functions
Publisher	Register new works or titles
	License mechanical, performance & synchronization copyrights
	Evaluate and market new artists
Record label	Sign new artists with commercial potential, including touring and merchandising
	Finance, distribute, promote, market and sell music CDs, DVDs, etc. through retailer relationships and on TV and radio
	Perform artist development
	Handles the sound recording copyrights
	May also perform some of the functions of publishers
Record producer	Produce the final record or arrangement (tracks), including working with instrumentalists and vocalists
	Interface with record labels
	Develop new artists for records labels
	Co-write songs
Copyright Administrator	Performs some of the duties of publisher on behalf of a copyright owner(s)
	Collects performance, mechanical, synchronization, print and foreign income for a commission
	All rights, including creative exploitation, remain with the copyright owner(s)

Source: Pitt (2010b, p. 66).

shows that in 2013—following the sale of EMI to Universal and Sony—the top three major music publishers accounted for approximately 87.10 % of all music distributed in the United States.

Table 8.3 Top 10 music publishers by ranked titles (year-end 2010)

Rank	Publisher	Titles	Share (%)
1	EMI[a]	233	22.15
2	Universal	230	21.86
3	Sony/ATV	183	17.40
4	Warner/Chappell	178	16.92
5	Kobalt	86	8.17
6	Bug music	52	4.94
7	BMG music	39	3.71
8	KASZ money publ.	19	1.81
9	Where Da KASZ at music	16	1.52
10	Peer music	16	1.52
	Total	1, 052	100
	Top 4 Cum. Share (%)		78.33

Source: Based on data from http://www.billboard.biz/bbbiz/charts/yearendcharts/2010/hot-100-publishing-corporations, and accessed March 13, 2012.
[a]At the time of writing, Universal Music and Sony were in the process of acquiring EMI, subject to a regulatory review.

Table 8.4 Major music publishers market share (%): by industry and record sales YE 2013

Publisher	Industry	Singles	Artist albums	All albums
Universal (%)	38.90	41.90	40.20	38.20
Sony	29.50	25.00	23.00	22.20
Warner	18.70	13.80	15.80	14.20
Sub-total majors	87.10	80.70	79.00	74.60
Others	12.90	19.30	21.00	25.40

Sources: Based on data from: *Top Music Distributors, 2013, Billboard*, January 1, 2014, accessed online: Business Insights Essentials,
http://bi.galegroup.com, document no.: I2502048396.
Market shares. Music Week, January 17, 2014, p.3, accessed online: Business Insights Essentials,
http://bi.galegroup.com, document no.: A361351656.

8.1 The Sources of Income for Songwriters, Composers, and Music Publishers

Table 8.5 illustrates the sources of income for songwriters, composers, music publishers, and record labels, where advances are recouped by music publishers or record labels. Recoupment is the music industry practice of recovering the recording, video, production, promotion, marketing, and other expenses associated with a song from the artist's royalty income. In general, the artists are paid only after the record labels have recovered these expenses (which may take years), and most artists may never achieve the level of record sales required to repay investments made by record labels.

Table 8.5 Selected music publisher and songwriter/composer sources of income: for copyrighted musical compositions and signed agreements

Music composition	Type	Payment	Terms
Used on Radio, TV, Internet, etc.	Performance	Varies[a]	Songwriters & publishers are paid separately and directly by ASCAP, BMI SESAC & SoundExchange
Sheet music	Print	$0.05 to $0.15	Writer's receipts for individual pieces of a song sheet
		plus 50 %	Of publisher's receipts from such use
Christian sheet music	Print	10–20 %	Publisher receipts from retail prices of hymnals, etc.
			Writer receives a pro-rata share of publisher's receipts
Folios	Print	10–15 %	Writer's share based on wholesale selling price, number of songs and writers in the folios
		12–20 %	If songs are designed around a particular writer/team
		plus 50 %	Of publisher's receipts from such use
CD, Tapes, Records, Downloads, & Ringtones	Mechanical	50 %	Writer's share of publisher receipts in the US
TV & Movie	Synchronization	50 %	Writer's share of publisher receipts from songs used in theatrical films and television programs
Commercials	Synchronization	50 %	Writer receives share of publisher receipts from songs used in radio, television, Internet ads
Home & Video games	Synchronization	50 %	Writer's share of all monies received by the publisher
Foreign exploitation	Foreign	50 %	Writer's share of all monies received in the US for sheet music, CDs. television, etc.
Merchandise	Other	Varies	Writer and publisher shares depend on "360" deal signed

Source: Based on Brabec and Brabec (2011, pp. 15–16) and Pitt (2010b, p. 69).
[a]Illustrated in Table 8.7.

In Table 8.6, we show the overall annual distribution of music publishers' share of collected royalty income by licensing type. In the year over year comparison, we see that royalty income from mechanical licensing declined as the sale of CDs continue to plummet. Revenue from performance licensing increased slightly, while synchronization licensing remained flat.

Table 8.6 Publisher's annual share of revenue by license type

License type	2011 (%)	2012 (%)	Y/Y Change
Mechanical	37	34	−0.03
Performance	31	32	0.01
Synchronization	29	29	0.00
Other	3	5	0.02
Total	100	100	

Source: Based on data from NMPA.

Table 8.7 Division of royalties among copyright holders and other artists: by percentage & less PRO administration costs

Copyright holders	ASCAP	BMI	SESAC	SoundExchange	Clear channel[a]
Songwriters/composers (%)	50	50	50	–	–
Music publishers (%)	50	50	50	–	–
Record labels (%)	–	–	–	50	50
Other artists					
Featured recording vocalist (%)	–	–	–	45	50
Non-featured musicians (%)	–	–	–	2.5	–
Non-featured vocalists (%)	–	–	–	2.5	–
Total (%)	100	100	100	100	100

Sources: Pitt (2010c, p. 90) and Christman (2012a). Note: Songwriters, composers, music publishers, and record labels are the copyright holders, the others are not.
[a]Clear channel has agreed to pay terrestrial royalties to recording artists and record labels as of June 2012.

As we discussed in Part One and in Pitt (2010a), performing rights organizations (ASCAP, BMI and SESAC) make separate and simultaneous distributions or performance royalty payments to publishers and songwriters, and their royalty payments are never *co-mingled* with the accounting systems of the record labels. This is sometimes referred to as the publisher's share (50 %) and the writer's share (50 %) as shown in Table 8.7. Songwriters and composers receive separate payments directly from ASCAP, BMI, SESAC, or SoundExchange for their royalty share of the entitled work, and the publisher or record label cannot recoup advances and other recording expenses. SoundExchange distributes 50 % of their royalties collected to the sound recording copyright owner (the record label), 45 % to the featured performer(s), and background musicians receive the remaining 5 %.

We will discuss the agreement between Clear Channel and Big Machine to share terrestrial radio revenue in detail in Sect. 8.6 on page 235. Tables 8.5 and 8.7 reveal why having a large catalog of past and current hits in every musical genre, including a mix of new and established artists are needed to sustain revenue for music publishers and income for songwriters.

8.2 Is a Digital Download a Sale or a License?

There is the dispute of whether music downloads should be classified as "sales" or "licensing." When downloads (from iTunes and the like) are classified as a sale, record labels treat downloads as "sales of records"—just as they did on sales of physical records in the pre-digital era—and a 10–20 % royalty rate, depending on sales volume, is applied to the artist's account. When downloads are treated as "licenses," the artist is owed a 50 % licensing percentage for his recording. The record companies argue that they should keep 85 % of downloaded music revenue because profit margins on digital sales are the same as the margins on physical records even though significant manufacturing and distribution costs have been eliminated.[3]

It appears that the issue of sales versus licensing was settled when the US Supreme Court recently declined to hear an appeal from Universal Music Group regarding the amount it pays artists for digital music sales. Universal was appealing a Ninth US Circuit Court of Appeals ruling from 2010 which stated that the labels should pay artists 50 % of royalties from digital music sales, rather than the 12 % rate that is common with physical sales because deals between Universal and iTunes were licensing of master recordings and not the sale of records. It is not clear how the ruling affects older recording contracts that are not up for renewal or renegotiation.[4]

8.3 Unethical Practices in the Music Industry

The music industry is often rife with unethical practices, particularly by publishers, managers, and producers who often claim credit for music in which they played no role in writing. A publisher, manager or producer demanding a share in the songwriting credits of a song is just one of the many unethical ways in which songwriters and recording artists have been exploited and cheated out of their rightful share of royalty payments in the past.[5] These are some of the types of legitimate copyright infringement claims that PROs are reluctant to pursue because of the fear of embarrassing their own member-publishers.

It has been reported that Irving Mills—a member of ASCAP and a notorious music publisher who couldn't read music and couldn't write a lyric—was well-known for his unethical practices by claiming both songwriting and publishing ownership shares in songs that he didn't compose. Mills served as both the music

[3]See Passman (2009, pp. 166–167) and Footnote number 25 in Chap. 5 on page 149.

[4]See F.B.T. Productions vs. Aftermath Records (2010).

[5]See Thall (2006) for numerous other examples of unethical behavior.

publisher *and* manager for Duke Ellington, the jazz composer and band leader. The lyrics to some of Ellington's early music was credited to Mills in a clear case of copyright infringement.

Disc jockey Alan Freed—who is credited with introducing the phrase "rock and roll" to radio listeners—is listed as a co-writer on Chuck Berry's *Nadine* and 40 other titles of that era and received publishing royalties for promoting the records. Freed's career was destroyed by the payola scandal in the 1960s. Payola is described as the illegal practice of undisclosed payments or other inducement by record companies for the broadcast of sound recordings on the radio in which the songs are presented as being part of regular airplay and not sponsored airtime.

Don Robey of Duke Peacock Records created the pseudonym Deadric Malone and assigned songwriting credits to himself on 100 songs recorded by his artists, making it nearly impossible to determine who wrote the music on his record labels. Many of the early rhythm and blues artists in the 1950s and 1960s were cheated out of performance royalties in this way.

Roulette Records president Morris Levy didn't even pretend to write anything—he just affixed his name to 340 songs, including *Why Do Fools Fall In Love?* Levy was not only receiving the publisher's share of royalty income, but was also getting a cut of the writer's share as well. In 1992, a jury decided that the *Why Do Fools Fall In Love?* authors were cheated out of their share of profits from the song. Emira Lymon, widow of Frankie Lymon, the singer on the original recording; Morris Levy, who bought the copyrights to the song; Big Seven Music Corp.; Roulette Records Inc. and Broadcast Music Inc. (BMI) were named as defendants in the case.[6]

McNally (2014, pp. 130–132) notes that "song plugger" and singing waiter, Irving Berlin (née Isidore Baline) was working at *Seminary*, Scott Joplin's New York music publisher, and his *first* big hit *Alexander's Ragtime Band* in 1911 was going to slightly resemble the *Real Slow Drag*, one of the songs in *Treemonisha*, an opera composed by Joplin. "Berlin would "appropriate" elements of African–American music including the minor third, pentatonic scale, expressive vocalisms, spare harmonies and improvisation, along with some other minor Jewish elements, essentially recognizing the value of black music and stealing it."

This was the pathological mindset of some of the charter members of ASCAP and will it have serious financial, economic, creative, artistic recognition, copyright infringement, and ethical repercussions for many African–American composers and songwriters in later years. With no musical training and rudimentary piano skills in which he could play only in the key of F-sharp, Berlin's seemingly inexhaustible, high productivity spawned many urban legends that his songs were written by others in a back room.[7]

Rather dubiously, given that many popular American songwriters are unknown, Berlin was later dubbed the "King of Ragtime," or the "King of American Songwriters," until his death in at 101 in 1989. Interestingly, at ASCAP's founding

---

[6]See Kimpel (2004); Neumeister (1992); McNally (2014, p. 278) and Murphy (2014, pp. 54–55).

[7]See Yagoda (2015, p. 37).

in 1914, Joplin was not a chartered member (he probably would not have been allowed to join even with a substantial body work), and out of 200 members, a mere two were African–Americans (classical baritone Harry T. Burleigh and classical composer James Weldon Johnson who is well known for what is considered the African–American national anthem, *Lift Every Voice and Sing*).

Recording artists will sometimes request a percentage of the publishing income on songs that they record but may not have contributed to the song's lyrics or melody. Some songwriters and composers will usually agree to this arrangement if the recording artist has the ability to sell a large quantity of songs in the millions.

8.4 Songwriters Regain Control of Their Intellectual Property

Performance royalty income can be an extremely lucrative long-term source of income for songwriters and composers whose music continues to be performed on radio, television and elsewhere long after their copyrighted songs stopped selling in retail stores. Songwriters, composers, and authors will be able to reclaim their valuable copyrights and control of their recordings under a provision in the 1976 Amendment to the US Copyright Act. Under the provision that applies to recordings released after January 1, 1978, songwriters (or statutory beneficiaries such as widows, widowers or children if deceased)[8] are able to reclaim ownership of a song's copyrights after 35 years by sending a *Notice of Termination* to publishers. Apparently, it was decided by Congress that 35 years were sufficient time for a label to recoup any up-front expenses (advances) paid to artists, and profit from the exploitation of a song.[9] For example, if a songwriter gave up ownership and control of a song to a record label in return for an up-front payment and released a song in 1980, the songwriter will be able to reclaim ownership of his copyrighted song in 2015 under the copyright statue commonly referred to as *Termination Rights*. The record label will no longer be entitled to royalty payments or able to exploit the copyrights without the songwriter's permission. This is likely to have huge economic and financial implications for songwriters, record labels, and performance and mechanical rights organizations as more and more popular recording artists reclaim the copyright ownership to their recordings that sold millions of copies and made billions of dollars in revenue for the major publishers and record labels.

Countless lawsuits—attesting to the long-lasting value of music copyrights—are no doubt in the works as songwriters attempt to reclaim their copyrights, and the record labels attempt to avoid termination by putting roadblocks in place. Publishers have added clauses to contracts asking artists to assign over the right to termination;

[8]Copyrights are intangible property rights.

[9]See Copyright Act (2011, Sections 203 and 304).

to give it up; let them have the first chance to buy it; remastering old recordings with different record numbers; or reclassifying the songwriter/music publisher relationship and musical compositions as "works made for hire." In addition, there are further complications in the right to terminate when the original copyright is held by several co-authors of a song title. Under works made for hire, the music publisher would be considered the "author" and owner of all copyrights associated with a musical composition, and the songwriter/composer would then be considered a regular employee with an employment contract or commissioning agreement.[10]

On May 7, 2012, in one of the first and important cases to interpret the copyright statue involving Termination Rights, a California court dismissed a lawsuit—filed by Scorpio Music and Can't Stop Music Productions, two companies administering the publishing rights to the Village People songs—preventing Victor Willis, former lead singer and lyricist of the 1970s disco group, the Village People, from terminating his share of the copyright grants to 33 songs. The courts case revealed that catalog material is valuable to music publishers and the songwriters as a source of "evergreen" revenue and income, and quite often, the leverage used to retain artists and prevent them from leaving for lucrative deals with other labels. Under the Copyright Act (2011, Section 203), Mr. Willis had earlier invoked his right to terminate, reclaim ownership and administer his share of 33 copyrighted songs after 35 years had elapsed.[11]

In their original lawsuit, Scorpio and Can't Stop Music argued in court that Mr. Willis could not unilaterally reclaim his copyright ownership in the songs because they were joint musical compositions that were co-written with other authors who had not elected to terminate their copyrights, and the Village People songs were all "works made for hire." Scorpio and Can't Stop Music later amended their lawsuit and withdrew their "works made for hire" claim. The Court rejected the publishers' claim that joint musical compositions required a majority of authors to terminate the grant of copyright ownership, and concluded that a joint author who separately transferred his copyright interest may unilaterally terminate the grant after 35 years under the Copyright Act. Furthermore, the judge in the case concluded that, "the purpose of the Act was to safeguard authors against unremunerative transfers

[10]See Passman (2009, pp. 298–325), Krasilovsky and Shemel (2007, pp. 110–121), Brooks (2009); Christman (2013); Van-Buskirk (2012) for a discussion of the related legal issues involved with Termination Rights.

[11]Can't Stop Music is the exclusive sub-publisher and copyright administrator in the United States of musical compositions published and owned by Scorpio Music, a French publisher. Mr. Willis's termination letter to the publisher, an exhibit with the 33 songs involved, the publishers' complaint to the court and other documentation in the case can be found here: Scorpio Music S.A. vs. Willis (2011). According to Christman (2013), it is not only Mr. Willis who has filed termination notices with the Copyright Office, other artists and their heirs such as Paul McCartney, Bob Dylan, Brian Wilson, Mort Shuman, Doc Pomus, Gerry Goffin, Carole King, Barry Mann and Cynthia Weil, Willie Nelson, Steve Cropper, Buddy Holly, Bo Diddley, Lloyd Price, Tommy Boyce, Bobby Hart, Daryl Hall, and John Oates have filed as well.

and address the unequal bargaining position of authors, resulting in part from the impossibility of determining a work's value until it has been exploited."[12]

Upon copyright termination with Scorpio Music and Can't Stop Music Productions, Mr. Willis is expected to reclaim his undivided ownership in the 33 musical compositions regardless of the wishes of the co-writers and the previous agreed upon revenue sharing deal. For example, if Mr. Willis were one of three co-authors of a composition, he would reclaim a 33 % undivided interest in the copyrighted composition rather than the 12–20 % royalty rate that he is paid in the original publisher's agreement signed in the 1970s. Mr. Willis may stand to reclaim up to a 50 % undivided ownership of his copyrighted songs when the legal dispute over song authorship is resolved at a later date.

The right to terminate court ruling is seen in the industry as a major victory for songwriters and composers. Songwriters and composers, who in the earlier stages of their songwriting careers (and with little bargaining leverage), negotiated away the valuable copyrights to their musical compositions to record labels in exchange for advances that had to be recouped from only the writer's share of revenue. In essence, the court ruling reinforced the Copyright Act that songwriters and composers who did not benefit from their songs earlier exploitation by music publishers should be the primary beneficiaries in the latter stages of a song's copyrighted revenue stream. Just looking at Tables 8.5 and 8.7 (even though they are in percentages of shared income between songwriters and record labels), you can see the enormous financial implications of songwriters deciding on how their intellectual property will be exploited with their permission. It is anticipated that this would be a great opportunity for composers, songwriters, and authors who will own their copyrights, have complete creative control over the marketing, sales and distribution of their songs and be able to negotiate better licensing deals without having to share income with record labels. On the other hand, record labels stand to lose a source of income, particularly if their catalogs consist of hit songs from 1978, the popular disco era. This may not be as bad as it appears on the surface as we discuss below.

8.5 Selected New Music Publishing Business Models

With all the turmoil and threats in the music industry, there are always opportunities for the innovators who are the least resistant to change. Just as it took small innovators like DMX, MCI, and Southwest Airlines to challenge the incumbent monopolists, independent music publisher, Kobalt is pushing an entirely new music-publishing model by delivering royalty payments with greater transparency and accountability.

[12] Additional details of the court ruling can be found here: Scorpio Music S.A. vs. Willis (2012).

Table 8.8 Kobalt's new music publishing model

Terms	Traditional publisher	Kobalt
Ownership of copyright	35 years	Short-term administration deals
		Artists keep control of copyrights
Administration services fee	50 %	5–15 %
Up-front advances	A year or more added to a contract	1–3 % against expected income
	Big advance tied to small royalties	Modest advance, but bigger share of royalties
Royalty collections lag time	2–3 years	1 year with direct collection from societies worldwide
Cash flow	Maximize publisher cash flow	Maximize songwriter cash flow
Accounting & transparency	Opaque accounting	Daily and weekly online reports
Maximize royalty payments	–	Purchases secondary data to match against collecting societies
A&R creative support	More	Less
Marketing plan	Cookie-cutter approach	Specific to each artist

Source: Based on Christman (2012b).

8.5.1 Kobalt's Music Publishing Model

The key features of Kobalt's new publishing model is summarized in Table 8.8. Several points are striking about Kobalt's new publishing model because they are not customarily done in the music industry, and only a few years ago it would have been considered insane. First, Kobalt is doing away with the traditional exclusive publishing agreement in which songwriters give up ownership and control of their copyright for 35 years, and the traditional 50/50 share of royalty income. Kobalt will charge only 5–15 % of revenue for its administrative services, and songwriters will retain control of their copyrights. Second, Kobalt is looking to recoup a 1–3 % fee against expected income from songwriters seeking an advance. Finally, Kobalt's new model encompasses many cost-saving technology enhancements that improve transparency and royalty accounting methodology. Those savings are passed on to songwriters instead of falling to the bottom line of publishers.[13] Parts of Kobalt's business model looks more like that of a copyright administrator in which they perform some of the duties of a publisher on behalf of copyright owners, collects performance, mechanical, synchronization, print and foreign income for a commission. All rights, including creative exploitation, remain with the copyright owner(s).

[13]See Christman (2012b).

Table 8.9 Partnership music publishing model

Budget support	Label expertise
Commercial	Sales, brand partnership and merchandising
Marketing	Promoting the artist on commercial radio and in the press
	Fan base research
Back office/supply chain	Physical manufacturing, accounting & digital distribution

Source: Based on Gordon (2011, pp. 194–195).

8.5.2 Partnership Music Publishing Model

In an interview with music industry executives, Gordon (2011, pp. 186–197) describes another business model when it comes to up-front expenses, similar in scope to the Kobalt model. Labels are offering a "partnership" under which the artist pays the initial up-front costs of creating an album. In return, the labels provide their expertise to the artist. Three budget-support choices are offered in which artists can select the best options that maximize revenue for them. Table 8.9 provides a description of the three budget-support choices that include commercial, marketing and back office/supply chain expertise. Other financing options include a modest up-front advance tied to a distribution fee. For songwriters and composers, lower advance payments may have a greater potential profit upside. The recording artist retains control of the master recording copyrights and a larger percentage of record sales. The distribution fee pays for the expertise and leverage of a large label. Many independent artists are no longer relying solely on investment and distribution support from a major label because the means of production in creating and distributing an album are now in the hands of the music creators.

8.5.3 Music Library Subscription Model

With synchronization proliferating on social media advertising, other new licensing models for supplying background music are taking root in which music supervisors—in an attempt to lower the cost of music licensing; avoid complicated royalty-payment rules; and prevent infringement lawsuits—are *not* using the registered copyrighted works in the repertories of PROs, record labels, and music publishers, essentially bypassing these incumbents. For example, Epidemic Sound is a start-up company that removes royalties from the music licensing equation by offering TV and video producers subscriptions to its library of 25,000 original musical tracks and sound effects for a monthly subscription fee. Epidemic Sound pays composers up-front for songs in exchange for complete ownership, meaning its users don't need to make royalty payments.[14]

8.5.4 TuneCore's Multiple Rights Licensing Model

In Table 8.10, we illustrate an entirely new music distribution, publishing and merchandising model by TuneCore, a digital music and video distributor, that bypasses the record labels altogether. In addition, TuneCore's publishing arm is looking to bypass the performing rights organizations as well. TuneCore may be an example of what Cardi (2007) refers to as a multiple rights organization (MRO) that consolidates the functions of record labels, PROs, and the Harry Fox Agency under one roof. TuneCore is a now a major supplier of music in the industry, and their model is lucrative for musicians who already have a following or can build one on their own.[15] For an annual subscription or flat fee, TuneCore will distribute worldwide any song or album on dozens of online music services such as iTunes, Amazon, Spotify, eMusic, and Rhapsody. In addition, TuneCore collects and distributes royalty payments from the sale of recordings.

8.6 New Sound-Recording Performance Royalty Model

The record labels and broadcasters have fought for decades over terrestrial performance royalty payments for recording artists whose only contribution to a song may have been that of a vocalist, and not in the writing of the lyrics or in composing melodies. Broadcasters had opposed the payment of performance royalties to recording artists and their labels because they argued that the performers earned enough from the promotional value (such as increased record sales and recognition) when their music played was played over the air.

In a new music industry innovation that has created another market-based business model that bypasses the outmoded PROs, Clear Channel Communications (the largest radio station group owner with 850 radio stations and 238 million listeners) devised a *terrestrial* or over-the-air radio revenue-sharing and holistic model with Big Machine, a record label. This is the first time that a deal has been negotiated in the music industry in which a *terrestrial recording-artist performance right* has been created. Clear Channel has agreed to pay sound-recording performance royalties for terrestrial broadcasts to a record label without a statutory requirement, Congressional involvement or costly litigation. None of the incumbent PROs

[14]See Karp (2013); Pakinkis (2013).

[15]See Sisario (2012a).

Table 8.10 TuneCore's multiple rights licensing model: selected terms and conditions

Terms/Features	Conditions
Grant of rights (non-exclusive)	Recording artists keep all rights
	TuneCore sells, copies, distributes and exploits recordings by all means and media
	TuneCore collects all income derived from such distribution
	TuneCore granted the right to use the name(s), photographs and likenesses, artwork, images, biographical and other information provided by the artists
Recording expenses	Recordings, images, and artwork are provided at the artist's sole expense
Flat fees for distribution to retailers	Require artists to purchase a recurring fee-based subscription
	Singles and ringtones cost about $10 a year and entire albums about $50 a year
	Music is available in most music stores in a few days after payment
Digital music stores	Recording artists can select the digital music stores that they like
	If Amazon On Demand is selected, music is available as a physical CD on Amazon.com
TuneCore's repertory	About 10 % or (2,000,000) of the songs on iTunes, about 4 % of all digital sales and 700,000 acts[a]
Signed singers/songwriters	Nine Inch Nails, Bjork, Aretha Franklin, Jason Mraz, The Civil Wars, Drake, Soulja Boy, 3OH!3, Ziggy Marly, Nevershoutnever, Keith Richards, Jay-Z, Cheap Trick, Moby, Joan Jett, Public Enemy and Slade
Royalty payments to artists	TuneCore pays 100 % of net income from consumer stores less taxes, fees and other expenses related to recording sales
	By using the TuneCore streaming media player, iPhone application or other applications as platforms for users to stream recordings, the artists waive their rights to digital, performance or other royalties
Accounting	Transparent accounting with 24/7 access to sales reports and royalty payments
Digital fingerprinting	Provides TuneCore's song identifiers (TCSI)
Music publishing (Songwriters and Composers)	TuneCore registers songwriters' works, collects royalties, police copyrights and issue licenses for a one-time setup fee & a 10 % cut of recovered royalties
Competitors	CD Baby and Zimbalam
Product integration	TuneCore service integration with the direct-to-fan music marketing and retail merchandising firm Topspin
	Combined distribution, publishing and merchandising under one roof

Sources: Based on data from http://www.tunecore.com, accessed May 7, 2012.
http://go.tunecore.com/topspin.
[a]Sisario (2012a).

(ASCAP, BMI, SESAC and SoundExchange) will be involved in this new form of "voluntary" licensing. Prior to this market innovation, record labels and recording artists (vocalists and background musicians) were paid royalties for digital broadcast performances through SoundExchange, while the songwriters, composers, authors, and publishers were paid performance royalties through ASCAP, BMI and SESAC as illustrated in Table 8.7.

Perhaps in anticipation of the rapid changes in the economics of radio broadcasting and its leverage in the industry, Clear Channel has provided one possible solution to the entrenched and broken royalty payment system that has not kept up with rapid changes in digital media. As part of its deal with Big Machine, Clear Channel will pay an undisclosed percentage of music advertising revenue for broadcasts whether they are heard online or over-the-air, instead of the legislatively mandated digital sound-recording royalty rate of $0.002. Royalty payments will be made directly to the label, which in turn will split those payments 50/50 with its recording artists.[16] The one drawback to this deal is that the terms are confidential and the record label receives the royalty payments for distribution to recording artists, subject to recoupment. This deal has happened at this particular time for several of the following reasons.[17]

First, the so-called *mobile computing cycle* is completely reshaping the music industry. The growth of online listening to music is shifting to mobile devices and is outstripping broadcasters' ability to monetize both online and mobile advertising. Smart phone (Apple's iPhones and Google's Android) and tablet (Apple's iPad and Amazon's Kindle) sales are outpacing PC (desktop and notebook) sales. Mobile web traffic, as a percent of total web traffic, is growing rapidly. Heavy use of smart phones is highly skewed toward younger consumers who are using the devices to make purchases.

Second, broadcasters, like Clear Channel, are hoping to accelerate the rapid growth in digital radio online audiences that has been stymied by the outdated Copyright Act and industry inertia that have that not kept up with today's consumer demand, innovations and technological changes.

Third, the deal between Clear Channel and Big Machine creates a predictable, holistic and transparent business model (partially transparent to Clear Channel and Big Machine, but not to the recording artists) that is likely to change the size and structure of royalty payments that have been set by federal statue. For example, to streamline the budgeting process and control future cost overruns, the agreement requires a fixed cap on the percentage of revenue paid out for performances, regardless of whether the broadcast is transmitted via radio, mobile phone or through a computer.

---

[16] See Christman (2012a).

[17] As discussed in Christman (2012a).

Clear Channel's new model is based on paying a percentage of advertising revenue instead of an "unhealthy" pay-per-play based model.[18] The CEO of Clear Channel has discussed his many reasons for needing revenue predictability in the music industry. The CEO is quoted as saying,

> I don't want to try and guess how much advertising I can sell— and if it's not coming in fast enough, can I slow down the song plays? Or should I do an interview show, or do more talk radio and news and sports, or maybe do more pre-1972 music programming? That's just a bad way to run—and even more importantly, try and build—a business. It encourages us to try and play as little music as possible.[19]

Finally, the decline in CD sales and the physical distribution of music deprived many recording artists of a source of income when consumers switched to purchasing music online. Terrestrial radio revenue sharing models of this type became a top priority for many recording artists. Recording artists stand to collect royalty payments from the 98 % of advertising revenue that comes from terrestrial broadcast radio instead of only collecting 2 % from digital radio music-advertising revenue. This new revenue sharing model between Clear Channel and Big Machine is expected to have wider and far-reaching repercussions in the music industry as other organizations negotiate similar deals. Perhaps, we will see a market-based solution in transparency that will make sure that recording artists get their 50 % share of royalties without the regard for recoupment when labels and publishers are directly collecting 100 % of revenue for later distribution.

8.7 Songwriter as a Self-Publisher

As a songwriter/composer becomes successful in the music industry, invariably it becomes a business in itself in terms of controlling the rights to the exploitation of their creative output. One option for the songwriter is to become a "self-publisher" using their own collection of songs as the primary assets of the company.[20] Self-publishers, by owning and controlling their own copyrights and masters, can negotiate their own non-exclusive licensing deals with multiple companies. This happens in the case of a songwriter having a large enough body of work and wants to avoid the overhead publishing and clerical expenses associated with copyright registration, demos, marketing, promotion, accounting, and so on.

Another option for the self-publisher is to subcontract out the clerical administration of copyright licensing to a copyright administrator (like Kobalt) or a sub-publisher who is paid a commission (or a flat-fee) without owning the copyrights. Multiple commission-oriented licensing firms can market a single song, if

[18]See the discussion by Robertson (2011) on why the current model of pay-per-play is called unhealthy.

[19]The quotation appears here: Christman (2012a).

[20]See Beall (2004); Wixen (2014).

the songwriter creates alternative titles or derivative titles for each composition. Each specific licensing organization can then have its own derivative song title with its own unique digital fingerprint to exploit. In this way, the songwriter avoids the administrative complications and confusion from multiple licensing deals brokered by several agents.[21]

As a self-publisher, the 50 % share of performance royalties from ASCAP, BMI, and SESAC that would normally flow to the music publisher would instead be directed to the songwriter, as well as the 50 % writer's share as shown in Table 8.7. In addition, as owner of the master recordings, the songwriter/self-publisher would receive the 50 % of digital performance royalties from SoundExchange. If the songwriter/self-publisher is also the featured vocalist, he or she will receive additional payments as well. The key difference here is that it is the songwriter/copyright holder who gets to set terms of the licensing deals associated with print, radio, television, film, the Internet and mobile music use, not the record label or music publisher. Wixen (2014, p. xiv) believes that, "[song]writers should retain their own copyrights and control them closely, and that alliances with multinational music publishing firms are rarely in the writers' best interests."

8.8 Who Should Own or Exclusively Control Data Intelligence?

With the widespread use of digital fingerprinting and other electronic data collection methods, there is now an incredible amount of data intelligence on music consumption patterns, which was never made available in the music industry. More importantly, the transaction costs of collecting and processing performances data have declined considerably with the use of electronic data collection methods. The collection of all of this type of data intelligence is leading to new insights into who is listening to music, the various platforms in which music is accessed, who is buying downloaded music, the music services where the music is bought, and which Internet traffic sites are promoting music content that are driving customers to music sites to make purchases.

Who should own (or even share) in this vast amount of collected data intelligence is creating controversy in the music industry among content providers (songwriters and composers), music service providers, licensing agencies, digital retailers, record labels, and music publishers. Independent recording artists—who own 100 % of their copyrighted songs and are self-publishers—are demanding access to user data from streaming or other music licensing services in order to identify potential fans, markets for live concerts and conduct more direct to consumer sales in order to maximize revenue. It has been an uphill battle for recording artists to obtain intelligence data on music consumption.

[21] See Wilsey and Schwartz (2010); Wixen (2014, pp. 54–67).

While the Copyright Act provides for royalty payments for musical performances, there is no provision on how much user, listener or on-site promotion data collected by the various licensing agencies and music services should be shared with songwriters, composers, and other musicians. As Castle (2012) observes, "from the point of view of property rights, why should the digital retailer own (or own exclusively) the artist's property right in data relating to their works? Since it is data created by the sale or transmission of the artist's work for which the artist has spent time and effort to make valuable, why should that value accrue solely to the digital retailer?" Some record labels and music publishers may already include extensive data collection in their licensing agreements with music streaming services, but this data is often not shared with recording artists due to the confidentiality clauses in licensing agreements that prohibit the release of such data.

Recording artists and copyright holders are now calling for changes in the anachronistic legislation and policies embodied in the various consent decrees to make sure that there are new policies and business models on how the valuable data intelligence-collected by PROs and music service providers should be shared with recording artists, content creators, and competitors. *Billboard Magazine* and their top 100 charts are now facing competition from start-up company, BigChampagne and their "The Ultimate Chart." The Ultimate Chart provides considerably more detail on song/artist rankings and includes factors that were not used before in chart compilations. Artists are ranked on a weekly indexed scale of 100 that includes "sales;" "radio," "online watching & listening," and "fans, friends and followers" categories making the process more transparent. For example, on March 17, 2012, top ranked recording artist, Adele received an "Ultimate Score" of 100, while the tenth ranked artist, Luke Bryan received a score of 29 based on the above categories. In response to such competition and other factors, *Billboard Magazine* announced on February 20, 2013 that they are now factoring in YouTube streaming data into their chart rankings, that also include digital downloads, physical sales, terrestrial radio airplay, on-demand audio streaming and online radio streaming.[22]

References

Bach, D. (2004). The double punch of law and technology: Fighting music piracy or remaking copyright in a digital age? *Business and Politics*, 6(2):1–33.

Beall, E. (2004). *Making Music Make Money: An Insider's Guide to Becoming Your Own Music Publisher*. Berklee Press, Boston, MA.

Brabec, J. and Brabec, T. (2011). *Music, Money and Success: The Insider's Guide To Making Money In The Music Industry*. Schirmer Trade Books-Music Sales, New York, NY.

Brooks, T. (2009). Only in America: The unique status of sound recordings under U.S. Copyright Law and how it threatens our heritage. *American Music*, 27(2):125–137.

[22]See http://www.ultimatechart.com and *Billboard, Nielsen Add YouTube Video Streaming To Its Platforms; Data Enhances Hot 100, Other Charts*, http://www.billboard.com/biz/articles/news/chart-alert/1549398/billboard-nielsen-add-youtube-video-streaming-to-its-platforms.

Cardi, W. J. (2007). Über-middleman: Reshaping the broken landscape of copyright music. *Iowa Law Review*, 92:835–890.

Castle, C. (2012). 'A Great Question from @ZoeCello: Should Digital Retailers Own the Artist's Fan Data?'. *Music Technology and Policy Monthly*. November 19, accessed online: http://musictechpolicy.wordpress.com/2012/11/19/a-great-question-from-zoecello-should-digital-retailers-own-the-artists-fan-data.

Christman, E. (2012a). 'Exclusive: Clear Channel, Big Machine Strike Deal to Pay Sound-Recording Performance Royalties To Label, Artists'. *Billboard Magazine*. June 5 issue, accessed online: http://www.billboard.biz, story:1007226762.

Christman, E. (2012b). 'Turning publishing upside-down: Aggressive. Transparent. Winning. Why Willard Ahdritz's strategies are working, and why his Kobalt Music is the future'. *Billboard Magazine*. January 28 issue, accessed online without illustrations: http://go.galegroup.com, story:7CA278171081.

Christman, E. (2013). 'Going for a Song'. *Billboard Magazine*, 125:28–29. March 30 issue, accessed online: Academic Search Premier, EBSCOhost, Accession Number: 86535006.

Copyright Act (2011). Copyright Law of the United States, United States Copyright Office, Library of Congress, Washington, DC, Circular 92. December, accessed online: http://www.copyright.gov/title17/circ92.pdf.

F.B.T. Productions vs. Aftermath Records (2010). No: 09-55817, ID: 7462343, DktEntry: 45-1, US Court of Appeals 9th Cir., Pasadena, CA. September 3, accessed online: www.âĂŐcdn.ca9.uscourts.gov/datastore/opinions/2010/09/03/09-55817.pdf, pp. 1–15.

Gordon, S. (2011). *The Future of the Music Business*. Hal Leonard, Milwaukee, WI, third edition.

Karp, H. (2013). Reaping profits from soundtracks. *Wall Street Journal*, page B6. December 16 2013, accessed online: http://search.proquest.com/docview/1468227178?accountid=35927.

Kimpel, D. (2004). *Who Really Wrote That Song? Music Connection Magazine*. March 15–28, pp. 48–51.

Krasilovsky, M. W. and Shemel, S. (2007). *The Business of Music: The Definitive Guide to the Business and Legal Issues of the Music Industry*. Watson-Guptill Publications, New York, tenth edition.

McNally, D. (2014). *On Highway 61: Music, Race and the Evolution of Cultural Freedom*. Counterpoint.

Murphy, G. (2014). *Cowboys and Indies: The Epic History of the Record Industry*. St. Martin's Press.

Neumeister, L. (1992). 'Two Songwriters Win Rights To Hit Song 36 Years After Writing It'. *Associated Press*. Accessed online: http://www.apnewsarchive.com/1992/Two-Songwriters-Win-Rights-To-Hit-Song-36-Years-After-Writing-It/id-b542816ef44f9b73bec72c206c677184?SearchText=morris%20levy%20roulette;Display_.

Pakinkis, T. (2013). 'PJ Bloom On Changing Sync Revenues and Opportunities for Rights-holders'. *MusicWeek.com*. March 21, accessed online: http://www.musicweek.com/news/read/pj-bloom-on-changing-sync-revenues-and-opportunities-for-rights-holders/054069.

Passman, D. (2009). *All You Need To Know About The Music Business*. Simon & Schuster, seventh edition.

Pitt, I. L. (2010a). *Economic Analysis of Music Copyright: Income, Media and Performances*. Springer, New York. Available online: http://www.amazon.com/Economic-Analysis-Music-Copyright-Performances/dp/1441963170/ref=sr_1_1?s=books&ie=UTF8&qid=1417266944&sr=1-1&keywords=economic+analysis+of+music+copyright.

Pitt, I. L. (2010b). Economic analysis of music copyright: Music publishers. In *Economic Analysis of Music Copyright: Income, Media and Performances*, chapter 3, pages 65–79. Springer, New York.

Pitt, I. L. (2010c). Economic analysis of music copyright: Songwriters and composers. In *Economic Analysis of Music Copyright: Income, Media and Performances*, chapter 4, pages 81–92. Springer, New York.

Robertson, M. (2011). 'Why Spotify can never be profitable: The secret demands of record labels'. *GigaOm.com*. accessed online: http://gigaom.com/2011/12/11/why-spotify-can-never-be-profitable-the-secret-demands-of-record-labels.

Scorpio Music S.A. vs. Willis (2011). No: 11cv1557 BTM(RBB), S.D.C.A. July, accessed online: http://archive.org/details/gov.uscourts.casd.357493, pp. 1–29.

Scorpio Music S.A. vs. Willis (2012). No: 11cv1557 BTM(RBB), S.D.C.A. May, accessed online: http://ia600708.us.archive.org/26/items/gov.uscourts.casd.357493/gov.uscourts.casd.357493.30.0.pdf, pp. 1–10.

Sisario, B. (2012a). 'Out to Shake Up Music, Often With Sharp Words'. *New York Times*. May 7. p. B1.

Sisario, B. (2012b). 'Sony Closes Its Acquisition of EMI Music Publishing'. *NYTimes.com*. June 29, accessed online: http://mediadecoder.blogs.nytimes.com/2012/06/29/passing-final-hurdle-sonys-deal-for-emi-publishing-is-approved-by-u-s/.

Sisario, B. (2012c). 'U.S. and European Regulators Approve Universal's Purchase ofEMI'. *NYTimes.com*. September 21, accessed online: http://www.nytimes.com/2012/09/22/business/global/universal-takeover-of-emi-music-is-approved.html.

Thall, P. (2006). *What They Will Never Tell You About the Music Business: The Myths, the Secrets, and the Lies (& a Few Truths)*. Billboard Books.

Van-Buskirk, E. (2012). Why 'Mastered For iTunes' Won't Defuse a Copyright Time Bomb. *Gizmodo.com*. March 1, accessed online: http://gizmodo.com/5889748/why-mastered-for-itunes-wont-defuse-a-copyright-time-bomb.

Wilsey, D. and Schwartz, D. D. (2010). *The Musician's Guide to Licensing Music*. Billboard Books, New York.

Wixen, R. (2014). *The Plain & Simple Guide to Music Publishing*. Hal Leonard, third edition.

Yagoda, B. (2015). *The B Side: The Death of Tin Pan Alley and the Rebirth of the Great American Song*. Riverhead Books, NY.

Chapter 9
Possible New Entrant

There is music industry speculation on a possible future "game changer" that could sweep the industry, a natural extension of direct licensing that was discussed in Part One. Figure 9.1 shows the current market place today of three competing music platforms, Apple, Google, and Facebook. All three of these companies have changed the way music is distributed from a musician to an audience. In addition, they have also changed the way music is purchased and consumed. Figure 9.2 depicts a hypothetical scenario of a merger of the *music media platforms* of Apple, Google, and Facebook. Although it is only a hypothetical academic theory, a possible merger of all three music platforms could create competition among the incumbent copyright collecting agencies and diminish the market power exercised by ASCAP and BMI as the consent decrees mandated. We would expect such a music-platform media merger—that is designed to create *open* technology and innovation—to raise concerns from the Department of Justice and music industry groups. There could very well be other possible mergers or combinations that reshape the music industry that we do not examine here.

An important question to ask is what is the likely outcome of such a merger? As a result, there are many important concerns about whether such a merger would create a powerful vertically and/or horizontally integrated company that could benefit society. One of the central issues here is the likely impact on the *transparency in pricing*—not technology—for consumers, musicians, and music users in a concentrated market that such a merger would create. Without transparency in pricing, it would difficult for customers to compare the cost of services from other service providers with compelling offers. In Table 9.1, we list additional concerns about a possible merger.

This is shaping up to be a promising area of research for economists, legal experts, and others. The research will help to clarify how restrictive patent and copyright laws may pose significant threats to innovation by discouraging creators from adapting the works of previous musicians because they may face huge losses from copyright infringement. Technology is the means by which market

I.L. Pitt, *Direct Licensing and the Music Industry*,
DOI 10.1007/978-3-319-17653-6_9

Fig. 9.1 Current marketplace

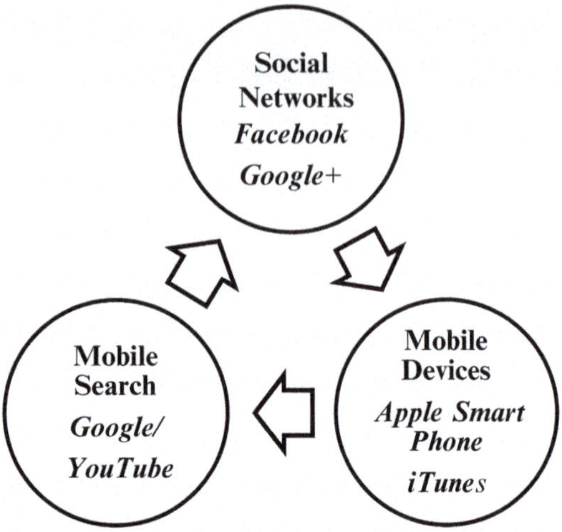

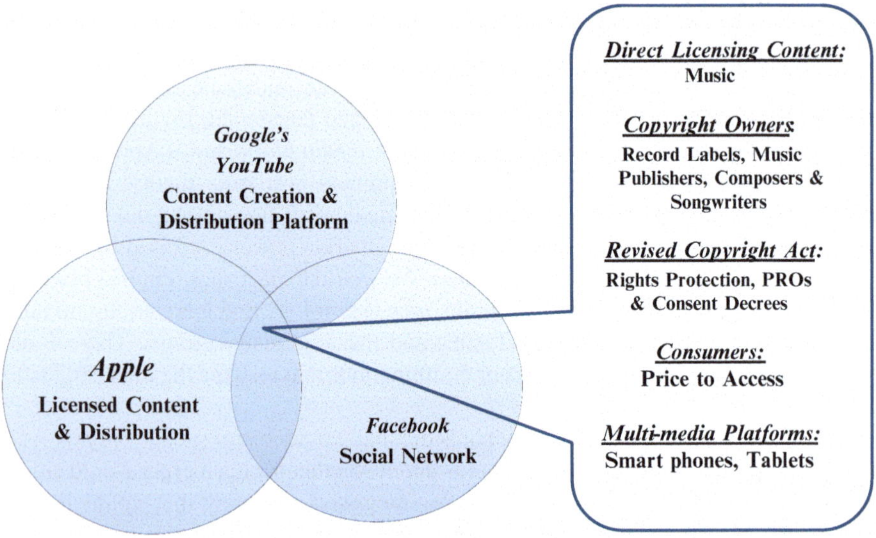

Fig. 9.2 Hypothetical merger and PRO competitor

expectations are created and satisfied. These "expectations can either be met—in which case copyright owners will make money according to those new markets and new expectations—or, as is often the case now, copyright owners can refuse to meet the new expectations, in which case consumers will go elsewhere to have their needs satisfied by others."[1] Table 9.2 shows the 2011 revenue generated by Apple, Facebook, and Google in 2011 and it appears that they each individual company

[1]See Patry (2011, p. 39).

Table 9.1 Concerns about a possible merger of music platforms

(a) Will it harm competition?
(b) Will it hinder innovation?
(c) Will it increase industry concentration?
(d) Will it discourage music/content creation?
(e) Will it increase excessive profits (rents)?
(f) Will it raise the barriers of entry for competitors in each individual line of business (smart phones, online searches, social networks, music publishing, music recording, music distribution and sales, licensing, etc.)?
(g) Will it yield too much bargaining power (considerable capital assets, intellectual property and exclusive deals) over songwriters, composers, independent artists, agents, managers, record labels, music publishers, consumers, and others in the music industry?

Table 9.2 Revenue ($B) by media platform 2011

Company	Revenue	Service	Value added	Consumer awareness	Consumer usage
Apple	$108.25B	iTunes	Devices, music content, distribution	High	High
Google	$35.76	YouTube	Content creation, distribution	High	High
Facebook	$4.04[a]	Facebook	Social network	High	High

Source: Financial data: Yahoo finance.
[a]Trailing 12 months (as of Mar 31, 2012).

dominates their respective markets. A fair question to ask is whether consumers, musicians, copyright holders, and others would prefer the convenience of having all of these individual services provided by a single and reliable company?

9.1 Apple: Devices and Music Content Distributor

By now, most everyone is aware of Apple's iTunes, Google's YouTube and Facebook, the social networking site. We will review a selection of the innovative aspects of each of these services. Apple and Google are two of the leading companies that have partially helped to destroy the old music distribution model with entirely new music content creation, distribution platforms, and music player devices.

Apple's contribution to the new music business model is that they have taken existing music content from publishers' music libraries—by combining their musical works into a single registry—that made distribution across multiple media platforms easier and cheaper. Many of iTunes' features were originally designed around the idea of a single jukebox on a single computer. A user's entire iTunes music library is now available on multiple platforms such as iPhones, iPods, iPads, personal computers, and cloud services. With Apple's paid services such iTunes Match, a user's music library of play lists and song data is entirely mobile, can go everywhere and stay "in sync" across the various Apple platforms. As part of Apple's iTunes Match subscription, the service stores uploaded songs to a central server that the user can access at his or her leisure, play back or download songs later to various devices. This is how Apple's iTunes has revolutionized the music industry. It has made it possible for music consumers to have their entire music library available to them wherever they may go.

9.2 Google: Content Creation and Distributor

On the other hand, Google has invested in infrastructure/content development platform and music licensing technology to make it easier for both amateur and professional content creation, marketing and distribution. YouTube is often described as an interactive on-line public communications and distribution network that allows users to upload original videos for public viewing. YouTube has also been described as an interactive music streaming service where music is delivered in real-time, and the user can choose to listen to any particular song whenever they want on the network. The YouTube platform was designed around the idea of user-generated content, that is, having producers of private musical and other video works supply the public with their creations. Among its many other uses, YouTube is often viewed as a low cost way for music creators to reach the public without having the marketing clout of record labels, radio stations, and music publishers. In addition, *Daily Variety Magazine* reports that "YouTube's parent

Google has acquired licensing and royalty reporting service, RightsFlow, with the aim of streamlining royalty payments to musicians and publishers. RightsFlow,[2] launched in 2007, uses a 30-million-song database and proprietary technology to match songs titles to publishers" (copyright holders) catalogs and manage royalty payments. By combining RightsFlow's expertise and technology with YouTube's platform, Google hopes to rapidly and efficiently license music on YouTube with the aim of making more music available to consumers to enjoy, and more money for the talented people producing the music.'[3] With a statutory fixed-rate license for musical performances (if enacted) that we discussed in Sect. 2.12 on page 101, and when combined with RightsFlow registry, Google can effectively compile its own music performance data from its YouTube platform and conceivably distribute performance royalties directly to songwriters, composers, record labels,

[2]RightsFlow, until they were bought by Google, competed with Harry Fox in processing mechanical licenses.

[3]See Barker (2011).

and music publishers without the intervention of performing rights organization, thus eliminating a costly, intermediary and inefficient layer in music licensing under the current system.

9.3 Facebook: Social Network

Facebook is now a publicly traded company and an advertising-supported social networking service. As of January 2012, Facebook claimed that it had more than 800 million active users, 50 % of whom use the service on any given day. On average, people on Facebook install application software (apps) more than 20 million times every day using a mobile device.[4] In one of Facebook's music functionality integration apps, it will automatically post whatever music the user is listening to on Facebook, and make it possible for friends in the user's social network to see it, click it, and listen along. The Gallup Organization reported that Facebook users posted 4.75 billion items of content; Twitter users sent 400 million tweets; Instagram users "liked" 1.2 billion photos and YouTube users watched 4 billion videos on a daily basis. Even with these impressive statistics of daily usage on social networks, the quantity and quality of such metrics can be highly dubious due to the double/triple/quadruple counting of multi-platform fakes and users.

Social media may not be the powerful and persuasive marketing force that many companies had envisioned. Companies that have invested marketing dollars into social media advertising are finding that increasing fans, follower counts and "likes" are not the same as increasing sales or revenue. The return on investment (ROI) for advertisers on social media—-when compared to other forms of social networking—has been disappointing because social media has little influence on the purchasing behavior of some consumers; consumers are using social media to interact with people that they know and not to engage with brand marketing; and Facebook fans or Twitter followers can be easily fabricated and purchased for pennies on the dollar at unscrupulous websites.[5]

9.4 Strengths and Weaknesses of Media Players

The debate is what such a merger could mean for the future of the music industry, if permitted by regulators. One benefit of such a merger would be that all the software, technology and music licensing would be in one place for both current and

---

[4]See http://www.facebook.com/press/info.php?statistics. The number of genuine and active Facebook users is in dispute due to a large number of fake and multiple accounts by individuals.

[5]See Elder (2014), Tavakoli (2013) and *The Myth of Social Media: A Majority of Consumers Say They Are Not Influenced by Facebook, Twitter.*, available here: http://online.wsj.com/public/resources/documents/sac_report_11_socialmedia_061114.pdf.

Table 9.3 Strength and weakness of music industry players

Firm	Strength	Weakness
Apple	Sale of licensed music & personal electronics	Lacks large audience for social interaction
	Dominant seller of single-track downloads[a]	
Google	YouTube platform & targeted search ad revenue	Lacks a social network and music subscribers
Facebook	Large web & mobile audience	Users connect to chat with friends. Relies on web advertising
	Personal information on users	Monetizing advertising revenue for mobile users
		Doesn't license music

[a]For the years 2007–2011 according to Christman (2012).

future music creators. Table 9.3 looks at the relative strengths and weakness of each player in the music industry in 2012, and summarizes what each company lacks in implementing the hypothetical merge model in the music industry. One observation that immediately stands out is that music ownership, content and copyrights will be key drivers of revenue as it is now in the industry.

Google has its popular YouTube site, but its social network platform, called Google Plus, "has been in a 'limited field trial,' with only those receiving invites able to join and create profiles. Unlike Facebook, Google Plus does not have a 'feed' for all users' online activity or a place for artists to post streams of their music or videos. "It also doesn't offer a way for developers to create add-on applications for direct-to-fan sales or content, something that Facebook is implementing." Furthermore, "Google Music" is not living up to expectations in terms of customer adoption rates and subscription revenue projections.[6] Google's Music was designed, in part, to compete with Apple's iTunes. It was thought that Google's marketing power and its 200 million Android users would be a major factor in the industry. The record labels welcomed the Google and Apple rivalry because of Apple's domination of music sales, Apple has been able at times to dictate music-licensing terms to the labels. The troubled start for Google Music comes as the music sector shifts attention away from downloads and onto subscription services, such as Spotify, Rhapsody, and Rdio. These companies sell consumers access to huge pools of songs for a monthly fee.[7]

Apple's biggest weakness is that it lacks the largest possible audience similar in number to Facebook's 400 million users a day that could launch or extend the reach of on-demand or paid subscription services.[8] Facebook may have a large audience,

[6]See Peoples (2011).

[7]See Sandoval (2012).

[8]At the time of writing.

but they did not license music at the time of writing. Apple and Google have already established licensing agreements with the major labels. Google's YouTube already has a direct license with music publishers for synchronization rights administered by the Harry Fox Agency. However, performance rights are not covered under the direct license.[9]

An Apple/Google/Facebook music platform combination could provide competition to the current incumbent PRO duopoly system in place by adding the direct licensing alternative to the traditional blanket license in the same way DMX has shown the industry. Google can seek a carve-out just like DMX and pay the copyright holders directly for musical performances on the Google network or platform. Google's YouTube has significantly reduced the huge costs of turning a musical composition into marketable content by essentially eliminating one of the functions of record labels. The copyright holders that will provide the content for such a combination could be the ultimate winners because they get to decide *how* their music is to be licensed and on *what* lucrative financial terms without the intermediate layer and legacy costs of incumbent PROs and publishers. As was pointed out earlier, there is a tremendous new opportunity for songwriters reclaiming their copyrights ownership, or joining forces with new innovators such as Kobalt who are no longer interested in owning copyrights, but maximizing income for the songwriter. We cannot be sure of what is likely to happen in the future, we can only help to point in the direction of future changes.

Google's and Facebook's current revenue model are based mostly on Internet advertising, while Apple's revenue stream consists mainly of selling electronic gadgets. A significant input cost for these ad-supported web-based business models is the cost of finding new users and retaining existing users. As the acquisition costs of finding new users increase, the revenue per user declines. One issue is whether Google will be satisfied with just advertising revenue for providing the software, technology, and platforms free of charge to future music creators, as it is currently doing now. Could an Apple/Google/Facebook combination emerge as a music publisher/record label itself—by negotiating directly with songwriters, composers and recording artists—and demand a share of copyright ownership from music creators, just as music publishers do today? Given the new paradigm shift in the music industry, it is not hard to imagine songwriters and other copyright holders demanding licensing deals that studios cannot offer.

It is unlikely that one business model is going to fit all content creators.[10] Table 9.4 looks at the new model in terms of the new merged entity as a non-exclusive distribution network focusing on both functions of a music user and a

[9]See http://www.youtubelicenseoffer.com for the key provisions in YouTube's direct license for synchronization rights with music publishers.

[10]See Cardi (2007), and Patry (2011) suggests other business models for creating efficiency in the music industry. See also the extensive examples of new business models in music, in addition to the way in which labels, artists, and songwriters are paid here: http://futureofmusic.org/sites/default/files/FMCnewbusinessmodels12.pdf.

Table 9.4 Merger model: non-exclusive distribution network

Role	Copyrights	Monetization ($ Revenue)	Functions
Music user	No ownership	On-demand rev.	Negotiate non-exclusive direct licenses with copyright owners
		Subscription rev.	Bundle performance, mechanical & synchronization rights
		% Advertising rev.	Royalty collection–copyright owners paid sooner and separately
		Per-stream rev.	Maximize income generation for copyright holders
		Per-performance rev.	Transparent accounting and audits
		Cloud services rev.	Revitalize older recordings for a new generation of listeners
		Statutory license	Open distribution network
Music publisher	Some ownership	On-demand rev.	Trade ownership in copyrights with music creators
		Subscription rev.	Songwriters as shareholders in a publicly traded entity
		% Advertising rev.	Negotiate ownership or commission fee structure
		Per-stream rev.	Provide financing choices for independent songwriters
		Per-performance rev.	Provide content creators with technology & creative platform
		Cloud services rev.	Develop a partnership with future music creators
		Statutory license	Negotiate pre-set non-exclusive distribution rights

music publisher. It will probably be to up the content creators and copyright holders to determine which model or (both combinations) best suit their own financial and creative goals.

New businesses are certainly going to be created to replace the economic value that has been lost in the traditional music publishing business and PRO organizations. As Table 7.1 on page 171 shows, many older technologies were displaced by newer versions, and new business models flourished that created incremental economic value. For future music creators, the copyright licensing process has changed dramatically, and it will become even more important to make sure that they are successful in profiting from their musical creations across a broad platform such as films, television, advertising, commercials, video games, merchandising, and Internet streaming services in a new environment.

References

Barker, A. (2011). 'Google acquires RightsFlow'. *Daily Variety*. December 12. p. 5.

Cardi, W. J. (2007). Über-middleman: Reshaping the broken landscape of copyright music. *Iowa Law Review*, 92:835–890.

Christman, E. (2012). 'iTunes On Top Again'. *Billboard Magazine*. May 12. p. 8.

Elder, J. (2014). 'Social Media Fail to Live Up to Early Marketing Hype: Companies Refine Strategies to Stress Quality Over Quantity of Fans'. *Wall Street Journal*. June 23, accessed online: http://online.wsj.com/articles/companies-alter-social-media-strategies-1403499658.

Patry, W. (2011). *How To Fix Copyright*. Oxford University Press, New York.

Peoples, G. (2011). 'The New Connectivity'. *Billboard Magazine*. October 1 issue, accessed online without illustrations: http://go.galegroup.com, story:7CA275974134.

Sandoval, G. (2012). 'Google Music not living up to expectations (exclusive)'. *CNET.com*. February 23, accessed online: http://news.cnet.com/8301-31001_3-57383531-261.

Tavakoli, J. M. (2013). 'Facebook Advertisers Beware'. *HuffingtonPost.com*. January 16, accessed online: http://www.huffingtonpost.com/janet-tavakoli/facebook-advertisers-bewa_b_2486921.html.

Chapter 10
Why the Merger Could Be a Viable Option

Today's social experiences are all integrated into the Google/Apple/Facebook media platforms, and it hardly matters if the music consumer is using a personal computer or smart phone.[1] An entire album can now be written and recorded on a laptop computer, while simultaneously released on iTunes and in traditional media outlets such as radio.

More importantly, established and next-generation recording artists can have massive hit songs on YouTube alone without a record label's promotional backing and radio airplay.[2] Songs are now released on YouTube; the popularity of YouTube videos leads to millions of "views," digital downloads and ringtone sales; this in turn leads to terrestrial airplay and then on to more sales.

Other social media platforms—such as Instagram—are used to bypass traditional music marketing and forge a direct marketing connection between an artist and his or her fan base or audience. Recently, superstar Beyoncé bypassed the traditional music marketing and promotion methods (radio airplay with an early single, booking as many TV appearances as possible and negotiating partnerships with big retailers and consumer brands) for generating marketing buzz for a new album. The artist used a stealth rollout of her latest album by first making a direct and surprise announcement to her eight million fans on Instagram and later offered her followers the entire multimedia album of 14 tracks and a music video for each track exclusively on iTunes for the price of $15.99. It is estimated that the artist sold approximately 365,000 albums on the first day in the United States, despite the fact that singles are the dominant sales unit.[3] Instagram is an online photo-sharing,

---

[1] See also the key findings in this report, Rideout et al. (2010, pp. 2–5).

[2] For example, recording artists, Cee Lo, Rihanna and others are cited in the following article that benefited from the viral influence of YouTube:*Billboard, Nielsen Add YouTube Video Streaming To Its Platforms; Data Enhances Hot 100, Other Charts*, http://www.billboard.com/biz/articles/news/chart-alert/1549398/billboard-nielsen-add-youtube-video-streaming-to-its-platforms.

[3] See Sisario (2013).

I.L. Pitt, *Direct Licensing and the Music Industry*,
DOI 10.1007/978-3-319-17653-6_10

video-sharing and social networking service that enables its users to take pictures and videos, and share them on a variety of social networking services, such as Facebook, Twitter, Tumblr, and Flickr.

In the information age, mergers and consolidation are not always as harmful to society as in the past because of the rapid rate of technological change and innovation that is occurring. For example, MySpace's—the older social media platform—decline was swift. Facebook was able to extinguish MySpace and become the dominant player for three reasons. First, consumers migrated to Facebook because of its network effects, that is, consumers flocked to Facebook because more of their friends were on that site and that increased its utility. Second, consumers found a better user interface on Facebook that was more appealing than MySpace. Finally, Facebook offered fewer advertising messages in its earlier incarnation. However, the sharp shift away from computer desktop technology to smart phones has left Facebook struggling to monetize its mobile product line because consumers do not like advertising on the relatively small screens on smart phones. Facebook's dominance is now being challenged by Twitter, Snapchat, and others who have developed applications for the smart phone. Recently, Facebook acquired Instagram and WhatsApp in multi-billion dollar deals because they faced disruptive threats from much smaller competitors with targeted applications in which Facebook could not build or did not possess.[4] For example, if consumers wanted to see just photos from friends? Instagram or Snapchat are applications that can do that. If consumers wanted to exchange text-messages with friends? Both WhatsApp and Snapchat are applications for those functions.[5]

While Apple's iTunes has dominated the market for digital music since the launch of its iTunes store in 2003, it was also facing a growing threat from music streaming because subscription streaming services such as Spotify and Pandora are beginning to cannibalize the sale of digital downloads. In May 2014, Apple decided to acquired Beats Electronics, a subscription-based music service and headphone device company, rather than expand it own iTunes Radio service. The acquisition of Beats also included the Beats headphone device that consumers were willing to pay several hundred dollars to obtain.[6] These mergers are likely to spur other companies to acquire assets that are more appealing to consumers.

Mergers can create efficiencies associated with both economies of scale and economies of scope in an Internet-only environment. It will probably take a merger—similar to the one that we discussed here—along with the combined financial resources to compete with Internet-based e-commerce businesses such as Alibaba. Therefore, changes to the Copyright Act and consent decrees should consider the future implications for copyright administration, given the speed in

---

[4]WhatsApp is a text-messaging application for smart phones.

[5]See also *Facebook Buying WhatsApp For $19B, Will Keep The Messaging Service Independent*: http://techcrunch.com/2014/02/19/facebook-buying-whatsapp-for-16b-in-cash-and-stock-plus-3b-in-rsus/.

[6]See Chen (2014), and Biddle (2013).

which Internet technology advances, transforms commerce and there is no longer the issue of scarcity. Alibaba Group Holding Limited is now a publicly traded Chinese company that is listed on the New York Stock Exchange. The company's mass-merchant business model appears to be a combination of Amazon, YouTube, Twitter, Ebay, PayPal, Yahoo, and a cloud computing service platform all rolled into a single entity. These efficiencies can be passed on to both consumers and music users in terms of lower prices, lower administration fees, and better service.

Indeed, this appears to be the pattern in the information age where successful (monopolists) incumbents are often forced to acquire smaller rivals who are a disruptive threat when they bring new innovations to the marketplace. In the acquisition examples cited above, all the apps were designed for use with a smart phone because customers who consume music, games, and video are no longer sitting in front of a computer, but are on the go. The scenario presented here could change depending on the success of the Google/Motorola merger where Google and Apple are rivals in the smart phone market. With declining CD sales and the demise of many physical retail music locations, music has now become a service, yet until recently music was monetized as a physical product.

10.1 Pandora Case Study

Peoples (2011a) estimated the royalty revenue opportunity for on-demand versus subscription streaming services using radio data, and his assumptions are shown in Tables 10.1 and 10.2. For example, under a best case scenario in which all time spend listening to audio is done with on-demand services, the average American would generate $45.55 per year based on a per-song royalty rate of 0.3 cents and $10.7 billion annually. If users listened to subscription services instead, the value of royalties would be $9.21 per person or $2.2 billion a year.

From his analysis, Peoples (2011a) concludes that "despite all the excitement surrounding subscription services, it remains to be seen whether these services

Table 10.1 Estimates of adults radio usage

Format	Minutes/day	Streams
Terrestrial radio	81.5	20.38
CD and tapes	18.9	4.73
Satellite radio	14.4	3.60
MP3 players	9.6	2.40
Audio stored on computers	8.1	2.03
Audio streams on computers	11.4	2.85
Audio on a mobile phone	1.9	0.48
Other sources of audio	19.2	4.80
Total	165	41.25

Source: Based on data from Peoples (2011a).

Table 10.2 Royalty estimates of streaming music

Activity	Royalties/person (per-year)	Annual[a] ($Billions)
Audio on-demand only	$45.55	$10.7*B*
Audio excluding talk & sports	$40.92	$9.6
Subscription services only	$9.21	$2.2

Source: Based on data from Peoples (2011a).
[a]Assuming a population of 234.5 million adults in the US.

will become profitable. Pay per-stream and a percent of revenue models have different cost considerations for music users, and revenue implications for copyright holders. Webcasters and subscription music services pay royalties on a per-play basis, which means the income that rights-holders earn is limited by the amount of time consumers actually spend listening to music. There is room for these services to grow from niche status into mainstream products, as webcasters' ad revenue eventually grows large enough that they pay a percent of revenue, instead of pay per-stream royalties. Recording artists, performers and labels would stand to profit from it."[7]

Robertson (2011) suggests that "the specifics [of the licensing deals] are even more onerous. Together they doom online audio companies to a life of subjugation to the labels." In Table 10.3, we summarize the secretive economic demands—barriers to entry—that affect profitability for every digital-music subscription service such as Spotify, Rhapsody, MOG, Muve Music, Slacker, Rdio, Xbox Music, and others.[8] Some of these economic demands are not well known because digital music service deals are often confidential. The sale of EMI to other music companies meant there are only three major labels. If a music service rejects terms offered by a label, then that service's offering will have an enormous hole in their catalog of 33 % or more of popular songs. In the business world, a monopoly leads to lopsided economics, and the subscription digital music business is a poignant illustration of that. "However, online radio services such as Pandora take advantage of a government-supervised license available only to radio broadcasters thus sidestepping dealing with record labels and their daunting economic demands." As Table 10.4 shows and at the time of writing, Pandora was still not profitable even with a government supervised license.

The financial statement revealed that most of Pandora's revenue is from advertising, and total revenue grew from $137,764,000 in 2011 to $274,340,000 in 2012, a 99 % year over year increase. A significant input cost is the cost associated with acquiring musical content, and that cost represented 52.12 % of its operating budget. As the year over year costs of acquiring content grew, along with other input costs,

[7]See Peoples (2011a).

[8]Based on Robertson (2011).

Table 10.3 Economic demands and barriers to entry in the music industry

Economic demands	Terms	Disadvantages
General deal structure	Pay the largest of:	Labels & PROs de facto set retail prices which limit the ability of music service to develop ancillary revenue streams
	(a) Pro-rata share of min. of $X/sub	
	(b) Per-play costs at $Y per play	
	(c) Z % of total company revenue	
	(d) Flat Fee	
Equity stake	Labels get partial ownership of the company	Labels get to set the price of the service and they also get partial ownership
Insider collusion	PROs prevent major publishers from signing direct licenses due to strong affiliation	Music users unable to secure rights to certain popular catalogs
Boycotts	Music users denied the right to use music in agencies' repertory	Alternative music sources required, if available
Up-front payments	Large amounts of cash payments are necessary	May stifle innovation in services & business models
Detailed reporting	Labels make additional demands such as overall market share reports, unrelated to payments to artists	The labels effectively offload their business analysis and the cost of such analysis onto the music services
Data normalization	Some labels provide their data in different formats	No standard method or format for referencing artists, tracks, and albums
Publishing deals	Deals require both record label & publisher approval	Services may have the rights to stream from labels, but unable to get the publisher rights
		May have unknown copyright holders
Most Favored Nation (MFN)	This could be a form of collusion since each label gets the best terms that other labels negotiate	This constricts the ability to work out unique contractual terms and further limits business models then benefits from the higher rates
	One label provides low-cost terms knowing others will demand higher rates,	

(continued)

Table 10.3 (continued)

Economic demands	Terms	Disadvantages
Non-disclosure asymmetrical information	Strict language prohibiting music services from revealing payments to labels	Disclosing licensing terms could jeopardize or invalidate license deal
	Labels receive payments for all entitled parties	Music services can't reveal payments to songwriters
		One party has more or better information than others
Publisher/label mergers	Completely new or different negotiation terms	Substantial catalogs can be pulled to force a renegotiation
Artist holdouts	Denial of access to new albums	Holdouts until massive royalties or advances are paid
Litigation	Rate court settles party disputes	Resources tied up in lengthy and costly legal proceedings as new competitors & technologies emerge
		Costs often exceed benefits

Source: Based on data from Robertson (2011).

Table 10.4 Pandora's selected financial results 2011 & 2012

(in $000)				
Pandora	2011	2012	2012 Share (%)	Y/Y Change
Revenue:				
Advertising	$119,333	$239,957	87.47	$120,624
Subscription services & other	$18,431	$34,383	12.53	$15,952
Total revenue	$137,764	$274,340		$136,576
Costs and expenses:				
Cost of revenue[a]	$11,559	$22,759	4.00	$11,200
Product development[a]	$6,736	$13,425	4.71	$6,689
Marketing & sales[a]	$36,250	$65,010	22.78	$28,760
General & administrative[a]	$14,183	$35,428	12.42	$21,245
Content acquisition	$69,357	$148,708	52.12	$79,351
Total costs & expenses	$138,085	$285,330		$147,245
Loss from operations	$(321)	$(10,990)		(10,669)
Net loss	$(1,764)	$(16,107)		$(14,343)

Source: Based on data from: http://www.sec.gov/Archives/edgar/data/1230276/000119312512099083/d306786dex991.html.

[a]Amounts include stock-based compensation expenses.

Pandora suffered a loss of $147,245,000 in 2012. Table 10.5 illustrates Robertson (2011) arguments by comparing the ratios of advertising and subscription revenue to content acquisition costs. Pandora's model relies mostly on advertising revenue, and for every dollar spent on content acquisition, the company generated $1.61 in

Table 10.5 Pandora's ratio of advertising revenue to content acquisition costs

(in $000)				
Pandora	2011	2012	Change	Change (%)
Revenue:				
Advertising	$119,333	$239,957	$120,624	101.08
Subscription services and other	$18,431	$34,383	$15,952	86.55
Total	$137,764	$274,340	$136,576	99.14
Costs and expenses:				
Content acquisition	$69,357	$148,708	$79,351	114.41
Ratio:				
Advertising rev./content acq.	$1.72	$1.61	−0.1069	−6.22
Subscription rev./content acq.	$0.27	$0.23	−0.0345	−12.99

online advertising revenue in 2012, a −6.22 % decline over 2011. A subscription only revenue model would not have been viable for Pandora to cover its content acquisition expenses, along with other marketing costs, and such a model would be unprofitable.[9]

Consumers will make the ultimate choice as to whether they want own music, or just want access to music via streaming, on-demand services or free access across a wide variety of platforms, including "in the cloud" technology. "In the cloud technology stores video, photos, data, music files and software applications on a central server that can be easily accessed by laptop computers or mobile phones with an Internet or wireless network connection."

"The cloud has changed how entertainment products are stored and delivered. Consumers can stream video or music without needing to store the files on the hard drive of their PC or mobile device. The cloud creates instantaneous on-demand access with little or no need to wait for entire files to download. It allows incredible amounts of user-generated content to be uploaded at sites like YouTube."[10] "The cloud has ushered in a new way to make money from entertainment. Money has normally been spent on discrete transactions—$1 for a song download or $20 for a DVD—and changes hands between buyer and seller each time a product is purchased. But the cloud has changed that relationship. Now consumers can pay to merely access music and video. On-demand video allows consumers to pay for a stream of a movie or TV show. Video and music subscription services allow unlimited streaming for a fee. Unlike sales from purchases, subscription fees are predictable and recurring. Purchasers only pay for what they buy, and weeks or

[9]This is typical of other Internet businesses as well where the growth in operating expenses often exceed the growth in revenue.

[10]See Peoples (2011b).

months can pass between purchases."[11] The choices that consumers make will determine how companies monetize their products and services in terms of offering free content, premium content, subscription or advertising supported revenue that fit in with digital sales and digital consumption patterns.

References

Biddle, S. (2013). 'Beat By Dre: The Exclusive Inside Story of How Monster Lost the World'. *Gizmodo.com*. February 7, accessed online: http://gizmodo.com/5981823/beat-by-dre-the-inside-story-of-how-monster-lost-the-world.

Chen, B. (2014). 'Apple to Pay $3 Billion to Buy Beats'. *New York Times*. May 29, p. B1.

Peoples, G. (2011a). 'Swelling Stream: What's the potential Value of the Streaming Music Market?'. *Billboard Magazine*. September 24 issue, accessed online without illustrations: http://go.galegroup.com, story:7CA267518925.

Peoples, G. (2011b). 'The quiet storm: Cloud computing has slowly crept from backroom and blog discussion to the forefront of every media executive's mind. Is your business ready for the winds of change?'. *Billboard Magazine*. May 14 issue, accessed online without illustrations: http://go.galegroup.com, story:7CA257217098.

Rideout, V., Foehr, U., and Roberts, D. (2010). Generation M^2: Media in the Lives of 8 to 18 Year-Olds. Technical Report, Kaiser Family Foundation, Menlo Park, California. http://www.kff.org/entmedia/upload/8010.pdf.

Robertson, M. (2011). 'Why Spotify can never be profitable: The secret demands of record labels'. *GigaOm.com*. accessed online: http://gigaom.com/2011/12/11/why-spotify-can-never-be-profitable-the-secret-demands-of-record-labels.

Sisario, B. (2013). 'Beyoncé Rejects Tradition for Social Media's Power'. *New York Times*. December 16. p. B1.

[11] See Peoples (2011b).

Chapter 11
Conclusion

Piracy was, more or a less, an obfuscation to shift the focus away from the structural changes that were occurring due to the widespread use of digital technologies where consumers were discovering and listening to music; and the creative ways in which to monetize the new digital services (free on-demand streaming with advertising or ad-free paid subscription models). Listening for free to streaming services—which was once considered piracy—was a crucial marketing plan for some of the streaming services to acquire new customers and build a loyal customer base to later up-sell or cross-sell other products and services. For example, in the Beats Music case, streaming was added in order to sell high-priced headphones. As streaming services increase the number of customers and revenue, they are beginning to increase royalty payments to songwriters, composers, and record labels as well, even though it may not offset the decline in revenue from CD sales and downloads.

Music publishers and record labels were unable to develop their own viable download sales or music streaming models because the publishers controlled their own distinct music catalogs, just like the PROs, that could not be licensed elsewhere. The music availability limitations of each record label's and PRO's respective repertories meant that music users and consumers could not benefit from the efficiencies associated with economies of scale and scope from the pooling of all available music in all repertories that could be accessed from anywhere. This meant that separate licensing agreements with PROs, music publishers, and record labels were required to obtain all music clearances. It took innovators such as Apple (iTunes and iPhone), Spotify (on-demand music streaming), YouTube (music and video synchronization) and Music Reports, Inc. (copyright ownership) from outside the music industry to create the new business models that involved the pooling of music repertories.

The music industry problems, as we discussed in the text, can be summarized as follows in Table 11.1:

Direct licensing and the partial withdrawal of digital rights have raised considerable doubts about the continued viability of the incumbent PROs in an industry that

I.L. Pitt, *Direct Licensing and the Music Industry*,
DOI 10.1007/978-3-319-17653-6_11

Table 11.1 Summary of music industry problems

(a) The failure to capitalize on consumer trends and changing consumer tastes that initially started with Napster, digital downloads and then moved on to music streaming services in which younger consumers did not care to actually own music but to have on-demand access across a wide variety of media platforms;
(b) A reliance on the self-serving status quo or cartel model for its benefits and perks;
(c) A failure to use econometrics to estimate the lifetime value of a single piece of intellectual property using the reams of historical royalty payments and performance data just sitting in databases waiting to be analyzed;
(d) A failure to understand multi-media platforms and differentiated (commodity) pricing;
(e) Erecting structural barriers to impede competition, innovation, productivity, and efficiency;
(f) The failure to adapt to structural and cyclical changes, new technology, and new markets;
(g) Independent music retailers with stand-alone retail outlets that could not compete with big-box stores who could subsidize music with other products or online digital retailers selling singles;
(h) Over-investment and mal-investment in infrastructure (brick and mortar outlets, recording studios, multiple offices in multiple locations, outdated technology and outmoded royalty payment systems);
(i) Retaining business models that were no longer sustainable, economical or profitable in a digital or Internet environment;
(j) Inertia, apathy, inflexible thinking, bureaucratic politics, dead-weight and figure-head personnel and a lack of imagination among executives that led to the inability to develop a coherent strategy in music licensing;
(k) Antiquated consent decrees and copyright laws that no longer made sense in a digital environment;
(l) Failure to understand how third-party aggregators (iTunes) were more efficient in connecting demand and supply in real time;
(m) A failure to understand the product life cycle in music; and
(n) A failure to understand the historical boom, bust and rebirth in the music industry.

is becoming more competitive with new entrants. Incumbent PROs may not be able to justify their double-digital costs of administering old-media blanket licenses for music performances because digital technologies have disrupted the most expensive and least efficient functions of administering the blanket license. The rate court battles may just be a bridge to buy time before the inevitable realization that the PROs economic value added to music publishers has been irreversibly eroded and it is a just a matter of time before they met their final demise. Future changes to the *Copyright Act* and consent decrees should address the Economic Demands and Structural Barriers to Entry in the Music Industry in Table 5.2 in Chapter Five on page 140.

Record labels are now adopting new business models that no longer rely on the old business model of owning copyrights. For example, there are now different types of licensing agreements between songwriters and record labels where the transferring of copyrights, lengthy terms of exclusivity and the methods for calculating and distributing royalty payments are completely different from years past. The old exclusive publishing model—where a single publisher represented all licensing deals with restrictions, transfer of copyright, and up-front advance payments—is slowly being replaced with a commission or fee-based marketing service using multiple agents. Songwriters are now pursuing new and more profitable non-exclusive licensing agreements with multiple companies without the transfer of copyrights. Both the songwriter and co-publishers share in the profits from successful multiple licensing deals, usually with licensing firms absorbing marketing expenses.

There are considerable concerns from organizations representing artists that the partial shift (as it is happening now) to the idea of direct or other forms of licensing may end up hurting the economic and creative future of artists. Songwriters and record labels face the challenge of finding equitable methods to allocate the pool of money generated from direct licensing fees because so many intermediaries are involved in royalty distribution payments. Table 11.2 provides a summary of the music industry concerns. These concerns are valid and deserve further academic study similar to the work already done on the traditional blanket license.

Table 11.2 Music industry concerns about music licensing

(a)	Is direct licensing going to "devalue" music?
(b)	Are music users trying to get more content for less money?
(c)	Is direct licensing anti-artist and anti-musician?
(d)	Will direct licensing reduce royalty income for musicians, songwriters, and composers?
(e)	Should publishers collect and distribute direct licensing royalty payments for all entitled parties?
(f)	What is the economic impact of direct licensing on incumbent PROs and record labels?
(g)	What are the economic benefits for independent artists versus artists controlled by labels?
(h)	How is government regulation likely to evolve to promote competition in a new technological age?
(i)	Should PROs acting on behalf of copyright holders prevent third-party technology innovations?
(j)	On what terms should licensed content be made available to consumers over the new Internet distribution media?
(k)	What is the relationship between copyright holders and licensed distributors in the digital era?
(l)	Is direct licensing going to create a more competitive marketplace?
(m)	How should regulators address the economic demands and barriers to entry in the music industry?
(n)	How should the Copyright Act be rewritten to match current markets to new technology?
(o)	Who should own the copyrights to long dormant works that are no longer released and are not profitable?
(p)	How will direct licensing affect the music industry market structure?
(q)	Should artists own the valuable music performance, listener and user data generated from downloads and streaming services?
(r)	Is there a need for a new organization for independent musicians who are self-publishers and own 100 % of their music?
(s)	How should streaming royalties be equitably distributed between mainstream artists with a large audience and independent artists with much a smaller fan base?

Any major change to the status quo in any industry that protects incumbents is likely to be controversial, whether it is caused by a market shift, iTunes, Last.FM, music subscription services like Spotify or revisions to copyright laws and consent decrees. Consumers are making important statements about the quality of music that they wish to purchase. We have come full circle in today's music industry where consumers have decided that it is a better economic value proposition to purchase "singles" (like they did in the 1950s and 1960s) in a virtual world with a more efficient distribution system, instead of buying an album with just one or two good songs in a physical location.

Direct licensing is not the only alternative to the blanket licensee that could benefit songwriters and composers. Creative Commons (CC) Licensing is another threat that the incumbent PROs are vigorously fighting because artists are releasing their music with a CC license. Songwriters and composers may decide to waive performance and mechanical rights compensation under a CC license depriving the PROs of their source of revenue. CC licensing is also a threat to record labels and a benefit for independent songwriters and composers, when they retain, control and exploit the copyrights to the master recordings such as negotiating the synchronization rights for film and television without the record labels sharing in the revenue.

Creative Commons is a relatively new, flexible, and a less restrictive licensing organization, that gives everyone from individual creators to large companies and institutions an alternative choice in copyright licensing. It is a simple and standardized way to grant some or all copyright permissions for the use of creative works. Content can be copied, distributed, edited, remixed, and built upon, all within the boundaries of copyright as long as the original work, depending on commercial or non-commercial exploitation, is credited appropriately according to the creator's restrictions.[1] It is not hard to see why independent recording artists find the CC license more advantageous: They already own the valuable rights to their master recordings by virtue of producing their own songs at their own expense and without the help of a record label; they get to keep a greater share of revenues from sales of their musical works; and success depends on their own initiatives. In addition, these songwriters, as owners of the sound recording, now receive royalties for certain digital public performances through SoundExchange, as well as the public performance royalties through ASCAP, BMI and SESAC as a songwriter/composer/self-publisher.

The PROs are barely holding on to their tenuous monopoly powers. As is evident, music publishers are willing to bypass the PROs. This is a decisive tipping point which reflects real and evolutionary structural changes in music licensing and the entire music industry. The publishers would hardly initiate the process for direct licensing if they did not mean to follow through with it. The PROs have been permanently weakened by exogenous technology, inexorable innovation, strong competition, and permanent structural changes in the music industry.

[1] See http://creativecommons.org/licenses.

The PROs were also internally undermined by the self-serving propensity of their own members or affiliates with their desire for a partial or full withdrawal of digital rights, and the creation of their own song title registries. Administration costs, the inherent inefficiencies of monopolies, and efficacy of PROs administering the blanket license for performance rights are major threats to their survival.

It was not hard to see why this was happening: CD and download sales continued to plummet and new-media streaming services were the new growth areas in music sales. However, streaming services revenue have not been able to offset the decline in CD and download sales. It is the familiar life cycle (boom, bust and rebirth) pattern that we have discussed in this text. Music publishers and songwriters are already envisioning a future without ASCAP and BMI, and the speed at which it is happening is truly breathtaking. For example, Universal announced in late June 2014 that they were planning to make all of their song catalog data available online, a move that would allow it to bypass both ASCAP and BMI. Sony/ATV is said to be working on a similar registry.[2]

The PROs' problems are increasingly visible, terminal, and cannot be easily solved with extended litigation or quick fixes to consent decrees. The inability of the PROs and music publishers to adjust to changing market conditions in music licensing—such as the need for new-media music users to acquire both public performance and sound recording licenses—can no longer be camouflaged. The publishers believed that consent decrees stand in the way of closing the gap between the payments for composition rights and sound recording rights and "because the two PROs were required under their consent decrees to issue a license to any music user who requested one, they could not adequately leverage their market power to negotiate a significantly higher rate for a license to publically [sic] perform a composition."[3]

Permitting a partial withdrawal of digital rights or allowing music publishers to determine how to use PROs to license music, even as a token, well-intended, flexible alternative to fixing the structural problems in music licensing caused by digital technologies, would actually make licensing problems much worse by permitting the incumbent PROs to cling for dear life to their only available lifeline, aided and abetted by amending consent decrees. The questions are (1) how exactly are music users going to benefit from the efficiency in music licensing by having to negotiate separate licensing agreements with music publishers, record labels, and PROs? and (2) how are songwriters and composers going to be affected by badly redesigned copyright laws and consent decrees if incumbent monopoly PROs are left in place?

It is now futile to merely ameliorate consent decrees or copyright laws to protect the outdated business models of PROs when so many struggling songwriters and composers are dependent on performance royalty as their only source of income. In revising copyright laws and consent decrees, perhaps by using a statutory fixed-rate for a musical performance across all media—as a freely functioning pricing

---

[2]See Sisario (2014).

[3]See *US vs. ASCAP & In re Petition of Pandora Media* (2014, p. 41).

mechanism that reflects the supply and demand dynamics for music licenses—might be one solution to the equitable distribution of performance royalties and to avoid situations of asymmetrical information in which music industry insiders can exploit outsiders in the licensing process. There is no reason why the availability (central registry of song ownership), terms (usage and duration), and pricing (cost per use) for an individual musical performance across all media platforms licensing cannot be done on a transparent and timely basis using a metering model and a digital asset management system for *directly* distributing royalty payments to all copyright owners.

It is going to take strong political will in public policy to deregulate the entrenched PROs in such a way that the removal of some governance does not open the door for fraudulent corporate practices and to do away with their outmoded and unsustainable business models, just as Judge Green did in the AT&T case.[4] It is important that any new changes in the system achieve the right balance of copyright law, regulation, supervision, ethics, and enforcement in which these PROs serve the legitimate interests of songwriters and composers.[5]

There is still going to need some form of judicial oversight to prevent abuse in a new licensing system, not to mention the risks of moral hazard as a special case of information asymmetry that may adversely affect songwriters and composers. PROs, music publishers, and record labels usually have more information than is made available to songwriters and composers, and in most cases, songwriters are at a disadvantage because they cannot completely monitor or audit these licensing agencies without incurring huge expenses.

In the Bruce Springsteen Case Study in Sect. 2.8 on page 84, we described how the interests (and the negative consequences of an inappropriate lawsuit) of a PRO and a songwriter are not always in alignment. But there is also the tension between the major music publishers—as they begin withdrawing digital rights—and songwriters within the PROs. The songwriters are justly concerned that when music publishers withdrew digital rights from PROs, the songwriters whose compositions remained would be burdened with the PRO's administration and overhead costs that include licensing; redundant, prestigious and expensive corporate offices in high-rent districts in multiple locations; exorbitant legal fees charged by expert witnesses, lobbyists and outside counsel for lengthy litigation; and the need to recover the amortized and mal-investment costs for long-delayed computer system upgrades. In essence, the songwriters are concerned that the PROs would become a mere third-party accounting administrator for the music publishers, similar to what the Harry Fox Agency has become with the decline in mechanical licensing.[6]

---

[4]See Kearney (1999), DiLorenzo (1996), Cairncross (1997), and Cauley (2008).

[5]Financial deregulation has received a bad rap due to the fraud associated with the savings and loan crisis in the 1980s and the role the repeal of the *Glass-Steagall Act* may have played in the 2008 financial crisis. In both cases, it was fraud committed by insiders who controlled the companies following deregulation. See Black (2005), Barofsky (2012), Galbraith (2014).

[6]See Stout (2012).

As we have pointed out in the text, the vast majority of songwriters and composers received minuscule royalty payments from the nearly $2 billion that ASCAP and BMI collect each year in performance licensing fees. It is only the top songwriters and composers and music publishers whose works are performed that receive the lion's share of performance royalties.

It is not just giving music publishers the flexibility to decide on how to use the PROs for music licensing, but as Patry (2011, p. 74) suggests, what is needed is a moratorium on new laws, a "fit-for-purpose" review of outdated copyright laws and the entire Copyright Act rewritten from scratch to reflect modern markets and rapid technological change. Music streaming services that need mechanical, performance and synchronization rights would probably benefit from the efficiency of negotiating with a single entity for those rights. It is most unlikely that all music use content could be directly licensed and so there will still be a need for third-party intermediaries in which multiple licenses are combined into a single agency.

References

Barofsky, N. (2012). *Bailout: An Inside Account of How Washington Abandoned Main Street While Rescuing Wall Street.* Free Press.

Black, W. (2005). *The Best Way to Rob a Bank is to Own One: How Corporate Executives and Politicians Looted the S&L Industry.* University of Texas Press.

Cairncross, F. (1997). *The Death of Distance.* Harvard Business School Press.

Cauley, L. (2008). *End of the Line: The Rise and Fall of AT&T.* Free Press.

DiLorenzo, T. (1996). The myth of natural monopoly. *Review of Austrian Economics*, 9(2):43–58.

Galbraith, J. (2014). *The End of Normal: The Great Crisis and the Future of Growth.* Simon and Schuster.

Kearney, J. (1999). From the fall of the Bell System to the Telecommunications Act: Regulation of telecommunications under Judge Greene. *Marquette University Law School Faculty Publications*, pages 1395–1472. Paper 505, accessed online: http://scholarship.law.marquette.edu/facpub/505, pp. 1395–1472.

Patry, W. (2011). *How To Fix Copyright.* Oxford University Press, New York.

Sisario, B. (2014). 'Sony Threatens to Bypass Licensers in Royalties Battle'. *New York Times.* July 11, p. B2.

Stout, L. (2012). *The Shareholder Value Myth: How Putting Shareholders First Harms Investors, Corporations, and the Public.* Berrett-Koehler.

US vs. ASCAP & In re Petition of Pandora Media (2014). Nos: 12 Civ. 8035 (DLC), 41 Civ. 1395 (DLC), S.D.N.Y. March 14, accessed online: http://www.business.cch.com/ipld/PandoraUSASCAP031414.pdf, pp. 1–136.

Appendix

See Fig. A.1.

I.L. Pitt, *Direct Licensing and the Music Industry*,
DOI 10.1007/978-3-319-17653-6

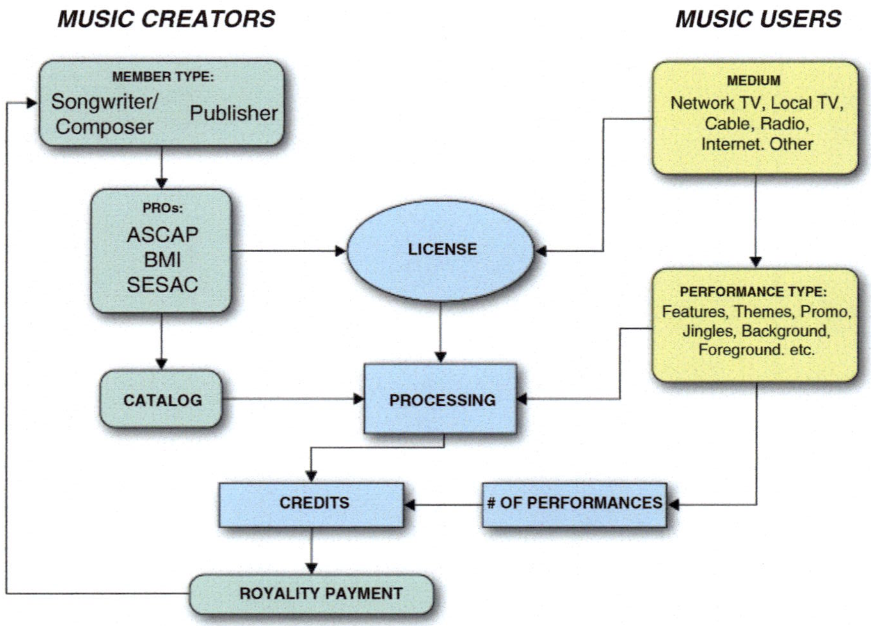

Source: Pitt. I. L. (2010a). *Economic Analysis of Music Copyright: Income, Media and Performances* Springer, New York. p. 8.

Fig. A.1 Royalty payment subprocess in a Performing Rights Organization

Bibliography

Books and Articles Cited

Alchian, A. and Demsetz, H. (1996). Production, information costs and economic organization. In Putterman, L. and Kroszner, R., editors, *The Economic Nature of the Firm: A Reader*, chapter 14, pages 193–216. Cambridge University Press, Cambridge, United Kingdom, second edition.

Alexander, P. (1994). New technology and market structure: Evidence from the music recording industry. *Journal of Cultural Economics*, 18:113–123.

Allen Consulting Group (2003). Economic perspectives on copyright law. Research Paper ISBN 1 876692 05 7, Centre for Copyright Studies Ltd, Strawberry Hills NSW 2012, Australia. The Centre is funded by Copyright Agency Limited, a copyright collecting society in Australia.

Anders, G. (2013). 'No Stores? No Salesmen? No Profit? No Problem for Amazon'. *MIT Technology Review*. November 7, accessed online: http://www.technologyreview.com/news/520801/no-stores-no-salesmen-no-profit-no-problem-for-amazon.

Anderson, C. (2008). *The Long Tail: Why the Future of Business Is Selling Less of More*. Hyperion, New York, NY.

Bach, D. (2004). The double punch of law and technology: Fighting music piracy or remaking copyright in a digital age? *Business and Politics*, 6(2):1–33.

Bacharach, B. (2014). 'What the Songwriting World Needs Now'. *Wall Street Journal*, page A11. January 23, accessed online: http://search.proquest.com/docview/1491047402?accountid=35927.

Barker, A. (2011). 'Google acquires RightsFlow'. *Daily Variety*. December 12. p. 5.

Barnes, B. (2014). 'After a Tumultuous Year, Hollywood Looks to 2015'. *New York Times*. December 22, p. B1.

Barofsky, N. (2012). *Bailout: An Inside Account of How Washington Abandoned Main Street While Rescuing Wall Street*. Free Press.

Baumol, W. (1982). Contestable markets: An uprising in theory of industry structure. *American Economic Review*, 72:1–15.

Beall, E. (2004). *Making Music Make Money: An Insider's Guide to Becoming Your Own Music Publisher*. Berklee Press, Boston, MA.

Besen, S., Kirby, S., and Salop, S. (1992). An economic analysis of copyright collectives. *Virginia Law Review*, 78(1):383–411. Symposium on the Law and Economics of Intellectual Property.

Biddle, S. (2013). 'Beat By Dre: The Exclusive Inside Story of How Monster Lost the World'. *Gizmodo.com*. Febuary 7, accessed online: http://gizmodo.com/5981823/beat-by-dre-the-inside-story-of-how-monster-lost-the-world.

I.L. Pitt, *Direct Licensing and the Music Industry*,
DOI 10.1007/978-3-319-17653-6

Blacc, A. (2014). 'Streaming Services Need to Pay Songwriters Fairly'. *Wired.* November 14, accessed online: http://www.wired.com/2014/11/aloe-blacc-pay-songwriters.

Black, W. (2005). *The Best Way to Rob a Bank is to Own One: How Corporate Executives and Politicians Looted the S&L Industry.* University of Texas Press.

Boldrin, M. and Levine, D. (2009). Does intellectual monopoly help innovation? *Review of Law & Economics*, 5(3):991–1024.

Brabec, J. and Brabec, T. (2011). *Music, Money and Success: The Insider's Guide To Making Money In The Music Industry.* Schirmer Trade Books-Music Sales, New York, NY.

Brooks, T. (2009). Only in America: The unique status of sound recordings under U.S. copyright law and how it threatens our heritage. *American Music*, 27(2):125–137.

Brynjolfsson, E. and McAfee, A. (2014). *The Second Machine Age: Work, Progress, and Prosperity in a Time of Brilliant Technologies.* W. W. Norton.

Budnick, D. and Baron, J. (2012). *Ticket Masters: The Rise of the Concert Industry and How the Public Got Scalped.* Penguin Group.

Bumiller, E. (1996). ASCAP Asks Royalties From Girl Scouts, and Regrets It. *New York Times.* December 17, accessed online: http://www.nytimes.com/1996/12/17/nyregion/ascap-asks-royalties-from-girl-scouts-and-regrets-it.html?pagewanted=all&src=pm.

Cairncross, F. (1997). *The Death of Distance.* Harvard Business School Press.

Cardi, W. J. (2007). Über-middleman: Reshaping the broken landscape of copyright music. *Iowa Law Review*, 92:835–890.

Carr, D. (2014a). 'Facebook Offers Life Raft, But Publishers Are Wary'. *New York Times.* October 27, p. B1.

Carr, D. (2014b). 'The Stream Finally Cracks The Dam of Cable TV'. *New York Times.* October 20, p. B1.

Carter, B. (2014). 'Overextended, Music TV Shows Fade'. *New York Times.* May 12. p. B1.

Castle, C. (2012). 'A Great Question from @ZoeCello: Should Digital Retailers Own the Artist's Fan Data?'. *Music Technology and Policy Monthly.* November 19, accessed online: http://musictechpolicy.wordpress.com/2012/11/19/a-great-question-from-zoecello-should-digital-retailers-own-the-artists-fan-data.

Cauley, L. (2008). *End of the Line: The Rise and Fall of AT&T.* Free Press.

Chen, B. (2014). 'Apple to Pay $3 Billion to Buy Beats'. *New York Times.* May 29, p. B1.

Chozick, A. (2013). Longing to Stay Wanted, MTV Turns Its Attention to Younger Viewers. *New York Times.* June 17. p. B4.

Christensen, C. (1997). *The Innovator's Dilemma: When New Technologies Cause Great Firms to Fail.* Harvard Business School Press.

Christman, E. (2008). 'Cashing In'. *Billboard Magazine*, 120:26–28. October 25 issue, accessed online: Academic Search Premier, EBSCOhost accession number: 34888428.

Christman, E. (2011a). 'EMI Music Publishing Taking Over Licensing Digital Rights From ASCAP'. *Billboard Magazine.* May 3 issue, accessed online: http://www.billboard.biz, story:1005167992.

Christman, E. (2011b). 'Sirius' Direct-Licensing Efforts Come Under Attack From Recording Academy, AFTRA'. *Billboard Magazine.* October 27 issue, accessed online: http://www.billboard.biz, story:1005445642.

Christman, E. (2011c). 'SiriusXM Attempting to License Directly From Labels'. *Billboard Magazine.* August 11 issue, accessed online: http://www.billboard.biz, story:1005312752.

Christman, E. (2012a). 'Exclusive: Clear Channel, Big Machine Strike Deal to Pay Sound-Recording Performance Royalties To Label, Artists'. *Billboard Magazine.* June 5 issue, accessed online: http://www.billboard.biz, story:1007226762.

Christman, E. (2012b). 'iTunes On Top Again'. *Billboard Magazine.* May 12. p. 8.

Christman, E. (2012c). 'Turning publishing upside-down: Aggressive. Transparent. Winning. Why Willard Ahdritz's strategies are working, and why his Kobalt Music is the future'. *Billboard Magazine.* January 28 issue, accessed online without illustrations: http://go.galegroup.com, story:7CA278171081.

Christman, E. (2013a). 'Copying The Left'. *Billboard Magazine*, 125:12. June 29 issue, accessed online: Academic Search Premier, EBSCOhost, accession number: 88430185.

Christman, E. (2013b). 'Going for a Song'. *Billboard Magazine*, 125:28–29. March 30 issue, accessed online: Academic Search Premier, EBSCOhost, Accession Number: 86535006.

Christman, E. (2013c). 'Pandora Ruling Has Far-Reaching Implications For U.S. Publishing Industry'. *Billboard.com*. December 23, accessed online: http://www.billboard.com/biz/articles/news/publishing/5847835/pandora-ruling-has-far-reaching-implications-for-us-publishing.

Christman, E. (2013d). 'Universal Music Publishing Plots Exit From ASCAP, BMI'. *Billboard Magazine*. February 7 issue, accessed online: http://www.billboard.com/biz/articles/news/publishing/1537554/universal-music-publishing-plots-exit-from-ascap-bmi.

Christman, E. (2014a). 'Dept. of Justice Sends Doc Requests, Investigating UMPG, Sony/ATV, BMI and ASCAP Over Possible 'Coordination''. *Billboard Magazine*. July 13, accessed online: http://www.billboard.com/biz/articles/news/publishing/6157513/dept-of-justice-sends-doc-requests-investigating-umpg-sonyatv.

Christman, E. (2014b). 'SESAC Facing New Anti-Trust Legal Challenge'. *Billboard.com*. March 14, accessed online: http://www.billboard.com/biz/articles/news/publishing/5937426/sesac-facing-new-anti-trust-legal-challenge.

Christman, E. (2014c). 'Sony/ATV's Martin Bandier Repeats Warning to ASCAP, BMI'. *Billboard Magazine*. July 11, accessed online: http://www.billboard.com/biz/articles/news/publishing/6157469/sonyatvs-martin-bandier-repeats-warning-to-ascap-bmi.

Christman, E. (2014d). 'The Digital Decline: What's Behind the First Downturn of the iTunes Era? And Can Streaming Save the Day?'. *Billboard Magazine*. January 18 issue, pp. 34–36.

Christman, E., Pham, A., and Peoples, G. (2013). 'Special Report: The Pandora Wars'. *Billboard Magazine*. August 10 issue. pp. 20–25.

Coase, R. (1996). The nature of the firm. In Putterman, L. and Kroszner, R., editors, *The Economic Nature of the Firm: A Reader*, chapter 7, pages 89–104. Cambridge University Press, Cambridge, United Kingdom, second edition.

Copyright Office (2014). *Music Licensing Study: Notice and Request for Public Comment, No. 2014-03*, Federal Register, Vol. 78, No. 51. May, accessed online: http://www.copyright.gov/fedreg/2014/79fr14739.pdf, pp. 14739–14743.

Copyright Royalty Board (2012). *Adjustment or Determination of Compulsory License Rates for Making and Distributing Phonorecords: Motion to Adopt Settlement, Docket No. 2011-3 CRB Phonorecords II*. April, accessed online: http://www.loc.gov/crb/motions/parties_motion_adopt_settlement_041112.pdf, pp. 1–33.

Copyright Act (2011). Copyright Law of the United States, United States Copyright Office, Library of Congress, Washington, DC, Circular 92. December, accessed online: http://www.copyright.gov/title17/circ92.pdf.

Cyert, R. and Mowery, D., editors (1987). *Technology and Employment: Innovation and Growth in the U.S. Economy*. National Academy Press, Dulles, VA. Accessed online: http://www.nap.edu/catalog.php?record_id=1004.

DiCola, P. (2013). Money from music: Survey evidence on musicians' revenue and lessons about copyright incentives. *Arizona Law Review, forthcoming*. Accessed online: http://papers.ssrn.com/sol3/papers.cfm?abstract_id=2199058.

Digital Millennium Copyright Act (1998). U.S. Copyright Office Summary, United States Copyright Office, Library of Congress, Washington, DC. December, accessed online: http://www.copyright.gov/legislation/dmca.pdf.

DiLorenzo, T. (1996). The myth of natural monopoly. *Review of Austrian Economics*, 9(2):43–58.

Dobbin, F. and Jung, J. (2010). The misapplication of Mr. Michael Jensen: How agency theory brought down the economy and why it might again. In Lounsbury, M. and Hirsch, P. M., editors, *Markets on Trial: The Economic Sociology of the U.S. Financial Crisis: Part B*, volume 30 of *Research in the Sociology of Organizations*, pages 29–64. Emerald Group Publishing Limited.

Downes, L. (2011). 'Leahy's Protect IP Act: Why Internet Content Wars Will Never End'. *Forbes Magazine*. May 16, accessed online: http://www.forbes.com.

Dredge, S. (2014). 'SoundCloud Financials Reveal Widening Losses'. *MusicAlly.com*. October 13, accessed online: http://musically.com/2014/10/13/soundcloud-financials-widening-losses.

Edwards, J. (2013). 'A Secret Cartel Keeps The Dying Broadcast TV Industry Afloat'. *BusinessInsider.com*. May 14, acccessed online: http://www.businessinsider.com/inside-the-madness-of-tv-upfronts-2013-5.

Einhorn, M. (2006). Transactions costs and administered markets: License contracts for music performance rights. *Review of Economic Research on Copyright Issues*, 3(1):61–74.

Einhorn, M. and Kurlantzick, L. (2003). Traffic jam on the music highway: Is it a reproduction or a performance? *Review of Network Economics*, 2(1):10–28.

Eisenhardt, K. (1989). Agency theory: An assessment and review. *Academy of Management Review*, 14(1):57–74.

Elder, J. (2014). 'Social Media Fail to Live Up to Early Marketing Hype: Companies Refine Strategies to Stress Quality Over Quantity of Fans'. *Wall Street Journal*. June 23, accessed online: http://online.wsj.com/articles/companies-alter-social-media-strategies-1403499658.

Fama, E. (1996). Agency problems and the theory of the firm. In Putterman, L. and Kroszner, R., editors, *The Economic Nature of the Firm: A Reader*, chapter 22, pages 302–314. Cambridge University Press, Cambridge, United Kingdom, second edition.

Fogarty, P. (2008). Major record labels and the RIAA: Dinosaurs in a digital age? *Houston Business and Tax Law Journal*, 9:140–173.

Galbraith, J. (2014). *The End of Normal: The Great Crisis and the Future of Growth*. Simon and Schuster.

Gapper, J. (2014). 'Publishers must become giants to take on Amazon'. *Financial Times*. May 28, accessed online: http://www.ft.com/cms/s/0/ab87b634-e5ad-11e3-aeef-00144feabdc0.html#axzz3GipACAWa.

Gardner, E. (2013). BMI Freaks Out Over TMZ Copyright Story. *Hollywood Reporter*. June 6, accessed online: http://www.hollywoodreporter.com/thr-esq/bmi-freaks-tmz-copyright-story-564170.

Gordon, S. (2011). *The Future of the Music Business*. Hal Leonard, Milwaukee, WI, third edition.

Grant, P. and Wood, C. (2004). *Blockbusters And Trade Wars: Popular Culture In A Globalized World*. Douglas and McIntyre, Vancouver, BC.

Harris, E. (2014). 'RadioShack: In Need of Rewiring'. *New York Times*. August 20, p. B1.

Hirsch, P., Friedman, R., and Koza, P. (1990). Collaboration or paradigm shift?: Caveat emptor and the risk of romance with economic models for strategy and policy research. *Organization Science*, 1(1):87–97.

Holden, M. (2001). Where's the beef?: PRO policies and the non-disclosure of music usage in America. *Film Music Magazine*. April 11, accessed online: http://www.filmmusicmag.com/?p=644.

Hutchinson, J. (1999). Can collecting societies survive beyond the digital frontier? *Film Music Magazine*. January 11, accessed online: http://www.filmmusicmag.com/?p=647.

Jain, S. (2008). Digital piracy: A competitive analysis. *Marketing Science*, 27(4):610–626.

Jefferson, C. (2010). 'The Music Industry's Funny Money: The Great Divide: Who Is Getting Paid (And How Much) In The Music Industry'. *TheRoot.com*. July 6, accessed online: http://www.theroot.com/views/how-much-do-you-musicians-really-make?page=0,0&GT1=38002.

Johnson, D. (2014). 'See How Much Every Top Artist Makes on Spotify'. *Time.com*. November 18, accessed online: http://time.com/3590670/spotify-calculator.

Kaiser, R. (2014). *'The Bad News about the News'*. The Brookings Institute. October 16, accessed online: http://www.brookings.edu/research/essays/2014/bad-news#.

Karp, H. (2013). Reaping profits from soundtracks. *Wall Street Journal*, page B6. December 16 2013, accessed online: http://search.proquest.com/docview/1468227178?accountid=35927.

Katz, A. (2005). The potential demise of another natural monopoly: Rethinking the collective administration of performing rights. *Journal of Competition Law and Economics*, 1(3):541–593.

Katz, A. (2006). The potential demise of another natural monopoly: New technologies and the administration of performing rights. *Journal of Competition Law and Economics*, 2(2):245–284.

Kearney, J. (1999). From the fall of the Bell System to the Telecommunications Act: Regulation of telecommunications under Judge Greene. *Marquette University Law School Faculty Publications*, pages 1395–1472. Paper 505, accessed online: http://scholarship.law.marquette.edu/facpub/505, pp. 1395–1472.

Kimpel, D. (2004). *Who Really Wrote That Song? Music Connection Magazine*. March 15–28, pp. 48–51.

Koenigsberg, I. (2002). *Performing Rights In Music And Performing Rights Organizations, Revisited*. White and Case, LLP, New York, NY.

Korman, B. and Koenigsberg, I. (1986). Performing rights in music and performing rights organizations. *Journal of the Copyright Society of the USA*, 33(4):332–367.

Krasilovsky, M. W. and Shemel, S. (2007). *The Business of Music: The Definitive Guide to the Business and Legal Issues of the Music Industry*. Watson-Guptill Publications, New York, tenth edition.

Laffont, J. and Tirole, J. (1993). *A Theory of Incentives in Procurement and Regulation*. MIT Press.

Langenderfer, J. and Cook, D. L. (2001). Copyright Polices and Issues Raised by A&M Records vs. Napster: "The Shot Heard 'Round the World" or "Not with a Bang but a Whimper?". *Journal of Public Policy and Marketing*, 20(2):280–288.

Leontief, W. (1983). National perspective: The definitions of problems and opportunities. In *The Long-Term Impact of Technology on Employment and Unemployment*, pages 3–7. National Academy of Engineering, Washington, DC. Accessed online: books.google.com/books?id=hS0rAAAAYAAJ.

Lepore, J. (2014). 'The Disruption Machine: What the gospel of Innovation Gets Wrong'. *New Yorker Magazine*. June 23 issue, accessed online: http://www.newyorker.com/magazine/2014/06/23/the-disruption-machine.

Liebowitz, S. and Margolis, S. (2009). Bundles of joy: The ubiquity and efficiency of bundles in new technology markets. *Journal of Competition Law and Economics*, 5(1):1–47.

Lohr, S. (2014). 'In Big Data, Shepherding Each Client Comes First'. *New York Times*. December 15, p. B1.

London, T., Pesner, B., Voss, Z. G., and Mingovits, V. (2009). *Outrageous Fortune: The Life and Times of the New American Play*. Theatre Development Fund.

Lunney, G. (2001). The death of copyright: Digital technology, private copying, and the Digital Millennium Copyright Act. *Virginia Law Review*, 87(5):813–920.

Lyons, D. (2014). 'The Real Reason Apple Needs Beats: It May Not Be the Headphones or the Streaming'. *Billboard Magazine*, pages 6–7.

McKinney, K. (2014). 'Book revenues are up – but without e-books, they'd be plummeting'. *Vox.com*. June 2014, accessed online: http://www.vox.com/2014/6/27/5849354/e-books-will-save-the-publishing-industry.

McNally, D. (2014). *On Highway 61: Music, Race and the Evolution of Cultural Freedom*. Counterpoint.

Mele, N. (2013). 'The End Of Big Business'. *Billboard Magazine*, 125:17. June 1 issue, accessed online: Academic Search Premier, EBSCOhost, accession number: 87933600.

Morgan, B. (2014). 'History of the Record Industry, 1877 – 1920s: Part One: From Invention to Industry'. *Medium.com*. Accessed online: https://medium.com/@Vinylmint/history-of-the-record-industry-1877-1920s-48deacb4c4c3.

Murphy, G. (2014). *Cowboys and Indies: The Epic History of the Record Industry*. St. Martin's Press.

Neumeister, L. (1992). 'Two Songwriters Win Rights To Hit Song 36 Years After Writing It'. *Associated Press*. Accessed online: http://www.apnewsarchive.com/1992/Two-Songwriters-Win-Rights-To-Hit-Song-36-Years-After-Writing-It/id-b54281 6ef44f9b73bec72c206c677184?SearchText=morris%20levy%20roulette;Display_.

Newman, M. (2005). Power Laws, Pareto Distributions and Zipf's Law. *Contemporary Physics*, 46(5):323–351.

Nye, W. (2000). Some economic issues in licensing of music performance rights: Controversies in recent ASCAP-BMI litigation. *Journal of Media Economics*, 13(1):15–25.

Olson, C. (2012). Changing tides in music licensing? BMI vs. DMX & In Re THP. *Northwestern J. Technology & Intellectual Property*, 10(3):277–293. Accessed online: http://scholarlycommons.law.northwestern.edu/njtip/vol10/iss3/8note.

Oxenford, D. (2009). 'ASCAP and BMI – Another Royalty Battle for Broadcasters? *Broadcast Law Blog*. October 3, accessed online: http://www.broadcastlawblog.com/2009/10/articles/ascap-and-bmi-another-royalty-battle-for-broadcasters.

Page, W. and Garland, E. (2009). The Long Tail of P2P. *Economic Insight*. Published by PRS, UK and accessed online: http://www.prsformusic.com/creators/news/research/Documents/The%20long%20tail%20of%20P2P%20v9.pdf.

Pakinkis, T. (2013). 'PJ Bloom On Changing Sync Revenues and Opportunities for Rights-holders'. *MusicWeek.com*. March 21, accessed online: http://www.musicweek.com/news/read/pj-bloom-on-changing-sync-revenues-and-opportunities-for-rights-holders/054069.

Passman, D. (2000). *All You Need To Know About The Music Business*. Simon & Schuster, fourth edition.

Passman, D. (2009). *All You Need To Know About The Music Business*. Simon & Schuster, seventh edition.

Passman, D. (2012). *All You Need To Know About The Music Business*. Simon & Schuster, eighth edition.

Patissier, F. (2012). Global economic survey of the royalties collected by the CISAC member authors' societies in 2010. Technical Report COM12-0093, CISAC (International Confederation of Societies of Authors and Composers). Accessed online: http://www.cisac.org/CisacPortal/initConsultDoc.do?idDoc=22951.

Patry, W. (2011). *How To Fix Copyright*. Oxford University Press, New York.

Peoples, G. (2011a). 'Swelling Stream: What's the potential Value of the Streaming Music Market?'. *Billboard Magazine*. September 24 issue, accessed online without illustrations: http://go.galegroup.com, story:7CA267518925.

Peoples, G. (2011b). 'The New Connectivity'. *Billboard Magazine*. October 1 issue, accessed online without illustrations: http://go.galegroup.com, story:7CA275974134.

Peoples, G. (2011c). 'The quiet storm: Cloud computing has slowly crept from backroom and blog discussion to the forefront of every media executive's mind. Is your business ready for the winds of change?'. *Billboard Magazine*. May 14 issue, accessed online without illustrations: http://go.galegroup.com, story:7CA257217098.

Peoples, G. (2013). 'AM/FM:Not Dead Yet'. *Billboard Magazine*. June 1 issue, accessed online without illustrations: https://web.ebscohost.com, accessed number: 87933587.

Peoples, G. (2014). 'Pumping Profits Into SoundCloud's Bottom Line'. *Billboard Magazine*. November 1 issue, p. 14.

Perlberg, S. (2014). 'Mobile Ads Breach Historic Barrier: Spending to Reach People on Their Devices This Year Will Eclipse Radio, Print'. *Wall Street Journal*. July 22, p. B1.

Perrow, C. (1986). *Complex Organizations: A Critical Essay*. Random House.

Pham, A. (2014). 'Streaming Made Up One-Fifth of U.S. Recorded Music Revenue in 2013'. *Billboard Magazine*. March 18, accessed online: http://www.billboard.com/biz/articles/news/digital-and-mobile/5937634/streaming-made-up-one-fifth-of-us-recorded-music.

Pitt, I. L. (2010a). *Economic Analysis of Music Copyright: Income, Media and Performances*. Springer, New York. Available online: http://www.amazon.com/Economic-Analysis-Music-Copyright-Performances/dp/1441963170/ref=sr_1_1?s=books&ie=UTF8&qid=1417266944&sr=1-1&keywords=economic+analysis+of+music+copyright.

Pitt, I. L. (2010b). Economic analysis of music copyright: Music publishers. In *Economic Analysis of Music Copyright: Income, Media and Performances*, chapter 3, pages 65–79. Springer, New York.

Pitt, I. L. (2010c). Economic analysis of music copyright: Songwriters and composers. In *Economic Analysis of Music Copyright: Income, Media and Performances*, chapter 4, pages 81–92. Springer, New York.

Pitt, I. L. (2010d). Superstar effects on royalty income in a performance rights organization. *Journal of Cultural Economics*, 34(3):219–236.

Pitt, I. L. (2013). Power laws and skew distributions: An application and analysis of performance royalty income. *Forthcoming: Journal of Income Distribution*.

Pitt, I. L. (2015). The Growth and Decay of ASCAP 1914–2014: Innovation, Disruption and Deregulation. *Working Paper*.

Pollock, B. (2014). *A Friend in the Music Business: The ASCAP Story*. Hal Leonard Books.

Price, J. (2011). 'Why Everyone But The Artist and The Music Fan is Doomed'. *Blog.TuneCore.com*. November 22, accessed online: http://blog.tunecore.com/2011/11/why-everyone-but-the-artist-and-the-music-fan-is-doomed.html.

Putterman, L. and Kroszner, R., editors (1996). *The Economic Nature of the Firm: A Reader*. Cambridge University Press, Cambridge, United Kingdom, second edition.

Rees, R. (1985a). The Theory of Principal and Agent–Part I. *Bulletin of Economic Research*, 37(1):3–26.

Rees, R. (1985b). The Theory of Principal and Agent–Part II. *Bulletin of Economic Research*, 37(2):75–97.

Reich, H. and Gaines, W. (1999a). 'Down And Out In New York: Depression-era America Was Dancing To Jelly Roll Morton's Tunes And Someone Was Getting Rich Off Them. It Wasn't Him'. *Chicago Tribune*. December 13, accessed online: http://articles.chicagotribune.com/1999-12-13/news/9912130109_1_jelly-roll-morton-letters-jazz.

Reich, H. and Gaines, W. (1999b). 'The Great Jazz Swindle: Jelly Roll Morton Helped Invent Jazz In America. Then, He Was Cheated And Discarded By The Industry He Ignited.'. *Chicago Tribune*. December 12, accessed online: http://articles.chicagotribune.com/1999-12-12/news/9912120442_1_music-industry-french-quarter-apartment-ferdinand-jelly-roll-morton.

Reich, H. and Gaines, W. (2003). *Jelly's Blues: The Life, Music, and Redemption of Jelly Roll Morton*. Da Capo Press.

Rideout, V., Foehr, U., and Roberts, D. (2010). Generation M^2: Media in the Lives of 8 to 18 Year-Olds. Technical report, Kaiser Family Foundation, Menlo Park, California. http://www.kff.org/entmedia/upload/8010.pdf.

Robertson, M. (2011). 'Why Spotify can never be profitable: The secret demands of record labels'. *GigaOm.com*. accessed online: http://gigaom.com/2011/12/11/why-spotify-can-never-be-profitable-the-secret-demands-of-record-labels.

Rosen, S. (1981). The economics of superstars. *American Economic Review*, 71:845–858.

Samuelson, P. (2006). The generativity of sony vs. universal: The intellectual property legacy of justice stevens. *Fordam Law Review*, 74:101–145. Accessed online: http://people.ischool.berkeley.edu/~pam/papers/Sony%20legacy%20FLR.pdf.

Sandoval, G. (2012). 'Google Music not living up to expectations (exclusive)'. *CNET.com*. February 23, accessed online: http://news.cnet.com/8301-31001_3-57383531-261.

Schap, D. (1985). X-inefficiency in a rent-seeking society: A graphical analysis. *Quarterly Review of Economics and Business*, 25:19–27.

Scherer, F. M. (1984). *Innovation and Growth: Schumpeterian Perspectives*. MIT Press.

Schumpeter, J. (1939). *Business Cycles: A Theoretical, Historical and Statistical Analysis of the Capitalist Process*. McGraw Hill, New York.

Silver, J. (2012). 'In Pursuit of a Global Music Registry'. *Future of Music.org*. June 27, accessed online: http://futureofmusic.org/blog/2012/06/27/pursuit-global-music-registry.

Sisario, B. (2011). 'Sirius's Move to Bypass a Royalty Payment Clearinghouse Causes an Uproar'. *New York Times*. November 7, accessed online: http://www.nytimes.com/2011/11/07/business/media/siriuss-move-to-bypass-royalty-agency-causes-uproar.html?_r=1&pagewanted=print.

Sisario, B. (2012a). 'Out to Shake Up Music, Often With Sharp Words'. *New York Times*. May 7. p. B1.

Sisario, B. (2012b). 'Sony Closes Its Acquisition of EMI Music Publishing'. *NYTimes.com*. June 29, accessed online: http://mediadecoder.blogs.nytimes.com/2012/06/29/passing-final-hurdle-sonys-deal-for-emi-publishing-is-approved-by-u-s/.

Sisario, B. (2012c). 'U.S. and European Regulators Approve Universal's Purchase of EMI'. *NYTimes.com*. September 21, accessed online: http://www.nytimes.com/2012/09/22/business/global/universal-takeover-of-emi-music-is-approved.html.

Sisario, B. (2013). 'Beyoncé Rejects Tradition for Social Media's Power'. *New York Times*. December 16. p. B1.

Sisario, B. (2014a). 'Chief Defends Spotify After Snub by Pop Star'. *New York Times*. November 12, p. B1.

Sisario, B. (2014b). 'Justice Department Plans to Begin a Review of Music Licensing Rules'. *NYTimes.com*. June 4, accessed online: http://www.nytimes.com/2014/06/04/business/media/justice-department-is-said-to-plan-a-review-of-music-licensing-rules.html?_r=0.

Sisario, B. (2014c). 'Music Industry Officals Agree on Need for Licensing Rule Changes, but Little Else'. *New York Times*. June 11, p. B3.

Sisario, B. (2014d). 'Pandora Suit May Upend Century-Old Royalty Plan'. *NYTimes.com*. February 13, accessed online: http://www.nytimes.com/2014/02/14/business/media/pandora-suit-may-upend-century-old-royalty-plan.html?_r=0.

Sisario, B. (2014e). 'Paying to Press Play: Premium Service for Music Coming From YouTube'. *New York Times*. November 13, p. B1.

Sisario, B. (2014f). 'Popular and Free, SoundCloud Is Now Ready For Ads'. *New York Times*. August 21, p. B3.

Sisario, B. (2014g). 'Sony Threatens to Bypass Licensers in Royalties Battle'. *New York Times*. July 11, p. B2.

Smirke, R. (2011). 'Universal Music Strikes Direct Licensing Deal With Last.fm'. *Billboard Magazine*. July 15, issue, accessed online: http://www.billboard.biz, story:1005279482.

Sobel, L. (1983). The music business and the Sherman Act: An analysis of the economic realities of blanket licensing. *Loyola of Los Angeles Entertainment Law Journal*, 3:1–44. available at: http://digitalcommons.lmu.edu/elr/vol3/iss1/1.

Solomon, S. (2014). 'For RadioShack, a Long History of Misses and Missteps. *New York Times*. September 17, p. B5.

Somaiya, R. (2014). 'The News, À La Carte—Using Algorithms, Facebook is Changing The Way Its Users Consume Journalism'. *New York Times*. October 27, p. B1.

Stanley, B. (2014). *Yeah! Yeah! Yeah!—The Story of Pop Music: From Bill Haley to Beyoncé*. W. W. Norton & Company, first edition.

Stockment, A. (2009). Internet radio: The case for a technology neutral royalty standard. *Virginia Law Review*, 95(8):2129–2179.

Stout, L. (2012). *The Shareholder Value Myth: How Putting Shareholders First Harms Investors, Corporations, and the Public*. Berrett-Koehler.

Streitfeld, D. (2014). 'Writers Who Support Amazon Speak Out on Dispute With Hachette'. *New York Times*. October 13, p. B6.

Tavakoli, J. M. (2013). 'Facebook Advertisers Beware'. *HuffingtonPost.com*. January 16, accessed online: http://www.huffingtonpost.com/janet-tavakoli/facebook-advertisers-bewa_b_2486921.html.

Thall, P. (2006). *What They Will Never Tell You About the Music Business: The Myths, the Secrets, and the Lies (& a Few Truths)*. Billboard Books.

Towse, R. (2008). Why has cultural economics ignored copyright? *Journal of Cultural Economics*, 32:243–259.

Ulin, J. (2014a). *The Business of Media Distribution: Monetizing Film, TV, and Video Content in an Online World*. Focal Press, second edition.

Ulin, J. (2014b). Internet Distribution and a New Paradigm: On-Demand and Multi-Screen Access, Cord-Cutting, Online Originals, Cloud Applications, Social Media, and More. In *The Business of Media Distribution: Monetizing Film, TV, and Video Content in an Online World*, chapter 7, pages 361–444. Focal Press, second edition.

Van-Buskirk, E. (2012). Why 'Mastered For iTunes' Won't Defuse a Copyright Time Bomb. *Gizmodo.com*. March 1, accessed online: http://gizmodo.com/5889748/why-mastered-for-itunes-wont-defuse-a-copyright-time-bomb.

Vermeulen, F. (2014). 'How Removing Copy Protection Increased Record Companies' Music Sales'. *Forbes.com*. January 27, accessed online: http://www.forbes.com/sites/freekvermeulen/2014/01/27/how-removing-copy-protection-increased-record-companies-music-sales/.

Verrier, R. (2014). 'End of film: Paramount first studio to stop distributing film prints'. *Los Angeles Times*. January 17, accessed online: http://www.latimes.com/entertainment/envelope/cotown/la-et-ct-paramount-digital-20140117,0,5245137.story#ixzz2qnhjeuov.

Williamson, O. (1996). The governance of contractual relationships. In Putterman, L. and Kroszner, R., editors, *The Economic Nature of the Firm: A Reader*, chapter 9, pages 125–135. Cambridge University Press, Cambridge, United Kingdom, second edition.

Wilsey, D. and Schwartz, D. D. (2010). *The Musician's Guide to Licensing Music*. Billboard Books, New York.

Wixen, R. (2014). *The Plain & Simple Guide to Music Publishing*. Hal Leonard, third edition.

Xie, F.-C., Lin, J.-G., and Wei, B.-C. (2009). Diagnostics for skew-normal nonlinear regression models with AR(1) errors. *Computational Statistics and Data Analysis*, 53:4403–4416.

Yagoda, B. (2015). *The B Side: The Death of Tin Pan Alley and the Rebirth of the GREAT AMERICAN SONG*. Riverhead Books, NY.

Court Cases Cited

AFJ2 (2001). *Second Amended Final Judgment, US vs. ASCAP Civ. No. 41–1395*, S.D.N.Y. June, available online: http://www.ascap.com/~/media/Files/Pdf/members/governing-documents/ascapafj2.ashx, pp. 1–19.

BMI vs. DMX (2010). No: 08 Civ. 216 (LLS), S.D.N.Y. July 26, accessed online: http://www.leagle.com/decision/In%20FDCO%2020100727985.xml/BROADCAST%20MUSIC,%20INC.%20v.%20DMX,%20INC, pp. 1–33.

BMI vs. DMX, ASCAP vs. THP CAPSTAR (2012). No:10-3429-cv, 11-127-cv., US Court of Appeals, 2nd Cir. June, accessed online: http://www.ca2.uscourts.gov/decisions, pp. 1–47.

BMI vs. Pandora Media Inc. (2013). No: 13-cv-04037 (LLS), S.D.N.Y. December, accessed online: http://docs.justia.com/cases/federal/district-courts/new-york/nysdce/1:1964cv03787/58544/61/0.pdf?1387564284, pp. 1–14.

F.B.T. Productions vs. Aftermath Records (2010). No: 09-55817, ID: 7462343, DktEntry: 45-1, US Court of Appeals 9th Cir., Pasadena, CA. September 3, accessed online: www.cdn.ca9.uscourts.gov/datastore/opinions/2010/09/03/09-55817.pdf, pp. 1–15.

Flo & Eddie Inc. v. Sirius XM Radio Inc. (2014). No: CV 13-5693 PSG (RZx), C.D.C.A. September 14, accessed online: http://www.soundexchange.com/wp-content/uploads/2014/09/Flo-Eddie-v.-Sirius-XM-Order-on-MSJ.pdf, pp. 1–15.

Flo & Eddie Inc. v. Sirius XM Radio Inc. and DOES 1-10 (2014). No: 13 Civ. 5784 (CM), S.D.N.Y. November 14, accessed online: www.soundexchange.com/wp-content/uploads/2014/11/2014-11-14-Order-on-Summary-Judgment-Flo-and-Eddie-v-Sirius-XM-SDNY.pdf, pp. 1–40.

Meredith Corp. v. SESAC LLC (2014). No: 09 Civ. 9177 (PAE), S.D.N.Y. March 3, accessed online: http://tvmlc.com/wp-content/uploads/2012/07/3_6_14-Court-Process-Decision.pdf, pp. 1–69.

RMLC v. SESAC (2013). No: 12-cv-5807, E.D.P.A. December 20, accessed online: http://www.fhhlaw.com/RMLC%20v%20SESAC%20injunc%20decision.PDF, pp. 1–40.

Scorpio Music S.A. vs. Willis (2011). No: 11cv1557 BTM(RBB), S.D.C.A. July, accessed online: http://archive.org/details/gov.uscourts.casd.357493, pp. 1–29.

Scorpio Music S.A. vs. Willis (2012). No: 11cv1557 BTM(RBB), S.D.C.A. May, accessed online: http://ia600708.us.archive.org/26/items/gov.uscourts.casd.357493/gov.uscourts.casd.357493.30.0.pdf, pp. 1–10.

State of Texas vs Penguin Group & In Re: Electronic Books Antitrust Litigation (2014). No. 1:11-MD-02293-(DLC), S.D.N.Y. June 5, accessed online: blogs.reuters.com/alison-frankel/files/2014/.../ebooks-cote6.5opinion.pdf, pp 1–45.

US vs. ASCAP & In Re Application of Cellco Partnership D/B/A Verizon Wireless (2009). No: 09 Civ. 7074 (DLC), S.D.N.Y. October 14, accessed online: www.eff.org%2Ffiles%2Ffilenode%2FUS_v_ASCAP%2FASCAP%2520v%2520Verizon%2520Order.pdf, pp.1–34.

US vs ASCAP & In Re Application of the Cromwell Group Inc. and Affiliates et al (2012). No: 10 CV 5210 DLC MHD, S.D.N.Y. January 30, accessed online: www.ascap.com/~/media/files/pdf/licensing/.../final%20order.pdf.

US vs. ASCAP & In Re Applications of RealNetworks, Inc., Yahoo! Inc. (2010). Nos: 09-0539-cv (L), 09-0542-cv (con), 09-0666-cv (xap), 09-0692-cv (xap), 09-1572-cv (xap), US Court of Appeals, 2d Cir. September 28, accessed online: http://caselaw.findlaw.com/us-2nd-circuit/1539469.html, pp. 1–49.

US vs. ASCAP & In Re Capstar (DMX) (2010). No: 09 Civ. 7069 (DLC), S.D.N.Y. December 1, accessed online: http://www.leagle.com/decision/In%20FDCO%2020101209735, pp. 1–87.

US vs. ASCAP & In re Petition of Pandora Media (2013). No: 1:12-cv-08035-DLC, 41 Civ. 1395 (DLC), S.D.N.Y. October, accessed online: http://www.digitalmusicnews.com/uploads/77/9f/.../pandoravascap.pdf, pp. 1–30.

US vs. ASCAP & In re Petition of Pandora Media (2014). Nos: 12 Civ. 8035 (DLC), 41 Civ. 1395 (DLC), S.D.N.Y. March 14, accessed online: http://www.business.cch.com/ipld/PandoraUSASCAP031414.pdf, pp. 1–136.

Viacom International, Inc. v. YouTube, Inc. (2013). No:1:07-cv-02103-LLS, S.D.N.Y. April, accessed online: https://www.eff.org/sites/default/files/yt2013opinion_copy.pdf, pp. 1–24.

About the Author

Dr. Pitt began his professional career as an economist with AT&T Long Distance in an era that is now seen as one of the most turbulent periods in the history of the modern telecommunications industry. The Communications Act of 1934—the statutory framework for regulating the telecommunications and broadcasting industries—was significantly revised, updated, and replaced with the Telecommunications Act of 1996 that now included the Internet for the first time. The Telecommunications Act was designed to increase competition by removing regulatory barriers to entry.

It was at AT&T that he witnessed the tumultuous technological changes that transformed the telecommunications industry in the early 1990s. All of those changes parallel many of the same changes that are occurring in the music industry today. The issues raised by competitors and new entrants are strikingly similar, and the industry's knee-jerk response and solution to protect the status quo are also familiar.

AT&T faced antitrust lawsuits in its more than 100 years old, illustrious history. Like the incumbent PROs today, AT&T was considered a natural monopoly and regulated by a consent decree. Between 1982 and 1984, AT&T had settled its antitrust lawsuits and agreed to be broken up into two separate and independent entities: The seven Regional Bell Operating Companies (RBOCs) that provided local telephone service was one, and the long distance, manufacturing, research and development was the other. In return, the US Department of Justice removed the 1956 consent decree restrictions that had governed AT&T. The long distance segment in the telecom industry was transformed from a monopoly to full competition with better, faster, and cheaper services and equipment for consumers and businesses.

As the 1990s progressed, countless restructurings, mal-investment, and ill-fated acquisitions could not save AT&T from fiber optic technology; economic uncertainty, fierce competition from hundreds of new entrants in the long distance market like MCI-Worldcom—that later collapsed under massive debts, corruption, accounting, and financial fraud and its CEO, Bernie Ebbers, was convicted and sent to prison—cable companies, and the onslaught of wireless phones. By the end of

I.L. Pitt, *Direct Licensing and the Music Industry*,
DOI 10.1007/978-3-319-17653-6

the twentieth century, the venerable institution that led the early development of the telephone, wireless communication, and the Internet infrastructure met its demise.

AT&T's executives faced a familiar dilemma: As fiber optic technology became ubiquitous and digital technology replaced analog systems, the "distance" in long distance no longer mattered and their old business models became irrelevant. Today, it is digital downloads, subscription streaming services, smart phones, and YouTube that are transforming the music industry and they call into question the relevancy of the PROs, record labels, and music publishing out-dated business models.

In later years, Dr. Pitt served as a marketing executive for several start-ups, including a cable network and a local exchange carrier before joining ASCAP as their Senior Economist. Dr. Pitt draws on his considerable experience in working for a large publicly traded company, and smaller start-ups that were competing in the space opened up by deregulation. This book reflects those valuable years and provides insights for future changes that may occur due to deregulation, competition, technology, and innovation. His most recent book is *Economic Analysis of Music Copyright: Income, Media and Performances*, Springer, 2010.

Author Index

I.L. Pitt, *Direct Licensing and the Music Industry*,
DOI 10.1007/978-3-319-17653-6

Subject Index

I.L. Pitt, *Direct Licensing and the Music Industry*,
DOI 10.1007/978-3-319-17653-6

The manufacturer's authorised representative in the EU is Springer Nature Customer Service Centre GmbH, Europaplatz 3, 69115 Heidelberg, Germany. If you have any concerns regarding our products, please contact ProductSafety@springernature.com

Printed and bound by CPI Group (UK) Ltd, Croydon, CR0 4YY
05/10/2026
02228127-0008